ACADEMIC PROFILING

Academic Profiling

LATINOS, ASIAN AMERICANS, AND THE ACHIEVEMENT GAP

Gilda L. Ochoa

University of Minnesota Press

Minneapolis

London

Portions of this book were published previously in Gilda L. Ochoa, Laura E. Enriquez, Sandra Hamada, and Jenniffer Rojas, "(De)Constructing Multiple Gaps: Divisions and Disparities between Asian Americans and Latinas/os in a Los Angeles County High School," in *Transnational Crossroads: Remapping the Americas and the Pacific,* ed. Camilla Fojas and Rudy P. Guevarra Jr., 143–70; reprinted by permission of the University of Nebraska Press; copyright 2012 by the Board of Regents of the University of Nebraska.

Published by the University of Minnesota Press
111 Third Avenue South, Suite 290
Minneapolis, MN 55401-2520
http://www.upress.umn.edu

Library of Congress Cataloging-in-Publication Data

Ochoa, Gilda L., 1965–
  Academic profiling : Latinos, Asian Americans, and the achievement gap / Gilda L. Ochoa.
  Includes bibliographical references and index.
  ISBN 978-0-8166-8739-8 (hc)
  ISBN 978-0-8166-8740-4 (pb)
  1. Discrimination in education—California. 2. Latin Americans—Education—California. 3. Asian Americans—Education—California. 4. Academic achievement—California. I. Title.
  LC212.22.C35O24 2013
  379.2'609794—dc23   2013030780

Printed in the United States of America on acid-free paper

The University of Minnesota is an equal-opportunity educator and employer.

20 19 18 17 16   10 9 8 7 6 5 4 3

For the students who shared their stories and
to all who have worked toward more just schools

CONTENTS

AP	Advanced Placement
API	Academic Performance Index
ASB	associated student body
AVID	Advancement via Individual Determination
BSU	Black Student Union
CAT6	California Achievement Test, sixth edition
CP	college preparatory
CSTs	California Standards Tests
CSU	California State University
H	honors
IB	International Baccalaureate
MEChA	Movimiento Estudiantil Chicana/o de Aztlán
NCLB	No Child Left Behind Act
PE	physical education
PSAT	Preliminary SAT
PTA	parent–teacher association
SCHS	Southern California High School
STAR	Standardized Testing and Reporting

TOK theory of knowledge

UC University of California

WASC Western Association of Schools and Colleges

On a June afternoon while meeting with twenty seniors in a transitional English class, I asked them about their four years at Southern California High School (SCHS).[1] At first, they joked about the school's yearbook; complained about student "drama"; and moaned about homework, mean counselors, and teachers. However, their carefree tone changed quickly when Albert Perez pounded his fist on his desk, glared at his classmates, and scolded, "Hey, I don't know if you've noticed, but we've been together all four years. It's almost like this is the Mexican class."[2]

Students initially responded to Albert's outburst with awkward silence and laughter. Slowly, they began discussing why they were confined to a non–college preparatory classroom removed from their largely Asian American schoolmates. First, Priscilla Mendoza whispered, "It's because of the Chinos." While Priscilla blamed Asian Americans, other classmates blamed themselves. They rationalized,

"We're different."
"We might be slow readers. We don't read as well."
"We like to party and have more fun than the honors students."
"We don't like to work as hard. We're lazy."

Shifting from individual explanations to school factors, Sam Ruiz interjected, "They've given up on us. They pay more attention to the honors students than to the students who are not college prep like us. They get all the awards and all the attention."

I first met Richard, Priscilla, Sam, and their classmates in June 2001 when I was finishing *Becoming Neighbors in a Mexican American Community* (Ochoa 2004). I had been interviewing adults on Mexican American–Mexican immigrant relationships and participating in a movement to save bilingual education in my community. In that project, schools were a crucial site influencing attitudes, relationships, and group boundaries long after high school. I wanted to learn how today's students were experiencing schools and how the practices of the past such as de jure segregation, curriculum tracking, and Americanization that I described in *Becoming Neighbors* were shaping current student dynamics.

My initial visits to SCHS were just months before President George W. Bush signed into law the No Child Left Behind (NCLB) Act in January 2002. This act reauthorized the 1965 Elementary and Secondary Education Act that sought to improve education for poor and working-class students. At the core of NCLB is accountability through strict standards and standardized testing. As part of the neoliberal policies of the Reagan-Bush era, NCLB and now Barack Obama's Race to the Top (RTTT) have dramatically influenced the discourses and practices within schools. The language of the achievement gap, accountability, and standards are used to justify the movement for structured curriculum and high-stakes testing where test scores are used to evaluate and make important determinations on students, schools, and teachers. In this age of assessment, test preparation and test results are all consuming—often overshadowing the unequal practices that plague schools. It is within this context that I visited several high schools in 2001, including SCHS.

I selected SCHS because of my familiarity with it and the surrounding communities. Raised and living in the area, my ties are strong, and for over a decade, I worked with my brother, Enrique Ochoa, to organize a mentoring and scholarship program at a neighboring middle school that eventually continued at SCHS. Given my commitment to the area, I approached the principal to discuss the possibilities of conducting research. Immediately, he directed my attention to the experiences of Asian Americans and Latinas/os—highlighting the academic disparities at the school. At the time, high-profile media accounts had been praising Asian Americans as so-called model minorities, while Latinas/os were being positioned as less committed to education. I knew that there was much more to the story than these facile characterizations, so I began my research by sitting in on various classrooms and listening to students.

Senior transitional English was one of the first classes that I attended. Before I entered the room, the principal explained that fewer than 5 percent of the over 40 percent of all Latina/o students at SCHS were in the honors and advanced placement courses. However, standing in front of the class, I realized that Latinas/os were not just underrepresented in the most prestigious courses; at 96 percent they were simultaneously overrepresented in this non–college preparatory class. Latino males, in particular, made up two-thirds of the class. Most were also from working-class households.

What I saw that June afternoon was painfully familiar. I had seen these patterns before in my own schooling, and older Mexican Americans had described such trends to me when I was completing *Becoming Neighbors*. They are part of a larger narrative where, in general, Latinas/os are a minority in honors and advanced placement courses and predominate in non–college preparatory classes (Oakes 1985; Ginorio and Huston 2001), and girls and women across race/ethnicity tend to outperform their male counterparts academically (Lopez 2003; Buchmann, DiPrete, and McDaniel 2008).[3] Despite these national trends, what students said that day was still jarring. That experience raised many disturbing questions that are the impetus for this work: (1) Why are there still segregated Mexican classrooms decades after the landmark *Mendez v. Westminster* (1947) and *Brown v. Board of Education* (1954) decisions?[4] In particular, why are students in different classes where they are prepared for unequal opportunities? (2) How do students describe their schooling experiences, and how do students and school officials account for differing educational outcomes? Furthermore, what are the implications of these explanations, and what is left out of these theories? (3) What are the factors influencing students' educational outcomes and their peer relationships? (4) How does focusing on a school with a predominately Asian American and Latina/o student population add to our understanding of the relational and interactional aspects of race, class, and gender? And (5) within the context of decades of exclusionary educational policies, what are the possibilities for changing schools, dominant ideologies, and everyday actions to foster more just spaces where no students are forsaken?

Following the two months of preliminary research in 2001 when I met the students in the transitional English class and interviewed several teachers and counselors, I returned with these larger questions to Southern California High School in May 2007 where I began extensive research. Since the research idea came from the school as a topic that concerned them, I was hopeful about how this work could be applied. The thought of collecting and sharing what I learned with SCHS aligned with my Latina feminist principles where research is social justice oriented and used for transformation.

Qualitative and Participatory Research

For eighteen months, I worked with nearly twenty students from the Claremont Colleges to complete 190 semistructured, open-ended interviews:

139 with SCHS students, 12 with parents, and 39 with school officials (3 school officials also had children who attended the school).[5] All participants generously shared their experiences and perspectives in lively interviews that ranged from thirty minutes to three hours, averaging sixty minutes in length. They described their family backgrounds, schooling experiences, perceptions of peers, dynamics at SCHS, and career and educational aspirations. Most of the interviews with students and school officials took place at lunch tables and in campus offices and classrooms. The interviews with parents were conducted in homes or local restaurants. With the exception of a few interviews where notes were taken, almost all the interviews were recorded, fully transcribed, and analyzed for recurring themes and patterns. The quotations appearing throughout this book are verbatim from the transcripts, but as is the custom in qualitative research, the names of participants and their schools have been changed.

Introducing the Students and Parents

Whether to counter romanticized perceptions of their school, have their "voice heard," "help out," "have fun," or simply "get out of class," students were motivated by a variety of reasons to share their experiences. That so many students wanted their stories heard punctuates the importance of creating such student-centered spaces that in the words of one student "let the truth come out." Sophomore Jung Kim explains, "There's a lot of propaganda going on covering the school. I want to puncture a hole and just let it all out."

As detailed in the appendix, on average, the students included in this book were nearing the end of their sophomore year in high school, and they are more likely to be women than men (60 percent compared to 40 percent). Of the sixty-seven Latina/o students, most identify as Mexican, Mexican American, Latina/o, or Hispanic. Most are the children or grandchildren of Mexican immigrants, but several are from families who have been in the United States for four or five generations, and a few are Central American or identify as multiethnic/racial. About one-quarter are from homes where one parent has received a college degree, but on average, their parents have high school degrees and jobs in construction, trucking, and sales.

In contrast, most of the sixty-three Asian American students moved to the United States as children or are the children of Chinese or Korean immigrants, the majority coming from Taiwan or Hong Kong.[6] Seventy-five percent have at least one parent who has received a college degree. On average, their parents have obtained nearly fifteen years of education and are likely to have middle-class professions in accounting and management. However, due to racial discrimination as well as language and licensing restrictions, not all are able to work in their areas of training. Some are in working-class positions, and multiple families have construction, computer, or restaurant businesses. Thus based on years of education and occupations, the Latina/o students are more likely to come from working-class and lower-middle-class households than their Asian American peers; however, racial/ethnic background and class position do not always correlate. Twenty-five percent of Latinas/os have at least one parent with a bachelor of arts, and a quarter of the Asian Americans do not have a parent who has completed college. Given the focus of this research and the demographics at SCHS, just 6 percent of students formally interviewed identify as White or Black. Their experiences add to the stories that emerge from the school.

Interviews with parents supplement the student interviews. By discussing their schooling experiences, parenting practices, philosophies on education, and perceptions of SCHS, the eight self-identified Mexican American parents, six Chinese parents, and one African American parent provide helpful context for understanding students' experiences. Three of the parent participants are also staff members at SCHS and are listed with them in the appendix.

Introducing the Staffulty

Generally, the thirty-nine interviews with the school staff and faculty, or "staffulty" as they are called at SCHS, were the longest. Most yearned for answers to address disparities in academic performance, but some were less optimistic about the possibilities for change. A couple of newer employees were fearful of retaliation by the administration, and a few people were downright defensive. In one extreme case, a teacher abruptly turned off the recorder multiple times during his interview. He was especially offended with questions about race/ethnicity, including ones asking about his own background and its relevance to his teaching. This, he believed, was not a "fair question," since he is "just a person."

At the time of our initial meetings, the twenty-eight teachers had been in the classroom from two to forty years. Several retired during the time I was at SCHS, and twelve were in their first five years. On average, they had been teaching for sixteen years. Over half are White, reflecting the demographics of the teachers at the school, and 60 percent are women. At 34 percent, more Latinas/os than the school's percentage volunteered to be interviewed, perhaps because of the topic of the research or because they perceived me as an ally due to my own racial/ethnic identity as Latina.

Combined, eleven counselors, administrators, and support staff were interviewed as well, and their demographic information is also included in the appendix.

Observations, Discussions, and Presentations

While interviews form the base of this book, I also include observations, discussion groups, and various exchanges I had at the school. I spoke informally with students and staffulty, led several student discussions, and with a few college students completed observations and field notes in classrooms and school events.[7] As part of the process of reciprocating for the time that members of SCHS shared with me and with the desire to help facilitate change at the school, I formally presented some of the research findings in the fall of 2008. After an initial presentation to school administrators and department chairs, I delivered two talks to the faculty and staff. I followed these presentations with an hour-long discussion that concluded with faculty and staff submitting in writing their ideas for improving the school. I also shared my schooling experiences and career path in various classes, and in fall 2009, I accompanied a group of students from the Claremont Colleges enrolled in a course I taught as they led class discussions in several classrooms at the high school on topics of teachers' choosing.[8] In collaboration with SCHS administrators and several Pomona College colleagues, I later applied for two grants to implement changes at SCHS.[9] All these exchanges were important for helping me better understand the dynamics at SCHS, and they reflect my ethos of reciprocity and commitment to education for social justice (for further discussion, see Ochoa and Ochoa 2004; Ochoa and Pineda 2008). They also helped integrate me into the school. As I became a familiar presence on campus, I recognized and was recognized by most staffulty and many students.

Although I do not claim that this research is necessarily applicable to all students or schools, each time that I have presented this work at Southern California colleges and universities, students and faculty have approached me convinced that I was describing their high school or their experiences. These affirmations remind me of the power of qualitative research where interviews allow for in-depth, detailed, and nuanced understanding, and case studies of institutions such as schools capture similar phenomena occurring in a variety of places. Nevertheless, the familiarity of these dynamics should not lull us into complacency; instead, students' testimonials make the need for change all the more urgent.

ACKNOWLEDGMENTS

This work was greatly enhanced by the contributions of the following people who supported me in the process of research, reflection, and writing. First of all, my family has been foundational in shaping all that I do, and they provided the encouragement and support I needed to complete *Academic Profiling*. My mother, Francesca Palazzolo Ochoa; brother, Enrique C. Ochoa; and niece, Elisa Ochoa-Kaup, read and commented on most chapters. Knowing that my mother, a retired public school teacher, was anticipating my biweekly updates, that my brother would review the final draft with a historian's precision, and that my college-going niece would apply a student's insider's perspective kept me motivated. Meanwhile, the home space and nourishment created by Eduardo Ruiz allowed me the requisite time and energy that I needed to write. The sharing of their own schooling experiences and continual words of encouragement from Ricky Ochoa-Kaup, Julie Kaup, Jesse Henderson, and Luce Palazzolo have also been significant. Similarly, years after his death, my father's messages still inspire me.

At the Claremont Colleges, I appreciate the support from my colleagues, including from the academic dean's office for funding student research assistants and the Intercollegiate Department of Chicana/o–Latina/o Studies and the Pomona College Department of Sociology. I thank María Tucker and Sergio Marin from the Draper Center, Sefa Aina from the Asian American Resource Center, and Martina Ebert for our collaborative efforts in trying to secure financial support to work with Southern California High School (SCHS) on addressing some of the disparities and divisions. The application process and the questions raised throughout it furthered my reflection on this work.

More than any other project that I've completed, this one benefitted immensely from the work of students at the Claremont Colleges. Dianna Moreno accompanied me for two months in 2001 to begin preliminary interviews and observations. Beginning in 2007, two separate research teams paid through Pomona College were particularly influential—one early in the research process and the second near the end. Laura Enriquez, Sandra Hamada, and Jenniffer Rojas participated in research meetings, worked with me as I presented the research idea to the staffulty, completed ethnographic field notes, and conducted and transcribed numerous interviews and focus groups. When this first research team graduated from college, Francisco Covarrubias, Markus Kessler, and Mai Thai worked as paid assistants for a shorter amount of time. They helped with interviewing, transcribing, completing field notes, and organizing data. These seven assistants were key to this research and in pushing my thinking.

At various stages and for shorter periods of time, the following students, also paid through Pomona College, helped with interviewing, transcribing, or reviewing the relevant literature or final versions of this book: Karen Ferreira, Isabel García, Sandra Huerta, Julie Juarez, Jordan Pedraza, Stephanie Roman, Johnny Le, Isaac Medina, Martin Barrera, and Kyra Martin. From Claremont Graduate University, Laureen Adams provided thoughtful comments on a draft of this book. Students enrolled in Los Angeles Communities and Chicanas/os–Latinas/os and Education with me opted to conduct and transcribe a couple of interviews, lead several workshops in SCHS classes, or complete literature reviews as part of their course credit: Dani Bernstein, Celia Camacho, Anthony Espinosa, Sara Farooqi, Chris Fiorello, Zoë Folger, Sarah Garrett, Alex Geonetta, Marisela Gutierrez, Sam Hanft, Kimberly Hartung, Markus Kessler, Maithili Naik, Jordan Pedraza, Eric Rios, Jennifer Roth, Camille Sheffield, Charity Soto, Mai Thai, Kendall Tripathi Parker, Jessica Villaseñor, and Ann Zhao. Finally, for one month through the Pomona College Academy for Youth Success, Laura Enriquez worked with then area high school seniors Marsha Boon, Marika Hoeckmann, Ming Johnson, Jose Juarez, and Taj Tucker to gather statistics, visit tutoring centers, and conduct and transcribe interviews. Together, all these students from high school to graduate school brought their enthusiasm and experiences to strengthen this project.

I am extremely grateful to SCHS students, parents, staffulty, and board members who graciously allowed me and students from the Claremont Colleges into their school and homes. They generously shared their perspectives, experiences, and aspirations. As I have, it is my hope that readers will also learn from their narratives.

Along with advice from colleagues and students at Pomona College, Cal Poly Pomona, University of California Irvine, University of Southern California, Riverside Community College, College of the Desert, and Columbia Basin Community College where I presented sections of this work, this research has benefitted tremendously from the financial support of Pomona College and the John Randolph Haynes and Dora Haynes Faculty Fellowship.

A special thanks to the University of Minnesota Press and Pieter Martin in particular for encouraging this project since the early stages of writing.

Academic Profiling at a Southern California High School

HECTOR DE LA TORRE: The punker guys, they are pretty much Mexican and White, and over there, you have Mexicans; they are skaters. Then the hip-hop kids are Black, light-skinned Black, and Filipinos, some Mexicans.

GEORGE PAZ: And there's the jocks—the football guys, the baseball guys I hang out with.

TOMAS MEDINA: They're Mexican and White.

GEORGE PAZ: Then you have the quiet Asians. I don't know where they're at. I think they're over there. They're hiding.

In most large school campuses in the United States, it is hard not to notice various groups of students clustered together. As high school sophomores Hector, George, and Tomas confer, they gather in distinct parts of their campuses—under trees, on benches, in hallways, and behind buildings. While over time and across schools, these groups' names might be different—such as "punkers," "skaters," "jocks," and "cheerleaders," the school spaces and the groups who occupy them are often unequally valued. At Southern California High School (SCHS), these peer groups also vary by race/ethnicity—leading one student to describe the clusters as "yellow" and "brown" to represent her primarily Asian American and Latina/o schoolmates.

In school classrooms, these patterns of distinct peer groups and their differential appraisals persist. This too is the case at the high school where its nearly two thousand students are separated into academic programs such as college preparatory, honors and advanced placement (AP), and International Baccalaureate (IB). These classes expose students to disparate expectations and curriculum. Whole classes and students are labeled "trouble makers" or "regular students" or greeted as "my bright shining stars." Like students across the nation, they are also largely segregated by race and class and sometimes by gender, too. Such distinctions, the messages they transmit, and the roles they play in perpetuating hierarchies of power and inequality are part of the hidden curriculum. They are among the many unspoken lessons transmitted at schools.

At Southern California High School, Asian Americans and Latinas/os are the two largest racial/ethnic groups, and such divisions and disparities are glaring. However, rather than interrogate the opportunity and social gaps that are engendered in schools and society, much of the discussion at SCHS and across the nation boils down to an emphasis on the "gap" in reference to an "achievement gap."

Often accompanied by calls for "accountability" and ascertained by high-stakes testing, in this age of assessment, the emphasis on the "gap" has become common parlance used by politicians, educators, journalists, and families across political persuasion. A concern for the "gap" gives an illusion that inequality is being addressed, when in fact school disparities and societal injustices are rarely challenged. Furthermore, at SCHS, this referencing of the "gap" perpetuates hierarchical and binary thinking— positioning Asian Americans and Latinas/os as polar opposites from one another and accentuating real and perceived group differences. The underlying reasons for inequalities are camouflaged, as are the variations that exist within these panethnic categories—such as by class, gender, ethnicity, and generation.

Too often lost within dominant discourses about so-called achievement gaps are enduring and pervasive forms of what SCHS teacher Manuel Cadena describes as "academic profiling." He observes such profiling when teachers and counselors are more likely to place Asian American students in academically rigorous courses over Latina/o students. Just as the police force and criminal justice system in general are known to use racial profiling to unequally pull over, arrest, and incarcerate Blacks and Latinos, individuals within schools and the educational institution overall also profile (Pizarro 2005, 240). At SCHS, the academic profiling of students involves disparate expectations and treatment by school officials *and* other students based on race/ethnicity, class, gender, course placement, and middle school attendance. Profiling occurs individually and is rooted in historic and systemic processes, and similar to police profiling, academic profiling teaches students their place in society. Thus, as much as students may resist narrow categorizations and unjust treatment, they are nonetheless schooled in unequal ways that have significant implications for their life trajectories and community relations.

Despite the continuing salience of racism, classism, and sexism in shaping schooling and students' life chances, since the civil rights movements of the 1950s and 1960s, the emphasis on confronting power, inequality, and discrimination in U.S. schools has receded. The movement to reverse racial/ethnic segregation and enhance students' relationships has also diminished. Overall, the social aspects of schooling and racial/ethnic interactions are underexplored and largely ignored. Instead, in the era of No Child Left Behind, A Race to the Top, and high-stakes testing, discourse on achievement gaps, standardized tests, and accountability consumes debates. This emphasis is part of neoconservative and neoliberal approaches that are actually exacerbating inequality and detrimentally shaping U.S. schools (Apple 2001).

Schooling in Neoconservative and Neoliberal Times

Starting in the 1970s and under Ronald Reagan's presidency, a backlash against civil rights gains resulted in the emergence of neoconservatism (Omi and Winant 1994). A neoconservative perspective assumes that we live in a meritocratic and so-called color-blind society where racism, sexism, and other forms of discrimination are believed to be something of the past. In popular discourse, some who accept this perspective argue that "we are all the same," that there is "a level playing field," and that programs stemming from civil rights victories are examples of "reverse racism." By failing to consider the larger societal factors that result in a stratified society, this approach blames individuals and groups for their positions in society. Most recently illustrated in the attacks on Mexican American studies in Arizona, neoconservatives support acculturation and a core Western-based curriculum. They oppose ethnic studies and bilingual education because they perceive them as threats to a U.S. national identity—narrowly defined as White, Protestant, middle class, English speaking, and heterosexual (see Schlesinger 1991). Thus, regardless of student demographics, the thrust is for homogenized or standardized curriculum that ignores the diverse histories, experiences, and cultures of the many groups who compose the United States.

While neoconservatives focus on "cultural restoration" and maintaining a core national identity (see Apple 2004), their perspectives merge with neoliberal ideologies that emphasize consumer choice and free market approaches such as privatization and deregulation of social services. Along with ignoring power differentials and the realization that not all have access to equal choices, neoliberal approaches have resulted in massive defunding of social programs in education, health care, transportation, social security, and public housing (Bonilla-Silva 2006). There has been a concurrent emphasis on individualism over a concern for community and the public good (Garcia and Martínez 2006).

Today's educational system has been dramatically shaped by reports and practices stemming from these neoliberal policies during the 1980s Reagan-Bush era and continuing under George W. Bush's No Child Left Behind Act and Barack Obama's A Race to the Top. In 1983, a commission appointed under Ronald Reagan's secretary of education released *A Nation at Risk*, a report critiquing the "rising tide of mediocrity" among U.S. schools in science, industry, and innovation in comparison with Japanese and Western European educational systems (National Commission on Excellence in Education 1983, 1). Although the report has been challenged as lacking evidence, "manufactur[ing] a crisis," and attacking America's public schools (see Berliner and Biddle 1995), *A Nation at Risk* became a rallying call for conservatives and ushered in a wave of criticism about the educational system. It opened the doors to the neoliberal school policies that are ubiquitous today: inflexible curriculum; standards-based teaching; high-stakes testing; reduced teacher autonomy; attacks on teachers' unions; and opportunities for greater privatization through tutoring programs, school vouchers, and charter schools (Pearl 2002).

Lost within our current period of schooling is a more holistic conceptualization of education, one where multiple aspects of students' development are considered and opportunities are provided to all. This type of education would be inclusive, nonhierarchical, and not driven by tests. Informed by a feminist and ethnic studies ethos, it would focus on relationships—fostering self-love and students' positive sense of their classmates; an understanding of multiracial/ethnic, class, and gender histories; global awareness; critical thinking; a passion for learning, and a commitment to working together to improve our schools and communities for the greater good (see Collins 1990; hooks 1994). Individual students, parents, and teachers alone would not bear the weight for what happens our schools. Rather than a framework of individual accountability that is measured by test performance, there would be *societal* accountability and assurance that schools and other social services were well funded and fully supported.[1]

Motivated by such a vision of schooling, I listened to students, parents, and school officials at Southern California High School to write *Academic Profiling*. As such, this study looks deeper into the student clusters, inequalities, and prevailing discussions of an "achievement gap" to uncover a significant and less told story about U.S. schools and their roles in influencing perceptions, opportunities, relationships, and inequalities. It considers the many faults within schools and society and depicts the diverse ways students make sense of their experiences, perceive their peers, and navigate an unequal educational pipeline. It deconstructs the dominant framing of an "achievement gap" and spotlights multiple gaps and hierarchies, their sources and consequences, students' responses, and strategies for change. It also considers the roles and reflections of administrators and teachers in classrooms and school culture. In so doing, it details the interactions between structure and agency: the structures and ideologies influencing students' lives at school along with students' and staffulty's roles in maintaining, challenging, and navigating these structures and belief systems.

The Value of Relational Studies

Despite extensive scholarship on the factors influencing students' educational outcomes, comparative research such as work undertaken for this book on how various students experience the same school and how schools shape relationships has been relatively limited. It was not until the late 1960s and early 1970s that a body of research on race relations in schools even began to develop (Schofield 1991). Much of that early research *quantitatively* explored the impact of desegregation on Black and White peer groups, largely ignoring the experiences of Asian Americans and Latinas/os and avoiding the role of schools in structuring students' relationships. In the 1970s and 1980s, there was important growth in qualitative research on race relations that began to detail how school practices such as curriculum tracking, classroom pedagogy, and extracurricular activities foster student divisions or collaboration (see Collins 1979; Schofield and Sagar 1979; Hallinan and Teixeira 1987). However, in general, that body of work continued to center on the experiences of Blacks and Whites. Since the 1990s, there has been increased attention on the effects of schooling on multiple racial/ethnic relationships (see Matute-Bianchi 1986; Conchas 2006; Kiang and Kaplan 1994; Ochoa 2004; Rosenbloom and Way 2004; Bejarano 2005). Seminal scholarship in this area includes work by Angela Valenzuela (1999) and Stacey Lee (1996, 2005). While Valenzuela's *Subtractive Schooling* details how Eurocentric curriculum and curriculum tracking limit relationships between Mexican American and Mexican immigrant students in Texas, Lee documents how admissions policies, curriculum tracking, extracurricular activities, and the belief that Asian Americans are "model minorities" foster racial tensions among students in Wisconsin.

Even with this newer research, comparative studies on the relational aspects of Asian Americans *and* Latinas/os remain scant. When Asian Americans and Latinas/os are included, scholars often focus on whether their experiences are more like Whites or African Americans, not considering Asian Americans and Latinas/os on their own terms or in relationship to one another (for exceptions, see Almaguer 1994; Saito 1998; Feliciano 2005; Pulido 2006; O'Brien 2008). Such approaches are limiting and incomplete, especially in places like California where Asian Americans are 12 percent and Latinas/os 51 percent of K–12 students.[2] They often share schools together and may be defined in relationship to each other.

Given the importance of understanding how schools simultaneously structure disparities and group relations and moving beyond a Black–White binary, this study heeds the call for qualitative research that "explores the diverse experiences of urban, ethnic minority students in multicultural schools, particularly where White students are not the dominant population" (Rosenbloom and Way 2004, 447). By considering the experiences of Asian American *and* Latina/o students, my comparative approach observes the warning of Denner and Guzmán (2006) about not reinforcing the positioning of one group above another in superior/inferior relationships. Similarly, I avoid the practice of "Oppression Olympics" (see Martínez 1999), where some forms of oppression are assumed to be worse than other forms. Such hierarchical thinking pits groups against one another and diverts attention away from the varied structures, ideologies, and intersecting inequalities that hurt us all in different ways.

At a time when higher education is more important than ever, schools across the nation are not reaching all students, and students are being unequally divided—stunting opportunities for growth, relationships, community building, and the sharing of resources. Thus intensive and comparative studies such as this one improve awareness of how educational inequalities can best be addressed. By listening to various experiences and perspectives, we are provided with more information to improve schooling and group relations for all.

SCHS and Its Communities: Past and Present

SCHS is a public high school in Los Angeles County. Surrounded by a major freeway to the north and hillside homes and a Buddhist temple to the south, it is located at the intersection of an established working-class Mexican American community and more recent middle- and upper-middle-class Asian American neighborhoods. As such, the nearly two thousand students at the school reflect the history and changing demographics of the region.

Mexicans have had a long presence in the area, especially in the neighborhoods north and west of SCHS. Historically, a few were members of Anglo-Mexican elite families who acquired Mexican land grants in the 1840s, but most of the original residents were dispossessed of their land and had a foreign language and culture imposed on them as a result of the U.S. conquest of Northern Mexico (Barrera 1979). While Whites dominated the area numerically and economically as landowners, Mexicans worked primarily as laborers in the walnut and citrus groves. They were later joined by Mexican immigrants who were recruited for work during World Wars I and II (Pinheiro 1960).[3] Through the 1940s, Mexicans encountered institutionalized segregation from Whites in schools, churches, occupations, theaters, barbershops, and swimming pools (Ochoa 2004). These historical precursors shape institutional inequities, public opinion, and the socioeconomic backgrounds of many Mexican Americans.

In the 1950s and 1960s as the Los Angeles freeway system developed and tract housing proliferated, more families made the area home. Stemming from this growth, SCHS was built in the 1960s just after an interstate freeway was completed.[4] Throughout the 1970s and 1980s, homes were constructed in front of SCHS and on the town's hillside, attracting more middle-class and upper-middle-class families. For the first ten to fifteen years, the majority of SCHS students were working- and middle-class Whites. However, there was a growing percentage of Latinas/os; most were working-class Mexican Americans, but some middle-class Mexican American families moved into the new housing developments along with Whites.

Following decades of legalized exclusion of Asians, immigrants from China and Korea began moving to the area after the 1965 Immigration Reform Act. This act dismantled the racist system of national-origin quotas by equalizing immigration rights for all nationalities; it included provisions for family reunification and an occupational preference system for highly trained people (Ong, Bonacich, and Cheng 1994). Previous to the act, there was a small percentage of Asian Americans near SCHS, primarily later generations of Japanese Americans who, until the Japanese internment and the elimination of de jure segregation in the school district, were also confined to the segregated and unequal school attended by Mexican American youth (Andriesse 1987; Ochoa 2004; Ling Nakano n.d.). However, these demographics changed with the 1965 Immigration Reform Act. The occupational preference system initially favored professionals to benefit U.S. labor demands in health care, engineering, and computer science (Teranishi 2010, 31). Therefore, many of these post-1965 immigrants from China and Korea were among a selective group of immigrants who were primarily middle- and upper-middle class (Danico 2004; Feliciano 2005; Lew 2006).[5]

As the percentage of Asian immigrants in the area increased, doubling in number from the 1970s to the 1980s, a Buddhist temple was built near SCHS. Reflecting assimilationist and racist assumptions about who belongs in the community, some of the longtime residents criticized the temple for its Chinese architectural style and claimed that it would increase traffic and parking difficulties. During this period, some of the White residents were moving to other areas east of SCHS.

In the 1980s and 1990s, transnational ties, the Mexican economic crises, and shifting priorities of the Mexican government influenced the migration of Mexicans (Ochoa and Ochoa 2007). While this period saw larger percentages of Mexican immigrants with college degrees, as in the past, most Mexican immigrants came as laborers and members of the working class. As of 2008, about 60 percent of Mexican immigrants in the United States over twenty-five years of age had less than a high school degree.[6]

The 1990s also brought growing numbers of highly educated Asian immigrants and significant amounts of financial capital to the region.[7] Those migrating in the early 1990s included skilled immigrants from mainland China as a result of the 1989 Tiananmen Square incident that resulted in the granting of permanent residency to Chinese students and visiting scholars within the United States (Zhou 2009). Also increasing migration was "the end of British rule and the return of Hong Kong to China in 1997, as well as the uncertain relationship between Taiwan and China" (Saito 1998, 20).[8] As a result of these migration patterns, nearly two-thirds of Taiwanese immigrants, almost 50 percent of immigrants from Hong Kong, and a third from Mainland China have at least four years of college education (Zhou 2009, 47). Reflected in the predominately 1.5- and second-generation Asian American students at SCHS, over 95 percent of Korean Americans are post-1965 immigrants and their children (Min 2011, 7), and nearly two-thirds of Chinese Americans are immigrants—most migrating after 1990 (Zhou 2009, 43).

The higher-than-average educational background and incomes of Asian Americans relative to other groups in the United States enhances their educational resources and opportunities for mobility (Feliciano 2005). However, as a whole, Asian Americans often receive lower returns on their schooling than Whites due to racism (Espiritu 2000). Furthermore, not all have access to well-paying and technologically advanced careers. As illustrated by the parents of some of the SCHS students, many have become entrepreneurs—making the region "home to the largest Chinese ethnic economy in the nation in terms of the number of ethnically owned businesses" (Saito 1998, 1), and as of 2002, there was one Chinese-owned business for every nine Chinese Americans (Zhou 2009, 50). Similarly, as of 2002, one-third of Korean families in the United States were self-employed. Faced with racial/ethnic discrimination and unable to transfer their educational and employment credentials in the United States, some have drawn upon their class resources and ethnic ties to establish small businesses (Lee 2002, 33–34).[9] Thus there are important class variations among Asian Americans, and 21 percent of Asian Americans at SCHS are designated socioeconomically disadvantaged.[10]

As a result of a history of institutional inequities, asymmetrical power relationships between the United States and Mexico, and differing immigration patterns and educational opportunities in immigrant countries, on average, the years of schooling for Latinas/os is less than the years of schooling that Chinese and Korean immigrants and their children often possess. While their Asian American schoolmates are likely to come from middle- and upper-middle-class backgrounds and have more recent immigrant ties, Latina/o students at SCHS who are primarily Mexican American tend to be second or third generation in the United States and from working-class and lower-middle-class households. According to the California Department of Education, nearly 60 percent of Latinas/os at SCHS are considered socioeconomically disadvantaged.[11] While there is a large poor and working-class community to the north and west of SCHS, the presence of middle-class and upper-middle-class Mexican Americans that began moving to the newer housing developments in the 1970s and 1980s is reflected in the small number of Mexican American students in this book whose parents are nurses, teachers, and lawyers.

Mirroring the demographics of the area, relatively equal percentages of Asian Americans (46 percent) and Latinas/os (43 percent) attend SCHS; the remaining student body is about 7 percent White, 2 percent African American, and 1 percent Native American. About 75 percent of the Asian American students and 25 percent of the Latina/o students included in *Academic Profiling* are from homes where at least one parent has a college degree. One in three SCHS students are eligible for free and reduced lunch, and over 10 percent are English language learners.

As is the case nationally, the school personnel at SCHS do not represent the current racial/ethnic demographics of the student body or the area. About half of the teachers and administrators are White, one-fourth are Latina/o, one-fifth are Asian American, and less than 3 percent are African American or Native American.[12]

Over the past ten years, the school has become known for having high standardized test scores and rates of college attendance. Based on such quantitative measurements, *Newsweek Magazine* has listed SCHS as one of the top one thousand schools in the United States. While the school initially taught non–college preparatory English classes such as the transitional English class I visited in 2001, these classes were eliminated during the time of this study and students are now placed in college preparatory, honors (H), or AP courses. In addition to these courses, the school offers two main academic programs: AVID (Advancement via Individual Determination) and IB. The AVID program works with students underrepresented in colleges, low-income students, and students who are the first generation in their family to attend college. There are twenty-five to fifty students in each grade who are enrolled in an AVID class where emphasis is placed on academic and social skills and introducing college opportunities. Likewise, combined there are twenty to thirty juniors and seniors in the school's IB program where they take courses such as the theory of knowledge, art history, and twentieth-century history. Students completing the required advanced courses, international examinations, extended essay, community service, and extracurricular activities graduate SCHS with an IB diploma.

In the context of the changing demographics occurring in communities throughout the United States, schools, such as SCHS, are ideal sites to understand the role of institutional practices and everyday exchanges on educational outcomes and group relations. With students spending about one-third of their waking hours in school, they serve as important places of socialization, and due to the historical pattern of neighborhood segregation, schools are one of the first places where there is the potential for extended and intimate cross-racial/ethnic and class contact of students from multiple neighborhoods (Goode, Schneider, and Blanc 1992). Furthermore, as microcosms of society, school practices mirror and reproduce dominant values, ideologies, and inequalities (Bowles and Gintis 1976; Giroux 1983). The demographics of SCHS are especially helpful for exploring the experiences and unpacking the variations that exist within the broad and diverse categories of the two fastest growing racial/ethnic groups within the United States—Latinas/os and Asian Americans. For theoretical guidance in framing what I learned from SCHS, I turn to the following literature.

Using an Intersectional and Multilevel Framework to Understand Schooling

To take students' experiences seriously, the approach I use shifts from an emphasis on the *product* of an achievement gap to one that focuses on the *processes* fostering multiple gaps—opportunity, social, and academic gaps and their ramifications. To this end, I use a tripartite macro-meso-micro framework that involves understanding the specific and intersectional aspects of macroscopic structural factors and dominant ideologies, meso-level school policies and practices, and microscopic everyday exchanges on educational outcomes and school relationships. Combined, these macro-meso-micro processes reinforce hierarchies and are experienced differently by the intersections of race/ethnicity, class, and gender. They also influence human, cultural, and social capital. Such an analysis enhances awareness of the interactional influences of structure and individual agency.

The Macroscopic: The Role of Histories, Structures, and Ideologies

Although the historical foundations, migration patterns, and demographic backgrounds presented earlier about the area of SCHS are often absent in popular discussions of education, they are not inconsequential. Similar factors have shaped towns across the United States, and such foundations influence group positions and opportunities for mobility. Working in tandem with the U.S. economic structure and the following ideologies, they are among the macroscopic factors and belief systems impacting perceptions, unequal schooling, and relationships.

Schools in the United States reflect the capitalist structure. Many systematically sort and divide students into different classes or curriculum tracks—preparing both middle- and upper-class students for managerial and high-wage positions while ensuring a pliable working class—often composed of Blacks and Latinas/os—that fills low-wage occupations (Bowles and Gintis 1976). Given deindustrialization since the 1970s with a decline in high-wage durable goods manufacturing jobs that do not require a college education, students tracked away from four-year colleges and universities are often limited to occupations in the military or minimum-wage service sector jobs.

In the contemporary period where neoliberalism drives education, government spending for schools has been slashed, and schooling is increasingly based on inflexible curriculum, standards-based teaching, and testing (Pearl 2002). Such defunding of public schools and the rigid approach to teaching and learning is experienced most harshly in Latina/o and Black working-class areas where students may encounter school closures and an emphasis on memorization and test preparation (McNeil 2005). Meanwhile, members of the ruling class such as the Gates and Walton Family Foundations are pushing the privatization of schools by funding the proliferation of charter schools and undermining teachers' unions (Russom 2012, 110). Some of these same neoliberal policies have taken their toll on urban and working-class communities where families experience job loss, poverty, and limited access to resources.[13]

Among the results of historical injustices and contemporary policies is a dramatic wealth gap in the United States, especially between White households and households of color. In 2009, the median net worth was $113,149 for White households, $78,066 for Asian American households, $6,325 for Latina/o households, and $5,677 for Black households (Kochhar, Fry, and Taylor 2011). While there are some variations within these panethnic categories, the overall differences in the amount of household net worth have significant implications for life chances, including having the ability to finance educational opportunities such as college educations.

In addition to the historical and economic factors influencing schools and households, it is also important to consider the role of dominant ideologies—prevailing systems of belief used to explain and justify the status quo. For example, the reproduction of a stratified labor force in schools through curriculum tracking has been reinforced by social Darwinist assumptions about the biological superiority of White Anglo Protestants and beliefs of cultural inferiority of immigrants and communities of color (Oakes 1985; Gonzalez 1990). In particular, despite the foundational role that Mexican workers have had in supporting the U.S. economy, Mexicans and Mexican Americans are often constructed as cheap labor and threats culturally, economically, and socially to the United States (Chavez 2001). Historically, Chinese, Koreans, and other Asian Americans were deemed "alien," "dirty," "heathen," and "dangerous." They were categorized by law as not White and thus were ineligible for citizenship. While today most Chinese and Koreans in the United States have a more recent immigrant background, a history of exclusionary policies and anti-Asian constructions have conditioned dominant perceptions and prevailing discourses (Chou and Feagin 2008, 5–9). At SCHS some of these same ideologies—in particular an assimilationist imperative and anti-immigrant sentiment—detrimentally impact intergenerational relationships, especially among Asian Americans students. At SCHS and as captured by Lee (2005) in a Wisconsin high school, some Asian American students attempt to escape the stigma of "foreignness" by distancing themselves from their immigrant and non-English-speaking peers (23–24).

Also, of particular significance are the processes of *racialization* where racial/ethnic groups are constructed in distinct and interactional ways that may also be based on class and gendered constructs. At SCHS, Asian American and Latina/o students are defined in opposition to one another, while Whites and Blacks are what I call "invisibly present"; as numeric minorities at the school, they are often not talked about, but hierarchical constructions of whiteness and blackness are ever present such that whiteness is the unnamed norm and blackness is stigmatized or associated with sports. Dominant ideologies are fundamental in such constructions, and the stereotypical representation of Asian Americans as "model minorities" who are perceived to be long suffering and hard working in comparison to Latinas/os who are depicted as criminals, teen mothers, or lackadaisical toward education is also hegemonic (Lopez 2003). This model minority myth first emerged in the United States during the 1960s social justice struggles at a time when Blacks and Latinas/os were demanding access into dominant institutions and engaging in mass demonstrations that critiqued U.S. society. Popular media such as the *U.S. News & World Report* praised Chinese Americans for being good citizens and advancing on their own because of their believed cultural emphasis on hard work and determination (Lee 1996, 6).

Since the 1960s, magazine and newspaper articles have promulgated the image that if Asian Americans can succeed without assistance, something must be wrong with African Americans and Latinas/os who are lagging behind educationally and economically. This myth persists, and various attitudinal studies find that in comparison to Latinas/os, Asian Americans and Asian immigrants are perceived as less likely to commit crimes and more likely to work hard and excel in school (Bobo and Johnson 2000; Suárez-Orozco and Páez 2002, 22).

As a result of such narrow categorizations, diverse Asian Americans and Latinas/os often experience racial lumping such that they are homogenized into these two broad panethnic categories. By casting Asian Americans as assumed models relative to Blacks and Latinas/os, this construction positions groups against each other, undermines the differing migration histories and the significance of racism and class disparities, and perpetuates the myth of a meritocracy because the belief is that anyone can succeed by just working harder. Such racialized assumptions are not simply isolated stereotypes. They are a part of larger systems that maintain and reproduce social, economic, and political inequality. They permeate all aspects of our society, including schools, and they reinforce racial hierarchies.

The Meso Level: School Policies and Practices

At the meso level, institutions such as schools shape, structure, and constrain relationships (Lamphere 1992, 4). The practices of most U.S. schools are based on division, competition, and hierarchies where different people possess unequal amounts of power, occupy different locations, and have limited opportunities for interaction. This is the case for adults who have unequal occupations and authority as well as for students.

Typically, school practices such as curriculum tracking, extracurricular activities, classroom structures, and course curriculum divide and rank students by race/ethnicity, English-language skills, class position, age, and gender. For example, curriculum tracking where students are placed into separate classrooms reproduces a stratified labor market and distinct peer groups (Gonzalez 1990; Valenzuela 1999). Likewise, zero-tolerance policies in schools, which are unequally enforced such that Black and Latino males are more likely to receive detentions and expulsions than their White counterparts, compound inequalities and may even fuel between-student resentment and suspicion (Kupchik 2010; Rosenbloom 2010).

Even in cases where there is the potential for cross-racial/ethnic friendships such as through extracurricular activities (Hallinan, Teixeira, and Williams 1989), especially if students work together toward a common goal (Moody 2001; Clotfelter 2002), not all students have access to them because of costs and time commitments. Also, school activities often confer different levels of status and prestige. In particular, students who are involved in the production of school-sanctioned dances, assemblies, newspapers, and the yearbook receive special status from school personnel in ways that consumers of school activities and nonparticipants do not (Eckert 1989). Students who are in charge of these activities are provided with leadership positions, greater freedom of movement on campus, and collaborative decision-making opportunities with teachers and administrators. They also are put in charge of leading and controlling other students. Since those students granted "school-endorsed power" are often White and middle class (Eckert 1989, 90; Clotfelter 2004; Gándara and Contreras 2009)—or as is the case at SCHS, are born in the United States, speak English fluently, and are in advanced courses—the unequal distribution of decision-making responsibilities can foster racial/ethnic and class divisions, hierarchies, and hostility. While discussed much less in the literature, I find that there are also differential responses to students' activities such that students involved in more overtly political and less assimilationist organizations may encounter greater restrictions and surveillance on campus, especially at SCHS where such students are often Latina/o and working class.

Assimilationist policies similarly divide and fuel disparities. A key function of schools in the United States has been socialization where an emphasis has been placed on integrating immigrants and groups of color into society (Parsons 1951). Historically, this has been carried out in segregated schools and classrooms through so-called Americanization and newcomer programs designed to teach the English language and U.S. laws and customs. Today, it persists in English-only policies and Eurocentric curriculum. Such practices are informed by and maintain hierarchies that privilege the English language and dominant values, norms, and expectations. They simultaneously ignore, undermine, or outright ridicule the cultures and communities of many SCHS students.

The Microscopic: Everyday Attitudes and Actions

In spite of the power of macroscopic factors and school practices, school staff and students have varied roles in constructing educational outcomes and relationships through their everyday attitudes and actions. For example, teachers' actions can strike at the core of a child and send exclusionary messages to all students in the classroom. As Fabienke cites, teachers' prejudicial and discriminatory treatment not only shape students' self-conceptions but also foster divisions and tensions among students (2007, 12). Since fellow classmates are aware of teachers' favored students—who as Luttrell (1993) found tend to be lighter skinned, more feminine, and middle class—this preferential treatment may result in a "circular process" that fuels excluded students' resentment and their harassment of favored students (e.g., see Rosenbloom and Way 2004). Individually, the power of school officials' actions is undeniable, but students are also active agents, and at an early age, young children internalize, act upon, and recreate racial/ethnic and class hierarchies (Van Ausdale and Feagin 2001, 3).

Combined, these macro-meso-micro processes work insidiously to differentially impact students' school-sanctioned human, cultural, and social capital. While all students possess and develop skills, knowledge, and networks, not all forms of capital are valued in schools and society (Stanton-Salazar 2004; Yosso 2006), and schools often provide students with unequal access to the most valued capital. Placed in different tracks, students in honors and advanced placement courses are the ones most likely to be encouraged to think critically, solve problems, and evaluate information—providing them with what Jeannie Oakes describes as the "high-status" knowledge required of college and important for enhancing the most valued forms of *human capital* (1985, 76). Similarly, enrollment in these classes and participation in prestigious school activities such as leadership, yearbook, and journalism provide select students access to school-endorsed *cultural capital* such as middle- and upper-class knowledge, cultural competencies, and worldviews (see Bourdieu and Passeron 1977). In contrast, the cultural capital that working-class and immigrant students and students of color often bring to school may be frozen, "subtracted," or outright depleted through English-only rules and Euro-centric curriculum (see Valenzuela 1999). Finally, separating students from their peers through curriculum tracking and other academic programs limits students' *social capital* since they are impeded from making con-nections, seeing themselves as parts of a larger community, and drawing upon the resources embedded in wide networks (Stanton-Salazar 2004). Taken together, these intersectional and multilevel dynamics compose the framework informing this book.

Organization of Academic Profiling

In the chapters that follow, I demonstrate how students at SCHS encoun-ter exclusionary ideologies and practices that divide and prepare them for unequal life chances. While the significance of racism, class inequality, and sexism are largely ignored at SCHS, they are ever present in ideologies, structures, practices, and interactions where discourses surrounding an achievement gap work in tandem with hegemonic constructions that cast Asian Americans and Latinas/os in hierarchical ways.

Relative to one another, Asian Americans appear to be privileged aca-demically while Latinas/os may be privileged socially. They then often have unequal access to school resources, experience differential policing, and maintain distinct peer groups. However, I argue that we all lose by such positioning. Systems of power and inequality remain intact, communities are divided, and students suffer in varied ways. Such dynamics negatively impact students' capital; they are provided with unequal access to skills and educational backgrounds, and separation from their peers limits their abilities to learn from and draw upon the networks and knowledge that each possess. Thus from myths about "model minorities" to practices that prepare students for different academic and career paths, intersecting macro-, meso-, and microlevel dynamics reinforce hierarchies, inequalities, and divisions. Simultaneously, the narrowing of curriculum and emphasis on standardized tests reveals how students are being schooled in ways that are confining and product centered rather than process based; holistic; and premised on creativity, exploration, and growth.

To capture the multifaceted factors influencing school dynamics and students' experiences, *Academic Profiling* is organized into three parts underscoring the interrelationships and the significance of macro-meso-micro processes. Following this introduction, part I focuses on dominant ideologies and school structures. Chapter 1 locates the frameworks that many of the administrators, teachers, and students use to understand dif-ferences in educational outcomes in larger ideologies and state and federal policies. Given the prevalence of "power-evasive" discourses in the United States that are apparent in neoconservative and neoliberal arguments that emphasize "color-blindness," individualism, and free choice, many at SCHS believe students and parents are largely responsible for their successes and difficulties in schools (Frankenberg 1993; Omi and Winant 1994).[14] As detailed in this chapter, such blame takes the form of (1) an emphasis on "an achievement gap" where over- and underachieving come to mean Asian and Latina/o; (2) biological arguments that naturalize race/ethnicity and gender and assert that some groups are inherently smarter than other groups; (3) cultural perspectives that assume that Asian Americans, in comparison to their Latina/o schoolmates, come from families and traditions that are more likely to value schooling and hard work; and (4) silence surrounding Whites, White privilege, and whiteness in general. These discourses ignore differing histories and panethnic heterogeneity, and they minimize the significance of structural and institutional inequality, including class disparities. They perpetuate the prevailing ideologies of individualism and meritocracy. With the false belief that some groups do not have the intellectual capacities or the cultural prerequisites, such arguments have been used to justify unequal treatment.

With these dominant discourses and myths about educational outcomes as a context, chapter 2 centers students' narratives as they describe the school structures and practices influencing their experiences. The chapter is organized around the implications of (1) segregated and disparately valued middle schools and (2) the inequalities attached to a rigid track system that includes placement in IB and AVID programs or nonhonors college preparatory (CP) classes. Woven in throughout this chapter are the significance of differing racialization and class backgrounds in shaping students' sense of selves and their opportunities.

Part II focuses on specific school practices and family resources. Chapter 3 shares the narratives of several students who reveal how academic profiling fosters unequal patterns of surveillance and regulation on campus. Chapter 4 discusses the intensification of a tutoring industry within the context of the growing weight placed on standardized tests. With some students receiving extensive amounts of paid tutoring in Chinese schools and from for-profit organizations and other students receiving none, the unequal access to tutoring is fueling academic and social differences and influencing teachers' curriculum and assignments.

Part III centers the microscopic relationships at SCHS. Chapter 5 focuses on the academic and social hierarchies that students perpetuate based on race/ethnicity and generation. By concentrating on how students navigate these hierarchical constructions, chapter 6 considers students' and staffulty's individual and organizational forms of resistance to the exclusion and judgment that they encounter. By claiming an identity, playing with stereotypes, and defying typification, students creatively carve out their own sense of selves and challenge others' perceptions. Organizationally, a smaller group of students and their teachers build alternative campus spaces that may be inclusive, oppositional, or even overtly political. However, given how entrenched power and inequality are, it is difficult to disrupt dominant perspectives and structures. Thus while some students' strategies may be personally beneficial, aspects of their maneuvering may reinforce hierarchies. In other cases, such as in the student organization MEChA (Movimiento Estudiantil Chicano de Aztlán), students and their supporters encounter additional policing and barriers when they contest stereotypes and counter inequality.

Chapter 7 reflects on my experiences sharing the research findings with the SCHS staffulty. It conveys both the urgency and the difficulty of change. While presenting on the institutional inequities and the prevalence of dominant beliefs at the school, I soon learned that some heard my analysis through the same frameworks that I aimed to critique. Others found it difficult to transform school practices in the age of assessment. Thus just as some of the students' strategies for contesting hegemonic constructions may unintentionally reinforce prevailing ideologies, I found this to be my experience as well.

In the final chapter, I discuss what SCHS teaches us about the detrimental impacts of the current state of U.S. schooling. In many ways, SCHS is any school, U.S.A. Just as it is premised on competition, individualism, and assimilation and focuses on a so-called achievement gap, it too overlooks the significance of opportunity and social gaps and the wealth of knowledge, experiences, and resources that its students, their families, and the surrounding communities possess. Dynamics such as these reveal what one school official in reference to SCHS describes as diverse, divided, and disillusioned—the three Ds. In spite of the many difficulties we are up against, I end with hope that the lessons learned from SCHS might be used to expand the debates surrounding schooling and help shift the direction of our educational system.

PART I

Prevailing Ideologies
and School Structures

CHAPTER ONE

Framing the "Gap"

Dominant Discourses of Achievement

Joe Berk remembered, "When I was applying for [this position], I said that there were two campuses at this same school—a high-performing campus, which is predominately Asian, and a low-performing one that is predominately Hispanic . . . This is not a [Southern California High School] phenomenon. Hispanics, in general, emphasize putting food on the table over education."

—*Field notes, February 1, 2007*

While at Southern California High School (SCHS), I frequently heard about "high-performing students," "low-performing students," and the "gap"—determined largely by standardized tests and course placement. Students more commonly described themselves and their schoolmates as "smart" and "stupid." These constant distinctions were made between the two largest panethnic groups at the school—usually referred to by school officials and students as Asians and Hispanics. These two groups were cast in opposition to each other, and analyses of their academic performances were often rooted in supposed biological and cultural differences, as when administrator Joe Berk describes an emphasis among Latinas/os on working to survive rather than working toward educational goals.

For generations, politicians, academics, and educators have offered various explanations for differences in educational attainment. These explanations range from arguments that blame individuals and groups for their supposed deficiencies to ones that critique biased school officials or unequal schooling facilities. The popularity of these theories has fluctuated over time and has varied in scope. However, the biological and cultural deficiency frameworks that are so pervasive at SCHS have been the most influential in shaping schools and the overall racial, economic, political, and social order (Gonzalez 1990).

Such deficiency frameworks largely dismiss the impacts of historical, structural, and institutional inequalities as well as systems of race, class, and gender on life opportunities. They are what Ruth Frankenberg (1993) labels "power-evasive," and they are part of a neoconservative perspective. At SCHS, with the exception of a small percentage of staffulty and students, these discourses inform explanations for educational outcomes. Much of the blame is placed on students and their families, deflecting attention away from the role of schools and society in perpetuating multiple gaps.

This chapter analyzes the individual and group-level explanations or frames that are often used by SCHS's staffulty to understand differences in educational outcomes. As Susan Rosenbloom (2010) describes, "Framing refers to the way people label and identify their worldview by relying on interpretations or maps that organize their experiences into discrete chunks of information" (6). Given the prevalence of power-evasive frameworks in the United States that claim we are in a postracial society, assume we have free choice and equal opportunity, and tout that we live in a meritocracy, many like Berk employ biological and cultural arguments. While heard less frequently, some at SCHS adopt what I refer to as power-aware approaches to understanding educational outcomes, where they consider disparities in resources and forms of discrimination. Given the magnitude of power-evasive approaches at SCHS and in U.S. society, they are hegemonic ideologies that shape people's perceptions and structure people's lives. Thus they are centered in this chapter.

At SCHS, Asian Americans and Latinas/os are the focus of these discourses, demonstrating the relational aspects of race/ethnicity—that these categories and racialized assumptions are not fixed or naturally occurring but are given meaning in relationship to one another. In contrast, Whites and Blacks are rarely discussed, but they are not absent in the school's racial/ethnic constructions. In particular, the silence surrounding whiteness—White identity, White privilege, and cultural practices—is considered in this chapter, while the positioning of Whites and Blacks at the school is considered in more detail in chapter 5.[1]

This chapter details four of the most common power-evasive discourses at SCHS ("the gap," biological deficiency, cultural deficiency, and the invisibility of whiteness) that set the context for understanding the disparities, divisions, and hierarchies at the school. Given their roles as institutional agents in influencing the school culture, the staffulty's perceptions take center stage. Occasionally, students' views are included, but their narratives are emphasized in subsequent chapters. Throughout this chapter,

I highlight some of the factors influencing the staffuly's frameworks and the implications of such perspectives. However, these perspectives are not fixed; people may adopt multiple explanations, or their views may change. Similarly, these perspectives are not simply products of individuals. They are part of the fabric of schools and society and mirror dominant ideologies. They are so entrenched that they may become accepted knowledge that few people question. Thus analyzing the frames that the staffuly use to understand schooling helps uncover the multiple structures and systems of belief that maintain unequal school practices and keep many Asian Americans and Latinas/os unequal and apart at schools such as SCHS.

Framing the "Gap"

A common frame in today's discussions about education is that there is "an achievement gap" based on race/ethnicity. While grades and rates of high school graduation and college attendance are sometimes considered, scores on standardized tests are increasingly *the* primary measurement of achievement, and each year newspapers and school marquees across the nation announce test scores—symbolically bolstering their importance. This emphasis on standardized tests emerged during the Reagan-Bush era and intensified with the policies of the federal government's No Child Left Behind (NCLB) Act of 2001. Accountability is at the core of NCLB, and test performance is used to assess students, schools, and teachers. Among the requirements of NCLB is annual testing in math and reading of children from grades 3 to 8 and at least once in high school. To determine how different groups of students are faring, test scores are disaggregated by race/ethnicity, limited English proficiency, and special education. Schools that do not meet their targeted competency scores or make what is referred to as "adequate yearly progress" receive increasingly severe sanctions. These sanctions range from paying for transportation for students who may transfer to other schools to funding private tutoring programs to being taken over by the state or closed entirely (Wood 2004). As well as diverting public funds away from schools in need, these sanctions fuel the movement for school vouchers, school choice, and charter schools (Hursh 2005). Thus these policies are part of a neo-liberal agenda to control the curriculum, evaluate teachers, and ultimately privatize public school education. They are fueled by "power-evasive" discourses because typically the extensive focus on the "gap" exists without a simultaneous interrogation of the larger factors influencing disparities and fueling the test-based movement in education.

Within the context of high-stakes testing, SCHS school officials begin each academic year by presenting data on students' performances.

Second-year teacher Laura Cooper explains, "From the moment we step into our teachers' meetings three days before school starts, it's 'results from testing; results from testing!' 'We are down again; we need strategies; we need this; we need to get students involved! We need; we need, and we need!'" Each year, this hurried pace of looking at data takes a similar format. Laura Cooper continues,

> The principal and assistant principal of instruction show the teachers last year's test scores and then this year's test scores. So we see that we went down by fifteen points or whatever. Then they put up a slide and do very little explanation of the slide; [they] just assume that everybody understands it the same way. Next thing that is put up is the achievement at the different grade levels. So three bar charts right next to each other, and you have that for Hispanic, Asian, and White; no other [group is presented]: just those three. Then you go through really quickly and see how the Latinos are performing versus the Asians. [The administration] says, "We've got to close that gap."

In large, rushed meetings, data are presented as accurate, meaningful, and self-explanatory. Limited consideration is given to the various factors influencing test performance, such as the construction of the tests; school and social inequalities; and students' diverse backgrounds, skills, and experiences.

There is minimal opportunity to digest, analyze, and reflect on the test scores. According to Laura Cooper, with no chance to process the data, discussions about what is even meant by "an achievement gap" are missing:

> You understand that there is a gap [when the data are presented], and when [the idea of] an achievement gap is brought up again, you make the association to these test scores. But it hasn't necessarily been defined . . . It's glossed over because I don't think that there is a set definition. It's mentioned over and over again like it has been defined, and it is just common knowledge at this point about what it's all about.

Thus while so much emphasis is put on a supposed achievement gap, much is excluded from the presentations that open each school year. Without dialogue, all this becomes "common knowledge" and accepted as the norm.

The racialized associations of achievement also become normalized. Simply presenting data by racial categories without discussion reifies differences and stereotypes. Laura Cooper illustrates,

You can put graphs up there all day long. But unless you are explaining what we see in the data and then come up with potential reasons why that data is the way that it is and then ultimately what can affect those things that we have identified in a positive way, nothing is going to change. You can say achievement gap all day; we know "achievement," and we know "gap." And we see the 150 points that are between our Asian population and our Latino population. I think what it is doing at least for the teachers is reaffirming their stereotypes. It is saying, "Well you know we are going to teach to the Asians."

When I asked Laura if she hears explicit stereotypes or if there are more subtle messages and beliefs, she clarifies:

No teacher here would say that [they teach to the Asians], and it is not because they don't want to [say it], but I don't think that they really consciously think that way. It's what they internalize. I think most teachers here feel that this is an equal opportunity education and they're not picking out certain students to teach to, but it is just [done] subconsciously.

When school administrators impart decontextualized and unanalyzed data that supports stereotypes, the internalization of the subconscious beliefs that Laura Cooper describes is facilitated. Similarly, presenting panethnic categories may reinforce the conception that Asian Americans and Latinas/os are diametrically opposed and that these categories are biologically and culturally natural instead of socially constructed as products of human social systems.

Just as there is no definition of the achievement gap or an interrogation of race/ethnicity, there is limited discussion of whether standardized tests are complete measurements of student learning. In fact, decades of research have demonstrated the many biases in standardized tests (see Gonzalez 1990; de León and Holman 2002). Students who have middle- and upper-class experiences are more likely to perform well on standardized tests because they often share the reference points and cultural backgrounds of those constructing the tests (Ochoa 2007, 176).

Not only may such biases skew test results, but also some teachers fear that the extensive emphasis on test performance and school rankings based on test scores is actually overshadowing student learning and personal growth. According to Laura Cooper, with a focus on improving the school's Academic Performance Index (API), a summary measurement used to evaluate school performance and progress on statewide assessments, the message within SCHS is as follows:

We have this achievement gap. We need to close it so we can bring up
our API. So *we* can win, not so Brian, who is sitting here, can win
when he graduates from high school and that a company that hires
him that assumes he can write a business letter [wins]. That's what it
needs to be.

Seventh-year teacher Beth Hill concurs that the focus is misplaced:

> I feel like [the administration] is so focused on [test performance]
> because they know that if our Hispanic students raise their scores,
> that will raise our API. *That* is why they are concerned. I don't get the
> general "I care about them, and they need to do better."

Fourth-year teacher Michelle Mesa also criticizes this hyperemphasis on
API scores and test-taking skills and how it deflects attention away from
how students are experiencing the campus:

> We are being very blind sighted if we only look at that by test-taking
> strategies in the classroom. I'm wondering if we didn't start giving a
> little more attention to the culture that we're providing, to the mes-
> sages that we're sending, and that perhaps that wouldn't be incentive
> enough for some of our students that are not performing to want to
> do better. If I am a student and I feel like I have no worth and there's
> nobody here that speaks to me on any level whatsoever why should
> I perform and give you what you want because at the end of the day
> you don't think I can do well anyway. As administrators and staff, we
> have to really look at how the subtle or not so subtle messages that
> we're sending are also impacting things like the API . . . It's not just
> all about test-taking strategies.

In such climates, the needs of students are overlooked. When test scores
drive schooling, this perpetuates a type of schooling that is based on what
sociologist Angela Valenzuela refers to as the "technical" or "aesthetic,"
where the impersonal and standardized are privileged over personal
connections and human affection (1999, 22). This type of "aesthetic"
schooling is "subtractive" and often divests students from what they
know and experience. As such, it can push students away from school in
the manner described by teacher Michelle Mesa.

Rather than attend to the needs of students, SCHS trumpets an ethos
of winning, competition, and rivalry. Returning to her critique of how the
administrators present the data to the faculty, Laura Cooper elaborates,

> And then the last slide that they put up is our scores in the content
> areas for the three different groups: Hispanic, Asian, and White for

our school against [another school in the district] . . . and the principal [says], "I just wanted to put that up there to see fairly comparable schools. I just wanted to let you know. It is not necessarily a rivalry thing." Of course it is a rivalry thing, of course it is! It is supposed to get us all fired up.

This emphasis on competition may even push students away from one another as they are encouraged to vie for higher scores against other students and schools. In the context of school rivalries fueled by sports, competition on standardized tests may also perpetuate divisions between schools. This overall focus on competition is antithetical to building collaborative and trusting relationships (Johnson and Johnson 2000).

Illustrating the normalization of test scores, their association with racial/ethnic groups, and how they foster divisions is the way that some students, typically Asian Americans enrolled in honors and advanced placement (AP) courses, comment on the school's API.[2] Without prompting, students explain how teachers' remarks, administrators' announcements, posters around campus, and public rankings of schools have made them aware of the value the school places on doing well on standardized tests. Junior Carmen Chu details,

We know about our API scores because we have video bulletins every Monday, and sometimes they'll talk about how the API scores are going down. [They tell us,] "We want to bring them up. This is our goal to have this certain amount when it comes to STAR [Standardized Testing and Reporting] testing."

Similar to their teachers, students also feel the pressure to do well for the school, and they hear racial/ethnic correlations on test performance and which groups are supposedly hurting the school's ranking. Senior Patty Song explains how some of her teachers even joke in class that "the Asian kids help us have a high API." She believes that "teachers and the administration kind of have it in their heads that the Asians are the smart ones, like they are the ones that make our API go high." In conjunction, students like junior Tommy Huie are "hearing from people outside our school that our API is kind of low because the Mexican people are dragging it down." Drawing on racist assumptions of academic ability, some teachers, administrators, and community members blame the school's perceived declining prestige to falling test scores supposedly caused by Mexican American students, and they put undue pressure on Asian American students.

Overall, the nationally imposed culture surrounding assessment and the excessive focus on the "gap" are detrimental to schooling and students' experiences. They reduce the attention on students' well-being and foster assumptions that standardized tests are fair and precise assessments of student learning. In addition, posting test performances by panethnic categories and without analyses of within-group hetero-geneity and the role of larger factors on test performance perpetuates the power-evasive framework that something must be wrong with those groups who are thought to be responsible for lowering scores. As Claude Steele (1997) has documented in his work on "stereotype threat," it could even become self-fulfilling so that Asian Americans rise to others' expectations and Latinas/os may underperform on tests in accordance with dominant assumptions. Finally, the narrow empha-sis on an achievement gap that leaves unquestioned standardized test results also positions Asian Americans against Latinas/os and fosters the invisibility of Whites and Blacks, who at SCHS are left out of the data or barely discussed. Given the relatively small percentage of Whites and Blacks at the school, their scores may not impact the overall ranking of the school. Thus their performances and such students are largely dismissed. As detailed next, this focus on standardized tests and decon-textualized presentations of students' performance work in tandem with the prevalence of individual and group-level frameworks on educational success. Together, they reinforce the legacy of biological and cultural deficiency arguments that further hierarchical constructions of Latinas/os and Asian Americans.

Individual and Group-Level Arguments for Educational Outcomes

> The approach to education might be like an Asian tradition. Since back for thousands of years, education has been *the* thing for like millions of years. Chinese dinosaurs probably took school seriously.
>
> —Sandra Wu, *International Baccalaureate (IB) senior*

Student Sandra Wu's comments rooting Asian educational success in the time of the dinosaurs capture other dominant frameworks. Such argu-ments posit that some groups possess and others lack the supposed biological or cultural attributes for progress and achievement. These arguments assume that racism and discrimination are passé and that the United States is a meritocracy. So the roles of class inequality and individual, institutional, and structural discrimination on educational experiences and life chances are largely dismissed. Furthermore, both biological and cultural arguments are essentialist and are used to pro-file students since all members of particular races/ethnicities, classes, and genders are perceived to possess defining traits. Within-group heterogeneity and the ways that race/ethnicity, class, and gender are sociopolitical, economic constructs are overlooked. Such perspectives have shaped popular discourse, and at SCHS, they are apparent in (1) biological determinist arguments that naturalize gender and race/ethnicity and assert that some groups are inherently more mature, more disciplined, or smarter than other groups; (2) cultural determinist beliefs that assume, for example, that Asian Americans and the middle and upper classes, in comparison to Latinas/os and the poor, come from families and traditions that are more likely to value schooling and hard work; and (3) the invisibility of whiteness. By glossing over student differences and ignoring macro-meso-micro factors fostering disparities in schools, broad categorizations of Asian American and Latina/o students and general designations of "high performing" and "low performing" reproduce dominant structures, maintain hegemonic gendered and racialized assumptions, pit groups against each other, and hinder the possibilities of change. Cultural determinist beliefs are also connected to assimilationist arguments and the "model minority" myth discussed in more detail in chapter 5. For now, we turn to the perspectives of the staffulty and the reinforcement of dominant ideologies.

The Belief That Biology Is Destiny: Naturalizing Sex, Gender, and Race

> Ninth-grade girls do well until they get the two Bs—boobs and boyfriends.
>
> —Tom O'Brien, teacher

> You grow up in a world where some people are just stupid and some people are smart. You assume that Asians are smart and that Mexicans are always stupid.
>
> —Monique Martínez, student

The comments made by Tom O'Brien before a faculty meeting and the reflections from junior Monique Martínez during an interview reveal the naturalizing of both gender and race/ethnicity as biological entities. Although some might interpret Tom O'Brien's remarks as a statement of students' changing interests over the life course, his specific reference to breasts implies anatomical differences and hormonal fluctuations that supposedly disrupt the academic performance of all ninth-grade girls, who he assumes are distracted by boys. Just as O'Brien claims that girls' academic performance dips with the onset of puberty, Monique Martínez's explanations of intelligence also suggest that biology is destiny. In this case, she has come to believe that Asians are naturally smarter than Mexicans. While such biological determinist arguments have long been disproved and replaced by theories of race/ethnicity and gender as socially constructed, some at SCHS reduce academic performance to biology and use assumed biological traits to profile students.

Rooting Sex and Gender in Biology

Although national statistics reveal an overall gender gap where women across all racial/ethnic groups have higher rates of school achievement and college attendance (Lopez 2003; Gándara and Contreras 2009), gender and educational outcomes were rarely discussed during the interviews. Similarly, school personnel reported that little was said at the school about their salience. Many did not seem to question this silence because as some indicated, they did not notice the significance of gender in their classrooms, or they figured that standardized test scores are presented by race/ethnicity. So they believed that the school simply draws on available data when trying to understand educational outcomes, and with the mandates of No Child Left Behind, test performance by race/ethnicity is emphasized.

Several of the school officials who described noticing gendered patterns in school performance naturalized them with comments such as "we all know that girls tend to perform better in school." A couple explicitly adopted a biological explanation by stressing differences in maturation. Teacher Jane King's comments are illustrative:

> English has a tendency to be a class that girls do better in because
> it's a linguistic-based class and, you know, the boys are not quite as
> talkative and not quite as social . . . I think honestly they're not ready
> for it yet, you know. They are when they're seniors; maturity-wise,
> they're where the girls are when they were freshman. You know,
> they're just not ready for it yet.

Believing that it is common knowledge that as two distinct groups all boys and all girls differ in terms of maturation, Jane King thrice uses the phrase "you know" to express her point. She is not alone in accepting this sentiment. Coach Jim Scott echoes her as he reflects on the students who have assisted him:

> The girls perform higher than the boys because of the maturation;
> girls usually mature faster than guys. There's like a five-year gap
> between the girls and the guys, maturity-wise . . . The people that

help me in my office, the good ones are the girls that are really good
on the computer and are able to handle the things I need done. I don't
think I've ever had a male office aide that was good on the computer,
so it's always been a female student.

Not only is sex and maturation conflated with gender identities, but such
biological determinist perspectives often foster unequal treatment. In this
case, young women are given the opportunity to work with Coach Scott.
This provides them with capital such as computer skills and social networks that young men may be denied. Similarly, just as young men are
restricted by this biological categorization, it may also reinforce gender
expectations of women's labor and the assumption that women are effective assistants and good with data entry.

Longtime teacher Margaret Albert extends this perception that there
are natural variations in maturation by sex and gender. As she explains,
in comparison to girls, boys have more energy, and this accounts for their
higher representation in remedial courses:

> When I had the remedial English [class], the majority were guys. We
> know that there are some differences in maturation . . . [I]t's pretty
> difficult with their energy level for them to have to keep still for as
> long as they have to.

According to Margaret Albert, these supposed differences make it hard to
force boys to sit in class for long periods of time. So she alters her teaching
strategies to accommodate for their perceived differences:

> [Guys are] more active. I'd need to have some of them run around the
> building a few times [to] get rid of that energy. And I need to have
> more hands on and moving around. It's cruelty to them to have to sit
> still that long.

Many people find it difficult to remain seated for hours each day in a
traditional classroom. However, rather than critique a lecture-based classroom structure that requires students to quietly sit next to other students
as they listen to the teacher and take notes, some such as Margaret Albert
instead locate the problem in males' supposed unique biological composition. Also underlying this teacher's comments is an assumption that
women are naturally more adept at sitting passively. Although Margaret Albert tries to accommodate the presumed high energy of males in
her remedial classes by changing her pedagogy, this does not address the
larger factors that lead to the unequal placement of young men in remedial classes, such as the transitional English class described in the preface,

that funnel students away from college. It also does little to disrupt the traditional one-way transfer of knowledge in the classroom that expects students to inactively receive information from teachers.

Similar to their teachers, students only occasionally considered gender as a factor influencing schooling. Nonetheless, a couple of students repeated a biological determinist argument that they learned in class. Eleventh-grader Margaret Kang explains, "Recently, we heard in English that girls excel in English and liberal arts and then guys are more logical thinkers."

Several students labeled girls as "hard workers" and guys as "lazy." Sometimes, guys were characterized as "chill"—which seems to contradict teacher Margaret Albert's description of boys having a lot of energy. For junior Summer Reyes, this apparent relaxed demeanor in comparison to girls' "more emotional" state is genetic:

> I think the girls are harder on themselves. I guess because girls are weaker or more emotional, so they get really stressed, so they work themselves really hard. The guys, they're chill about everything . . . I think it's just in their genes. Girls are just more caring about things.

Senior Jean Kim concurs with Summer that "guys are more laid back; just naturally they're laid back. Even if they're smart, they're laid back." She adds that girls "take [more] initiative and actually try to work harder than guys, but then sometimes guys are smarter. They don't even need to try; they just are smarter." The assumption in such comments is that in comparison to men, women are not inherently smart; they are just harder workers.

Remarks such as these reveal how some at SCHS equate sex with gender. Such conflating ignores the ways that gender is not natural. Instead, gender is a sociopolitical economic construction that is influenced by socialization from family members, peers, schools, the media, and others. Gender is also performed in everyday interactions and embedded in cultural expectations and institutional disparities (Risman 1998). Furthermore, such comments assume that one's biological sex always matches one's gender identity and that genders are genetically distinct from each other. In spite of research demonstrating that the two-sex (male–female) and two-gender (man-woman) system is constructed and that there are more variations *within* the categories of males and females than between males and females (Epstein 1988), such conflating of sex with gender persists. This discourse perpetuates the belief that both sex *and* gender are biological and that variations between sexes and genders are normal. It is alleged that girls and boys differ biologically and that these differences produce fundamentally distinct people. Expecting changes in academic performances is thus futile because the assumption is that boys and girls are just naturally different. Such sentiments may then become self-fulfilling to the extent that students are profiled based on these assumptions and encounter unequal treatment and expectations.

Employing Biological Constructs of Race/Ethnicity and Intelligence

In comparison to discussions surrounding sex and gender, school officials were much less likely to provide such explicit biological arguments when explaining academic differences by race/ethnicity. Instead, they were merged with cultural deficiency arguments or their language was racially coded. For example, coach Marilyn Garcia combined biological and cultural explanations in her assessment of students' coordination:

> Asians, they're more oriented to academics, to their studies. They'd rather not play softball or hit the ball, or they don't have the coordination. But then, the Mexican kids are a lot more fun in terms of sports because they're not studying hard at home. There's no one really to beat them up to do the school work because the focus seems to be different.

Although few school officials adopted such traditional racist beliefs linking race, biology, and performance—in this case that Asian Americans lack coordination—there were indications that some school officials still accept the belief that intelligence is biological and that select people are innately more inclined to certain subjects. For instance, during an IB meeting with students, a school official instructed "natural-born mathematicians" to enroll in an additional calculus class, while those who are "not the brightest light as math is concerned" should take statistics.[3]

Teacher Manuel Cadena also reinforces conceptions that intelligence is biological:

> If you're lucky enough, you are on this side of the tracks. You're given students that are unbelievably bright. You've got three people [at SCHS] that scored perfect on the SATs. Here, if you get something below 1200, something's wrong with you. We've got all this raw talent, but then you get these kids from the other side of the train tracks that are not prepared. So you can only do so much.

While unstated, race/ethnicity and socioeconomic status are embedded in Manuel Cadena's train tracks metaphor. In comparison to the primarily poor and working-class Latina/o neighborhood on "the other side of the train tracks," SCHS is situated in a more socioeconomically privileged and racially diverse area—factors that, according to Manuel Cadena, result in students with "raw talent" in comparison to other students who he believes "can only do so much." Such references to talent and brightness in this context reinforce assumptions that intelligence is not only innate but also correlated with class and race/ethnicity. His equation of SAT scores with talent also overlooks years of hard work studying for the test and unequal resources such as differential access to tutors and paid preparation courses.

Whereas during their interviews most school officials tended not to equate race/ethnicity to biology, students frequently used phrases such as "smart" and "stupid" to refer to different racial/ethnic groups, as in Monique Martinez's opening quote. It was not always clear if such labels and racial/ethnic associations were linked to an underlying belief in biological differences, but the associations are made so frequently that some students start to deduce, as Monique does, that "Asians are smart and that Mexicans are always stupid." According to at least one group of friends, such comments are as frequent as saying "Hi" at school.

Some of what students hear emanates from their teachers. Sophomores Jenn Vanderhol and Fran Padilla reflect on the power of teacher's comments:

> JENN: He would just talk about how Asians are smarter. How we are not smart 'cause "you're not Asian."
>
> FRAN: He was always joking around, but it's like even if you're joking around there is always some form of truth to it. It has to come from somewhere.

As Fran suggests, even though her teacher may be joking, these racialized messages from authority figures may be internalized and reproduced. After all, Fran believes that such so-called jokes must bear some "truth."

Mexican Americans Rebecca Ramos and Gloria Camacho accept similar beliefs, and they too draw upon a teacher's lesson to prove their points. When asked why one of the two middle schools that many SCHS students attend is perceived as better than the middle school they attended, Rebecca and Gloria offer the following explanation:

> REBECCA: They're all Asians over there . . .
>
> GLORIA: They're probably just born smart.
>
> REBECCA: Yeah, and well, our first period teacher was showing us how many people go to college, and Mexicans were last. First, it was Asians and then it was White people, then it was Black people, then it was Mexicans.

While their teacher's intent in sharing current demographic information on educational attainment was not clear, if the data were presented without interrogation as the standardized test results are presented to teachers, a phenomenon similar to the one teacher Laura Cooper described earlier may occur for students. That is, like some teachers, students may also interpret such statistics as confirmation of a racial/ethnic hierarchy where Asian American students are positioned as smarter than other students.

These biological arguments from some school officials and students are not isolated. For much of history, biological deficiency perspectives dominated academic and public discourse, and they have bolstered school practices. Through the 1950s, White middle- and upper-class researchers and educators often used biological arguments to justify de jure segregation, Americanization programs, and vocational courses for students of color. For example, proponents of biological determinism believed that Mexican American students were naturally inclined toward sex rather than education, were predisposed physically to perform agricultural labor, and lacked the mental capabilities to excel in academically rigorous courses (see Gonzalez 1990). These theories justified separate and unequal schools that punished those who spoke languages other than English, emphasized U.S. patriotism, and prepared students for low-wage and gender-specific occupations. Meanwhile, Euro-American students were largely schooled to fill higher-paying occupations in accordance with their gender and class positions.

More recently, there have been several high-profile cases illustrating the endurance of biological arguments, including in 2005 when, at an economics conference, then–Harvard University president Lawrence Summers attributed the underrepresentation of women scientists in senior positions to genetics (Goldenberg 2005). In 2009, a Harvard PhD student completed a dissertation arguing that immigrants have lower IQs than White Americans. The content of the dissertation was made public when a well-known conservative think tank aimed to use it to bolster their argument against immigration reform (Wessler 2013).

Even though the idea of superior and inferior sexes, genders, and races/ethnicities has long been disproved scientifically, biological arguments persist. They seep into dominant ideologies, people's imaginations, and even our language. Furthermore, along with some of the cultural determinist arguments detailed in the following section, they have maintained and reproduced a race-based capitalist and gendered labor system that divides and ranks students.

Cultural Determinism: Fostering Homogenization and Hierarchies

> The Asians seem to be motivated and driven. The Latinos don't seem
> to value education in the same way. [Their] parents don't seem to be as
> involved the way the Asian parents are.
>
> —*Anthony Castro, teacher*[4]

Notwithstanding the existence of some biological assumptions, cultural explanations such as those presented by fifth-year teacher Anthony Castro were more commonly provided during the interviews. These arguments emphasize supposed differences in values, parental expectations, and work ethics. As in the biological arguments surrounding race, in most cases, Asian Americans—believed to possess the preferred cultural and familial predispositions necessary to excel—are positioned in opposition to Latinas/os. However, at times, Asian Americans are judged just as harshly as Latinas/os but still in binary ways, with Asian Americans characterized as being overly involved or demanding too much academically of their children and Latinas/os as being too lax when it comes to school. Similarly, some teachers also use a "culture of poverty" explanation when they argue that the poor and working classes are "apathetic" toward education (see Lewis 1966). Thus, just as these cultural determinist arguments homogenize groups and overlook systems of power and inequality, they also foster racial/ethnic and class hierarchies.

The assumption that Latinas/os and Asian Americans are diametrically opposed in their support for and involvement in education is ubiquitous. Comments such as the following by school official Jackie Towne are typical: "The achievement gap is going to be there because the mind-set of the Asian culture and the mind-set of the Hispanic culture are different. They're just different." Teacher Jane King, who earlier attributed supposed biological differences in maturation to gendered performances in English language courses, agrees with Jackie Towne that "culture" and "family life" are preeminent factors in influencing educational outcomes:

> Whether or not somebody is academically successful? What influences
> that? Oh, first and foremost, their family life, how they were raised,
> the culture of the family, what the family believes—100 percent, and
> that's why we have a gap at this school between the Asian population,
> Hispanic . . . You're going to see the number one difference is what's
> going on in the home, not what's going on in the classroom.

Along with referring generally to the undefined but apparently understood "gap" at SCHS, Jane King is quick to dismiss any role that the school may have in creating and perpetuating inequalities. According to her and many of the staffulty, "the culture of the family" is 100 percent liable for student performance. This discourse of the family is pervasive; it reinforces assumptions of good and bad families, and it ignores the multiple economic and political contexts infringing on household resources and opportunities. The implication is that educational outcomes cannot be changed unless families and cultures are altered.[5] Schools and society are held unaccountable.

Framing Latinas/os

Even when the staffulty do not explicitly compare Latinas/os with Asian Americans, these assumptions of cultural difference and a cultural hierarchy are rampant. Teacher Manuel Cadena, whose views span biological, cultural, and power-aware arguments, is one among several school personnel to offer a scathing critique of what he refers to as "the attitude" of Latina/o parents:

> Latino parents have no involvement in what their kids are doing . . . The attitude of the village needs to change. The entire Latino village needs to change the way it raises kids to understand the value of being educated and realize they're a big population that can be heard.

While study after study reveals that Latina/o students have higher aspirations to go to college than do students from the general population and that 94 percent of Latina/o parents say they expect their own children to go to college (Delgado-Gaitan 1992; Kao 2000; Pew Hispanic Foundation/Kaiser Family Foundation 2004), sweeping generalizations are made about Latinas/os not valuing education. Incidentally, earlier in his interview, as described in the section on biological determinism, Manuel Cadena argued that students on "the other side of the train tracks" (read: Latina/o and poor or working class) are "not prepared. So you can only do so much." In this current example, he criticizes Latina/o parents for not valuing education. Yet members of the same Latina/o community that he castigates across the tracks who attend SCHS are actually "choice students." These students and their families made the decision to leave their home schools to attend the more highly ranked school in the district with the hopes of increasing their educational opportunities. One such student, sophomore Daniela Gutierrez, explains her parents' decision: "My brother was coming here, and I guess they thought that [SCHS] was a better school . . . They have higher test scores or something like that." Thus while some working-class and Latina/o families are actually investing significant time to enroll their children in SCHS and then driving them several miles each day to and from school, Manuel Cadena dismisses these efforts by assuming that parents do not value education. Instead, he seems to equate valuing education to attending school meetings:

> If you look at the parents of these kids in [my non–college prep. course], you'll see a difference in their parental attitude compared to the parents of kids in [my college prep. course]. Parent conference night, for example, I'll see one or two sets of parents from two kids from [my non–college prep. course]. The rest of the fifty-some parents that I see are from my [other class].

This belief that attendance at school meetings is a crucial indication of parent caring is a fallacy accepted by many who possess stereotyped perceptions of Latina/o families and narrow conceptions of parent participation (Lareau 1989; Quijada and Alvarez 2006).

Not only do parents believe that all forms of raising children are critical, including providing food, clothing, and verbal encouragement (Williams and Stallworth 1983; Gándara 1995), but working-class, immigrant, or Latina/o parents may also be more likely to expect that schools and teachers are responsible for student learning since they are officially trained for this undertaking (Lareau 1987). However, given the hegemony of middle-class and upper-middle-class frameworks of parent participation, these broader views may be ignored by the staffulty. Likewise, by blaming parents' cultures, the responsibilities of schools in creating spaces inclusive of all parents—including working-class, immigrant, and non-English-speaking—are overlooked.

Also overlooked in cultural deficiency frameworks are the ways that class position and previous experiences with institutions of higher education may influence families' cultural and social capital. In particular, low-income and Latina/o families may not have the same forms of school-expected cultural capital (knowledge of how the school system works and what it values) and social capital (access to institutional agents) than middle- and upper-class students who are often White and Asian American (Lareau 1989; Gándara and Contreras 2009, 68). However, rather than examining how schools may assume that all possess the same forms of capital or that schools bear no responsibility for providing information and access that may be taken for granted by more privileged parents, Latina/o families are blamed.

While only mentioned in regard to Latinas/os, a couple of school officials drew on classic cultural deterministic arguments that blame what has been referred to as a "language handicap" for hindering academic success (see Chavez 1991). Fourth-year teacher Mike Williams expounds,

There's a huge language issue because they're taught Spanish first
and then they come to an American school where everything is done
in English. So they're already behind because they don't have that
language acquisition. They don't have the language to function academically, so that already is an enormous setback for most.

Rather than seeing bilingualism as an asset or faulting schools for the elimination of bilingual education, Mike Williams assumes that Spanish-speaking
students are deficient—that they lack "language acquisition." This sentiment
was common, especially through the 1960s when much of the academic
scholarship on bilingualism was premised on the belief that English-language
learners experience impairment in speech, intellect, confidence, and original-
ity of thought (Soto 1997, 3). Disproving such biased assumptions, more
recent studies indicate that when students are provided the opportunity to
acquire two languages through dual-immersion programs, they demonstrate
superiority in concept formation, mental flexibility, and verbal problem-
solving abilities relative to their monolingual peers (Lindholm 1995, 247).

By only focusing on Latinas/os and the Spanish language, teacher Mike
Williams assumes that Latinas/os are the group most held back by language or that they are more likely to come from non-English-speaking
households. However, as documented by the California Department of
Education, equal numbers of Latina/o and Asian American students (about
one hundred each) are designated English-language learners at SCHS.
Although no group should be the target of such a fallacious statement that
they lack "language acquisition," this sentiment is also unequally applied.

Framing Asian Americans

In contrast to Latina/o parents, who are typically described as not valuing education, Asian American parents are often characterized as just the
opposite. Second-year teacher Alison Adams's comments capture this sentiment: "I see honors/AP as your high achievers, and that tends to be
your Asian kids. I think it's cultural. I took a class once, and we talked
about that, and culturally Asian parents tend to push more. They're very
involved in education." Dominant representations of Asian Americans as
a so-called model minority who are believed to really "push" education
prevail, and in the case of Alison Adams, she learned this in her teacher
education program. Teacher Mike Williams bases his assessment on his
observations:

Education, from what I've seen in most Asian families, is something
that is held in the highest regard. If you want to get anywhere in

your life and become successful and prosper and be a professional, education is that key. What I've noticed even with little, little Asian American children is, "School, school, school, work work, work. Study your butt off." And because knowledge and education is so revered in so many Asian American families, that's quite naturally what a lot of Asian American students bring to school with them.

While his qualifying language of "most" and "a lot" tempers Mike William's simplifications, he nonetheless casts a broad stroke in describing Asian Americans. Likewise, he conveys his assumption that "education is that key" to success, "to get[ing] anywhere in life." Such a sentiment supposes that there is just one path and one conception of success, that everyone has equal access to education, and that education necessarily results in prosperity. In contrast to these assumptions, relative to Whites, Asian Americans do not receive comparable returns on their education, and they often face blocked opportunities to career advancement, especially in managerial positions (Woo 2000; Chen 2006). Some suggest that it is precisely these *structural* barriers that are a product of racial discrimination that lead some families to do all they can to encourage education for their children in hopes of reducing the impacts of racism (Louie 2004). Like their Latina/o immigrant counterparts, studies suggest that Asian American parents place much hope in their children's education. However, at SCHS, the financial resources and knowledge of educational institutions of Asian American and Latina/o parents often differ because of parents' variations in class-based resources and educational backgrounds.

While school officials tend to praise Asian American families for what they believe is a strong emphasis on education, underlying some of these cultural arguments is that Asian Americans might just "push" their children too much. Veteran teacher Margaret Albert reflects,

> The bad side of that is that some Asian parents have, and again I'm lumping all Asians and it's very different being wherever you're from, but sometimes, it's so unrealistic that their parents are pushing them that that creates a lot of problems. You know, it's unrealistic that everyone's going to go to UC [University of California] Berkeley.

Softening her generalization of Asian Americans by mentioning geographic and ethnic differences, Margaret Albert cautions Asian American parents from being "unrealistic" and "pushing" too hard. However, like many, she does not challenge the structure of society and schools that are based on competition and driven by hierarchies that rank schools and individuals. The push to achieve greater and more rewards is embedded in society and schools. As described earlier, SCHS's emphasis on its API score is just one of many examples of this culture of competition in schools. Rather than critique this culture, the supposed culture of Asian Americans is targeted.

The image that Asian American parents are not just "unrealistic" but even downright abusive has, according to teacher Beth Hill, become part of the student lore. She shares, "The students always joke, 'You have no idea what beating I would get if I get a B.' That's like a big joke, but I don't know if it really is." While Asian American students may be playing with stereotypes of their parents when they make these comments to their teachers, Beth Hill hears such comments so often that she is even beginning to believe them.

Just as some critique Asian Americans for "pushing" their children in what they perceive as too much, a few such as Beth Hill belittle families for being insistent with teachers:

> I have a student that was absent a lot and his mom has been e-mailing me. Since he got a C for the semester and a B– [overall], and I didn't advise him to go on to AP because I feel like the absences are really going to [hurt him], she e-mailed me, "Please."

Parents have the right to request that their children be placed in advanced courses. However, Beth Hill believes that this request was too demanding and emblematic of some of her exchanges with Asian American parents. To punctuate her point, she continues with a second example:

> One [family member] I had asked to change a grade. [The student] took my sophomore class as a junior for honors because he was in IB and he needed a better grade than a D. He still got a D in my class his junior year. That aunt [said], "Please, can you just change it?" I'm like, "No." They come, and they push.

While it is unclear how often teachers encounter this second example, where they are asked to change a grade, some teachers may equate these two interactions with Asian Americans parents only. However, middle-class and upper-middle-class children and parents in high curriculum tracks such as the International Baccalaureate program or those with high socioeconomic status may be more likely to make such requests because of their own privileged positions and sense of entitlement in school and society (Lareau 1989). As education scholar Lisa Delpit (1995) has documented, they may possess a variation of the "culture of power" in knowing what to expect and what to ask of the school to best serve their interests.

Typically ignoring within-group variations, many school officials describe
the supposed cultures between Asian Americans and Latinas/os as static,
homogenous, and diametrically opposed. When asked about within-group
differences, many seem unaware or reluctant to discuss them. This was
especially the case for White administrators and faculty, who often accepted
dominant beliefs or were raised in areas where, as the numeric majority,
they did not think about the significance of race/ethnicity. For example,
thirty-year teacher Harriet Andrews remembers being raised in an area
where "people didn't concentrate" on racial/ethnic backgrounds. Instead,
during her childhood, there was the idea of "the so-called melting pot,"
where it was believed that all groups would interact and boundaries would
eventually blur so that people's backgrounds would become insignificant.
It was thought that they would lose their ancestral ties and assimilate into
the dominant U.S. culture (Waters 1990). As a result of this perspective,
Harriet Andrews believes that Asian American students' ethnicities, along
with her own, which she defines as American, are "irrelevant":

> I have an awful lot of Asian students. The school percentage is some-
> thing like 53 percent or maybe more, and in the honors classes it's
> probably 80 or 90 percent, and I've taught so long that I forget what
> anyone is, and I certainly don't know the difference between a Korean
> and a Japanese and a Chinese in general. I might because someone
> told me or they have a Japanese last name. It occurred to me that all
> of that, especially in being older, it becomes irrelevant. If I were a new
> teacher, I'd be more aware of it.

It is unclear why she speculates that she might be more aware of students'
ethnicities if she were just starting to teach since even some newer teachers are also unaware. Newcomer Alison Adams, who earlier shared how
she learned in a class that "culturally Asian parents tend to push [educa-
tion] more," confesses here that she actually knows little about students'
backgrounds:

> I wish I knew the different socioeconomic [backgrounds] because I
> don't know the differences. That's one thing that I don't . . . I guess
> it's good and bad. I don't know the difference between the different
> Asian ethnicities. So I don't pinpoint that.

Ironically, while the school focuses so much on Asian American and
Latina/o educational outcomes in the form of standardized tests and so

many profess that there are cultural differences between groups, teachers such as Alison Adams are uninformed of the histories and backgrounds of those who compose these categories. This confirms teacher Laura Cooper's earlier critique that outside of students' test results, little information is provided about the various students at the school. Initially, Alison Adams is concerned that she does not know these differences, but then she reflects on how not knowing may be good. She seems to imply that if she knew, she might treat students unfairly.

Not only is there little awareness of varied histories and ethnicities, but staff ulty tend not to distinguish between socioeconomic status. In fact, with comments such as "It's a touchy subject" and "People don't want to go there," several outright avoided any discussions about class disparities. Since so many accept a cultural determinist view rather than a more structural analysis on group position, the assumption is that one's socioeconomic position is somehow a reflection of a person's worth or merit. To some, to be poor is perceived to be a negative indictment on one's values, work ethic, or abilities rather than a critique of an unequal class system or an awareness of differing migration patterns. In the eyes of one SCHS administrator, "To say you're poor is more of a slur [than to say you are Mexican]." She believes that the prejudices and stigmas against the poor and Mexicans are so strong that people not only avoid identifying as such, but there is a culture of silence surrounding class and race.

These claims about averting awareness of differences are a more contemporary spin on the melting pot approach that was popular during teacher Harriet Andrews's childhood and through the early 1960s. The melting pot approach emerged in the 1930s and was a liberal challenge to biological determinist beliefs that assumed a biological hierarchy of racial/ethnic groups (Omi and Winant 1994, 14). In contrast, the view articulated by new teacher Alison Adams became pervasive in the 1970s in opposition to the civil rights struggles and an analysis of systemic power and inequality. The backlash against civil rights gains resulted in what has been described as neoconservatism. Some who accept a neoconservative perspective may say that they do not see class or race, or they may equate being class or race conscious with being exclusionary. While melting pot and neoconservative ideologies developed during distinct time periods and represent different political perspectives, they are both variations of a cultural-determinist and power-evasive view because they minimize class inequality, racism, sexism, and other forms of discrimination (see Omi and Winant 1994). Cultural arguments, as opposed to historical, political, economic, and social ones, are then used to explain group position. However, in a society and school stratified by class, race/ethnicity, gender and migration and when these backgrounds *are* salient for people's experiences, not noticing them or believing that they are "irrelevant" can reinforce stereotypes, inhibit understanding, and camouflage the role of larger factors in perpetuating inequality. They are also assimilationist because all are expected to become the same, such as by melting away their differences. In these examples, the assumption is that all Asian Americans are the same and that unequal resources as a result of class disparities are irrelevant in influencing schooling.

In spite of a general tendency among school officials to homogenize racial/ethnic groups, some made within-group distinctions. However, this was more common when describing Latinas/os, and such acknowledgments of heterogeneity often came from Latina/o teachers. For example, while many teachers were silent on the impact of class differences on educational outcomes, several emphasized that poor and working-class Latina/o families in particular were the ones who did not value education. Fifth-year teacher Anthony Castro clarifies:

> There is a lot of "apathy" [from low-income Latinas/os]. Both students and their families don't place importance in education. The Latino families [at SCHS] are economically disadvantaged. Socioeconomic status is so correlated with family instability. Their parents don't have as much education, and they don't value it in their children. If there weren't different class statuses then there wouldn't be a difference, a gap. The Latinos in the upper-level classes are the Latinos that come from the Asian neighborhood. They have the high test scores and GPAs [grade point averages].

Raised in a Mexican American family, Anthony Castro may be more inclined to see the diversity among Latinas/os. However, as someone who is college educated and the third generation of his family in the United States, he may wish to distinguish himself from working-class Latinas/os because of the extensive stereotypes that lump all Latinas/os together. Upon first glance, Anthony Castro's arguments about class variation appear helpful for acknowledging some of the differences among Latinas/os and highlighting how many Latinas/os at the school are working class. Nevertheless, his arguments also perpetuate detrimental assumptions. First of all, they assume that something is allegedly wrong with low-income Latina/os who Anthony Castro stereotypes as not valuing education. In contrast, he says little about how class inequalities influence access to resources such as computers, tutoring programs, and other forms of support that enhance educational opportunities. Second, by claiming that the eradication of class differences will eliminate racial/ethnic disparities,

Anthony Castro overlooks the significance of racist beliefs and practices. Finally, a common assumption made by this teacher and others is that all Asian Americans are economically advantaged. Thus while some recognize class differences among Latinas/os, Asian Americans are still cast as monolithic and held up as the group to model. Popular misperceptions that all Asian Americans are middle and upper class lead some to overlook how nearly 11 percent of Asian American families in the area of SCHS, including one in five Korean families, are living below the poverty line (U.S. Census 2000).

Gendered and Racialized Assumptions

Just as some acknowledge class variation among Latinas/os, a small number of school officials link gender and race/ethnicity to argue that there are more gender differences between Latinas and Latinos than between Asian American women and men. As teacher Anthony Castro proclaims, for the Hispanic group, the guys are less motivated to do well. For Asians, "guys and girls are equally motivated." In making such assessments, the emphasis is again on allegedly different values between Latinas/os and Asian Americans.

In fact, a few staffulty, such as teacher Margaret Albert, drew on hegemonic constructions of race and teen pregnancy to characterize Latinas as more sexually active and desirous of children in comparison to other groups of students on campus:

> I've felt there was a marked difference between the Hispanic female, and I remember reading a very interesting article on how it was a status symbol practically, you know, you're proud that you're pregnant at an early age . . . If you're in one part of the subculture, it's kind of cute for the girl to walk around pregnant. And she's young and then he's young and then there's the limit to how much education you can get.

Despite research indicating that Latina adolescents are less likely to be sexually active than European American and African American girls (Blum et al. 2000, as referenced in Denner and Guzmán 2006, 4) and that having a child as a teenager is linked to class resources, the assumption is that Latinas/os as a group favor young mothers. Teacher Margaret Albert expounds on her essentializing of Latina hypersexuality and young parenthood in comparison with her beliefs of Asian Americans:

> Among the Asian population, generally dating and really getting involved in boyfriend-girlfriend relationships is something that is

delayed a great deal. And therefore they have more time to do other things.

Such categorizations are also pervasive in the media, and they position Latinas and Asian American women into racialized and gendered binaries. During various historical periods, Latinas and Asian Americans have been cast as sexually promiscuous and flaunting their sexuality or as asexual and virgins until marriage. In contrast, Latino men are often stereotyped as "Latin lovers" or hypermasculine, whereas Asian American men may be feminized (Ramírez-Berg 1997; Espiritu 1997). These representations are confining. They divide groups into whore/virgin and masculine/feminine dichotomies; they do not allow for the individual agency of Asian Americans and Latinas/os in determining their own sexualities, and they assume that education is necessarily sidelined by relationships and pregnancy. The few studies centering the perspectives of Latina teens actually suggest that motherhood increases educational aspirations for some teens (Russell and Lee 1994, as referenced by Trejos-Castillo and Frederick 2011). With so much focus on the supposed values of racial/ethnic groups, young Latinas are derogatorily cast as "at risk" and seen as the source of the believed problem of teen pregnancy (Garcia 2012). Meanwhile, sex education remains absent in most schools, limiting students' opportunities to learn more about their bodies, relationships, and sexual health (Fields 2008).

Several school officials noted that they believe Latinos in particular have more "behavioral" problems than other students, and Latinos were typically named as the root of the problem. Teacher John Alvarez, who at first faulted the school for eliminating vocational classes that might appeal to some students, reverted to a cultural explanation by clarifying that "within the Hispanic culture, [boys] like to get involved with their hands. They like to work with cars." Even Alvarez, who believes that SCHS needs to provide more course options for students, reverts to an underlying assumption that Latinos, in comparison to other students, have a predilection for working with their hands. Arguments such as these permeated rationales used through the 1950s to confine Mexicans to manual labor in the agricultural fields, brickyards, and mines (Gonzalez 1990).

In spite of the variations in people's emphasis on supposed cultural differences, such explanations prevail in the dominant representations of Asian Americans as an assumed "model minority" in comparison to Latinas/os. These beliefs divide Latinas/os from Asian Americans, and as history teaches us, these same frameworks are used to justify differences in academic achievement and to shape school practices. With groups of color defined as the "problem," attention is also diverted from Whites and White privilege.

"The White Elephant": Whiteness Is Largely Unmarked

Early during my research, a member of the staffulty referred to the achievement gap between Asian Americans and Latinas/os as the "white elephant" because few people actually discuss it. As previously described, staffulty mention the "gap" constantly but only look superficially at the quantitative data. They do not delve into the complexities behind the numbers. When I heard this "white elephant" phrase, I understood it as a mistaken reference to the popular idiom of "an elephant in the room" used in reference to a taboo topic that people ignore. The addition of the word "white" is apropos given the overall silence regarding Whites, White privilege, and the normative cultural practices sustaining the racial/ethnic hierarchies at the school. As part of the power-evasive discourse at SCHS, whiteness is one of the elephants in the school. Few White staffulty reflected on their own identities or the manifestations of White privilege. These silences are as significant as the biological and cultural arguments for maintaining disparities and for illustrating the dominance of power evasive thinking.

"I Never Thought about [My Racial/Ethnic Identity]": White Invisibility

In spite of all the staffulty's continual references to "Asians" and "Hispanics," few talk about or even mention Whites at the school. Actually, interviews with the White staffulty reveal that although they are generally comfortable talking about Asian American and Latina/o students and parents, some are much less accustomed to thinking about their own racial/ethnic identities. Several even confessed that they never thought about their identities.[6] This lack of acknowledgement of Whites' own identities and positions in contrast to the extensive focus on Asian American and Latina/o students is glaring and reflects the normalization and privileging of whiteness that permeates the United States.

Older White teachers and administrators who were raised in predominately White communities outside of California were least likely to have thought about their identities. Comments by established teacher Elaine Cobb are illustrative:

> I never thought about this ever, ever, ever. I thought of myself as an
> American, and over the years it seems to me it's not good enough to

be American anymore. You have to identify with something, and we weren't raised to identify with anything really but being an "I pledge allegiance to the flag" kind of person. So it is difficult for me when people make a big issue over "I'm a this; I'm a that" 'cause I never thought of those terms until recently. Every form you fill out wants you to identify with something.

Until lately, Elaine Cobb's racial/ethnic identity has gone unquestioned. As a light-skinned and blond White woman, her race has been the unnamed norm affirming sociologist Ruth Frankenberg's point that "White stands for the position of racial 'neutrality,' or the racially unmarked category" (1993, 55). Within the United States, where many Whites have been taught to think about race/ethnicity only in relationship to people of color and not to themselves, Cobb identifies simply as "American" and emphasizes her "allegiance to the flag." Now, presumably because of the growth in people of color, she is resentful at what she perceives as a change in expectations surrounding identification and assimilation into "Americanness."

In an extreme case, longtime teacher George Larkin got very nervous when he was asked how his racial/ethnic identity is relevant to his teaching. He blurted, "I'm just a person helping everyone." Larkin's defensive reply suggests that he believes it is not good to see peoples' differing racial/ethnic identities, histories, and experiences. He insinuates that even naming his own identity might imply that he is a traditional racist who treats students unfairly.

Coming of age in White communities in the 1950s and early 1960s and then becoming teachers at SCHS at a time when most students were White, these older members of the staffulty have been in positions of privilege where their experiences, perspectives, and cultures have been the unmarked norm. Assimilationist imperatives that all should shed their identities and practices to become "American" and the popular discourse purporting that "race does not matter" also seem to influence their ideas. Within this context, they have adopted a power-evasive framework to their own positionalities. From their positions of not having to name or think about their racial/ethnic identities, they have a difficult time understanding why all racial/ethnic groups in the United States cannot or do not just ignore their backgrounds. These staffulty appear unaware of the historical and contemporary dynamics circumscribing the identities and experiences of many people of color in the United States, where their "Americanness" and identities are often contested. Unlike the experiences of many Whites where their racial/ethnic identities may be taken as the standard, can be considered "symbolic," or can be regarded as something enjoyed during holidays or represented in special foods (Gans 1979; Waters 1990), for many people of color—including students of color at SCHS—race/ethnicity continues to be imposed, required, and involuntary. Also, there is a generational gap based on immigration between the White staffulty and many of the students that may impede understanding. Compared to the White staffulty whose families have been in the United States for multiple generations, many of the students at SCHS migrated at a young age or are the children or grandchildren of immigrants. These differing experiences and perspectives have important implications for the type of climate that is constructed in the classroom and on campus.

Highlighting the prevalence of white invisibility, a couple of newer staffulty members expressed similar forms of resentment and bewilderment surrounding racial/ethnic identities, White privilege, and the significance of racism. Nancy Gardiner was the most vocal. She grew up in a small town in the Midwest, where she remembers, "We probably had one Mexican American student and one family from India." Even though Gardiner spent the next twenty years in more racially/ethnically diverse communities in Southern California, she was shocked when she was recently asked about her background:

> One of the staff turned to me and said, "Well, what race are you?"
> I've never been asked that question before. I go, "What? Well, I'm
> White, you know." The correct answer to that was "I'm German
> and English." I never had anybody ask that. I had to stop and think,
> "That sounds really different to more and more people." German and
> English, you know, in a way, it's like, "Don't be afraid of me."

Similar to Elaine Cobb's bitterness that increasingly "you have to identify with something," Nancy Gardiner implies that as a result of changing demographics, she is a minority in California. She even wonders if people will fear her because of her perception that being German and English is so unusual.

This sentiment and her feeling of being "really different" were intensified when she first saw all the SCHS students at a school event:

> I walked into the gym, one of the first times I met the students here,
> and it is the sea of nothing but black hair. You know, I'm more of a
> minority as each year has gone by in my life. So that's been interest-
> ing, and I try to experience it in a healthy way.

Rather than state the racial/ethnic demographics at the school, Gardiner focuses on hair color to demarcate students' differences relative to her own as a blond White woman. Nancy Gardiner's use of hair color as opposed to naming racial/ethnic backgrounds illustrates what Frankenberg describes as using "polite" language or a "euphemism" to avoid "naming power" (1993, 149). In this example, the assumption is that hair color is what distinguishes socially and politically constructed races/ethnicities. This failure to name power differentials between staffulty and students as well as the position of Whites over communities of color is especially apparent when Gardiner proclaims that she is "more of a minority as each year has gone by." This proclamation ignores the fact that as a group Whites constitute more than half of the staffulty at SCHS and that they predominate within the United States and continue to wield most of the power.

Ignoring and Asserting White Privilege

In a society seeped in racism and where race and ethnicity influence opportunities, a few staffulty who ignore their identities also overlook the multiple forms of White privilege—what Beverley Daniel Tatum describes as "the systematically conferred advantages they receive simply because they are White" (1997, 95). Ranging from the ability to shop without being treated as suspect by clerks to being seen as an individual rather than as a representative of her race, in her now classic piece, Peggy McIntosh (1995) lists forty-six daily benefits of White privilege. Sociologists Oliver and Shapiro (1995) document the state policies fostering a cumulative legacy of White privilege and white supremacy that has resulted in vast wealth differentials between Whites and African Americans. These include unequal access to loans, a history of restrictive housing covenants, contemporary residential segregation, and differential rates of home appreciation based on the racial composition of communities. A lack of awareness of such everyday, institutional, and structural advantages granted to Whites relative to people of color reproduces the racial order. It also maintains the idea that individuals are solely responsible for their positions in society (McIntosh 1995).

This limited consciousness of privilege was most apparent in Joe Berk's retelling of his schooling and career trajectory. Raised in Southern California in the 1960s and 1970s, Joe attended a Catholic high school with a majority of White and Latina/o students. For him, school was "easy," and he "got along well" with his teachers, who were virtually all White. As has been the pattern in the racial skewing of course placement, he was placed in the top classes away from his Latino friends, who were put into courses that were several levels below his. This practice of being pushed up the educational pipeline continued throughout his life: after he became a teacher, he was selected to be a counselor, a director, and eventually an administrator. Recounting his experiences, Joe piped, "Everything I did, I always got pushed into some leadership role." This experience of what Williams (1995) describes as the "glass elevator effect" contrasts with the "glass ceiling" often encountered by women and people of color who face multiple barriers to academic and career advancement. Nevertheless, Joe did not initially understand his experiences as an example of White and male privilege. Instead, he stumbles to explain why he was pushed up the career ladder:

> I don't know why. I, I just, I don't know why. Ummm, it's like even when I was finishing up at high school umm and I was asked by the coaches to come out and help coach in the spring of my senior year. Why they asked me, I don't know. Then when I was, when I first started teaching umm, I was pulled into a role as a counselor . . . I was just being pulled into those roles. Ummm, one of the things I remember that was written on my observation when I was doing my student teaching was that they felt that I would eventually be suitable for an administrative position.

Joe Berk's multiple false starts, repetition, and lengthy pauses suggest that he is uncomfortable or even nervous answering the question. Such "rhetorical incoherence" increases when people discuss sensitive topics (Bonilla-Silva 2006, 68). This difficulty contrasts with the ease at which Joe characterized Asian Americans and Latinas/os at the beginning of this chapter.

As Joe explains his current position, he continues in a similar manner of rhetorical incoherence and without an analysis of the advantages his race/ethnicity and gender have had on his promotions:

> I've always been kind of trusted with these leadership roles. Umm, I was thrust into uhh the role at [a private high school] as a counselor. And, before I left there, they, they were thrusting me into a disciplinary position as a leader. Then when I started teaching at the public school, after my second year there, I got pushed into department chairmanship. I got pushed, kind of, uhh into taking the athletic director's role.

Flustered to understand why he was so trusted and promoted, Joe eventually attributes his advancement to "showing an interest" and people being "happy to give" him high status roles. However, at the end of our two interviews spanning multiple weeks, Joe shared an epiphany: after the first interview, he started considering how he might have been pushed up in curriculum tracks and in job promotions because he is White.

While Joe Berk's narrative illustrates how people's perspectives can change, it also highlights how the invisibility of whiteness is similar to biological and cultural arguments in that it shifts attention away from structural and institutional causes of inequality and the salience of race/ethnicity, gender, and class. For staff member Nancy Gardiner, her ignorance of White privilege—including, as described in the previous section, her unawareness of her own identity—leads her to invert the reality of power differentials and to blame immigrants for "ruin[ing]" the United States:

> NANCY GARDINER: Sometimes I resent it. It's like, "Wait a minute. You came in and you think this is all about you. Excuse me." You just sometimes feel run over. I mean, some of my more defensive emotions might be, "Well, you came here to America for the good that America has to offer, but then in so many ways, a lot of people seem to ruin it."
>
> GILDA OCHOA: What do you mean? Are there any examples you can think of?
>
> NANCY GARDINER: I feel that a lot of people take advantage of what's given to them and do not respond in an appreciative way. In some ways, things have been made too easy for people who have needs or people who come illegally. I might be wrong, but a lot of my perception of poverty and crime for example are from a lot of people who are here illegally and take advantage of the system in America like free medical, free public education, communicating in your primary language.

By failing to note power and privilege, Nancy Gardiner overlooks the many hardships immigrants encounter living and working in a new country. She also inaccurately reverses who is really advantaged within the United States and who benefits from our current system. Rather than critique the role of U.S. economic and military policies that impel people to migrate and that are also impacting the livelihoods of working people within the United States, she faults undocumented immigrants. This framework allows her to ignore how immigrant labor forms the base of the U.S. economy so that the low wages paid to immigrants advantage capitalists and consumers. These low wages and immigrant labor subsidize the food, clothing, electronics, and services that many people in the United States consume, and the economic policies and military actions of the power elite—primarily upper class White men—serve elite interests.

Psychologically, Nancy Gardiner's anti-immigrant perspective also provides her with a scapegoat for her difficulties finding a job:

> In my own [experience] seeking employment, I was becoming very concerned and frustrated that so many of the schools were looking for

someone who could speak Spanish. That was upsetting to me. And a
lot of the job positions were bilingual. It changed from desirable or
preferred to desired, to required.

Instead of considering the possibility that others are more qualified than
she is and that bilingual staffulty are assets in schools, she exerts a sense
of entitlement that she deserves to be hired:

> It became very discouraging and upsetting. It's like, "My God, here
> I am an intelligent adult. I just paid for a master's degree. I have the
> qualifications, the credentials to be hired . . . just being more mature,
> having been a parent and my work in schools, a lot of other things in
> my background that were very desirable to be hired, even in schools
> where I knew people." But I felt I was not getting hired because I
> could not speak Spanish.

When she was not immediately hired and she could not benefit from her
social connections, Nancy Gardiner claimed discrimination and recon-
structed the history of the area to suit her interests:

> I was being discriminated against. And that brought various
> thoughts and feelings like, "Wait a minute, this is America and
> our primary language, our national language—whether by default
> or whatever has been English. Why can't I get hired and all these
> people who didn't even have an education could get hired just like
> that?" And here I went and invested in a master's degree, and I felt
> like I was being discriminated against. So that made me angry at the
> whole system.

Conceiving of the region as English speaking, Nancy Gardiner adopts
mainstream ideas that selectively forget that the area where Los Angeles
was founded in 1781 started as a Mexican pueblo. Similarly, even when
Southern California and the rest of the Southwest were forcefully incorporated by the United States in 1848, cultural rights were to be protected
under the Treaty of Guadalupe Hidalgo. As Vigil notes, "Mexican cultural
customs and patterns were to be given equal consideration with Anglo
culture; this meant recognition and accommodation of the Spanish language and Catholic religion" (1980, 127). By overlooking this history and
contemporary demographics, she accepts an image of Southern California and the United States as White and English speaking.[7] Furthermore,
Gardiner speaks in generalities about "all these people" who were being
hired over her. She does not name their racial/ethnic backgrounds, but the
implications are that they are less qualified, do not have an education,
and are not from the United States. Her focus on the Spanish language

appears to be a code word for Latinas/os and her belief that unqualified Latinas/os are taking these jobs. Nancy Gardiner assumes that she has more of a right—an entitlement—to be hired, possibly because "this is America," and she is White. In spite of the privilege Whites receive in a racially stratified society and the legacy of discrimination against people of color, this example of claiming discrimination or "reverse racism" is a noted strategy employed by some Whites who believe people of color are responsible for taking college slots, jobs, and promotions from Whites. As Eduardo Bonilla-Silva explains, such "racial stories" of not getting jobs because of people of color help "make sense of the world but in ways that reinforce the status quo, serving particular interests without appearing to do so" (2006, 75). Despite such racial stories, the number of reverse discrimination cases actually filed with the Equal Employment Opportunity Commission is small and the majority of the cases are rejected for lack of any foundation (83).

Nancy Gardiner's description of applying to a tutoring center reflects her framework of ignoring and asserting White privilege:

> I found it very interesting that when I went into the interview, everybody was Asian. People at the reception desk were speaking Chinese to the parents coming in. Again, I thought, "Oh my gosh." It's like I grew up and moved to another country. I thought, "Oh boy, it's not going to work here either."

Although this is a private tutoring business run by members of the Chinese community, Nancy was enraged when she saw who participated in the center and that Chinese was being spoken to parents. This space did not fit her white image of the United States, even though there has been a long Chinese presence in this country, especially in California. As she did throughout her interview, Gardiner defends White privilege by proclaiming an exclusionary definition of America and Americanness belonging to and populated by Whites and English speakers.

When Nancy Gardiner's assumptions that she would not be hired at the center were disproved, she celebrates what she perceives as her niche—inverting the reality that the English language is hegemonic:

> But in the interview with the president of the company, she was very complimentary; she was very impressed. She wanted to hire me . . .
> One of the things she said was that they were interested in me being a teacher because I was a native English speaker. I am going, "Wow!" There is a market for me somewhere . . . I finally decided there are so many languages around me that my strength is on the native English speaker.

While a cultural hierarchy within the United States positions the English language over other languages, Gardiner seems to believe that the power of the English language and her role in education is threatened. She resolves this concern by embracing a belief that she has a value that others have somehow not yet realized—she is a "native English speaker."

Gardiner is unique in the amount of time she devoted during her interview to revealing her White privilege and concurrent sense of entitlement. Most staffulty said nothing about white advantage individually or institutionally. At SCHS, where Asian Americans and Latinas/os are consistently talked about, this silence surrounding whiteness and White privilege are obvious. As Frankenberg writes, "Whites are the nondefined definers of other people" (1993, 197). Such silences surrounding whiteness and White privilege are damaging. They lead to the overlooking of the macro-meso-micro factors perpetuating white supremacist practices such as assimilationist expectations. Likewise, they simultaneously advantage those who fit dominant constructions of whiteness—such as being light skinned, speaking English, being born in the United States—and disadvantage those outside of this socially constructed norm.

Silences Surrounding the School Culture

Along with not recognizing their own positionalities, most White staffulty said little about the school culture and the multiple factors influencing it. Absent was a critique of the power structure and the racial/ethnic gap between the staffulty and students. At SCHS, three-quarters of the administrators and half of the teachers are White. In contrast, 90 percent of the students are of color (California Department of Education 2008). As illustrated throughout this chapter, this racial/ethnic gap between the staffulty and students may be one of the factors fueling the school culture with deficiency and assimilationist perspectives. These perspectives are known to inhibit understanding of students and to impede more inclusionary approaches in schools (Sleeter 1993). As Valenzuela also found when analyzing the gaps between teachers and students in her Texas high school study, "Teachers see the differences in culture and language between themselves and their students from a culturally chauvinistic perspective that permits them to dismiss the possibility of a more culturally relevant approach in dealing with this population" (1999, 66). While changing the racial/ethnic demographics of school officials is not the answer to altering perspectives and the campus climate, studies suggest that increasing the percentage of teachers of color may have a positive effect on race/ethnic relations in schools by better addressing inequalities (Goldsmith 2004;

Ochoa 2007). As will become apparent in the forthcoming chapters, the silences surrounding the school culture at SCHS compounded with an acceptance of power-evasive perspectives allow for the continuance of Eurocentric course curriculum and school activities.

Overall, power-evasive frameworks such as these biological and cultural arguments and the absence of an interrogation of whiteness are dangerous for what they expose, justify, and camouflage. They reveal deep-seated biases that are rooted in larger ideologies that dichotomize, homogenize, and perpetuate hierarchies. Biological and cultural deficiencies justify inequality and shape everyday perceptions and interactions, including how staffulty perceive students. They can become self-fulfilling, especially when the focus in education is on standardized tests and students' worth is simply defined by quantitative measurements. Similarly, the absence of a discussion of standardized tests and whiteness prevent an analysis of their impacts on student learning and the campus dynamics. As detailed in the upcoming chapters, students experience the power of these constructs to the point that most Asian American participants reference the limiting expectation that they be "model minorities" while Latina/o students often discuss being seen as "troublemakers." As long as such confining categorizations persist and remain uncontested, dominant discourses will inhibit the discussions necessary for dismantling larger injustices. The causes and justifications of disparities and divisions will remain intact.

To more thoroughly understand the factors influencing students' educational experiences, chapters 2 through 5 focus on the school structures, practices, and everyday dynamics that work in conjunction with the dominant discourses presented in this chapter to influence students' opportunities and peer relations. By interrogating dominant discourses and educational practices, we are better positioned to reconstruct paradigms and rebuild institutions in the movement to change exclusionary perceptions and create more equitable realities.

Welcome to High School

*Tracking from Middle School to
International Baccalaureate Programs*

> It should not be so separated because it makes people feel different.
>
> —*Rebecca Ramos, sophomore in college preparatory (CP) classes*

By the time students begin Southern California High School (SCHS),
many are aware of the racialized and classed reputations that mark the
middle schools feeding into the high school and the students who will
soon be their schoolmates. The images of the two neighborhood middle
schools—La Montaña and Maple Grove—are stark. As detailed in this
chapter, these reputations and unequally valued schools interact with
the segregation structured in SCHS's tracking system. This system sorts,
divides, and treats students disparately, fueling their separation and the
feeling of being different and unequal, which Rebecca Ramos critiques
in the previous quote.

While there are important variations, in general, Asian Americans and
middle-class and upper-middle-class students are concentrated in La Montaña Middle School and in the high school's International Baccalaureate
(IB), honors (H), and advanced placement courses. In contrast, Latinas/os
and working-class students predominate in Maple Grove Middle School and
in nonhonors courses that are designated college preparatory (CP). With
students in La Montaña and in SCHS's top classes experiencing higher
expectations and greater educational opportunities, a binary, racialized,
classed, and hierarchical construction of students is perpetuated. This construction is propelled by and reinforces racialized and classed discourses.
Consequently, rather than greeted with inclusion and optimism at the
high school gates, students are funneled into a system of inequality and
competition where their peer groups are disparately and separately formed.

While the impacts differ across middle schools and curriculum tracks, The emphasis on quantitative measurements and structured curriculum impedes holistic student-centered learning and relationship building.

"That's What I've Been Taught": What Happens in Middle School Doesn't Stay in Middle School

Located less than two miles from each other in distinct neighborhoods, La Montaña and Maple Grove middle schools differ by race/ethnicity, class, and academic performance—narrowly defined by students' scores on standardized state tests. Primarily middle-class and upper-middle-class students attend La Montaña; nearly 55 percent of the students are Asian American, about 32 percent are Latina/o, and 12 percent are White. It also boasts the highest possible Academic Performance Index (API) score, a 10. Maple Grove is attended primarily by working-class and lower-middle-class students who are nearly 70 percent Latina/o and 20 percent Asian American. About 7 percent are White and 3 percent are African American. On a scale of 1 to 10, the school's API score is a 5. In the context of the racialized constructions of Asian Americans and Latina/os, these differences combine to foster (1) disparate perceptions of the two middle schools and the students who attend them and (2) separate friendships. Together, these dynamics fuel academic and social hierarchies.

At an early age, many students learn that La Montaña is perceived as the academically stronger and more resourced school. For example, sophomore Elizabeth Villa first heard such comments by her peers: "I've talked to some people from La Montaña, and they think Maple Grove's like 'ugh.' 'The school is just ghetto.'" As juniors Robert Wong and Art Casas reveal in two separate interviews, adults are often responsible for transmitting these messages:

> During the whole time I was in middle school, all the teachers told us, "La Montaña's the best school in the district, and look at our API score." Parents and teachers have all agreed on this. So I just assumed that was true too (Robert Wong)

> . . . . [W]e've had substitutes going to our school, and they're just talking about how much better La Montaña is than other schools (Art Casas).

With peers, teachers, and parents conveying such messages, most students, including the following, are aware of the middle schools' differing demographics and their skewed reputations:

> Everyone just talks about how all the kids from La Montaña are Asian. All of them are smart. (Monique Martinez, junior)

> They probably say Maple Grove was ghetto because there were a lot of Mexicans. (Claudia Macías, sophomore)

> La Montaña is known as a pretty good school in the district. Our scores, and our people, 'cause some schools are kinda ghetto, or they say, "Stupid people go there." (Mary Hwang, sophomore)

While API scores are used as a key factor determining school quality, as these students' comments reveal, the significance of class and the role of racialized images are also paramount in shaping opinions. Apparent in students' narratives are the interchange of the labels "ghetto," "stupid," and "Mexican" in comparison to "Asian" and "smart."[1]

The association of Asianness and smartness with La Montaña and the equation of Mexicanness, stupidness, and a poor school with Maple Grove is pervasive. In a group interview, self-identified Hispanic and "mixed" Hispanic and European females who attended La Montaña offer the following analysis:

> VICKI PARDO: Our school was like 97 percent Asian. So everyone thinks that our school is smart just because of the Asians.
>
> JENN VANDERHOL: Yeah, we could be smarter than *them*, and they wouldn't even notice.
>
> VICKI: It sucks for other schools 'cause when our school sees other schools, they are always like, "Oh my god. They are so dumb." Everybody is getting judged just because of their race, and then they eventually fall into it.

These friends are cognizant of the way that race, academic ability, and middle schools are correlated in the minds of their peers. Similarly, they realize how such racialized assumptions and a competitive school climate reproduce divisions between students and middle schools. As Vicki attests, others' perceptions may become self-fulfilling. While the images of Asian Americans as "smart" made Vicki and Jenn feel invisible at La Montaña, in their opinion, Asian Americans were hyperpresent—leading them to believe that 97 percent of the students at their school were Asian American. However, at the time that they were students, Asian Americans were less than 60 percent of the school population. By overestimating the number of Asian Americans, Vicki and Jenn inadvertently reproduce the very invisibility of Latinas/os that they experienced and despise.

Even if they begin SCHS unaware of these stereotyped perceptions of their middle schools, students often learn early what others think. As a senior, Maple Grove alumnus Christopher Zuniga will "never really forget" when his ninth-grade teacher pulled him aside to discuss the low B that he was receiving in her class and stated, "Oh, you're not doing too well. It's probably because you're from Maple Grove." Christopher respected this teacher who was trying to reach out to him, but he believes that she was implying that "'Cause that school's majority is Mexican, they kind of have a bad rep." Students from Maple Grove may deduce from such comments that their school is stigmatized because Mexicans attend it, and as products of this school, as is the case for Christopher, as Mexicans, they too are labeled with a "bad reputation."

To the extent that such labels influence students' perceptions, some students carry a stigma and others possess high self-esteem. In contrast to Christopher, who felt Maple Grove and maybe even he by association had a negative reputation, La Montaña students such as Margaret Kang gain confidence from the glowing image attributed to their school, "[I feel] good 'cause I go to La Montaña, and it boosts my self-esteem when I get good grades from that school."

Just as these perceptions fuel *academic hierarchies* that position La Montaña, Asian Americans, and middle- and upper-class students above Maple Grove, Latinas/os, and working-class students, there are also *social hierarchies* where the reverse order is fostered. Although students discussed it less often than they did academic reputations, several believe that Maple Grove students are more prepared socially than La Montaña students. Senior Karla Ortiz's comments are illustrative: "La Montaña prepared me school-wise, but not social-wise . . . Here [at SCHS], everything is more interactive. Over there [at La Montaña], they didn't push people to do it." Echoing the value of acquiring social skills from Maple Grove, self-identified American-born Chinese Ricky Liu offers his theory on why he believes students from his alma mater are more prepared socially:

> Maple Grove was more diverse. A person would be a lot more normal if they went to our school. 'Cause at La Montaña, it's heavily Asian, like Asianified; everything is Asian. At Maple Grove, there were Mexicans, Blacks, Asians, Whites; there are lots of different types of people, so we get exposed to different types of things. So people just grow up more normally—if people are willing to get out of their little groups.

Expanding on his conception of "normal," Ricky concludes,

> I'll call it calibrated. It's when you see a person walk into a situation,
> the way they act, the way they talk, their body language, or just how
> they interact with different people . . . You get that instant thought,
> "That's weird; they're acting really weird." And normal would be the
> way they act; it's more acceptable. It's not socially retarded.

Ricky finds strength in the precise factors that others use to diminish Maple Grove. He critiques the conditions of La Montaña that foster social awkwardness and segregation and inhibit interaction with people from varied backgrounds. To the extent that schools such as Maple Grove are racially/ethnically heterogeneous and there are opportunities for interaction, students may develop the experience and knowledge to more comfortably interact across differences. Despite these benefits, these experiences are undervalued in today's schools and society, and places such as Maple Grove remain stigmatized because they do not excel in the standardized measurements of so-called high-performing schools.

With people viewing the middle schools and the students who attend them unequally academically and socially, it is no coincidence that for many students, peer relations fall along race/ethnicity and middle schools. Senior Jean Kim from La Montaña reflects,

> I don't think in La Montaña that the Asians and the non-Asians
> would really hang out. They did when we were young like sixth
> grade, but by the time we were in eighth grade, it was completely
> different. But in Maple Grove, no matter what, you just hang out.
> A couple of my friends who went to Maple Grove, they were like,
> "Oh yeah, when I was in junior high, I hung out with the Hispanics.
> Then as soon as I got into high school, I started hanging out with the
> Asians."

As Ricky Liu discussed earlier, Jean also believes that Maple Grove friendships are less racially segregated than at La Montaña. However, she observes that regardless of middle school, by high school, peer groups become more separate. This separation may stem from a growing consciousness of racial/ethnic identity that often happens around middle school (Tatum 1997), but such division is also institutionalized in distinct middle schools and then high school classes.

With SCHS doing little to address student divisions, some students explain that in high school, they have a difficult time crossing middle school and racial lines. Junior Tommy Huie, a Chinese-identified student, describes, "Going to La Montaña, we grew up with each other . . . Pretty much, we knew all the Asians. So coming here we didn't really know anyone, and we stuck together in our own cliques." These experiences suggest that the segregation within and between middle schools and the racialized beliefs about the middle schools condition the segregation of peer groups at SCHS.

Rather than contest the racist and classist middle school reputations, deconstruct the limited criteria used for ranking schools, or name the disparities in resources, many adults and in turn students accept and reinforce the middle school images. This ensures that the dominant ideologies presented in the previous chapter remain intact. Thus by fostering perceptions of unequal student abilities, the constructed academic and social divisions at La Montaña and Maple Grove pave the way for similar hierarchies and divisions at SCHS. In high school, these dynamics are intensified by a rigid track system and the unequal allocation of resources.

Tracking Inequality

Before students begin SCHS, standardized test scores, middle school courses, and staffulty's recommendations are used to place them into courses and programs ranging from honors/advanced placement (H/AP), AVID (Advancement via Individual Determination), and CP courses; students may also apply for the pre-IB program, where they complete honors and AP courses and may become IB students their junior and senior years.

As teacher Emily Saldana proclaims, these disparate courses and academic paths fundamentally influence students' opportunities, access to resources, and their relationships:

> When a kid comes in from junior high, that is the most significant turning point if that kid is going to go to college or not . . . They are categorized early on without knowing their abilities because we don't know the students. We go off of what the junior high teachers tell us . . . [Y]ou are now tracking a student saying, "You are going to be in an integrated class [non–college preparatory course]." It's going to be very hard for you to go from an integrated course to an AP course . . . If you are AP/IB, you are what we call a pre-IB student; you are going to be put into the best classes with the best teachers.

Rooted in a legacy of racism and class inequality, tracking exacerbates the hierarchical academic and social binaries apparent in the middle schools. By schooling students in separate and unequal conditions, tracking continues the history of detrimentally shaping students' capital and reproducing systemic inequality.

Tracking and the ideologies that maintain it are ingrained in how schools such as SCHS are organized. As the status quo, tracking typically goes unchallenged or is rationalized—often by the teachers, students, and families in the top courses—as the best way to teach students. Tracking is usually perceived as "the tradition" and believed to allow students to progress at their own pace without hindering the advancement of other students (Oakes 1985). However, tracking and the criteria used to place students into courses and programs are not neutral.

The practice of placing students into different courses based on perceived capabilities can be traced to the changing demographics at the turn of the twentieth century, the growth of factories, and prevailing ideologies. In particular, tracking emerged during a period when access to public schooling was increasing and growing numbers of poor, immigrant, and second-generation children from southern and eastern Europe were entering school. During this period, the ideologies that shaped the formation of schools and the system of tracking included social Darwinist assumptions about the biological superiority of White Anglo-Saxon Protestants, cultural deficiency perspectives that justified Americanization programs and vocational tracks for immigrants and groups of color, and scientific management-based models of the factory as the most efficient way to educate a mass citizenry (Oakes 1985). The history of allocating students to distinct educational and career paths by race/ethnicity and class position has reproduced inequalities and maintained the capitalist system by ensuring managers and owners and a ready supply of laborers (Bowles and Gintis 1976; Gonzalez 1990).

Today, exclusionary ideologies and racial/ethnic and class skewing in track placement continue. As illustrated in the previous chapter, the biological and cultural deficiency ideologies of the past emerge in contemporary discourses, and they intersect with the myth of meritocracy to explain and even justify differences in education. Furthermore, the criteria used to place students in courses—such as standardized tests and staffulty recommendations—remain biased. Just as standardized tests are biased against working-class, Latina/o, and African American students and in favor of middle- and upper-class English-speaking White students whose backgrounds tend to reflect those designing the tests (Oakes 1985; Gonzalez 1990), Asian American and White students with similar standardized test scores as Latina/o and Black students are more likely to be placed into rigorous courses (Oakes and Guiton 1995). Thus placement may be skewed by school personnel's perceptions of students' abilities, work ethics, and aspirations often based on race/ethnicity, socioeconomic status, and behavior (Oakes 1985). At SCHS, a couple of staffulty confess that because of "the school's reputation" and perhaps because of the belief that Asian Americans are a so-called model minority, students from La Montaña are often given the "benefit of the doubt" when determining which ninth-graders to place into honors courses. In contrast, Latinas/os are often assumed to not belong in honors. Tom Delgado, a ten-year member of the staffulty, shares how certain teachers convey these messages:

> This one student was a female who was Hispanic; she was a freshman a couple of years ago, freshman's honors class, and the teacher asked her, "What are *you* doing here? You are in the wrong class." She said, "No, I'm in the right class." The teacher said, "This is an *honors* class." . . . The teacher made her feel that [because] she was Mexican, she didn't belong there . . . The student checked out of the class a week later.

These exclusionary expectations are among the factors shaping unequal track placement. Reflecting national trends, middle-class and upper-middle-class Asian American students are significantly overrepresented in IB, AP, and honors courses while working-class Latinas/os are underrepresented (see Oakes 1985; Ginorio and Huston 2001). During the time of this study, Asian Americans and Latinas/os represented 46 percent and 43 percent of the student population, respectively, yet school data revealed that they constituted 86 percent and 10 percent of the students in the AP courses. At 95 percent and 5 percent, the divide in the IB program was even more glaring. There were twenty-one seniors in the program, but just one was Latina/o. In comparison, Latinas/os predominate in SCHS's special education courses. According to the California Department of Education (2005), over 60 percent of the students labeled with a learning disability at SCHS are Latina/o, and, according to staff member Sandra Perez, most of the students in special education courses are Latino men. In contrast, 3 percent of the students with this designation are Asian Pacific Islanders. Overall, just 11 percent of Latina/o seniors at SCHS had completed the necessary course work with a C or better to attend a California State University (CSU) or a University of California (UC) school immediately after graduation. Compare this with over 50 percent of Asian Americans, 40 percent of African Americans, 30 percent of Whites, and 25 percent of Native Americans (California Department of Education). An analysis of what happens in SCHS's IB, AVID, and CP courses underscores how tracking is manifested in today's schools where racism and class inequality prevail.

"My Bright Shining Stars": The IB Program

When I met teacher Margaret Albert in her combined AP and IB class, she praised the students as "the top students—even when they don't look like they're working, they get the job done." In a class of just eight Asian American students, another teacher welcomed the IB seniors as "my bright shining stars." These characterizations of the IB students are common. The headline in the 2007 school's yearbook introduces the IB students as "I think therefore IB"—illustrating the perception that these are among the school's smartest students.

At SCHS, the IB program is an honors college preparatory program that select students take as an overlay in addition to AP classes. Students completing the required advanced courses, international examinations, extended essay, community service, and extracurricular activities graduate with an IB diploma. In printed materials, the school describes the program as "offering an academic challenge to bright, motivated students." Upwards of two to three hundred first- and second-year students apply for and are designated pre-IB students, but the retention rate is very low; only thirty to forty juniors and seniors continue with the program. Most students leave the program before the start of their junior year—often because of the workload and the view from students that little is gained from it.

IB programs were initially started in 1968 for students in international schools, and they were primarily in private schools geared toward political diplomats' children (Kyburg, Hertberg-Davis, and Callahan 2007). However, they have since expanded to public elementary, middle, and high schools worldwide. According to the International Baccalaureate Organization, there are nearly 2,300 IB high schools in 139 countries, including over 800 in the United States and 87 in California alone. The aims of the program are to (1) develop students' critical thinking skills, (2) enhance international understanding, (3) provide internationally qualified courses to students seeking acceptance into higher education, and (4) educate the whole person—intellectually, socially, and emotionally (International Baccalaureate Organization 2007). The IB web page lists part of the mission as "aim[ing] to develop inquiring, knowledgeable and caring young people who help to create a better and more peaceful world through intercultural understanding and respect."

In spite of its admirable goals and especially its aim of "intercultural understanding and respect," SCHS staffuly express great ambivalence, if not outright disagreement, with the implementation of the IB program at their school. Some critique it as a "top-down program" imposed by school board members as a way to keep interested middle-class and upper-middle-class Asian American students and their families from leaving the school district. Longtime teacher Mallory Tate even insinuates that familial interests of one school board member may have been influential in why the program was started at SCHS:

> Members on the board were noticing that we were losing some top students to [a neighboring school district] . . . So they were going to set up a program here so that we would not allow them to leave the district for such a program. I had the son of one of the school board members in my classroom, and he said that it was coming.

Coupled with the imposing of this program is an even more prevalent critique of the amount of resources allocated to it. Teacher Mallory Tate continues,

> And then it came here. We were being shipped off to here, there, and everywhere [to get trained] at humongous expense. The expenses are still there because if you're a school that's having the program, then there's an amount you pay [each year]. And then the kids pay for tests at twice the AP cost; it's very expensive for them . . . And they typically don't have seminars nearby, so you go off to Canada someplace. We've sent administrators to San Juan, Puerto Rico, paid for by the district.

Some administrators and other teachers not only critique the program's expenses but also contest the fact that only a tiny fraction of students are privy to the resources provided to the IB program:

> We spend a lot of money on IB, and we influence the smallest amount of kids. I'd like to see that grow. (Joe Berk, administrator)

> I know some of that money is used for conferences. But why is it that teachers can go and get trained, and fly to New Mexico, Laughlin, or Vancouver, and I got to go? Why do they get to go for that kind of training to work with these kids that really don't need any help or direction because they're going to do it no matter what? What about everybody else? (Chris Tapia, administrator)

As Chris Tapia explains, of particular concern is how the resources funneled into the IB program are going to students who are already doing well academically and are on their way to top-ranked universities. These staffulty see a replication of inequality as the students who are excelling and are typically from more economically privileged backgrounds are provided with even more support while the majority of students are overlooked.

Even though IB students are a small fraction of the school's nearly two thousand students, they receive a disproportionate amount of attention and other resources. For example, with their AP classmates, they often are enrolled in smaller classes. During the 2005–2006 school year, their junior and senior English literature courses had ten fewer students than the college preparatory English classes (twenty-six to twenty-seven students compared to thirty-six students). Similarly, they enroll in specialized and often small seminar-based courses such as theory of knowledge, studio art H/AP, art history, and history of the Americas. Furthermore, with a teacher and a counselor co-coordinating the program, they have access to an IB-designated counselor.

In spite of such criticism, the IB program has remained at the school for over ten years, serving primarily middle-class and upper-middle-class Asian American students. At the time of this research, most of the IB students were the children of college-educated Asian immigrants primarily from Taiwan and Hong Kong but also from Korea. Many of the students attended La Montaña, and as will be described in chapter 4, they participated in after-school enrichment programs such as Chinese school from K–8 and SAT prep courses—enhancing their academic opportunities and fostering the development of strong peer and parental social networks. A few students even learned of the IB program from adults and students in these after-school programs.

At an estimated ratio of three to one, young men predominate. As one of the IB coordinators explains, "Girls are more likely to be involved in other activities—ASB [associated student body], annual staff, and journalism," implying that the academic demands in the IB program inhibit the participation of students who are very involved in campus activities.

As is the case with the following three IB friends, students' experiences in the program augment the multiple forms of capital—human, social, and cultural—that they already possess. Many enter the program knowing each other, even as friends, having benefitted from supplemental educational programs. Within the IB program, these forms of capital intersect with high expectations, rigorous curriculum, Socratic classrooms, and easy access to staffulty. However, for some, the experiences and treatment they receive fuels a sense of entitlement that they are the "elite." Through a process of "concerted cultivation" at school, which Annette Lareau has described in reference to what occurs in middle-class families, these students are taught to "question adults and address them as relative equals" (2003, 2). They may come to expect a certain type of treatment and even manipulate school rules to their advantage. SCHS is building the elite relative to their AVID and CP schoolmates.

"Supposedly, We're the Elite People in School":
Billy Su, Mike Song, and May Lee

At the time of our meeting, Billy, Mike, and May were looking forward to graduating as part of the small group of IB diploma candidates. Having completed their course work and finals, their theory of knowledge teacher allowed them to join me in two hour-long discussions. Longtime friends from La Montaña who also attended Chinese school since they were seven and SAT classes in high school, they were relaxed and eager to talk.

Warned that the IB program would be "rigorous," they laugh and confirm that it was. Despite the workload, they were committed to staying in the program, and their social ties proved instrumental in their persistence. While May describes her parents as giving her "no choice" but to complete the program because her older brother had, Billy credits his friendship with Mike:

> I joined IB because he [pointing to Mike] influenced me, and I was like, "No, I don't want to," and he's like, "Come on!"

As Mike emphasizes, these ties helped them during busy nights of homework:

> Me and May, we'll stay up all night [online] finishing all of our work. We'll be really tired. The whole year, each day we slept like three hours. That's it, max.

The structure of the program builds on these relationships by distinguishing IB students symbolically and physically from other students on campus.

Key to fostering a sense of collectivity among the IB students and drawing divisions away from other students is the school's designation of IB students as the "elite." Billy and Mike explain,

> BILLY: The coordinators try to motivate us by saying [May laughs nervously] we're the best in school, or we're supposed to be the best in school.
>
> MIKE: There's this one time in IB where I guess we weren't acting as elite students. So they made us write an essay about how we would have all of the IB qualities to be a top student.
>
> BILLY: It was like a page and then we had to write the attitudes we're supposed to have.

The "elite" label is one that some IB students accept, but Billy ponders its accuracy as it applies to him:

> Supposedly we're the elite people in school [May and Mike chuckle]. They have high expectations for us because we're the elite group. But then, it's really not that 'cause you can get into IB if you apply. And I

had bad grades, and they still let me in. So I don't think the elite thing is actually accurate.

Although Billy questions this categorization because, as a ninth-grader, he failed a class and was nonetheless accepted into the program, the fact that he still uses the school's label to describe his classmates and to evaluate himself reveals the strength of the descriptor.

According to teacher Margaret Albert, fostering this sense among IB students that they are "very special" is a goal of the program, one that she too contemplates: "The negative of it is then are you becoming elitist, and are you being an elitist teacher and an elitist little group?" This concern that the school may be fostering elitism by creating elitist students and teachers who participate in the program is significant since this category is accompanied by many privileges that also differentiate IB students.

"High-Status Knowledge" and Skill Building: Course Curriculum, Pedagogy, and Assignments

As the program advertises, many of the IB requirements focus on developing students' critical thinking, analytical capabilities, and public speaking abilities—skills crucial to students' growth and preparation for college. Required to complete an extended essay and oral examinations and other tests as part of the program's internal assessments in six subject areas, Billy and Mike add that their IB coursework enhanced their social skills and knowledge of contemporary issues. In particular, they praise the theory of knowledge (TOK) seminar, a course required for IB seniors:

> BILLY: I got less shy afterwards 'cause I volunteered for stuff like leading junior IB people.
> MIKE: We have these presentations about homelessness or we choose an issue that's around the world and we present it to the juniors in the IB program. . . . For example, homelessness or like—
> BILLY: [interrupts] Global warming.
> MIKE: Global warming, that kind of stuff. So then we present it to the kids . . . Plus, it also makes us more aware locally too, 'cause in TOK we have to write TOK journals. Every Monday we have to present a TOK journal where we talk about some issue and connect it to TOK stuff. So it makes us think more logically and makes us more aware of what's going on around us.

The TOK course is run as a college-level seminar where students present, analyze, and discuss various topics. An IB teacher explains,

[It] is an opportunity to help students learn how to be critical thinkers and help them to evaluate claims that are made in all different areas. So it's kind of a theoretical course, [but] it's also very practical in the sense that students will be using it for a long time.

The knowledge, vocabulary, and confidence that students develop in this seminar were apparent during this research where students such as senior Yi Lin comfortably applied their course language to describe campus dynamics:[2]

From my TOK class, we learned that there are different paradigms. And they're cultural differences, and I think that has a lot to do with everything because not only do we Asians have different paradigms about other races, other people do too.

Given the size of the senior IB cohorts, the TOK course is small relative to the other classes at SCHS. It ranged from eight to fifteen students during the times I observed. Class size and the use of the Socratic approach where teacher and students sit in a circle discussing and posing questions facilitate community building, active participation, individualized attention, and an asset-based approach to education where students are expected to actively contribute to the learning process. Together, the teacher and students are able to explore topics and readings in depth, ask questions, and dialogue with one another. One teacher even explains that the TOK class "helps *me* to understand the world and how we know what we know." This pedagogical approach contrasts with most courses at the school that are larger (thirty to thirty-seven students), organized in rows, teacher-centered, test-stressed, lecture-based, and increasingly PowerPoint driven. Thus, along with developing students' critical thinking, analytical abilities, and verbal skills, by encouraging students to express their own thoughts, they learn that their perspectives are important. Precisely because of this approach to teaching and learning in the TOK course, veteran teacher Val Sherman believes that it should not be limited to IB students:

Our theory of knowledge is a wonderful course. Both of the instructors who have taught it have done a fantastic job of getting the students to think about truth, reality, about themselves, about how they are in relation to others and other things—how math relates to English, how history relates to math. That's the kind of course that not just our IB students but a lot of students could really benefit from.

Since the structure of TOK provides students with the opportunity to explore topics in detail, another privilege for IB students is that their course materials differ from the work required of the students in what are referred to as "regular" or CP classes:

> BILLY: Some people have regular classes and they do a lot more harder stuff that we don't do.
>
> GILDA: Can you be more specific?
>
> MIKE: I think they [the regular students] do more work 'cause we already went through it 'cause we're taking AP classes. We should be able to already do this stuff that the regular kids do. I think that's why we can skip all the hard work and go into the more deeper [work]. It's like they're covering a whole bunch of shallow stuff compared to smaller areas.

Not only may IB students have a different type of work because it is assumed they already know what students in the CP courses are covering, but the emphasis on depth over breadth may be among the factors making learning enjoyable in less structured courses such as TOK. Rather than feeling like they have to know a lot of information superficially, such classes may allow students to delve into topics and explore their ideas. They are positioned as creators of knowledge as opposed to passive consumers of large amounts of information.

Similarly, relative to CP courses, some of the IB and AP courses appear to be more loosely defined, allowing for more creative versus structured and regimented assignments. Using the examples of his younger brother and himself, Mike compares his assignments with those of students in CP English:

> MIKE: The work that he [my brother] gets from his English teacher kind of makes me mad 'cause it's very unreasonable, and it's pointless.
>
> GILDA: What do you mean by unreasonable?
>
> MIKE: I had to grade his essay once and when I grade it I have to fill out a form. I have to put a happy face here and then underline stuff. Usually when you grade papers you just proofread, but there's all these steps you have to follow for the grader and it's really maddening [May chuckles]. And then, their research paper has to be ten pages. If it's not ten pages you can't get an A. So six pages, if you ace that then you get a C max. So I think she's kind of grading it on length instead of quality over quantity.

The ease at which Mike offers his critique is a reflection of the content of his criticism. That is, while he and other IB students are encouraged to express their views, develop their ideas, and even critique others—in this case teachers—it appears that his brother in college preparatory courses may be taught to follow orders and take directions. As Oakes (1985) has documented, courses designated as honors courses often provide students access to higher-level thinking and decision making necessary for managerial and professional careers. Thus the more open-ended and flexible assignments expected in the TOK course foster the development of more than academic skills.

In spite of the flexibility in the TOK course and even honors classes, this characterization does not always apply for all advanced-level courses. In fact, several teachers critique the prescriptive standards dictating teaching in the junior and senior AP courses that require them to prepare students for AP tests. Jane King's comments comparing the honors and AP courses are illustrative:

> I get the sophomore honors, so I get kind of the cream of the crop and I get to have fun, and I get a group of kids that we can have these really intelligent conversations with, but because they're sophomores, the curriculum is pliable. So I can do what I want with the curriculum. Whereas, if you teach honors at the junior or senior level it's prescribed; it's very strict because you're teaching AP standards.

Jane prefers the less rigid curriculum in the ninth- and tenth-grade honors courses because this enables more spirited discussions with students.

This more flexible approach to teaching and learning is a method favored by other teachers who fear that some of the students in the top classes may become too structured in their approach to learning. Teacher Marie Silva argues, "They are learning more just to regurgitate the information than to grow personally. They don't necessarily want to be challenged in their thinking." As teacher Beth Hill explains, this lack of creativity that she observes among students in her honors courses diminishes the joy of teaching:

> The thing that was the most challenging for me is teaching the honors . . . You can't give them an open-ended project. I mean, you can, but it bothers them. I'm very open-ended where I'm like, "Do this, this, and this." They are like, "Well, how much is it worth? How much is this worth?" So you are kind of like, "This is not fun" . . . Like thinking about analyzing a quote, they want what I have to say, not what *they* think.

Thus, while the TOK course and other classes may provide students in the IB program with opportunities to develop their own ideas, this is not always the case in their AP classes. Similar to the overall testing culture, where assessment is foundational to what is happening in many schools, the emphasis on following strict standards for AP tests and achieving high GPAs (grade point averages) may stifle both teacher and student creativity.

In contrast to their general praise of their courses, May, Billy, and Mike raise a concern echoed by some of their classmates that "teachers assume that we know things, and they don't teach a lot of stuff." As May explains, "Then I'm just lost." They give an example from their Spanish class:

> BILLY: Her assignments that she gives us assume that we're Spanish 4 AP level.
>
> GILDA: But you are taking Spanish 4? You don't feel like you're at that level yet?
>
> MAY: Yeah.
>
> BILLY: Yeah, so we need help with stuff, and she always gives us essays, which I don't think help us [May laughs nervously]. 'Cause we don't know Spanish, and you're going to make us write in Spanish.

Experiences such as these suggest that the labels "IB," "AP," and "elite" can work against students' interests because some teachers may inaccurately expect them to know certain material that they either have not been taught or have not fully learned. Once students are designated AP, they may be pushed up in the tracks even if they are struggling with course materials. Thus, while these three friends criticize some of the CP teachers for covering too much information in their classes, more students could benefit from access to that material as well.

Building Capital with Staffulty

Just as the pedagogy involved with the TOK course fosters less authoritarian relationships between teacher and students, IB students are also provided with the resources to develop significant relationships with other adults. As part of the 150 hours of community service, extracurricular activities, or athletics that are required through the IB program, students are encouraged to volunteer at the school where they can help teachers or assist with campus events such as parent conferences. Just as these experiences integrate students into the life of the school and help them feel more comfortable with the staffulty, the relationship the students have with the IB counselor is also important. These relationships add to students' social capital by helping them navigate high school and prepare for college. They also learn to interact with institutional agents, providing a form of cultural capital that teaches them how to make demands of people in authority, expect special treatment, and bend the rules in their favor. Mike describes the following:

You know in the [school's main] office, sometimes they stop you. [They say,] "Oh you can't meet with your counselor unless you have an appointment." [I say], "Oh, I'm an IB student." And then they're just, "Okay, *you* can come in."

As Mike and Billy laugh about this, Mike expands on the relationship they have with the IB counselor through group sessions that are designed only for IB students:

[Our counselor's] really close to us. We had stress group with her, and we could tell her anything; we're really cool with her.

Beginning in the second semester of their junior years, IB students are given this relaxed space to talk confidentially about topics of their choosing such as school, dating, family, and friends. Along with providing a valuable outlet and support network, these groups enhance students' relationships with their counselor. IB senior Sandra Wu recalls,

My counselor only has twenty-two seniors to deal with because there are twenty-two of us in IB. So when it came to writing college applications, it was really easy because we just walked in. Plus, last year, we had this thing called stress group. We had an hour every week with a certain group, and we would just go and talk about what happened that week, and we'd rate our stress level . . . [O]ur counselor got to know us rather than as a name on a piece of paper . . . She called me out of class a couple of times just to ask me about what I wanted on my application or my letter [of recommendation]. It was a really friendly thing, like a real personal contact.

Billy concurs:

I just talked to her on Friday too, 'cause I had problems with college, and I don't know what to do. And I just go up there and talk to her. And then, when you want classes that you didn't get or got to get, she'll work favors for you—talk to teachers and then get you in. It's kind of unfair for other people but—[Mike, Billy, and May laugh].

The goal of making IB students feel "very special," as described earlier by teacher Margaret Albert, seems to be working. These friends not only feel that their counselor is "cool" with them but also seem to relish the superior treatment they receive where school practices are changed to meet their interests.

Easy access to their counselor and the stress group are the most frequently named perks that SCHS IB students cite. During a daylong Saturday IB boot camp for fifteen pre-IB sophomores, the IB counselor said, "Walk into my office; it's never locked." IB students value this relationship with the counselor, and they realize its importance for improving their educational trajectories. A counselor who knows students more than "a name on a piece of paper" can write stronger and more individualized letters of recommendation, refer students to scholarship opportunities, and connect students to other resources. Thus this relationship not only enhances students' chances of being admitted to top schools and receiving awards but also can have larger implications for the types of jobs and future networks available to them.

This support compares drastically with the experiences of other SCHS students. Mari Ramirez, a member of the staffulty, frequently observes such disparate treatment by counselors. However, unlike with Billy, Mike, and May, anger—not laughter—fills her voice when she recalls this inequality:

> For everyone else, "Oh no I cannot do anything; I cannot change your
> schedule now; it is too late in the year." An IB student comes in, "Oh,
> OK." You just told this other student it cannot be done, but now you
> are doing it for this student! I don't understand. Even me as a parent,
> and I work here and my sister tells me, "You have to have some sort
> of pull; you work there tell them to change [your child's] classes." I
> am scared to go to the main counselor who is there.

Students in the school's honors and AP courses concur. Not only do they rarely see their counselors, but rather than welcomed with an open-door policy, some are rudely turned away. Junior Eric Han reveals, "I go in there and ask, can I talk to a counselor? [I'm told,] 'Honey, I'm sorry, we don't have time. Get out of here. Get out of here.'" Three sophomore friends add the following:

> LAUREN CHAN: It doesn't seem like they give a lot of advice, and we
> don't really see them a lot and then they are so busy they don't *want*
> to see you.
> TERRA LEE: Like, if you go to the office, you have to have a reason or
> else you won't get help.
> VANESSA CHEN: Or the lady will yell at you.

Some students realize that their mistreatment is compounded by the fact that IB students are treated more favorably, causing even more frustration. Junior James Tuan details how the so-called higher students on campus are the ones most likely to be seen by time-strapped counselors: "There's too little counselors to go around. I mean, they're always busy and they don't have much time to talk, and if they do talk it's usually to the IB students, which are even higher [than AP]." Senior Jessica Su observes how rules are changed for IB students:

> IB students always get first pick for summer school. For example, you can be an IB student who turns in the paperwork the day it is due and then they will pick the IB student over the average student who turned it in on the first day they gave the summer apps [applications].

Echoing these critiques, a school counselor also contests how some students strategically sign up for pre-IB their first two years in high school just to receive some of the school's perks, but they drop the program their junior years. She explains, "The community has learned to play the game. They know, 'If I go into pre-IB, I'm gonna get the classes that I want and then I'll get out.'" So just as students are granted their preferred courses and easy access to counselors, the IB program also teaches select students how to navigate the school system in their favor.

Despite the multiple privileges IB students receive, at times, the treatment from staffulty can be daunting. The high expectations can inspire hard work, but IB students may be granted little leeway in the classroom. As a student in several honors classes, senior Maggie Cordova sees firsthand the "much higher standard" teachers hold for IB students:

> This IB kid, I don't think he was feeling well. He was sick or wasn't in the mood to really do his assignment. The teacher pulled him aside, and was like, "You're an IB kid. What are you doing? I expect so much more from you. You're in these classes for a reason."

In spite of her enrollment in honors courses, Maggie never remembers receiving the same message as her IB classmate. Feeling badly for the student, Maggie realizes, "If you're labeled an IB kid, you're expected to do so much more. When you're having an off week, and you don't perform, everyone still expects you to." Observations such as these capture some of the difficulties that come with labeling students and treating them unequally—no matter how positive the label and treatment may seem. Labeling allows little room for variation, and labels and unequal treatment push students further apart.

Reflections on Class, Race/Ethnicity, and Building the "Elite"

These compounded experiences are among the factors that may fuel teacher Margaret Albert's concern about breeding elitism. This elitism where a small group of students receive exclusive treatment and some even come to expect such treatment is also evident in the actions and beliefs of some of the IB students, especially in how they perceive non-IB students. These attitudes are antithetical to the IB organization's larger goal of "intercultural understanding and respect." Instead, SCHS is fueling hierarchies, divisions, and antagonism based on an unequal and unjust system of tracking.

The language and attitudes expressed by the three friends reveal clear boundaries between IB and non-IB students. This was especially salient during a conversation about cheating where Mike castigates CP students and condones the behavior for his AP classmates:

> BILLY: The issue in I think every school is cheating. 'Cause I think a lot of students cheat.
>
> GILDA: And why do you think they cheat?
>
> MIKE: Lazy.
>
> GILDA: Really, you think it's laziness?
>
> MAY: Yeah [nervous laugh].
>
> MIKE: They're like, "Ahh, I don't want to study but I still [want to do well]." Cheating is worse for people who are in the upper classes like AP and honors level 'cause we have so much other stuff to do. I'm not saying I do it, but [May laughs] I'm just saying like maybe, "Oh, this class takes up most of my time, and then I have a test tomorrow for this class so I don't know how to balance it out." I think that's why people [cheat], "Oh, this class load, this class is really easy to cheat in so maybe I'll just cheat in this class. So one time only; let's use it to get by." Then they continue to do it, and that's the mentality I think of the people in AP and honors.

After Mike reflects on the demands faced by AP and honors students to understand why students may cheat, he returns to his initial comment that people who cheat do so because they are lazy. For him, this explanation is applicable to students in college preparatory courses or what he and most students at SCHS refer to as "regular students":

> And then for the regular classes or the lower end of the students, I think they're just lazy. They're like, "Oh I don't really care. So if I get caught then it doesn't really matter."

Mike's explanation for why students in different tracks cheat parallels deficiency or "blame the victim" theories that have been used to understand and justify class inequality (Ryan 1976). Even the commonly used language in schools of "upper classes" and "lower end" students that Mike employs mirrors the class-based system in the United States. Mike's statement and deficiency theories in general assume that students in the "regular classes" and people who are economically poor are lazy compared to the "upper classes." Also, the common misperception is that they have nothing to lose if they are caught cheating. This framework disparages students and people in the so-called lower end by blaming them for their positions in schools and society. Furthermore, it simultaneously privileges the so-called higher classes who are almost excused from cheating because it is believed that their workload leaves them little option but to cheat and that some teachers make it so easy to cheat that such students simply cannot resist.

Interestingly, when he begins discussing cheating, Mike claims, "Cheating is worse for people who are in the upper classes." However, it is unclear if he is implying that cheating is more rampant among students in the AP and honors courses or if the ramifications for getting caught are worse for these students. Listening to teachers in the AP and honors courses such as Mallory Tate talk about cheating suggests that Mike means the former:

> There are a lot of kids who don't do the reading, and they find ways around it. People tell them, "This is what happened in the story." And they copy homework. There's just a gross amount of cheating going on, much more with Asian students than with Latino students.

Importantly, while not all Asian American students are in the IB, AP, and honors courses, they compose the vast majority of students in these classes, suggesting that these are the students who Mallory Tate describes since she teaches these classes.

The underlying sense of superiority that some IB students possess is apparent in other arenas as well. For example, Mike's belittling of students in CP courses continues as he recalls with his friends his experience in a CP summer school class he completed at a neighboring high school:

> When I took Algebra 2 regular, there's a bunch of *seniors* in that class. Like, "What did you take freshman year to be in Algebra 2 in your senior year?" I guess they kind of slacked off . . . The IB students or AP students would totally dominate that class [May chuckles]. We would get over a hundred percent, without even trying. It's ridiculous . . . I really just pwned that class.

While Mike uses the language from computer games to claim that he "pwned" or owned the Algebra 2 class, another IB senior Charles Lin conveys a similar level of condescension toward students not in his classes,

"I'm really not sure of people in the lower classes 'cause I wouldn't want to hang out with them or anything like that. It sort of like bugs me . . . they choose to just stay in classes and do easier work." Revealingly, Charles is referring to the different tracks at SCHS, but his disparagement of "the lower classes" makes it easy to see the parallels between tracking and a class-based system where students in CP courses and members of the working classes are maligned.

The school's tracking system is instrumental in fostering such stark student hierarchies. Within such a system, students are kept separate, unequal, and unaware of one another. Perhaps because of their academically privileged position, IB students seem more confident and, as illustrated by IB senior Art Chen, they may be uninformed of their classmates:

> IB is sort of like the elite group, but some of the elites don't choose IB because it is so much work, and then I don't know about AVID, but I know they exist . . . Regular students, umm, yeah, I'm not too sure about what they are up to or what they are into.

This lack of awareness is even pronounced for Art, who was unique among the IB students because he critiques the "disparity between Asians and Latinos" at SCHS as an "[un]healthy environment for kids to be around 'cause it's not reality."

At SCHS where course placement is distorted racially/ethnically and by socioeconomic class, this elitism also intersects with racist beliefs about Asian Americans and Latinas/os. Ashley Cordero, a junior previously enrolled in the IB program, observes,

> IB students could get kind of big-headed at times because it's only Asian . . . and then I'm Hispanic. It's kind of recognized as the Asian thing because the Asians are supposed to be the smarter ones.

Examples such as these illustrate how tracking and the elitism structured into the IB program manifests itself in students' attitudes and peer groups. These patterns parallel other research documenting how school practices such as the confinement of students in different classes foster racial/ethnic tensions and conflict among students who in turn adopt different identities and draw boundaries around themselves and in opposition to others (Matute-Bianchi 1986; Valenzuela 1999; Henze, Katz, and Norte 2000; Bejarano 2005).[3]

Not all IB students feel a sense of superiority that the elitism at SCHS fuels. As detailed in later chapters, a couple of students feel marginalized within the program. Nonetheless, the climate created at the school and replicated in some students' sentiments is an indication that the mission

of the IB organization to "develop inquiring, knowledgeable and caring young people who help to create a better and more peaceful world
through intercultural understanding and respect" (International Baccalaureate Organization 2012) is lost at SCHS. Reflecting on this goal, Billy
scoffs,

> When I went to the IB meeting, they talked about world peace and
> stuff and like, "Whoa, whoa what's this? I just came for school." And
> then they say, "You're in an IB program because when you graduate
> you will use your academic knowledge to benefit everyone around
> you." That's so exaggerated [Billy, May, and Mike laugh].

While Billy may have just come to SCHS for what he thought was simply
school, he and his schoolmates are being socialized to maintain a system
of power, privilege, and inequality.

AVID and Building the "Middle"

In contrast to the predominately middle-class and upper-middle-class
Asian American students in the IB program who are designated the "elite,"
as administrator Joe Berk explains, the primarily Latina/o students in the
school's AVID program are characterized as the "middle":

> One of the first things I said we'd do is get an AVID program so that
> the kids that are right in that middle, and a lot of those kids are our
> Hispanic kids, can get that little extra push to make sure that they're
> accessing those advanced classes too.

The language of the "middle" is part of the discourse of the national AVID
program, where the emphasis is on increasing the achievement of students
in the academic "middle"—those earning Bs, Cs, and Ds (Lozano, Watt,
and Huerta 2009; Swanson, Mehan, and Hubbard 1995).

Established in 1980 by a high school English teacher in San Diego, California, to address concerns about how students being bused to San Diego's
Clairmont High School under court order would fair at an academically
acclaimed school, AVID is offered currently in more than 4,800 elementary
and secondary schools and 16 other countries, where it serves over 400,000
students. Many students are the first generation in their families to attend
college and are students of color; about 50 percent are Latina/o. AVID's
mission is "to close the achievement gap by preparing all students for college readiness and success in a global society" (Advancement via Individual
Determination 2012). It is considered an "untracking program" because of
its aim to place students in rigorous courses (Pitch et al. 2006).

Encouraged to apply by teachers, counselors, parents, and friends, AVID students are selected based on standardized test scores, course grades, and teacher recommendations. At SCHS, cohorts of twenty-five to fifty students enroll in a required AVID course as one of their electives each of their four years of high school. These courses focus on organizational and study skills, provide peer tutorials and academic assistance, and include guest speakers on college and careers. Ninth-grade classes tend to be larger than later years because of some attrition, especially by young men. Thus young women predominate, particularly in the junior and senior classes, where at the time of this research there was an estimated ratio of six to one women to men. Most students are Latina/o. They are also likely to come from working-class families where they will be the first generation to attend college.

The first cohort of about twenty-five AVID students was preparing to graduate the year I completed my research. As the following friends share, their participation in AVID has been instrumental in enhancing their capital and preparing them for college. They, like their IB schoolmates, emphasize the special treatment they receive at school. However, rather than being schooled as the "elite," the messages they receive, their curriculum, and the relationships built within AVID fuel a sense of being students in the "middle."

"The Middle Students Are in There": Monique Martinez, Art Casas, and Laura Cadena

Friends since their days at La Montaña, Monique Martinez, Art Casas, and Laura Cadena were in their third year in AVID when we sat down to talk. The two previous years, I was a guest speaker in their AVID classes, so we had met before. Their friendship and our familiarity facilitated the flow of our two-hour conversation.

Encouraged by their parents to join AVID, they have persisted in spite of a significant number of students who have left the program:

> LAURA: My parents wanted me to get in because they thought, "Oh college!" They help us get into college.
>
> MONIQUE: AVID, first year, we had so many kids in that class; we had two full classes of forty. So that's like eighty kids my freshman year. I think it's 'cause their parents wanted them to try the class. But since we had a bad teacher who didn't teach well, a lot of kids were like, "We don't like AVID." Everyone thought it was stupid. So our eighty kids dropped to forty or less.

Notwithstanding their criticism of their first AVID teacher, the friends still credit him with maintaining high expectations and fostering a sense of solidarity among students, even if it was against him. Realizing the overall benefits of AVID, the three students persevered. AVID has been instrumental in strengthening their ties to one another and to the school. This has facilitated their and their classmates' paths to college.

Echoing administrator Berk's earlier quote, AVID students also adopt the language of the organization to describe themselves. This language categorizes students and influences their sense of selves and their perceptions of their peers. Laura Cadena explains, "In AVID, the middle students are in there. Like, people that aren't the smartest, but they could be bright." AVID juniors Laura Luna and Elisa Vasquez concur. They describe themselves as "not too smart, not too lower—like in the middle." Laura and Monique reveal how this discourse is shaped by quantitative measurements used to rank students, in this case grade point average:

> LAURA: We don't have 4.0s, but we don't have a 1.0.
>
> MONIQUE: In the middle, like 3.5.

Some may question how a 3.5 GPA could be considered a "middle" GPA, but at schools such as SCHS where there are multiple courses in honors and advanced placement where students earn an additional grade point per class, valedictorians and salutatorians often have 4.5s or higher. For Laura and Monique, GPAs converge with the language of AVID to reinforce perceptions of intelligence, as is seen when Laura uses certain terms like "smartness" and "bright."

AVID junior Stephanie Yep uses similar language, but she emphasizes curriculum track rather than GPA to understand intelligence:

> AVID is for students in the middle, who don't know exactly if they're super smart or not that good. IB and AP are for the students who are really high up there; they're like class speakers and stuff . . . I'm in AVID, 'cause I'm not really good in all those academic stuffs, but I'm not like super bad. I'm just right in the middle.

School-determined markers of academic worth such as high GPAs and course placement are assumed to be indicators of greater intellectual ability. Teacher Beth Hill reveals how because of the belief that such indicators are meaningful, AVID is often stigmatized by students:

> BETH HILL: At the current time [students in AVID] have a 2.0, 2.5, like the average, middle. They are not the highest . . . So on campus everybody is saying it's for the dumb kids.

GILDA OCHOA: Who are the students that are saying that?

BETH HILL: I think most of the time it's the honors kids.

AVID juniors Laura Luna and Elisa Vasquez find that students in honors classes are not the only students who look down on AVID. They observe students in college preparatory courses, saying, "Oh, you're in AVID because you are not smart" or "You're in AVID because you can't do it yourself. You don't know how to do it." For some students, this sentiment fuels a sense of shame. Laura Luna remembers, "In the beginning, I was like, 'Oh yeah [voice lowers], I'm in AVID'—kind of embarrassed."

The prevailing language of the "elite," "honors," and the "middle" reinforces these experiences. In the binary framework of "smart" and "stupid," AVID students are believed to fall in-between. Thus, while their IB schoolmates are listed in the school annual as "I think therefore IB," just a few pages later, the AVID students are designated as "potential thinkers." Apparently, they are not yet thinkers—like their supposedly "smarter" IB counterparts—but they have promise.

At SCHS, the framing of AVID as students in the "middle" is not innocuous. Instead, it intersects with racialized constructions of intelligence and a hard work ethic to reinforce racial/ethnic and academic hierarchies. The racial/ethnic and class skewing of student enrollment in IB and AVID perpetuates the beliefs apparent in the middle schools that Asian Americans are smarter than Latinas/os. Speaking frankly about these perceptions, Monique, Art, and Laura reveal the following:

> MONIQUE: We established that the Asian kids are usually in the IB program. There are a couple of Mexicans, but I think it's because Asians work harder.
>
> ART: [Asians] know that they're smarter than us, and they treat us like that.
>
> LAURA: Yeah.
>
> ART: I guess it works both ways. Because we look at them like, "Oh—"
>
> MONIQUE: Yeah, we look at them like, "Oh you're so smart. Help us."
>
> ART: Yeah, we go up to Asians for help in our classes mostly.
>
> MONIQUE: [If] my friend needs help, [we say], "Ask the little Asian kids."

Based on observations such as these, junior Jennifer Cortez deduces that her Latina/o AVID classmates have internalized assumptions that they are not smart: "A lot of them tend to put themselves down; they say that they're dumb. But I see that with them, they actually are trying to do better, even if they struggle." Dominant ideologies about Asian Americans, differential and unequal course placement, and everyday exchanges work in tandem to foster these racialized assumptions and interactions.

Despite its dominance, not all AVID students accept the pervasive trope that they are in the "middle" or "not as smart." Ninth-grader Miguel Cortez clarifies,

> The AP students, they want to study really hard, like every night, possibly, and the AVID students, most of us are the ones who are having trouble sometimes. So it's not that we're not as smart; we just haven't tried hard. 'Cause a lot of the kids are really smart, they just need to try.

Demonstrating his awareness of prevailing assumptions of students in different academic programs, Miguel challenges biological arguments. However, he replaces this framework with another individualizing one that still blames students for their academic performance. He attributes course placement to work ethic. While this perspective may help motivate him, it assumes that students are provided with equal opportunities to excel and that students in AP courses try harder than students in AVID. With limited access to power-aware frameworks that consider the macro-meso-micro factors impinging on their academic opportunities, such students adopt the individualizing discourses detailed in the previous chapter and even in their program's name—Advancement via *Individual* Determination. Students in AVID may come to believe that they are to blame for their position in the school and that they are lacking in intelligence or a hard work ethic.[4]

Skill Building: Expectations, Cornell Notes, and Tutorials

Despite the program's emphasis on increasing academic achievement, many AVID students feel unmotivated in classes with teachers who apparently have low expectations:

> MONIQUE: I think some of the teachers don't push us hard enough.
> ART: All of them. Yeah
> LAURA: Yeah. Yeah.
> MONIQUE: Our AVID teacher is one of the only teachers that likes to push us hard.
> ART: No motivation in other classes.
> MONIQUE: Yeah, well [our Spanish teacher] motivates us a little . . . The other teachers are just like, "Do your work. OK then, bye."

Sophomore Edmund Sosa adds how other than his AVID teacher, "the teachers just want you to pass the class."

Feeling unchallenged and uninspired in most of their classes, AVID students said little about their courses. An exception was Art who was one of the few students in the program who was enrolled in an AP course. As a junior, he had just started taking AP literature, where he immediately noticed a difference in teacher expectations between his college preparatory English 3 class and the AP course:

> I remember one assignment in English 3. It was like, "Answer one or two questions on a reading." Now I'm doing essays. I'm reading a book; I have to read five chapters this weekend. I have to grade a paper that I wrote. The essay I'm doing, I have to compare the essay I wrote to a really good essay, and then I have another homework assignment that's really big . . . She thinks that we're really smart.

While the amount of work assigned is not necessarily an indication of teacher's expectations, the quality of the assignments in the two classes differs vastly. In the CP class, students were required to answer a couple of questions from a reading. Now Art is being assigned books and essays—work that will enhance his critical thinking, writing, and analytical abilities. The message conveyed to him by the teacher is that the students are "really smart."

While AVID students were generally quiet about the content of their classes, especially compared to how the IB students gushed about their theory of knowledge seminar, they nonetheless talked at length about the components of their yearly AVID course. Building organizational skills is at the crux of these AVID courses where students learn how to complete class notes and maintain school binders with course handouts, homework schedules, and personal goals. These binders are graded regularly on content, order, and neatness, and a major component are their required notes that constitute most of the writing completed in the AVID course. AVID students are expected to follow the Cornell method of note-taking developed in the 1940s by Walter Pauk, emeritus professor from Cornell University (see Kerstiens 1998). As part of this Cornell method, students write notes on the right side of papers and questions and headings on the left. A paragraph summary is included as well. Students describe spending much of their AVID class time taking notes. For students such as Jose de Leon, this is a repeat of what they have already learned: "During AVID, right now we're just practicing to take Cornell notes, mostly what we did in junior high for AVID."

Rather than feeling challenged, some students find the extensive and overly structured note taking tedious. When given the option to complete binders and Cornell notes or to enroll in a course elective, some opt for an elective and leave AVID altogether. This is the case for sophomore Maria

Castillo, who dropped AVID after just one year because she believes "you waste a lot of time on learning how to take notes. It was like taking notes on taking notes. It wasn't worth giving up an elective." This highly controlled method of taking notes does not allow for different styles of learning and engaging with course materials. In contrast to the IB theory of knowledge course, this requirement of the AVID program emphasizes following directions and regurgitating material over active engagement and critical thinking.

Another significant aspect of AVID is biweekly tutorials. Twice a week during their AVID class, students work in small groups with college tutors to discuss questions from their other courses. This process is designed to be collaborative. Students bring questions for help, and with the guidance of college tutors, peers offer their assistance. Ninth-grader Rosalyn Saldana explains,

> We did one yesterday. We did questions that we don't know and then
> we were in groups and we write them on a board and then whoever
> knows the answer, they show us how to get it and then we just write
> the answers in the back and that's how we know the answers.

As discussed in more detail in chapter 4, many AVID students rely on this support. Teacher John Alvarez has heard from AVID students how much they value this resource and the way the tutorials are based on an ethos of collaboration:

> They like the idea of having a period where they can work in groups,
> and if they are struggling in, say, mathematics, then they will get help.
> So there is this sort of helping from each other; some students who
> are stronger in other areas help each other. The nice thing is that you
> have a teacher that is strictly there for support.

However, similar to the Cornell note-taking system, there is a structured format for conducting, preparing, and participating in tutorials. While this highly regulated approach may work for some students, a few find it less compelling and overly complicated. For example, ninth-grader Susan Drake questions, "We do these tutorials, which I do not get at all. I don't get the point; I don't even know how to do it right."

In spite of some students' criticisms, the organizational skills and the cooperative peer relationships AVID is inculcating are adding to students' cultural and social capital. Just as the AVID requirements are enhancing students' note-taking abilities, study skills, and time management, they are also building a sense of community as students working together. Reflecting on his first year of high school, ninth-grader Eduardo Telles captures the growth experienced by many AVID students:

AVID has helped me a lot in improving my grades, doing my homework, and being time efficient and not just wasting time sitting there doing nothing. It's helped me become organized 'cause I used to have a big mess in my backpack before. It's also helped me become a better student by helping other students with their problems in school.

While AVID students appreciate such improvements, none describe having access in their courses to the critical thinking, extensive writing, and open-ended assignments that their IB and AP schoolmates detail. This silence may not indicate its absence, but when combined with their more structured assignments, it suggests that students in these two programs are being schooled unequally and prepared for differing life paths.

Building Capital within AVID

The relationships established through AVID are significant for enhancing students' social and cultural capital. Since many AVID students are the first members of their families to attend college, relationships with caring educators who assist them with the information needed to make the transition to college are crucial. The AVID teachers and counselors are instrumental in this process, and many students credit an AVID teacher for being the person most responsible for helping them academically. Junior Iris Pedraza admires her AVID teacher so much that she hopes to follow in her footsteps:

AVID has helped me a lot, has brought my vision of getting into college, and it helps me decide which college I wanna go to; I really wanna go to Cal State Fullerton, because [my AVID teacher] went to that one, and she became a teacher there . . . I wanna be a teacher.

Equally important in students' lives is the AVID counselor. Students in AVID and IB have the same counselor, and like their IB schoolmates, AVID students praise their unique relationship with her:

MONIQUE MARTINEZ: We have the best counselor in the whole wide world . . . She's freaking awesome. AVID and IB are the two special programs we have here. So anything that has to do with us we get first choice, first pick in anything we want. For summer school classes, we just write down [our counselor's] name, and we get the class. No matter what we want, or if we have a problem with our schedule, we can just go up to the office and be like, "We don't like it." She'll be like "Okay." She'll ask us, "What's wrong? What's going on?" She's very understanding.

Sophomore Edmund Sosa confirms the special treatment granted to AVID students:

> She's very helpful. She really looks out for me. Even when I mess
> up she fixes it for me . . . Sometimes when I'd be off the due date
> [for completing necessary paperwork, such as enrolling in summer
> school], she'd take it and put it in the system still.

This supportive relationship where AVID and IB students "get first choice" contrasts with what Monique has observed from the other school counselors:

> She's not like the other counselors [who are] like, "Okay. Wait. Come
> back in a couple of days; we'll see what happens." She's more like,
> "Do it now. Do it now." And she tries to push us hard . . . She's like,
> "I think you should take this class instead because it'll be better for
> college."

Access to a counselor with high expectations is instrumental in motivating students and ensuring that they take the necessary courses to put them on a path to a four-year college or university (Espinoza 2011).

In addition to the close ties they have with their AVID teachers and counselor, students are introduced to weekly or biweekly guest speakers who discuss their schooling experiences and career paths. Ninth-grader Susan Drake thinks this is one of the strengths of AVID: "The guest speaker thing is pretty cool 'cause you get to know other people's experiences and you can relate to people." Similar to the AVID staffulty, these motivational speakers provide students with helpful information and important connections to colleges and jobs.

Finally, AVID students also work closely with college students, and they visit several area colleges each year. As Mandy Esquivel indicates, these experiences expand her resources, influence her vision, and demystify higher education, "AVID has helped me see how college is and how to get there too, and I think that if I'm not in AVID, I wouldn't be as motivated to go to college."

Despite these networks of support, some believe that AVID is missing an important component—a stronger connection between the school and the community. Member of the staffulty Jackie Towne expresses her concern:

> My understanding of how the program is supposed to work is that
> you really need to have support services because you're looking at the
> Hispanic students that could do it but just need those extra supports.
> I don't think that we really have that in place to help them.

Jackie Towne expounds on the type of support she envisions by critiquing the school's unequal practice of reaching out to the Chinese American community and neglecting Latina/o parents:

The community has to be involved, and it's not. We have a Chinese
parents group. Do we have a Hispanic parents group? No, I know
we had a Hispanic liaison and she's out ill, but have they bothered to
replace her? No.

As Towne highlights, this lack of connection with the Latina/o community is glaring, especially when one considers that the school has created
a paid position in the administrative office for a Chinese parent liaison
who meets with Chinese parents; invites counselors to parent meetings;
and hosts informational sessions on college, scholarships, and other relevant topics.[5] The school's Chinese parent liaison has facilitated a strong
support network through the Chinese American Parent Association. As
teacher Beth Hill explains, this helps parents and students share information and resources:

Asian parents, they all know each other and know the kids . . . [A] lot
of the parents [whose children I teach] have a relationship. They all
know each other and they all talk about different things.

The additional support that comes with the school's paid Chinese parent
liaison is significant, and a similar liaison who speaks Spanish could also
help build a stronger web of assistance for Latina/o students. Such a liaison could be an advocate for Latina/o students and parents at the school
and provide more support for students. Since there is not a comparable
Latina/o community liaison, the school's current practice is unequal and
may actually hinder the goals of the AVID program.

Finally, although one of the goals is to ensure that students in AVID are
accessing advanced classes, the separation of curriculum tracks makes it
difficult for AVID students to know about the IB program and to befriend
students outside of AVID. When asked about their relationships, most
students reveal that their friendships are dependent upon who is in their
classes. Sophomore Felipe Perez's comments are exemplary, "Well, obvi-
ously, I'm friends with everybody in AVID, but I don't think I have any
friends in AP or IB." Few AVID students report having friends in IB, and
most have only heard about the program. They do not know the specif-
ics. Even AVID junior Art Casas, who has a cross-section of friends in CP
and AP courses, is unsure about the details of IB: "I don't really know
what IB is. All I know is if you do it and graduate, you get some diploma,
and you can go to that school Oxford and get in, I think." This lack of
awareness reveals the segregation of the programs and the students in
them. By not knowing about the IB program, students' opportunities
for participating in it and building their social capital by forming friends

with people outside of their courses are dramatically reduced. This lack of awareness also demonstrates the school's failure in fulfilling a program goal of "closing the achievement gap." With curriculum tracking sorting and dividing students into different courses, it hinders their social, cultural, and human capital (see Moody 2001; Goldsmith 2004; Stanton-Salazar 2004).

Reflections on Building the "Elite" and the "Middle"

Similar to their schoolmates in IB, AVID students receive some special treatment, most noticeably in their relationships with their counselor. As Susan Drake, a ninth-grader in AVID, critiques, this treatment is also reflected in teachers' attitudes:

> AVID and IB are treated differently . . . They're treated like they're better than the other students. I don't think so, but I think the teachers have more respect for them. [They think], "Good job, you're enrolled in good classes."

While such privileged treatment is exclusionary and it has the potential to be divisive, it is not the same for both groups of students in these two academic programs.

First of all, the origins and rationales for the two groups of students' treatment vary. Given their overall class advantages as primarily middle-class and upper-middle-class students and their privileged positioning at the school, IB students are among a group who already tend to have access to the most valued forms of capital and other resources. They are enrolled in honors and AP classes and receive school awards and other praise. Similarly, many of their parents and the students are also more connected to school officials and other social networks. Likewise, the IB program was established by the school district to keep many of these wealthier families from fleeing the district—revealing their parent power to influence school district decisions and their capital to access schools that serve their interests. In contrast, the AVID program, while still excluding other students who could also benefit from it, is trying to remedy unjust school practices that typically overlook students in the so-called middle. It is doing so by giving primarily working-class and first-generation college students support, encouragement, access to resources, and a push to enroll in honors and AP courses. Thus the IB program at SCHS is an example of hypercurriculum tracking with all of its faults of reproducing a system of racial/ethnic and class inequality. At SCHS, AVID is a reform program that seems to acknowledge unequal access and is trying to work around it for a small group of previously excluded students.

Second, the ramifications of the differential treatments also diverge. Since the "elite" label is so embedded with unequal treatment and the assumption that Asian American students are stronger students, IB students are more likely to exude a sense of confidence, entitlement, and even superiority over students in other curriculum tracks. This demeanor was absent in the interviews with the AVID students. Instead, a sense of being in the middle and working together to achieve their goals of attending college is present. As sophomore Mandy Esquivel shares, there is a feeling of we-ness among AVID students:

> [AVID] is mixed but mostly more Hispanic. I think there's like three Asians in there, but we don't see it different. We're like, "It's just our class." We say it's our class. It's not just, "Oh, it's a Hispanic class in there."

With so much focus on individualism, this collectivist sentiment is unique in schools. For students in AVID, it may be fostered by their biweekly tutorials and by being with the same classmates for all four years. Most importantly, their awareness that they are primarily first-generation college-going students and Latinas/os and perhaps less expected to succeed academically may be among the factors that bind them.

In contrast to the IB program, this collaborative ethos does not pit curriculum tracks against each other in a competitive or hierarchical manner. This sense of "we-ness" does not assume a negative juxtaposition to other students. Rather, there is a concern that other students should also have access to the support and encouragement they receive. Laura Luna, a junior in AVID, advocates,

> If there are kids that are struggling, they shouldn't ignore them. They should try to help them too. If they have a program for AVID, for us kids, and then they have one for honors kids, why can't they have one for the lower class so that they can become an AVID student or an honors student? . . . They put the honors students first, but I think it should be all equal.

While Laura uses the language of the school to distinguish between different students—AVID, honors, and lower class—she does not adopt a hierarchical and competitive framework. Instead, like many of her AVID classmates, she advocates providing more opportunities for all students. Since students in AVID are positioned in the middle, they may have a unique angle of vision where they are better able to see and critique the privileges select students receive and the relative lack of support provided to college preparatory students.

In spite of their differences and distinct origins, at SCHS, both IB and AVID contribute to stratification within the school and society. These programs perpetuate a racialized and class-based system of tracking, even if unintentionally in the case of AVID, which is referred to as an untracking program. Since students are unequally labeled, schooled, and supported, they are being disparately prepared as they make their ways through SCHS and into institutions of higher education.

The "Rest": CP Students as "Regular" and "Average"

> There's the honor, AP, IB courses, and then there's the rest, which I think almost all of them now are designated college prep.
>
> —Mark Durand, Southern California
> High School (SCHS) teacher

> I'm an advocate for the average kid and below average kid . . . They've done a good job promoting the top echelon people. But I don't feel there's been enough for the average kid, and I see the gap widening.
>
> —Jim Scott, SCHS teacher

With the exception of some electives and classes for English language learners or special education students, nearly all the courses at SCHS are college preparatory. Thus, as teacher Mark Durand defines, after considering the students in honors and advanced classes, students in the CP classes represent the "rest" of the student body. However, at nearly 1,200, they compose the majority of the campus. They are over 65 percent of the student population—not an insignificant amount. Nevertheless, the language often used to describe them, as well as the limited resources and support they receive relative to students in the IB and AVID programs, are among the reasons that, in the words of teacher Jim Scott, a "gap is widening" between the "top echelon" and the students considered "average."

"IB, AP, Honors, and Just Regular": Maria Castillo, Becky Cruz, Isabel Fuentes, and Julia Rios

While the fifty-minute lunch period was a short time for their interview, sophomores Maria Castillo and Becky Cruz wasted no time delving into their schooling experiences. The students huddled together outside on the floor and ate and talked just yards away from where their group of friends were eating. Two of their friends—sophomores Isabel Fuentes and Julia Rios—were also being interviewed at the same time. The four of them have known each other and most of their friends since they were at Maple Grove Middle School.

Aware of the academic programs at SCHS and how, as Becky describes, "the IB kids mostly stick together because they have the same classes," Maria and Becky proudly describe their ten friends:

> MARIA: We're really mixed.
>
> BECKY: She's in softball. I'm in cheer. I don't hang out with the cheerleaders. Marilyn is in cross-country. One girl is in drama. The other one is in choir . . . [W]e're the people who don't like to hang out with what we do. We like something separate.
>
> MARIA: A lot of my softball friends, they hang out together. I'm the only one who's separate.
>
> BECKY: Yeah, me too. I'm the only cheerleader who's separate . . . Almost all of [our friends] came from Maple Grove, except for maybe two or—
>
> MARIA: Three.
>
> BECKY: They are other people's friends, and they came in and now we're all friends.

Just as their interests are varied, so too are their placements in curriculum tracks. Maria is in CP courses and Becky was in honors courses her ninth-grade year and will be in AP courses her junior year. She opted out of honors classes her sophomore year because "it was really hard," but she reports, "I want to get back into it next year." Julia Rios is a pre-IB student, and a couple of their friends are in AVID.

Their cross-track friendships are unique, and they provide Maria, Becky, Isabel, and Julia with a "dual frame of reference" from which to compare and contrast their varying experiences (see Ogbu 1991). Since they talk about their experiences with each other, they are aware of the differing treatment and resources provided to students. Together, their perspectives convey how students in CP classes are considered "regular" or "average," how they encounter unequal practices in classes, and how they receive limited assistance from their counselors.

Labeling the "Regular" and the "Average"

In nearly every interview, staffuly and students such as sophomore Araceli Castro refer to students in CP courses as "regular" or "average"—implicitly or explicitly comparing them with students in honors, AP, and IB courses:

> I call mine regular. I'm not dumb, but I'm not Einstein. I'm pretty average, when it comes down to it.

These references are more than labels; they are often value laden, occasionally associated with levels of intelligence, and they influence perceptions and expectations of entire classes. Despite the prevailing discourses used to label students, a few teachers explicitly contest dominant perspectives that position students in CP classes as less than others. A critic of today's schooling, where indicators such as standardized test scores and GPAs are the sole measurements of success, teacher Marie Silva demonstrates how the labels "average" and "regular" may be contradictory when applied to students in her CP classes, who she characterizes as creative individuals who may not abide by other's mandates:

> I have had some very brilliant students, probably more brilliant than some of the students in my honors class. The honors students, who aren't as smart as these other kids, have bought into [the system]; they go through the routine; they go through the motions. The other students are free thinkers. They color outside of the lines. They get Cs and Ds, not because they are not smart but because they don't buy into the whole system. They think in a different way and they think in higher levels and they are thinking beyond, but they don't turn in the homework.

Such observations call into question who is really "regular" and what are the factors inhibiting more "free thinkers" in schools. By recasting how students in CP courses are typically perceived, Marie Silva questions the traditional system of ranking students. She also contests the homogenization where students are schooled to obediently follow others' expectations and conceptions of success. Nevertheless, in her critique she uses dominant labels to designate students and evaluate their levels of intelligence in ways that still perpetuate a hierarchical system.

Similarly, teacher Jane King also praises students in the CP classes. Earlier, she critiqued AP classes for being too prescriptive, and she shared her joy of teaching sophomores in honors classes because the curriculum is more "pliable." However, here, she explains why "junior regulars" are her preferred group of students:[6]

> I like teaching junior regular kids because they are like the heart of the school . . . [I]t means that I'm getting those regular junior kids that are down to earth, and they're like how I was when I was a student . . . [T]he junior regulars, they are definitely my favorite. If I didn't teach those [students] next year, I'd be sad.

Though Jane King uses the common label of "regular" in her description, she is not being pejorative. Instead, she includes herself in this category and identifies with the students in her CP classes. She considers them "down to earth," perhaps compared to some of the students in the IB and AP classes, who are schooled to believe that they are better than others.

Schooling for Learning? (Dis)Engaged Teaching and Curriculum

Despite the asset-based approach that teachers such as Marie Silva and Jane King use to praise students in CP classes, students in these courses echo similar concerns as some of their schoolmates in AVID. They often feel uninspired by unmotivated teachers, traditional teaching practices, and removed curriculum. They critique an educational approach that is highly structured—where a premium is placed on test performance and student behavior. Within these classrooms, teachers and textbooks are positioned as authorities and students are assumed to have little or nothing to offer. This "banking method" of education perpetuates a one-way transfer of knowledge where students are lectured at and expected to passively receive information (Freire 1970). For many students, these teaching approaches and the curriculum are rigid, distant, and disconnected from their lives. There is an emphasis on rules, policies, and the technical aspects of schooling rather than *how* students are experiencing the classroom environment and whether they are actually learning (see Noddings 1984; Valenzuela 1999). The impacts of such schooling include disengagement and inequality. Students crave more forgiving, compelling, and interactive teachers, classes, and curriculum. So do some of their teachers, but they encounter similar practices as the students enrolled in their CP classes. This, in turn, hinders teaching and learning.

Almost immediately into their interview, friends Maria Castillo and Becky Cruz capture a recurring desire for "teachers that care more." They plead for teachers who "try" and don't "give up." Instead, they have to contend with a math teacher whose grading and testing policies are so narrowly defined that they are negatively impacting student desire:

> MARIA: My math teacher, she gives up on her students. There's like five students that don't come to class, and half the class is asleep or not trying.
>
> BECKY: She won't give you a test because she says there's no point if you're failing.
>
> MARIA: Yeah, I gave up because she's that bad . . . I was doing all my homework and all my work and I got an F, and most teachers would at least give you a C and she wouldn't. So there was no point in trying, so I stopped taking the tests.

By basing most of the course grade on test performance and denying students the opportunity to complete tests if they are failing, this teacher delivers powerful messages that she has forsaken students. She squelches students' incentive to submit their homework, and some students opt out of the class entirely by sleeping or ditching. Rather than encouraging students to persist and exploring other options for engaging students, this teacher's policies fuel low morale in the classroom, among students, and perhaps even for the teacher.

Just as teachers' testing policies may lower some students' drive and hinder possibilities for improvement, grading procedures that mark students down for behavior may also have detrimental impacts. They may lower students' grades and convey the idea that behavior is more important than knowledge of the course material. This has been sophomore Daniela Gutierrez's experience:

> DANIELA: My Spanish class is easy for me. That's why I talk because it's easy; I don't really pay attention in that class because I know Spanish.
>
> GILDA OCHOA: How are you doing in terms of your grades for your classes?
>
> DANIELA: In Spanish, I have a "C" because she takes off points for talking and stuff. Actually, I have a "D."

Not only does Daniela feel unchallenged, but she also finds that she is barely passing her class because she is being penalized for her behavior. As in the previous example with the math teacher, there seems to be greater emphasis on having students follow rules and pass tests than changing teaching approaches and curriculum to reach more students. Just as sociologist Nancy Lopez (2003) found in her research in a New York school, some students may engage in "willful laziness" when they feel unchallenged in classes, either because the classes are easy or because the teachers are less invested. The result may be a self-perpetuating cycle where students stop trying and spend class time talking with friends. In turn, teachers may funnel more of their energy into controlling the class and teaching less.

Part of the regimented approach to education underlying some CP courses is reflected in how teachers construct the classroom space, including the seating assignments. Research assistant Sandra Hamada documents in her field notes what she learned from one teacher:

> The class is divided by grades. There is an As and Bs section, then Bs and Cs, and then Ds and Fs section. [The teacher] said it was something she was trying out . . . because she felt that some of the students were bringing other students down. She told me that the students

knew right away that they were being seated in this order. I think she
did not tell them, but once they saw who was seated in each section,
they figured it out.

This seating arrangement can be just as detrimental as the math teacher's
testing and homework policies. In this case, students are visibly ranked
based on academic performance. These rankings can become self-fulfilling
such that students may begin to see themselves as other people do and
respond to their evaluations. As senior Melvin Jackson tells research
assistant Laura Enriquez, such designated seating arrangements can also
become distracting:

> The first day of school, I try and sit with the people that I know will do
> their work and be quiet. But always when they come out with the seat-
> ing chart I am next to all of the noisy students who like to talk during
> class and not do their work. I'm always with these loud students.

Regulating where students sit may have the unintended impact of actually
hindering student performance. It may define students' abilities and not
allow for the fact that students can change—either their grades or their
behaviors.

Students also critique the equally unforgiving lecture-based approach
used in many classrooms. Sophomores Isabel Fuentes and Julia Rios detail
the following:

> ISABEL: I would change the teacher methods, the way they teach.
> JULIA: Like out of the book for the tests.
> ISABEL: Like [teach] like they know it. Play games, you know.
> JULIA: And not straight from the textbook.
> ISABEL: Yeah, and just copy notes. 'Cause, we don't really learn that
> way . . . It's boring . . . All we do is copy from the book, and I'm not
> learning it. I'm just writing just so I can get it done.

While teachers may be constrained by mandates that force them to cover
certain standards in preparation for district, state, and federal tests, lecturing directly from the textbook is not compelling, and, as Isabel argues,
it hinders student learning. Sophomore Claudia Macías adds, "The teachers just talk all day." These classroom environments where students are
expected to sit quietly and listen for hours at a time make for "boring"
classes and disengaged students (Shor 1992). They do not provide students or teachers with the chance to critically reflect, apply, discuss, or
challenge the material. They fuel a perception that knowledge is fixed and
something to be consumed.

These teacher-centered and lectured-based classes also limit student interactions. Students are expected to listen to the teacher instead of interact and learn with their classmates in free-flowing classrooms. As a result, students such as Claudia Macías crave "more hands-on stuff" rather than "the same routine over and over again." Isabel and Julia explain that even in their college preparatory chemistry class, where completing experiments could be one avenue of applying what they learn, they have only conducted two labs the entire academic year and one of them was completed by the teacher at the front of the classroom.

In some cases, the course curriculum is as disconnected, irrelevant, and disengaging as the teachers' pedagogy. As implied earlier by IB friends Billy, Mike, and May, the curriculum and assignments appear more structured, allowing less space for interpretation than the IB and honors courses. As sophomore friends Isabel Fuentes in CP English and Julia Rios in honors English compare their class assignments, the differences in how students are being educated are revealing:

> ISABEL: My English class sucks . . . I really like to write, and I really like to learn new words, and I've been there [with that teacher for two years], and he doesn't make us do anything. I don't want to write about Julius Caesar and something about the tyrant. I want it to be on the more personal level—you know, that *makes* us want to write.
>
> INTERVIEWER LAURA ENRIQUEZ: Like what?
>
> ISABEL: Like, give us quotes and we have to think about what the quote means. Say, "Write an essay on what you think the quote means," or "Write a story or compare yourself to this person in this book." Just not Julius Caesar. And I would like to read some good books, like *To Kill a Mockingbird.*
>
> JULIA: They have us read it in honors English.
>
> INTERVIEWER LAURA ENRIQUEZ: [W]hat are the differences between those two classes?
>
> ISABEL: Her teacher's cool.
>
> JULIA: Yeah, she's cool. Wait, how many books did you guys read? Um, *Julius Caesar*?
>
> ISABEL: No, we didn't read the book *Julius Caesar*. We read it from the interactive reader.
>
> JULIA: Oh, we read the book.
>
> INTERVIEWER LAURA ENRIQUEZ: What is that [interactive reader]? Is that the whole book, or is it just pieces?
>
> ISABEL: The textbook. It's just like a summary.

Isabel expresses a love of writing and learning new materials; however, she is not enthused by the course assignments in her CP class. She wishes

they were more open-ended and allowed students to make personal connections and offer their own reflections rather than simply describe what
they are reading. Similarly, Isabel looks to Julia's honors class to emphasize the types of books she would like to read, such as *To Kill a Mocking
Bird*. However, one wonders if even this book would lose its appeal if students in CP classes are only assigned sections of it from a course reader.

Coupled with the belief that CP homework assignments constrain students' thoughts, some students feel that the workload is heavier than what is
expected in AP classes, where students appear to have more liberty of expres-
sion. Senior Alicia Vasquez, who is enrolled in AP and CP classes, exposes,

> I've noticed that AP classes tend to be easier than regular classes.
> Sometimes we get more work; sometimes we get less. But whatever
> the work is, it's pretty easy. It's like, "Whatever you think it is. There
> is no right or wrong answer."

As the students in IB classes also argued earlier, Alicia believes that there
is more leeway granted in AP classes. As a result of this difference, she is
strongly committed to staying away from CP English and enrolled in her
AP classes:

> I was thinking next year of not taking AP English, but I was like,
> "No, I don't want to go back to the regular English and do a lot of
> work!" You're open to more discussion in AP classes.

Observations such as these reveal more than the disparate forms of education students receive. They also suggest that CP students are being
schooled in more controlled environments where their perspectives are
discouraged and they may be assigned *more* course work, while their
schoolmates in honors and AP classes receive an extra grade point for
each of their classes.

Although there are important examples of teachers and course assignments in CP classes aiming to create engaging learning experiences, these
opportunities seem to pale in comparison to what is provided to students
in honors and AP classes. Isabel Fuentes and Julia Rios illustrate,

> ISABEL: We read *Twelve Angry Men*. I really liked that one, and we got
>   to act it out. So that was really cool.
> JULIA: Yeah, we went to go see it.
> ISABEL: Because she's in honors, and I'm not.
> JULIA: Yeah, we got to go see it in LA. We got to spend a whole day in
>   LA by ourselves. It was awesome.

Even the one reading in her CP English class and the acting assignment
that accompanied it that Isabel found appealing were upstaged by the

resources provided to the sophomore students in English honors. Teacher Beth Hill details,

> We went on the best field trip with the honors class to Los Angeles. We saw *Twelve Angry Men* at the Ahmanson and then they got to go everywhere. They got to go to the Cathedral, the Contemporary Art Museum, the Disney thing. They could walk to Olvera Street. We gave them a map with all the different places, and we told them this is how much time you have . . . They just loved it.

Continuing, Beth Hill ponders whether she would trust students outside of the honors courses with such liberty:

> That is something I would love to do, but everybody worries, "Oh well maybe you couldn't do it." When you get the honors kids in there, and they were so good. They all showed up to the play on time. They went and had lunch . . . But I think, "Could we do this with our just college prep kids?" You hate to say that, but the attitude, the behavior is so different that you worry.

The concern that students in college preparatory classes cannot be trusted illustrates how some apply the track labels to more than individual students or to academic skills. Entire classes of students are seen as possessing the right "attitude" and "behavior" befitting a trip to Los Angeles.

When asked to describe interesting classes, students emphasize the importance of teachers who demonstrate caring, respect, and more relaxed or interactive approaches. For Isabel Fuentes, her math teacher epitomizes these qualities:

> He talks to us. Then he'll find ways for us to remember. He gets life stuff, and he'll say, "Oh, you know, like this." Then you think back, "Oh, OK! Like, he said that is like—." He just doesn't teach; he talks to you.

Isabel makes an important distinction between *teaching* and *talking*. Based on her and her schoolmates' comments, teaching involves removed and disconnected lecturing. This can be very structured and even come directly from the textbook. In contrast, talking to students is about relating. It entails interacting with them, drawing on what students already know, being flexible, and connecting course materials to life concerns.

Overall, underlying students' critiques of their CP classes is a challenge to the regimented approach in the classroom. This traditional approach schools students for passivity, following orders, and the uncritical acceptance of information. It contrasts with the seminar-based dialogical and student-centered theory of knowledge class provided to IB seniors where teacher and students are learners together. It also differs from the AVID class where twice a week students collaborate with college tutors to review course work. These more student-centered and interactive spaces better allow for the emergence of students' voices and new, more creative ideas.

Students in CP classes are not alone in critiquing the constraints and types of education they are receiving. Some of their teachers also contest the disparities in education fueled by the school.[7] CP teacher John Alvarez was horrified when he was blocked from using particular books in his classroom because they were reserved for students in honors classes:

> If I take you to the media center [where the class books are located], Mrs. Peterson made it very clear, "These are honors," [when I said,] "I would like to have that set right there, can I? I would like to take a copy of that book and read it." She said, "No you can't." I said, "Well, I'm sure I can go and ask permission." But it's wrong. They have a much better selection. If you look at the college prep books, there is just not a wide selection.

Experiences such as these, along with the smaller class sizes in honors classes, have led to John Alvarez's critical analysis of the school's privileging and exclusion:

> It's almost like the honors are special classes. The AP classes are special classes. So they are anointed. They get the blessing and my other kids basically get whatever is left. In a sense that's really what it comes down to is that they don't get class reduction size, but they are expected still to score well on the SATs just as well as AP classes. If their scores don't go up, then we are going to hear about it. Well, the API scores are probably not going to go up if you continue inflating our college prep courses.

As Alvarez clarifies, even though CP teachers and students are provided with fewer resources and opportunities, the same tests are used to evaluate them and their counterparts in honors and AP classes.

Limiting Capital: Inhibiting Ties, Opportunities, and the Transfer of Information

While the students in IB and AVID know their counselor well and relish being able to see her when needed, many students in college preparatory courses have just the opposite experience. Some do not know their counselor's name because they rarely meet, and when they do see a counselor their time is limited. Staff member Mari Ramirez observes,

> The average students, the ones who are just trying, they never get seen [by their counselors] because they never get sent up to the office for discipline. They are not way up there knowing what to do on their own. They just schedule their classes, and they never see them.

Sophomore Rebecca Ramos, who is enrolled in CP courses, concurs: "They don't really talk to me 'cause they only talk to you if you're really bad, like if you need help or have a F." In our current era of education, where the ratio of public school counselors to students is upward of a thousand to one (Romo and Falbo 1996), counselors face increasing workloads, including bureaucratic paperwork tied to the intensification of testing. This makes it difficult to devote more time to students. However, because of the privileged access provided to IB and AVID students, the disparity in counselor contact is especially alarming at schools such as SCHS, where the ratio of counselors to students is about 350 to 1.

For students in CP courses, their limited access impedes their abilities to build relationships with a key institutional broker at the school, and it hinders their opportunities to plan for their futures. But more than just this exclusionary access, students also report cold and downright hostile receptions from their counselors—the very people they hope will help them. Sophomore friends Maria Castro and Becky Cruz detail the following:

> MARIA: We talked to her once for summer school.
> BECKY: She was rude.
> MARIA: And she got mad.
> INTERVIEWER SANDRA HAMADA: What happened?
> MARIA: We wanted to get into Algebra 2 for summer school and—
> BECKY: The class was full and we asked her if there was a different class we could do, and she told us to get out the late slip. And we asked her if it was first come, first serve . . . I wanted to take AP and honor classes next year so I went in to ask her what are the right classes, and she told me to talk to my teachers, and I told her I had gone to talk to the teachers already and they told me about the class but they didn't tell me if I could get into it, if I had the right grades. So I went to talk to her and she said, "I can't tell you what classes to take. You have to talk to the teachers and you have to figure out if it's right for you." I told her I already did that; so then she kept going in circles about that. I told her it was OK; I would just do it myself.

Compared to the IB and AVID students, who are greeted with an open-door policy by a counselor who contacts them and stretches the rules, Maria and Becky encounter animosity, bureaucratic regulations, and the runaround. They are left to navigate the schooling system on their own. Parent Christina Perez reports that her daughter in CP classes is actually "afraid to go to the counseling office" because of the way the staffulty speak to students. According to her, "They don't make them feel comfortable. So how are they going to turn to this person when there is a problem? My daughter is like, 'No, I'm not going in there.'" Even Christina's multiple phone calls to her daughter's counselor remain unreturned.

When searching for college information, senior Samuel Fujimoto encountered similar types of unresponsiveness from the counseling office:

> If you go to 'em and say, "Can I talk to my counselor?" They go,
> "What about?" And you're like, "College." Then they go, "Oh, it's
> too early for that." I'm like, "We're gonna graduate in two months."

Experiences such as these are particularly detrimental for first-generation college students, who may not know the requirements for college or how to enroll in AP courses. The larger patterns at SCHS suggest crucial information is being withheld from students in college preparatory classes. Teacher Ana Camacho corroborates, "The counselors go in and visit the honors classes and the AP classes and give them more information about college than they do the regular classes."

Given the racial/ethnic and class skewing in course placement, Latinas/os and poor and working-class students are most likely to be denied access to their counselors and to crucial academic information. Teacher Michelle Mesa details,

> Some of the Hispanic students come to me and ask where can they
> find information about this 'cause I'm an advisor for one of the honor's
> society on campus and like, "Well, your teacher should've mentioned it
> or the counseling department." But they only advertise it to the AP and
> honors classes, and here the majority are Asian students anyway . . .
> [I]t's those sort of things where students feel, "Well, they just didn't
> want me to take it or they didn't care enough about me or they didn't
> think that I had it within me. So that's why we weren't told about it."

These discriminatory patterns block opportunities and convey larger messages to Latina/o students about their perceived worth and abilities.

CP students are also divided from students in other tracks, inhibiting their awareness of different academic programs. While such divisions and limited information are detrimental for all students, given their lower academic positioning at school, this lack of knowledge is especially detrimental for students in CP classes because it makes access to more opportunities completely unfathomable when students do not even know that various programs exist. The dialogue between sophomore friends David Kim and Araceli Castro about the school's AVID and IB programs is telling:

> ARACELI: I think AVID's to help you—
> DAVID: All of 'em are to help you.
> ARACELI: No, but I mean to help you with—I don't know . . .

They know even less about the IB program:

> ARACELI: I don't know what that is.
> DAVID: What is IB? I never heard of it. I've heard of AP, honors. I've heard of all that stuff, but never heard of what, IB? Does it really go that high? Is that higher than AP?

When asked about IB, Araceli and David stumble with the acronym, are surprised that the program exists, and are stunned that there is a program at the school that is considered higher than advanced placement. Exchanges such as these capture the disparate information provided to students and how unequal forms of capital are reproduced. While students in CP courses receive much less support from staffulty and little information about the school resources, students in the IB program who have access to more capital—economic, social, and cultural—are typically the most likely to receive additional capital.

Reflections on Maintaining and Creating the "Regular"

> The community, the district, and also the school have a certain mentality that maybe some kids can't, don't deserve to be [in the IB and AP classes]. Maybe they believe that they don't have what it takes to be in those classes.
>
> —Tom Delgado, staffulty

> So many of the students stay in the same courses . . . If they are honors freshman, they tend to stay in honors for four years. If they are not [in honors], they tend to stay not [in honors]. There are very few people who move between tracks.
>
> —Marie Silva, teacher

Staffulty Tom Delgado and Marie Silva's comments underscore the rigid assumptions and track placements that permeate students' experiences.

Students are schooled in different conditions, with varying levels of school support and under disparate expectations. Students in CP courses are treated as "the regular" and "the average," and there is limited mobility between tracks. However, just as CP students are maintained in the tracking system, it appears that within the conditions of today's educational mandates, many students are being schooled in ways that might be characterized as average. That is, they are going through the motions, abiding by school-sanctioned expectations and with little demonstration for a love of learning. Thus more than just the students in CP courses are being schooled to be "regular" in places such as SCHS.

Compared to the greater flexibility in leaving IB, AVID, AP, and honors courses, students in CP courses have to struggle to get into honors courses. Teacher Beth Hill explains,

> This year I had a girl go to the office because she chose to fight to get in. We have to let them in if they want to. We have to offer it to every-body. We say it's an application process and a lot of the kids don't understand that they can go to the office and fight to get in . . . She just had her parents come in and demand that she was put in it.

Beth Hill's language of "fighting" reveals the near permanence of these tracks—especially when moving into the school's more highly regarded courses. Moreover, she exposes how the theory that students have access to honors and AP classes is not always the practice. As teacher Michelle Mesa made clear earlier, most students in CP classes are not given information on applying for honors and AP classes. So one can deduce that even fewer are told that a parent can demand a change in courses. Second, students have such a difficult time accessing their counselors that it seems nearly impossible that students would be able to make the necessary course changes.

By withholding information from students and requiring additional paperwork, not only are CP students excluded from honors and AP classes, but even parents may not know how to navigate the school's bureaucracy. Parent Cristina Perez, who is determined to enroll her youngest daughter in honors courses, believes that there is little she can do because her daughter does not perform well on standardized tests. As Cristina notices, early performances on standardized tests are often used to determine course placement. However, they are not the only factor. Perhaps if the phone calls Cristina has been making to her daughter's counselor were returned or if there were a comparable Latina/o parent liaison or parent group as there is a Chinese parent liaison, critical information would be available.

Once students do all they can do to enter honors and AP classes, they may find that the different types of assignments expected of them in CP classes have not sufficiently prepared them for the switch. AVID student Monique Martinez explains, "It's easier if people have been in honors since they were younger because they're so used to getting the work. They're just like, "Got this; got that." They know what's expected of them." Together, these differing educations and blocked opportunities maintain students in their designated positions.

Similarly, while the labels "average" and "regular" are not typically applied to students outside of CP courses, the comments by several teachers and students throughout this chapter suggest that schooling in general may be fostering a sense of disengagement and regimented teaching and learning that is typical in classrooms across curriculum track. To the extent that an extensive focus on preparing for standardized tests such as within AP courses structures curriculum and fuels what Marie Silva describes as "regurgitation," there may be an overall squelching of creativity and passion that may actually make many students lackadaisical toward schooling. Within these structured and standardized contexts, students may appear regular or average as they uncritically abide by district, state, and federal dictates to move up the educational pipeline.

"I See the Gap Widening": Conclusion

Lost in the dominant framing of an achievement gap and the prevalence of biological and cultural deficiency perspectives presented in chapter 1 are significant opportunity and social gaps between students that are structured in schools such as SCHS. Students first arrive to SCHS from two distinct middle schools with different reputations. They then experience race/ethnicity and class-based skewing in tracked courses where they encounter dominant messages about their academic abilities and receive different forms of support and education. Together, these structures and messages exacerbate the academic, opportunity, and social gaps that were apparent in middle school.

This cycle reproduces hierarchies where students are funneled into different life trajectories. Students are steered toward the "elite," the "middle," and the "regular." While some cross these tracks academically or socially in their peer groups, many are driven apart, leading to the "widening gap[s]" described by teacher Jim Scott. The school practices, family resources, and racialized climates detailed in the next three chapters reinforce these divisions. However, as students' and teachers' narratives unfold throughout the book, so too do their forms of resistance detailed in chapter 6.

PART II

School Practices and Family Resources

CHAPTER THREE

"I'm Watching Your Group"

Regulating Students Unequally

Everything is caged in, lots of bars. It's like they don't trust us, like we're just going to run away and not come to school if there weren't any bars. I don't like that.

—*Andrew Moreno, senior in college preparatory (CP) classes*

I call it concentration camp, our school, 'cause we're not allowed off campus, or on campus when we're outside, we're constantly being watched; there's a security guard right there.

—*Jung Kim, sophomore in CP classes*

Senior Angelica Vega believes that SCHS feels "like a prison." Rod iron gates enclose it, several security guards patrol it, and occasionally drug-sniffing dogs scour it. Security and punishment are part of what has been called a discipline regime in public schools (Morris 2006; Kupchik 2010). These practices of social control are part of the movement from a welfare state to a penal state characterizing the neoliberal agenda (Fleury-Steiner 2008). Emerging in the context of "tough on crime" polices and fueled by a culture of fear and the demonizing of youth of color, schools are increasingly using prisonlike tactics, including zero-tolerance policies where students caught violating school rules face stricter penalties, including suspensions, expulsions, and maybe even police interventions (Beres and Griffith 2001; Noguera 2008; Nolan 2011).

While physically SCHS is "barred," not all students encounter the same monitoring, restrictions, and punishment. Due to the racialized academic profiling that pervades the school, Latinas/os and students outside of the International Baccalaureate (IB) program are more likely to describe being constrained, surveyed, and assumed guilty. Women may encounter a sexualizing masculine gaze and school practices that attempt to contain their bodies. Some Asian American students describe receiving harsher punishments for actions that are presumed unacceptable for presumed model students. Finally, students with school-sanctioned middle-class social and cultural capital may be able to avert detection and escape punishment. Taken together, track placement, differential racialization, gendered constructs, and class shape how and when students' bodies and behaviors are regulated. Some are given multiple chances and others no chances at all. These disparate experiences influence students' relationship to school, their sense of belonging, and racial/ethnic, class, and gender hierarchies.

Track Placement and a "Free Pass"

When students make their way around campus, some are keenly aware of the disparate restrictions influencing their movement. As AVID (Advancement via Individual Determination) junior Sandy O'Brian explains, these inequities are often linked to track placement:

> Well, obviously the teachers are a lot harder on the honors and AP [advanced placement] kids than they would be on the regular kids. But at the same time, they don't discipline the honors kids as hard as they would discipline the regular class kids because the honors kids, normally they are more intelligent, so they're more mature in a way, so they don't have to discipline them as much.

Thus, while honors and AP students have higher academic expectations placed on them, they appear to be disciplined less than their schoolmates in CP classes.

During the lively two-hour focus group meeting with his two IB friends described in the last chapter, Mike Song confirms Sandy's analysis about track placement and regulation. He raves how his status as an IB student not only grants him access to the counselors' office but also helps him avert punishment:

> It's kind of like a privilege, you know. If you're in trouble [and they ask,] "Hey, what are you doing outside?" [I say,] "Oh I'm an IB student," and they're like, "Oh, OK."

When I asked for clarification about when this might happen or with whom he might use this identity, Mike expands,

Oh, security guards. Like, one time, I was out of class 'cause I really had to go talk to the counselor, and it was like, "Oh, you're not supposed to be here." Then I was like, "Oh, umm, I'm an IB student." And then, they're like, "Oh, OK, then you can go." And in the office, sometimes they stop you, "You can't meet with your counselor unless you have an appointment." "Oh, I'm an IB student." Then they're, "Okay, *you* can come in."

In this example, Mike is able to bypass two control mechanisms on campus—the security guards and the staff members. Despite the fact that security guards roam the campus, making sure students are in class and gatekeepers in the school's office prevent most students from meeting with their counselors without an appointment, IB students such as Mike are able to exert what he has come to realize as his privilege to receive the attention he demands.

A month after my focus group discussion with Mike and his friends, some of the advantages that they boasted about were on display at a day-long IB boot camp. Organized by SCHS counselors and teachers on a Saturday in July from 8:00 a.m. to 5:00 p.m. this camp was designed to facilitate the transition of pre-IB sophomores into the IB program. Along with discussing the IB requirements, this camp provided the only fifteen students in attendance with specialized attention. Most relevant for this discussion is how the students were allowed to engage in the following three activities that left me wondering if their actions would have been permitted for students outside of the program.

While entering the school's media center for the start of the camp, I was immediately drawn to the behavior of the following students:

Three Asian American guys walked into the media center before me. They were bouncing two large balls, and they continued bouncing the balls on top of the tables. No one said anything, even when one of them threw a ball at a student who walked in after them. (Field notes, July 12, 2007)

The media center is the school's library and computer center. It is also where the staffuly hold their meetings. During the school day, students' actions in this space are heavily regulated—so much so that a month earlier a Latina Pomona College research assistant, perhaps confused for a high school student, was reprimanded by a staff member for entering the media center with gum in her mouth. She was abruptly told to discard it. Students are expected to whisper and work quietly in the center. Thus that the three IB students were able to enter bouncing balls on the tables was a stark contrast with other observations I had made of the activities condoned in the space.

Halfway through the camp's activities, I was again struck by what I perceived as the privilege of IB students. This time it was the opportunity to speak openly and critically about their teachers in front of school officials without condemnation. Three IB seniors were introduced as having "made it through their junior year." A school official explained that the students would be presenting an "overview of next year's teachers. So pay attention to what they are saying." These are "honest opinions designed to help you." The students delivered a PowerPoint presentation titled "Junior Year for Dummies," where they described the workload, expectations, and quality of each of the teachers the juniors would be having the following year. In general, the descriptions appeared nonjudgmental and focused mainly on the workload, homework assignments, and preparation for AP tests. Since students were providing each other with tips that could enhance their performances, they were sharing their cultural capital. However, in at least two cases, the seniors' descriptions were more personal. They critiqued a teacher's "boring, monotonous tone" and how "she talks to nobody." "Students won't pay attention to what she says halfway through the year," since "she loves to digress." A second teacher was characterized as an "evil person" who "hates everyone." "He'll lose homework and even tests." Students were instructed to "avoid eye contact" so that "he'll pick on you less." That students feel this way about select staffulty is not surprising. However, I wonder if all students would be given the floor during a school event and allowed to openly criticize their teachers.

During the IB boot camp, there were two outdoor games involving water balloons for what a faculty member referred to as "team-building activities." One of these games was "capture the flag," where students tried to get the flag without being hit by a water balloon. The second activity entailed covering the eyes of several students and then playing catch with the water balloons. During this activity, one of the blindfolded students accidentally ran into a tree, cutting his lip and scratching his nose. However, the game continued. Notably, water balloons are listed on the school's contraband list as forbidden because they can "endanger others or cause a disturbance on campus." Students are warned that all contraband items will be "confiscated." The school's policy states, "Discipline procedures will be enforced for all contraband items. Discipline may include parent conference, detention, suspension, and/or expulsion." In spite of the school's rules, no IB students were punished that day. After all, the staffulty had initiated these team-building activities, and a latent message of them was that school rules can be avoided when planning events for IB students. Such leeway granted to IB students, when combined with their additional resources and support as described in the previous chapter, may explain how a sense of entitlement may develop where they come to expect privileged treatment and are in turn given more liberty.

In spite of the ability of IB students to avert some school rules, this is not always the case. During her interview, Asian American teacher Val Sherman, who primarily teaches the IB and AP students, made a point of letting me know that an Asian American student in the IB program had recently been caught with drugs on campus:

> We just heard that one of our students got suspended and probably expelled for having drugs. And, um, not that it's—not that there's a stereotype but—there isn't—because we've got kids of all groups— into drugs. But this was an IB student who is Asian and, you know, not who I would have said would be my first choice, but on the other hand, I'm not really surprised to hear it 'cause he's, he's the kind of kid who's kind of quirky . . . I guess we had the dog come on campus, and it was in his car, and they sniffed it in his car.

Teacher Sherman uses this example to illustrate the fallacy that IB and Asian American students are immune from getting in trouble. However, in spite of trying to challenge track-based and racialized assumptions, her halting language and comment that the student would not have been her "first choice" when asked who does drugs seems to suggest that she, too, may have accepted some stereotypes.

Reflecting on the extent of drug usage among the IB and AP students she teaches, Val Sherman concludes,

> We don't see it as much. I don't see it as much because my students either hide it very well or aren't into it. But I know when I talk to some of the other teachers who teach the regular classes, they say, "Oh yeah, it's happening everywhere."

Val's speculation that maybe the IB and AP students are more adept at hiding their drug usage is an interesting point, especially considering that the student who was recently caught was able to hide the drugs in his car, at least until the drug-sniffing dogs were brought to campus and taken to the parking lot. Access to a car is a class-based privilege that may be more common among the IB and AP students, given the class skewing of who is in the school's top courses. While Val Sherman's reflection that students in her courses might hide their drug usage may disrupt assumptions about who uses drugs, there is still talk among teachers that drugs are "happening everywhere" among students in the so-called regular classes. Such sentiment might fuel and justify further monitoring and searches of students in those particular classes.

While as a whole, IB students may have more control over their movements, actions, and decisions, some students in the general college preparatory track encounter just the opposite experience: they feel that they are more highly scrutinized. For example, in contrast to Mike Song, who earlier named the IB program as the highlight of the school because of the privileges he receives, sophomore Albert Ortiz, who is enrolled in college preparatory courses, "hates" SCHS. He wants to change one of the school administrators because "he's too strict with everybody. He doesn't give anyone chances . . . He just comes and starts getting mad." Albert ponders the differential disciplinary policies that he believes he receives compared to students in IB and AP courses:

> [Students in the higher classes get] more liberty, I bet, and more choices to get more stuff around here. They probably have [a] better chance of staying out of trouble if they do something wrong, or if they do [something wrong, it's] like, "Oh, let them just go." Like, they'll just have a free pass through all high school.

He expands on the academic profiling where some students are easily suspended and others receive a "free pass":

> Like me doing something bad, [the administration thinks,] "I'll give him a Saturday, or give him a two-hour detention, or suspend him." Most of them [in the top classes], it's like, "Oh, just let them go. They messed up." It's different with people like me. We start complaining: "Oh, why did I get suspended?" And we get more in trouble.

While Mike Song is able to exert his status as an IB student and talk back to school officials when asked why he is out of class, if Albert asks why he is suspended, he is given a harsher punishment. Such unequal experiences convey which students are trusted and given a voice on campus, thereby reinforcing some students' privileged positions relative to their schoolmates.

Like Albert, Asian American sophomores Nat Punyawong and Mark Ku, who are also enrolled in college preparatory courses, sometimes feel that they too are denied extra chances and the benefit of a doubt. Resigned, they declare the following:

> NAT: A lot of teachers here, if you mess up one time, they think that you're a screw-up for the rest of your life.
> MARK: They have no hope in you.

This hopeless feeling that Nat and Mark find among some of their teachers penetrates how they feel about school. It also influences what they want conveyed from their focus group:

NAT: Even though we come from different backgrounds, we're still people. And we should be treated with the same respect if you try or not.

MARK: Yeah, like no matter what race you are or anything.

NAT: Yeah, no matter what grades you get. Just because you get a bad grade or good grades doesn't mean you're smart.

As college preparatory students who believe that too much value is placed on grades and race/ethnicity, Nat and Mark vehemently critique the unequal assumptions that are made of them and their classmates. Their call for respect indicates their awareness of how race/ethnicity, class, and other identities influence people's perceptions of them and the type of treatment they are accorded.

"It's Like 99.7 Percent Hispanic": Policing Young Men by Gender, Race, Class, and Style

Two weeks before graduation, I had a forty-minute informal discussion with seven seniors—two Latinas, four Mexican American males, and one biracial Black and White male. Their teacher excused them from class to speak with me, and we gathered together on outdoor benches. It did not take long for them to open up about their experience. The question that sparked the dialogue was a simple one: "What have been some of your most memorable moments at SCHS?" As part of their responses, they casually recalled lunchtime with friends, a couple of "chill teachers," school rallies, food fights, and prom. However, the first and last topic named and the one that garnered much of their attention was Mr. Johnson, a school administrator. They explain the following:

RAUL MELENDEZ: Mr. Johnson, the remarks he makes to certain students make him a dick.

MARCOS RIVERA: Yeah, he told me, "I'm surprised you could afford the prom."

NICK MESA: He picks on people who look like troublemakers, like Mexicans, gang members, skinheads.

TRAVIS JACKS: He goes after Mexicans and Blacks.

RAUL: He told me and my Black and Filipino friends, "I'm watching your group."

Illustrating this constant watching and disciplining, the students angrily recalled a time when they received detention simply because they were having a "thumb war" during lunch.[1] Our brief conversation revealed how Mr. Johnson's constant surveillance has left an undeniable mark on these students' schooling experiences. Such policing is part of larger patterns of profiling Black and Latino young men as troublemakers.

During a larger discussion with these same seven students and their twenty classmates, several students described similar forms of surveillance by campus administrators who monitor not only their behavior but also their clothing. Young men pointed to a female student wearing a t-shirt with a woman and a gun on it and explained how they could not wear the same shirt to school, implying that there were double standards in the enforcement of the school's dress code. Sociologist Nancy Lopez (2003) describes a similar pattern of unequally enforcing dress code policies in the New York public high school she studied. She notes that since working-class Black and Latino masculinity is constructed as adversarial, young men were constantly reprimanded for breaking the school's dress code that prohibits wearing hats (75). In contrast, this policy was not enforced for young women for whom wearing hats was equated with fashion (86).

Teacher John Alvarez is all too familiar with how Latino youth encounter strict punishment by school administrators for wearing certain clothes:

> I noticed [one of my students] wasn't turning his work in. It's the third or fourth week already, [and I told him,] "Hey Danny, you've got to start turning work in." "Oh yeah, teacher, you're right." Very respectful young man. Then I would see him absent for two or three days straight, and he seemed to be suspended . . . [W]hen he got back, [he said,] "Well, you know, so and so got ahold of me. I was wearing my Raider's shirt." . . . Apparently when one of the APs [assistant principals] took it away from him, he said that the AP was accusing him of being a gangbanger. He said, "I'm not a gangbanger. I just happen to like the Raiders."

John Alvarez knows student Danny Garcia as a "very respectful young man." Nevertheless, a school administrator suspended him when he wore a football jersey from the school's list of banned apparel. As John denounces, some of the Latino students are picked on because they "might dress a little different; maybe they have a particular style of dress or they cut their hair short." This repeated policing of students' dress can wear on students who find that they are in a continual struggle over how they look, and it can also impact concerned teachers such as John Alvarez. Furthermore, this emphasis on students' appearances has been shown to fuel tensions between staff1y and students, and it diverts time and energy away from classroom instruction (Valenzuela 1999; Morris 2006).

Given the strong rapport John Alvarez has established with students, he is privy to the constant haranguing Latinos encounter on campus, especially by administrator Johnson:

There have been several Latinos who have said, "He doesn't like us. He doesn't like Latinos. He's always picking on us." We were hanging around over here in the back, and he came around and started trying to break up our group. He said, "Is that one of the gangbangers?"

These student testimonials confirm for John that race/ethnicity, class, and students' styles shape student treatment:

This administrator does not understand the culture of Latinos. He doesn't understand that these kids have been influenced by their cousins or where they live in [a working-class Latina/o community]. They don't live in million dollar homes . . . There's a breakdown in understanding where these kids come from . . . Honestly, I think he's not aware of what's going on, or maybe it could be a form of xenophobia.

As John argues, the racial/ethnic and class gaps between such administrators and select students could be among the many factors shaping students' experiences on campus. When individual staffulty lack familiarity with students and their communities, they may be more inclined to misunderstand them and perceive them in inferior ways (Noguera 2008, 103). However, these racist attitudes are more than individual. They are institutionalized in dress code rules, disciplinary practices, and the equating of Latino youth and particular styles of clothing with gang affiliation. Since clothes are often a reflection of how students see themselves and their communities, such regulating of students' styles is also assimilationist and can be an attack on their identities. As John explains, students "have been influenced by their cousins or where they live," and when their presentations of self do not conform to hegemonic expectations, they are forced to contend with suspicion, labeling, and punishment (see Valenzuela 1999; Morris 2006).

Conversations with staff member Mari Ramirez confirms that almost all the students sent to the principal's office on referrals are Latinos. She proclaims, "It's like 99.7 percent Hispanic; rarely do I see Asians." The charge against most of these students is "defiance"; it is believed that "they don't listen, and they don't want to do the work." This disparity reflects national trends where poor, working-class, Latina/o, and Black students are more likely to be punished at school and to receive harsher punishments than their middle- and upper-class, Asian American, and White schoolmates (Skiba et al. 2000; Nolan 2011).

Some Asian American students are very aware of this unequal treatment. Given the demographics of the college preparatory classes, where there are larger numbers of Latinas/os, Asian American students in these classes observe firsthand the disparate treatment. The following exchange with Asian American sophomore friends introduced earlier captures such differential disciplining:

> KATHY HSIN: There are different kinds of teachers here, and some are like racist. Some are mean, and some like picking favorites.
>
> INTERVIEWER MAI THAI: What do you mean that some teachers are racist?
>
> KATHY: Some people only like Asians because they're Asian.
>
> MARK KU: 'Cause they're like, "They're smart."
>
> NAT PUNYAWONG: They think there's some difference, you know?
>
> MARK: Like Mexicans, they're like, "Oh, he doesn't try." But they judge the book by its cover.
>
> NAT: Yeah, like if you come late to class or something, and you tell them your PE [physical education] teacher let you out a little late, they'll be like, "Oh, it's OK." And then a Mexican guy comes and says that, and they're like, "Oh, go to the office."

Unlike IB student Mike Song, who relishes the privileges he receives, this group of students criticizes such favoritism. These friends realize that this profiling and discriminatory treatment hurt not just their Mexican American classmates. They too are unfairly judged by the assumption that all Asian Americans are smart. Perhaps their experiences as Asian American students who fall outside of the IB or AP/honors track expected of them provide them with an enlarged perceptive where they are better positioned to see and understand the experiences of others in ways that students who are in more privileged positions may not.

These unequal patterns of punishment are frustrating for staff member Mari Ramirez. At a meeting where I presented this research, she pleaded for answers from her colleagues:

> As someone in the office, it is usually Hispanics that I see. I want to know what I should tell students who ask why they are sent to the office when other students were also involved.

A teacher unsatisfactorily responded,

> Some students act more defensively. They question why they got in trouble, and those are typically the students who then get in trouble.

Just weeks before this meeting, a school administrator had given me the same justification. This blaming of students for unequal treatment confirms what sophomore Albert Ortiz explained earlier. Some students, perhaps those in the school's top programs and who possess the cultural capital or know-how to interact with institutional agents, have the privilege of a "free pass." Rather than ask questions in a method that may be perceived as disrespecting authority, being defiant, or acting defensively, they may have developed the expected capital to speak with school officials. This could involve speaking confidently that they are correct, as when Mike Song simply declares, "I'm an IB student." However, it could also include being able to establish an ongoing relationship with administrators that is enhanced by class position and parental participation at school. Senior Melvin Jackson, whose middle-class African American mother is well-known on campus for her involvement in the PTA (parent-teacher association) and the booster club, describes just how he is able to eschew punishment:

> Like Mr. [Berk] and Mr. [Johnson], I go talk to them and say, "Hi."
> We're cool. Other students say I'm sucking up, but I'm just being
> respectful. But I am late to first period a lot and the teacher likes to give
> me detention. So I go up there [to the front office] and talk to them, and
> they just rip it up. My friends, they get detention or Saturday school.

Students such as Melvin who come from households where parents have the resources to participate in campus activities, such as sporting events and the PTA, and who have the expected mannerisms and style of dress may be permitted to talk their way out of trouble without fear of being tagged as "defiant."

The staffulty's interpretations of students' demeanors and whether students are cited for defiance are subjective. As Aaron Kupchik finds in his research on school discipline, conceptions of noncooperation and disrespect are "in the eye of the beholder" (2010, 183). In the schools he studied, compared to White students, Latinas/os and Blacks were much more likely to report being punished for defiance and disrespect, offenses based on more "subjective appraisals" than offenses involving the possession of weapons or drugs that are a bit more clear-cut and more evenly distributed by race/ethnicity (183–84).

For some students, this monitoring extends beyond the school gates. This surveillance and the assumption of guilt has become commonplace for senior Christian Sandoval. He equates it with being a young Mexican American man living in Southern California:

> The cops usually tend to harass you a lot more . . . There are times
> where I am coming out of my house and it is dark and they just for no
> reason flash the lights in my eyes, and they will pull you over sometimes
> and be like, "What are you doing?" "I'm going to my friend's house."

Christian's Mexican American working-class community is heavily policed, and in his daily activities such as driving or walking outside, he is questioned and harassed. These are constant reminders that he and his community are stigmatized.

Assumed guilty, Christian has been made to realize that even his employers do not trust him. After playing football and running track for his first two years of high school, Christian redirected his focus from sports to work and education:

> I wanted to get a job and get some money because I didn't want to be depending on my parents for everything. And I wanted to focus more on my homework and my studies. I wasn't struggling when I was doing sports, but I just decided to get more education. I am not going to get a scholarship for sports. I would rather get an academic scholarship.

Responsibly, he started working at a neighborhood fast food restaurant, but it was short-lived:

> It was going OK until there was a little incident. I was supposed to be at the front cash register and they had me open two registers, one in the drive thru. I was supposed to be in charge of running the front. Well, eight people were working that register, and somebody stole money, and since it was my register I was blamed for it.

There was no evidence of who had stolen the money, but Christian was fired:

> I asked them to look at the cameras, but the cameras weren't working, so they had no way to prove it. So I was blamed for it. They just had me doing everything that day. The manager was telling me to do this person's job and this person's job.

Even though Christian was following the manager's many requests that took him away from his register, he alone was considered guilty.

Taken together, these examples of disparate treatment reflect the dominant constructs that pervade SCHS and U.S. society in general. The mainstream media often depicts Latina/o youth as uncaring about education and Latino men in particular as criminal, undocumented, inferior, or lazy (Ramírez-Berg 1997). These depictions have significant implications for how youth are labeled and treated. Across the nation, they have fueled legislation and practices empowering law officials to stop, question, and disproportionally arrest young Latino and Black males because of an assumption of gang affiliation or undocumented status. As a result, as sociologist Díaz-Cotto describes, Latinos and Blacks are "overrepresented in juvenile arrests, juvenile correctional facilities, adult jails, and prisons" (2006, 17). Latinos and Blacks also predominate on law enforcement databases where youth may be listed unbeknownst to them as a gang member for meeting loosely defined criteria such as interacting with alleged gang members, having perceived gang graffiti on their personal items, or using assumed gang hand signs (Beres and Griffith 2001, 760–61). In one region of Los Angeles County that includes the now infamous Rampart Division, where extreme corruption was uncovered in their CRASH (Community Resources against Street Hoodlums) antigang unit, about two-thirds of the people listed on the database were Latino and the other third Black (Beres and Griffith 2001, 762). A 1992 report by the Los Angeles County district attorney's office found nearly half of Black men in Los Angeles County between the ages of twenty-one and twenty-four were on the database, leading the then chief of police to explain that non–gang members may have been inadvertently included (Stolberg 1992).

More recent research reflects these continual patterns of racial profiling. For example, a 2012 civil liberties report on the New York Police Department's "stop and frisk" activities reveals that 87 percent of the nearly 700,000 people who were stopped in 2011 were Latina/o and Black, although these communities represent about 50 percent of New York City's residents. In particular, at just 5 percent of the city's population, young Latino and Black men between the ages of fourteen and twenty-four accounted for 41 percent of these stops. Over half of the people stopped were frisked, and although young Latino and Black men were *more* likely to be frisked than their White counterparts, they were *less* likely to have a weapon. These findings, along with the fact that nearly 90 percent of the people stopped and questioned received no ticket or arrests, attest to the continuing prevalence of racial profiling and how it is backed by policies.

As staffuly member Tom Delgado reveals, the following practice at SCHS of defining groups of Latino students as an "unofficial gang" reflects these national patterns:

> We've always had a Hispanic group, maybe between five to ten students, that hang out together. They are a group. In my line of work, maybe four or five in a group and they give themselves a little name. To us, unofficially, that's called a gang . . . I don't really know if they are actually gang members, but they are well on their way to it. And if they are not members, they are known associates of the gang. We might have seen them tag up a restroom with their gang. So once they put their name, their gang name, we relate to it. To us, unofficially, they are actual known gang members.

This racist practice of relating to groups of Latino students as a gang helps account for the hostile campus climate that some Latinas/os and Blacks describe. This labeling and treatment persists in spite of the fact that, according to Tom Delgado, SCHS has "almost zero gangs." He believes that Asian American gangs have "disappeared" from campus and that there are just "a couple of Hispanic gang members, but they don't really start trouble here." It is unclear how Tom is basing his evaluation of gang membership. However, if he is using the aforementioned criteria, just as the numbers of Latino gang members may be overestimated, the number of Asian gang members may be underestimated.

Overall, these unequal experiences influence students' outlooks toward school (Lopez 2003). Constant monitoring, questioning, and punishment can shape how students perceive their place and how they relate to staff/staffuly and other students. Such negative experiences may fuel unequal educational outcomes, especially when punishment entails excluding students from classes and learning opportunities (Gregory, Skiba, and Noguera 2010). As a result, some students may eventually scale back their aspirations and increase their desires to get out of school as quickly as possible.

"Checking Out the Girls": Young Women, Gender, and Sexuality

As revealed in chapter 1, there is a general silence in the interviews about gender and sexism at SCHS. However, several school personnel and students reveal disturbing experiences that highlight the significance of gender for young women's everyday lives, one where their bodies are hyperscrutinized, sexualized, and patrolled. Gendered constructs also intersect with processes of racialization to foster increased patrolling of Latinas compared to Asian American women.

One pattern is the sexualized attention some young women receive based on dominant constructions of beauty. In particular, teacher Marilyn Garcia is very concerned that "prettier girls with bigger breasts seem to get [certain male teachers'] attention more." She reveals that this pattern has had several detrimental impacts including (1) unequal practices by a couple of male teachers known for granting select female students desired classes and (2) a severe case of negligence by a teacher who overlooked a student accident involving an Asian American male because the teacher was believed to be "checking out the girls." Thus while some of their Latino and Black male schoolmates might be watched suspiciously, women may experience objectifying gazes that reduce them to their body parts.

Some male students have also noticed gender disparities in teacher attention. Junior John Jansen explains, "The girls are favored more. Our coach specifies more on the girls. He says, 'Good job, good job,' like motivates them, but he never motivates us." Just as the sexualization of young women in schools sends powerful messages about women's worth, to the extent that they are ignored or not encouraged, young men may also be hurt by these teacher-student exchanges. They may push them away from school and not provide them with crucial support.

In addition to gender differences in the types of attention young men and women may receive, as described earlier, restrictions on dress also vary. During the class discussion where a few of the men complained that women can wear certain clothes (such as the t-shirt with a woman and gun on it) that guys cannot, one young woman quickly corrected, "There are dress codes for the prom. We can't wear low-cut dresses or ones that are cut down the back." Thus, while young men critique a double standard where women are perceived to be granted more liberty, some women feel limited by the school's dress code that stipulates, "Dresses, skirts, and shorts shall be within the bounds of decency and good taste." Given sexualized media representations where girls and women are often evaluated by their bodies and clothes, some may support dress codes as a way to combat these sexist and consumerist media pressures.[2] Unfortunately, most schools like SCHS do not make this case for such restrictions or provide students with opportunities to deconstruct media representations. Instead, SCHS emphasizes "decency and good taste"—subjective constructs that are influenced by multiple factors including age, generation, culture, religion, and socioeconomic status. It is assumed that all at SCHS share or should share the same conceptions as the school's primarily White middle-class staffulty who regulate students' dress. The assumption then is that those who do not share this conception are somehow indecent and have poor taste. As part of schooling students on mainstream norms, students who break the dress code are sent home to change, or they are forced to wear loaner clothes.

Comparable to the dress code, the reasons behind these differential restrictions are also gendered, and students realize this. When asked during class why the school has dress codes, students answered, "So different gang members don't fight or cause tension." However, as one Latina quipped, "The dress code doesn't make sense because there are still going to be gangs." Regardless of their effectiveness, the dress codes that appear to be more vigilantly enforced on young men are framed as an attempt to contain gangs and violence, activities typically associated with young men of color in particular. Meanwhile, women's bodies are policed to constrain their perceived sexualities and to enforce what sociologist Julie Bettie (2003) has described as school-sanctioned femininity that is based on middle-class gender norms. Likewise, considering some of the heteronormative and biological arguments presented in chapter 1, the "decency" dress codes may assume that young men are unable to control their sexuality if girls' tops are low and shorts high. In fact, the dress code policy includes a sentence that clothes should "not distract or interfere with the educational environment," implying that women's bodies need to be covered to avoid distraction.

Of the young women who shared their schooling experiences, Latinas were more likely to describe being policed on campus, revealing that they are not immune from some of the negative exchanges doled out to their Latino and Black schoolmates. While some encounter the same type of watching and typecasting that Latinos describe, as the following testimonials illustrate, there are gender-specific aspects to their surveillance, especially if they are perceived as transgressing gendered expectations.

"The Administration Seems Really Sketchy": Maggie Cordova's Story

When asked about her contact with campus adults, senior Maggie Cordova echoes the negative exchanges some of her Latino and Black schoolmates have had with administrator Johnson. But she finds the actions of all the school's White male administrators troubling: "Something about the administration seems really sketchy—weird. I'm not very fond of them." Maggie's use of the words "sketchy" and "weird" implies that she does not feel safe with the administration—that they are untrustworthy maybe even creepy. When she is asked why she feels this way, she initially tries to convey a general sense she has about them and then she provides an example:

> There's something about them. I just don't like how they treat people . . .
> The way Mr. Johnson approaches situations, it's like he thinks you're
> guilty no matter what. He came up to me; I guess I was chewing gum,
> and he comes up with the attitude like I'm a bad troublemaker, and I'm
> like, "No, I never get in trouble. I don't do anything bad."

For chewing gum, Maggie is stopped and questioned in a manner that appears unnecessarily confrontational. Interactions such as these where one is presumed guilty and a troublemaker can take a toll on students. Fortunately, Maggie is confident in her assessment of herself and uses this knowledge to cope with the similar judgmental treatment she receives from teachers:

> I don't like how he and other teachers here do it too. They come up to
> you with this attitude like they automatically assume you're a bad kid,
> and they put you in the wrong. I'm like, "No, wait. Breathe. Take a

look at the situation. Figure it out, and then you can accuse me if I'm
doing something wrong."

As a student on the school's newspaper staff, on the cheer team, and in
honors and AP classes, Maggie is well positioned to draw on her educational successes to maintain a strong self-concept. Overall, she believes
she has had a "good high school experience," even though she is "so over
it" and "ready to move on with life," which involves deciding on whether
to attend the University of California or the California State University
in the fall. Unlike Maggie, not all students have these school-sanctioned
positive identities and experiences to pull from, making it more difficult
to constantly combat others' negative interactions.

"Watch Out! Here Comes Tyson": Angelica Vega's Struggles

Similar to Maggie, senior Angelica Vega also abhors the assumptions
made by school administrators:

> Sometimes, they just assume things. They assume that just because
> you're part of a group and they're doing bad things, that you're gonna
> be doing the same things. And it's not just the security. It's also with
> Mr. Johnson. More Mr. Johnson than anyone else . . . It seems like
> he's too stubborn to understand kids, and he's more bossing kids
> around than trying to understand—"I'm the administrator; you're the
> student. You listen to me."

Mr. Johnson's judgmental and authoritarian demeanor, coupled with his
unwillingness to give Angelica a second chance, has left an indelible mark
on her life.

During her sophomore year, Angelica became friends with a group of
girls who she later found out were doing drugs. After about a month
of using drugs with them, Angelica quit and helped her friends stop as
well. When her mother found out about Angelica's past drug usage, she
quickly reported this to the school. Along with receiving the majority of
the punishment from the school, Angelica also encountered ostracism and
fistfights from her former friends who confronted her because her mother
reported the drug use to the school.

Rather than being praised for stopping her drug use or receiving assistance during a very difficult stage, for the rest of high school, Angelica has
been branded with a negative reputation:

> Because of all that with those friends that got involved with drugs and
> I got in a fight with them, Mr. Johnson still thinks I'm the same type

of person. Yet I don't hang out with them. I don't have any interaction
with them, and yet he still judges me from back in the day. It's like,
"C'mon. I'm focused on school."

Despite her attempts to establish a new identity and friendship group,
Angelica must also contend with enhanced surveillance:

> Just the way security is, they'll sit there [in front of the campus]. They
> look at the same people to see what they're doing, to see where they're
> going but not new faces . . . Like me, they'll just watch and watch.

At times, this constant watching is combined with public ridicule by security officers:

> They always give me problems. Like [saying,], "Here she comes. Be
> careful." I remember this security guard saying, "Watch out! Here
> comes Tyson," 'cause they know me as fighting. So they call me, "Oh,
> here comes Mike Tyson. She's gonna hit you."

Not only are these school officials' comments humiliating, especially for
a student trying to alter a negative image, but the labeling of Angelica
as "Tyson" has other implications as well. First of all, Angelica experiences masculinizing name-calling perhaps because it is assumed that
women do not engage in fistfights. Second, such labeling reinforces racist
constructions of Black men as aggressive, violent, and ready to strike at
any moment (see Feagin 2001). Similarly, in this case, to be nicknamed
"Mike Tyson" is to be stigmatized. At SCHS where there are only a
couple of African American staffulty and little is taught about Blacks in
the school curriculum, this labeling is especially pernicious. Blacks are
almost completely absent in the school, and as detailed in chapter 5,
they are often mentioned in stereotyped ways that maintain racial/
ethnic hierarchies.

Each time she is berated, Angelica does all she can to cope with such
harassment by thinking,

> Get over it. I'm not gonna do anything. Yeah, I'm known for fighting.
> Whatever. It's not like I'm gonna start a fight with anybody . . . They
> just start talking. I don't like that. Knowing me as a person now, you
> wouldn't think the same. But I can't do anything about it.

Angelica cannot remove the stigmas that have been assigned to her. Thus,
when we met her in March of her senior year, she could not "wait to leave
this school." This sense of urgency to "get out of here and start college"
was palpable. It was one of the first things she said when she introduced
herself.

Angelica's difficulties early in high school have had an enduring impact on her experiences at SCHS and even on her life goals. In fact, she wants to work with youth in a way she wishes she had been treated:

> I just want to get into my career, which is criminal justice, and I really want to make a difference 'cause teenagers, they need help. I've learned from my mistake. You know, I got over it. I'm done with it.

Angelica's determination to "make a difference" demonstrates her resilience, and her desire to prove them all wrong is discussed more in chapter 6.

"There's Discrimination": Summer Reyes's Activism

Junior Summer Reyes, a student leader in MEChA (Movimiento Estudiantil Chicano de Aztlán), a national Chicana/o student organization established during the civil rights movements of the 1960s, finds that politically active Latinas may also be extensively observed. Furthermore, she believes that the school administrators judge her more harshly than they do the group's male president because she has played a crucial role in organizing campus events and has been outspoken in her struggles with administrators to ensure that these campus activities are not cancelled:

> As a Hispanic, there's discrimination, and I think gender-wise there's discrimination too. I noticed that for the president of MEChA, they've never given him dirty looks, or they're never watching what he does, and for me, they are . . . I guess because they always notice me. They kind of know who I am. They don't know my name, but after all that was going on with MEChA and they weren't letting us do things, I started noticing that they were watching where I was going . . . I'm the one who did mostly all the stuff for MEChA this year.

Summer believes that as a self-identified Hispanic woman, she is already subjected to racial and gender discrimination. However, this discrimination is heightened because of her participation in an antiracist, social justice, and overtly politicized organization that, as she explains, works to "empower Hispanics." Since SCHS's administrators are predominately White males, one is left wondering if Summer encounters more surveillance than her male counterpart because not only is she involved with an organization known for challenging the status quo, but by calling attention to racism and anti-immigrant practices, she is also transgressing normative raced and gendered expectations of acquiescence and passivity.

Given her critical awareness of inequality and her unwillingness to concede to the administrators' attempts to cancel MEChA's campus-wide events,

Summer feels that she is subjected to retribution in the form of constant surveillance, where the administration is almost waiting to punish her for any infraction of the school rules. At times, this monitoring takes the form of sexualized policing:

> There's a lot of couples around school and they are constantly making out, and no one ever tells them anything, and me and my boyfriend are just talking and I can see the administration. They're just standing right next to us. And I'm like, "We're not even doing anything." It kind of gets me angry that they don't do it to anybody else. They just do it to me.

While Summer may be especially aware of such supervising of her interactions with her boyfriend, this experience must be seen in the context of the overall climate on campus where relative to their Asian American schoolmates, Latinas/os were much more likely to describe feeling marginalized. In particular, the sexualized profiling Summer feels may also be influenced by dominant constructions of Latinas as supposedly hypersexual. Just as the mainstream media often derogatorily casts Latinas as sexually promiscuous and teen mothers, as highlighted in chapter 1, some of the staffulty also reproduce judgmental assumptions that Latinas are more sexually active and desirous of children than other students.

Like Maggie Cordova, Summer Reyes is also an involved student on campus. In addition to MEChA, Summer is active in the school's leadership and is one of the few Latinas enrolled in honors and AP courses. Nevertheless, these identities do not shield either of these Mexican American women from constant surveillance, indicating that much more than track placement influences which students believe they are denied a "free pass."

"A Higher Standard": Asian Americans' Experiences

In general, Asian American students across gender rarely spoke about feeling patrolled or disciplined on campus. However, when they did, there were qualitative differences. The following examples capture the significance of racialized academic profiling on punishment and a staffulty's support for a hidden surveillance technique.

First of all, students describe what I believe is a punishment gap that differentially privileges either Latinas/os or Asian Americans depending on dominant racialized constructions. As portrayed earlier, the characterization of Latinas/os as criminals and troublemakers seems to provide them with fewer opportunities when it comes to tardiness and assumed "defiance." In contrast, the prevailing image of Asian Americans as model students may give them fewer leniencies than Latinas/os when it comes to academics. During a group interview with two of her friends enrolled in her English honors class, sophomore Lauren Chan illustrates the following:

> LAUREN: They let some students do some things and other students don't get to.
> INTERVIEWER KENDALL PARKER: What do you think determines whether they let certain students do things?
> LAUREN: Well, if they're Asian.
> INTERVIEWER KENDALL PARKER: If they're Asian? What sort of things *wouldn't* they let them do?
> LAUREN: Turn in homework late.

This racialized double standard when it comes to academics is most strongly expressed by Asian American students outside of the school's IB and AP courses or by those who are struggling academically. Since as a whole Asian Americans are assumed to be academically inclined, those who do not meet others' expectations may be more harshly punished for their schoolwork. During their group interview, sophomores Nat Punyawong and Mark Ku, who earlier critiqued teachers for unequally punishing tardy Mexican Americans, here echo Lauren's comments that when it comes to submitting late schoolwork, Asian Americans may be the ones who are treated unjustly:

> NAT: Like, Asians, you're supposed to be smart.
> MARK: I guess teachers treat you differently.
> NAT: Yeah, dude, we mess up one time, and they go all like anal-retarded on us.
> MARK: [They go,] "You're an A+ student, why aren't you good at—?"
> NAT: Yeah, if it was like a Mexican guy, I don't want to be racist or anything . . . if he gets a good grade, they're like, "Wow, this guy's so good!"

Experiences such as these have made Nat, Mark, and Kathy very critical of people who "judge the book by its cover." Since they are perceived to be high achieving and smart, Asian American students who do not receive the school's top grades may be judged harshly and have their backgrounds questioned. Thus, to the extent that a strict binary exists in which it is assumed that Asian American are A+ students in comparison to Latinas/os, Asian Americans who do not fit within such discrete categories may incur teachers' wrath. Such academic profiling does not leave space for students to be understood as individuals with their own interests and capabilities.

Sophomore Nathan Yi also feels that the higher academic expectations placed on Asian Americans can result in harsher punishment. Like Nat, Mark, and Kathy, Nathan is enrolled in college preparatory courses in which he is often one of the few Asian American students in his classes. He believes that this has especially hurt him in his science class, where he notices that his Asian American teacher more heavily penalizes him. He explains that students often curse the teacher in "low tones, sometimes loud tones" when she humiliates them with comments like the following:

> She disses them on an academic level. Say I don't know how to do a problem [and I ask,] "Can you help me?" Then she'll be, "You don't know how to do this problem because you don't ever study. That's why you don't do good in your class! That's why you're having an F and blah, blah, blah, blah." People feel really embarrassed.

In such degrading situations, perhaps some students curse under their breath to try to reclaim their pride in front of their peers. Nathan observes that these students are not reprimanded for cursing in the way that he recently was:

> Last time, I slipped out a curse word, and she was like, "Go to the office." I was, "Okay," and then after that, everyone was cursing. They didn't get any referrals, so I was pissed off at that.

Reflecting on why he might have been treated differently, Nathan deduces,

> I think it's pretty much racial profiling to me personally. 'Cause like there's not a lot of Asians in that class; [the teacher] she's Asian, right? When I curse she sent me to the office. When everyone else curses they don't get anything else but "Watch your mouth." How come I'm the only one that got in trouble? Most of the times I didn't do anything wrong. I just sit there and be quiet, and she doesn't even let me go to the rest room because I don't do my work.

He continues,

> She expects Asians to have a higher standard. I hate that kind of stereotyping because I'm getting bad grades doesn't mean I'm any lesser than anybody else. Just because I'm Asian doesn't mean I have to get all straight As and study all the time.

Perhaps confirming Nathan Yi's belief that Asian American staffulty have higher expectations for Asian American students is a drug-monitoring technique that staff member Ah Kum Chan encourages the Asian Americans she knows to use on their children:

> I told a lot of parents, if they suspect that their kids are using drugs, a
> very good way to tell is to use their hair. Just cut a little bit, or maybe
> get some hair from the bed. You can pick it up and get it tested.

This secretive use of students' hair follicles for drug testing is one of the
latest forms of intensive surveillance sold to parents and schools as a mechanism to monitor children's activities. It, like the varied forms described
throughout this chapter, can breed resentment and suspicion among youth.
They may feel that their rights have been violated and that they are not
trusted, in this case, possibly impeding open communication between parents and their children.

While Nathan believes that his Asian American science teacher is
stricter on him because they are both Asian Americans, sophomore Vanessa Chen finds that at least one of the three Latina/o security guards is
sterner on Asian Americans and may actually favor Latinas/os:

> Like the campus security, there's this one and she is really mean. We
> think she is kind of racist, but we don't know. Like, if we're after
> school and there are Asians here and Mexicans over there, she'll make
> us leave. Then if we come back, she'll yell at the Asians.

Experiences such as these reveal how stark the racial/ethnic divides are at
SCHS and that many students are attune to unequal restrictions.

Where Is the "Hope"? Conclusions

At a time when standardized tests and bureaucratic policies drive education, schools such as SCHS expend increasing amounts of energy on the
"achievement gap" and practices that differentially monitor, restrict, and
punish students. As staff member Mari Ramirez argues, lost in this climate of test and control are the everyday lives and struggles of students
and parents:

> All the counselors and the discipline issues and there is nobody there
> really to talk to the students or help the parents; there have been par-
> ents that come in asking for help. Their words are, "Help me I don't
> know what to do with my son or my daughter."

Rather than finding understanding, supportive, and nonjudgmental
staffulty to work with students or assist parents as Mari pleads, too many
students experience school as alienating, unequal, and disempowering.
So much so that some feel that the staffulty have simply given up on
them. They are granted no "free pass" and no second chance, regardless

of how much they have been able to overcome or change. Instead, they are greeted with more monitoring, restrictions, and punishment that are counter to educational success and send a message that, in the words of sophomore Mark Ku, there is "no hope" for students.

Included in the message of hopelessness is one that schools students on their supposed place in society. The racialized, gendered, and class-based treatment reinforces and justifies prevailing ideologies and a hierarchical system where one's background and styles are integral to how one is seen and treated. While students demonstrate impressive amounts of resilience and the resolve to persist, the tolls of these detrimental messages and a punishment gap are undeniable, and as detailed in the following chapter, they are intensified in the unequal allocation and expectation of private tutoring that is increasingly shaping education.

CHAPTER FOUR

"Parents Spend Half a Million on Tutoring"

Standardized Tests and Tutoring Gaps

> So wealthy family, you produce smarter kids, and low-income families produce what? Average students because their lack of resources. That's terrible. I think that's terrible.
>
> *—Mei Chee, parent*

Taiwanese immigrant Mei Chee is angered by what she observes as the reproduction of inequality within education. The inequalities detailed in the previous chapters are aggravated by the rapid growth of a tutoring industry that reverberates throughout families and schools.

Globally, tutoring is a multibillion-dollar enterprise, and tutoring franchises are increasingly popular for investors to open and to trade publically (King 2011). For example, with its 26,000 centers around the world, the fifty-year-old Japanese company Kumon reported over $800 million in annual sales in 2008 (Davidson 2008). In 2009, the Kaplan Review, one of the largest test preparation companies, earned over $190 million in revenue (Butler 2010).

Within the United States, the intensification of standardized tests and businesses that seize on the fears of families and students determined to gain admittance into desired colleges and universities have made tutoring a lucrative industry. In fact, as the role of SAT scores have increased in college admittance, so too have private SAT prep courses (Buchmann, Condron, and Roscigno 2010; Byun and Park 2012). Likewise, the No Child Left Behind Act (NCLB) has also been a boon to the tutoring industry. Under NCLB, Title 1 schools that for three consecutive years do not make what is referred to as adequate yearly progress on tests must provide free supplemental tutoring through private organizations to low-income students.[1] With federal money from public schools reallocated to fund private tutoring, leading companies have experienced skyrocketing enrollments and revenues, in some cases quadrupling in students after the implementation of NCLB (Karla 2004, 2; Wood 2004). There was nearly a 50 percent increase in federal funds allocated to such supplemental educational services, from $1.75 billion in 2001 to $2.55 billion in 2005 (Koyama 2010, 60).

At SCHS, some students and parents also feel compelled to subsidize public school education by paying private entities and individuals to boost test scores and increase college options. However, as parent Mei Chee critiques, tutoring fosters greater inequalities and allows larger questions to go unexamined, such as what is being taught in schools and what is expected of today's youth:

> Most parents send their children to take SAT tutoring. It costs
> $1,000! I feel so sad for low-income families because obviously
> the tests you are giving to students are too hard. Why are so many
> students complaining math is so hard? Why are students complaining
> science is so hard? And we have to send our students to tutoring that
> costs a lot of money? What about the low-income families?

Mei Chee is saddened by such a system where schools are basically ignoring the needs of students and limiting their life chances.

Echoing Mei Chee's concerns, Ah Kum Chan, a parent and a member of the staffulty, tabulates the prohibitive costs of tutoring:

> My husband says SCHS parents spend half a million on tutoring
> classes . . . Just high school: The chemistry tutor, $250. Then $85 per
> week for the SAT prep. That's just considering SAT I. SAT II is more.
> The math tutor, at least $30 to $40 an hour. Then how about the English
> tutors? How much money? A lot of students have three to four tutors.

The amount of money that some parents are able to spend is astronomical. Thus at SCHS, where tutoring feels expected, students left without this resource are at a severe disadvantage.

As detailed in this chapter, while the price of tutoring is high, the costs of unequal access are more than monetary. Compared to their schoolmates, middle-class and upper-middle-class Asian Americans enrolled in the International Baccalaureate program (IB) and advanced placement (AP) courses are more likely to have concurrent and accelerated tutoring.[2] In contrast, few Latinas/os describe participating in private tutoring. Unless they are enrolled in the school's AVID (Advancement via Individual Determination) program, which provides peer tutorials, when Latinas/os need academic assistance, many ask friends, go to the school's peer-tutoring program, or utilize the free after-school tutoring provided by teachers. In a few cases, Latinas/os may also enroll in private tutoring programs, but these tend to focus less on accelerated tutoring and SAT preparation and more on concurrent tutoring—helping students with their current schoolwork.

A school culture where tutoring is perceived by some as the norm and yet some do not have access to this service has significant effects on students, teaching, and public school education. Along with reproducing disparities—including human, social, and cultural capital—it fuels what I refer to as a tutoring cycle. Individually, this is characterized by a progression of some students who move from being tutees to eventually becoming paid tutors. Institutionally, a tutoring cycle is reflected in a public school system that becomes reliant on and subsidizes private tutoring for student learning. Furthermore, in a period where standardized tests shape students' opportunities, tutoring programs that focus on rote memorization and test preparation contribute to an educational system premised on narrow measurements of success. Thus, while tutoring may aid individual students, it is not a panacea, especially when it breeds inequality, squelches creativity, reduces the joy of learning, and silences questions about the direction of schooling.

Separate and Unequal: Tutoring by Type and Frequency

Just as there are quantitative differences in how much families can afford to pay for tutoring, there are also *qualitative* differences in the types and length of tutoring, the material covered, and the opportunities for building students' capital. These differences fall along a tutoring continuum by type and frequency.

For students at SCHS, along one end of the continuum are standardized test preparation courses and accelerated classes where students as young as three and four are often introduced to concepts and course materials before they are covered in school. Bearing names such as Ivy, Stellar, Apex, and Yale, these private, predominately Chinese-owned businesses are often referred to as cram schools, college preparation centers, and enrichment programs. They offer a range of after-school, weekend, and summer programs, including SAT test prep and course tutoring. Classes in these programs progress as students advance through the educational pipeline, ensuring that students continue for multiple years.

Moving along this continuum is a popular tutoring franchise—Smith's Learning Center. It too is a private program with classes provided after school, on the weekends, and during the summer. However, students from SCHS seem to access these programs more sporadically and for concurrent and remedial tutoring in addition to test preparation.

Along this continuum are Chinese schools. Since their emergence in San Francisco in the 1880s, Chinese schools have been important spaces of identity formation and the forging of community ties for Chinese Americans in the United States. The over one hundred Chinese schools throughout Southern California are diverse in size, course offerings, and fees. While most offer Chinese-language courses, math, science, and English, some include classes as varied as speech, sports, college preparation, and Chinese history (Zhou 2009, 156–57). As sociologist Min Zhou (2009) describes, "Most of the children of Chinese immigrants have been to a Chinese school or a Chinese-language class at some point" (157). Students start at a young age, and at SCHS, Chinese and some Korean American students attend Chinese school in elementary and middle school, helping them to form strong connections with peers and instructors. Parents also cement ties with other families in these schools.

At the extreme end of a tutoring continuum is free assistance provided by high school students at the community library or at SCHS by teachers. These high school students and teachers may help students with their current course work on an as-needed basis several days a week. For AVID students, area college students provide biweekly tutorials.

These distinct programs reveal the range in variations where tutoring is (1) private or public; (2) accelerated, concurrent, or remedial; and (3) long term or as needed. With students of different racial/ethnic identities, class backgrounds, and curriculum tracks usually accessing these various forms of tutoring or no tutoring at all, the school's divisions and disparities are intensified.

"You Will See Little Babies There All the Way to High School": *Acceleration, Capital, and the Tutoring Cycle*

While IB senior Yi Lin's estimate—that "99 percent [of IB students] are all going to one or the other [tutoring program] like Ivy and also Stellar"— might be high, most in the IB program do participate in private tutoring programs and summer classes. Teachers such as Beth Hill agree that this is also a pattern for ninth and tenth-graders in the school's honors program, who she describes as "going to SAT school all summer." National studies report similar findings; just as students from wealthier families are more likely to enroll in private SAT examination courses, so too are East Asian Americans (Byun and Park 2012). The results are higher SAT scores, admittance into more selective colleges and universities, and greater opportunities for merit-based scholarships and awards (Buchmann, Condron, and Roscigno 2010; Gándara and López 1998).

For many of the Asian American students in SCHS's IB and honors courses, there is a progression from elementary school through high school of accelerated and concurrent academic programs. This progression is part of the tutoring cycle, and Yi Lin's narrative captures how this cycle assists the academic performance of participating students.

Yi was eleven years old when he left China and his grandparents to join his mother, who had moved to the United States years earlier following a divorce. His parents were both doctors in China, but after the divorce, Yi's mother left the country to start a business. When this did not materialize, she found a job in a California casino. After making friends and establishing herself, she called for Yi to join her.

Yi remembers elementary school in the United States as "really hard." He tried to adjust to a new country and language where "everything was brand new," and he "didn't even know how to say hello or good-bye":

> The teachers and all the students were basically different races than my race, and some of them were Asian looking. So I thought they were going to be Chinese, but in the end I wasn't able to communicate with them, because even if they were [Chinese], they weren't able to speak it.

As a young child in a different environment, Yi was not provided with any home language assistance at school. He had to fend for himself in class and on the playground, making schooling very difficult.

While the English language was new to him, Yi recalls math being easy. When he was in fifth grade, students were being assigned problems he had covered in second or third grade in China. So this relieved some of his academic transition.

Almost immediately, Yi's mother placed him in a private after-school facility near their home to help him learn English. This was the beginning of his U.S. experience in privately run programs used to augment his public school education:

> I was sent there because my mom looked it up in the newspaper or through friends, and she thought that I should be sent there because at the rate that I was going, she didn't think that I was gonna make it through high school and definitely not in the IB program.

Her financial resources and established network of Chinese friends and the local Chinese community helped Yi's mother find this after-school center. She relied on a common pattern of middle- and upper-class families in East Asia of sending their children to tutoring programs as early as kindergarten (Lew 2006, 40). Such programs are prevalent primarily in urban areas across the world. However, relative to other regions, tutoring appears to be highest in East Asia because of school systems where college entrance examinations are rigidly used to place students into selective universities (Dang and Rogers 2008, 163; Aurini and Davies 2004).

As an immigrant, Yi initially felt more comfortable with the primarily Chinese students and tutors than with the teachers in his public school: "To me, it's more secure . . . I know there's a Chinese-speaking person, at least the principal or the supervisor, or whoever's in charge, the teacher maybe. They are the same race." Yi began establishing social ties with the other students and the program's staff, and he advanced through the after-school classes for the next six years:

> At first it was me with all these little kids studying grammar. It was sad because they all knew what was going on and I was just sitting there like, "Okay, I'm memorizing these vocab words about college." I was there throughout the year, all the way 'till last year because after each class there's the PSAT [Preliminary SAT], or eventually you go to SAT—the SAT math, SAT verbal, writing, all those tests.

From English classes to SAT preparation, such programs provide step-by-step assistance to aid students through each academic hurdle. For Yi, this meant many hours:

> When I was in the lower classes, it was basically every day after school. I think Mondays and Wednesdays were math classes from 3:00 to 6:00 or 3:30 to 6:00 and we get a break. Then on Tuesdays and Thursdays it's English, and then on Fridays, it's writing. After, I moved to SAT, it was on Friday afternoon; you come in and take the practice SAT test every week! That's three hours long. And then Saturday morning you come back and you start at 9:00 until 4:00 in the afternoon. Of course, you get a break in the middle, but it's a long time. There's also summer session. I took one or two; you start from 9:00 in the morning and you go there every single day.

Along with providing the human and cultural capital that facilitated his familiarity with the SAT, Yi's tutoring program was also an effective broker that nurtured his social networks. In particular, the program's principal shared key information with Yi's mother about SCHS's IB program:

> After eighth grade, they were like, "What's the best thing for me to do?" At that time, [the principal] thought that I was the type of person where I have to be pushed. Like if you don't push me, I'm just gonna do whatever. But if you push me, I could do a lot of great things. So he's like, "At SCHS, there's an IB program. At [a neighboring high school], there is no IB program." My mom's, "Okay, send him to wherever you think is best."

New to the United States, Yi and his mother were unfamiliar with the school structure or what their neighborhood schools offered. Thus the program's principal connected the Lins to other organizations—in this case SCHS. The fact that the principal speaks Chinese could have also enhanced the relationship he had with Yi's mother, especially relative to many public schools where immigrant families may have a more difficult time interacting with English-speaking staffulty (see Byun and Park 2012).

Just as he did with Yi's mother, the principal shares information about the IB program with others in the tutoring program. Thus some of Yi's tutor mates eventually became his classmates at SCHS. This connection solidified ties Yi and his mother had been establishing over the years, and these classmates and parents continue exchanging information and being resources for one another. Students encourage one another, provide assistance with homework, and develop a camaraderie based on their shared backgrounds and experiences in class. Yi reflects on how the parents also compare notes and students' progress:

> Among parents, they have nothing better to talk about besides their kids, sometimes. When they gather, they say, "Oh, I heard that Stellar Studies is pretty good. I sent my child there and the score increases a hundred points a week" and that kind of stuff. And it's "Oh really? Okay!"

Marisa Yep, Yi's IB classmate, concurs that these social ties are strong and persuasive:

> My mom is influenced by a lot her friends, and then my Chinese school principal, her son came here and did the IB program. She thought it was really good for him. So then she recommended it for all the parents. So then a lot of the IB students, I knew them since Chinese school because she recommended it, and then because my mom heard it, she's like, "Oh, you have to do it, Marisa."

This sharing of information and the long-term support fostered through such Chinese schools and Chinese-run tutoring programs is one Jamie Lew (2006) also documents in her research on middle-class Korean Americans in an elite high school in New York. She learned that even before beginning high school, many Korean American students and their families know each other because they participate in the same churches, community organizations, and tuition-based tutoring academies. These relationships are crucial for helping students navigate schools, especially because in comparison to U.S.-born middle- and upper-class White students, many immigrant families do not have the same ties to mainstream institutional resources and opportunities (Lew 2006, 42).

Having completed all the courses at his tutoring center and the SAT required for college admittance, like several of his IB classmates, Yi was finishing his senior year at SCHS as a paid tutor. He uses the knowledge and techniques he acquired during his years as a tutee to work with high school sophomores in Algebra 2. This experience continues to provide Yi with the opportunity to enhance his skills, and it expands his capital as he meets new students, earns money, and prepares to begin studying at one of the top University of California schools in the fall.

"Every Tuesday and Thursday We Have Tutorials": AVID and Concurrent Tutoring

As described in chapter 2, many of the AVID students name the biweekly tutoring they receive by college students as a valuable aspect of their program. As AVID junior Sandy O'Brien's narrative indicates, this support enhances their educational opportunities, especially given their positions as primarily working-class and lower-middle-class students without access to paid tutoring.

The daughter of a factory worker, Sandy is always being pushed by her family. Her mom tells her that she "wants me to turn out better than she did." This motivates Sandy. However, as much as her mother supports her, Sandy is not always able to have her questions answered about coursework:

> My mom tries her best to help me, but the material that I'm learning now is a lot higher than she learned in high school. So I know she finds it frustrating 'cause she wants to help me more and she can't.

Sandy raves about the support she receives from AVID precisely because it provides her and other students with academic assistance.

As someone who would not have access to consistent tutoring without AVID, Sandy advocates for free and accessible tutoring for all students. Her collectivist ethos even leads her to freely share with others the knowledge AVID provides her:

> I'm always there if they need help, I'm always there to tutor them if they need anything. If they have any questions, they can always call me or ask me in class.

As described in chapter 2, part of this emphasis on collaboration, rather than progressing individually and competing against one another, is integrated into AVID's use of tutorials where class time is devoted for students to aid one another. This process allows students the opportunity to enhance their skills and solidify some of their relationships as they help one another.

While students such as Sandy are accruing additional human, cultural, and social capital through their AVID tutoring, the benefits they obtain are different from the ones recounted by Yi Lin and many of his middle-class and upper-middle-class IB classmates. Just as the AVID students are *not* receiving the extensive and accelerated tutoring that many IB students are privy to, the social capital they are building is also distinct. At SCHS, the social capital of AVID students appears to be concentrated in other AVID students, their AVID coordinator, and college tutors. They do not seem to have access to the network of parents and the institutional brokers from the tutoring agencies that many of the students in the IB program have. Nevertheless, the racial/ethnic and class positions of AVID students and the structured opportunities for peer support may be instrumental in nurturing a sense of community among AVID students as they support each other as best they can through the educational pipeline.

"An Hour a Week": Concurrent and Remedial Tutoring

Unlike many of the primarily middle-class and upper-middle-class Asian American IB and AP students who spend many hours and multiple years in private classes or the students in AVID who have biweekly tutoring, the few Latinas/os and some Asian Americans outside of these programs who describe using tutoring do so on an as-needed basis for significantly less time. Teacher Bryan Lee explains, "About 10–15 percent of my college prep students have outside tutoring." Much of the tutoring for students not in IB and AVID is concurrent or remediation that is occasionally private but is usually free and provided at SCHS. Similar to the accelerated tutoring, such tutoring assists students with their courses, and the tutors may also be helpful institutional agents who provide additional capital. However, since it is accessed on an as-needed basis, by the time students are tutored, they may already be struggling. Some may have fallen behind, especially in cumulative courses such as math and science. Also, students seem not to develop the length and depth of relationships many of the IB students establish in their tutoring programs.

Parent Ramon Vasquez describes the type and frequency of private tutoring used by his daughters, who are enrolled in AP courses:

> If they weren't as good as they should be, then we would get them
> a tutor. They'd go to Smith's Learning Center. And in high school,
> several times, I had tutors come into the house to help them with their
> subjects . . . If they were having trouble with any subject, they would
> ask for a tutor.

Ramon Vasquez finds that tutoring is helping his daughters with their math and science courses, a similar pattern repeated by many students.

With high expectations and realizing that many of his daughters' classmates in the honors and advanced placement courses have tutoring, Ramon Vasquez feels compelled to use what he refers to as "supplemental education":

> We've instilled that it's so important to do as well as you can, to challenge yourself . . . The competition in class is fierce; everybody's driven. They're driven to excel. And my kids would often be the only non-Asians in the class—certainly the only Latinos. And they have to work very, very hard to keep up, including going to supplemental education.

As a first-generation college student from a Mexican American household, Ramon provides all he can to his children. Believing that he did not always have the knowledge or the resources to help him when he was a student, he is able to use his graduate-level schooling and financial assets as a judge to support his daughters in their educational quests. At SCHS, where tutoring is pervasive in the top classes, he senses that without these resources, his daughters would not be in contention.

Like Ramon Vasquez, Cristina Perez is also Mexican American and fiercely committed to her children's education. With a desire "to give them every opportunity that I can to succeed," Cristina searched the telephone book for tutoring centers close to her home to aid her daughters in their college preparatory courses. She initially tried Smith's Learning Center as well, but she was not happy with their workbook approach to tutoring, where the emphasis was placed on completing the center's worksheets as opposed to using her daughters' school books as a foundation for studying. Now she pays for her two daughters to attend another tutoring program:

> An hour a week I take them. I've seen the difference. My daughter was failing a class in junior high. Now she went all the way up to an A in a semester. So I know my kids can do it.

As well as this weekly hour-long tutoring, Cristina solicited the advice of one of her daughter's teachers, who suggested that she purchase workbooks to prepare her daughters for the California Achievement Test (CAT6).

The additional academic support that Cristina provides her daughters may be helping, but her oldest daughter is still struggling in math and science. The once-a-week tutoring and perhaps even the CAT6 workbook focus more on math tricks and test-taking skills. While this may be sufficient for her ninth-grade daughter, her older daughter requires further explanation to understand her more advanced course work. Referring to her youngest daughter, Cristina praises,

> She got a really good tutor . . . [M]y daughter has learned so many
> different shortcuts to math that I couldn't teach her because, honestly,
> [when I was in high school,] we weren't required to take algebra. I'm
> taking it now, and now I can help her. But it helped them a lot. She
> has done really well. We're going to continue it in the fall. Right now
> they are taking the summer off.

Several distinct patterns are apparent in the tutoring Cristina Perez is able to provide her daughters. First of all, she relies on the phone book rather than being able to select a tutoring program by referrals from friends or students. Compared to Yi Lin's mother, Cristina is not part of a social network that shares information about the type of educational resources she seeks. There is no indication from their weekly tutoring that she and her daughters are establishing the embedded forms of social capital fostered in the more sustained private tutoring programs or in the AVID program. Consequently, Cristina and her daughters do not receive comparable forms of support and information about educational resources and opportunities from these organizational agents. The once-a-week tutoring and its focus on tricks and strategies may also be less substantive than other forms of tutoring. Finally, while Cristina is currently taking an algebra course at a community college, this course was not required when she went to high school. So unlike college-educated parents who often have the benefit of familiarity with their children's course work, Cristina is not always able to assist her daughters with their homework. Thus, as much as she aims to give her daughters "every opportunity," the inequalities persist.

Realizing the need to assist students in their course work, SCHS's teachers and peers offer free concurrent and remedial tutoring after school. Students value these forms of tutoring as well, but they have their own limitations, and they disadvantage select students. In particular, staying after school is difficult for students who work, who have family responsibilities, or who are "choice students" and live outside of the school's neighborhood. Teacher Beth Hill explains,

> My Hispanic students, a majority of them have to find a ride home.
> They might be in [a neighboring town]. So they can't stay because
> they get a ride from somebody that they've arranged.

A significant percentage of choice students come from the neighboring Latina/o working-class city, so staying after school without access to transportation may make tutoring impossible for the very students who are least likely to be able to afford or know about private tutoring. Similarly, teacher Michelle Mesa considers how even for Latinas/os who are available for tutoring, the racial/ethnic divisions and misperceptions on campus may be a deterrent for peer tutoring:

> Most of the tutors tend to be the Asian students and as a Hispanic student there's no one that looks like me when I walk in for tutoring, and so there's that kind of weirdness that exists. It's like, "Well, you're part of the problem, but yet I'm supposed to come and sit down with you for about an hour to get tutored by you? I already feel really low and then I have to get instructed or tutored by you." So there are those hidden dynamics that our tutoring program isn't diversified.

As parents and students strive to enhance their opportunities, their different resources are not only unequally reproduced but also kept separate. As conveyed in chapter 2, students in the IB and AVID programs are part of distinct peer groups who typically do not participate in one another's tutoring programs and friendship circles. Thus they are not able to share their resources, keeping students and resources separate and unequal. In a context where tutoring has become so integral to the advancement of some students, as detailed in the next section, for students without any tutoring, the ramifications of a tutoring gap are even more glaring.

Going without Tutoring

Margaret Kang, a Chinese American student enrolled in several AP courses, realizes that her wealthier friends can have higher goals than she can simply because they are provided with the added support to excel. She explains,

> I have a friend that goes to prep school like 24/7, and she's expecting to get 2400 on the SAT. I think she can set such a high goal for herself because she has the extra preparations that other people don't get.

As Margaret argues and as the following students elaborate, these gaps are damaging. They can widen disparities, and in some cases, when students observe the inequities in their classes, they may even fuel resentment and the desire to give up. Nevertheless, as students also reveal, tutoring can be stifling, especially if it becomes too regimented in its approach.

"There Wasn't Much Tutoring Offered for Me": Rose Gonzalez's Critiques

As the daughter of Mexican immigrants, senior Rose Gonzalez will be among the first in her family to graduate high school and attend a university. She is also one of the few Latina/o students at SCHS to have completed the IB program since its inception. Initially, Rose found it "really intimidating because of all the Asians, and a lot of them didn't talk to me at first." She was a self-described "loner," but eventually her IB classmates "warm[ed] up" to her. Given the demanding workload expected of IB students and the unequal amount of academic support Rose is able to receive relative to many of her classmates, Rose's accomplishments are especially impressive.

Education is "extremely important" to Rose's parents, particularly her father, who has a "vision" that she will "become a doctor or a lawyer." Rose's entire family encourages her, and her family's struggles motivate her. Her family has inculcated a sense of independence and a strong work ethic, but in contrast to her IB classmates, many of whose "families are doctors and their sisters and brothers are going to UC [University of California] schools," Rose feels she has no one in her family who can help her with her course work:

> My dad, he went through some college, but he never graduated. He doesn't really know my homework; he doesn't really understand. My stepmom, she can kind of help me, but even she struggles. So when it comes down to my homework, I have no help.

According to Rose, the structure of the IB program and its intensive workload make it nearly impossible for students to fully digest and acquire course knowledge without assistance. She pleads with teachers,

> Just offer more help, more tutoring for AP and IB classes. They should have study sessions or something extra because for our classes, they give tons of homework. So you're in a rush to do the homework; you cannot really learn the other material. You're just focusing on, "Okay, I gotta get this done." You're not taking time to read everything because there's so much that you can't really read it.

The amount of work and the fast pace in the IB and AP courses hinder student learning. Rose is just trying to complete her homework. There is simply too much information to comprehend. Thus students such as Rose feel the need for tutoring to aid understanding.

While some teachers offer after-school assistance, this help does not address the underlying problem of what is happening in classes and the high demands placed on students. Rose explains why she is unable to stay after school for assistance, and she proposes expanding access to free tutoring:

> There wasn't much tutoring offered for me. Teachers offered help, but it was hard because they were, "Okay, well come after school." I couldn't come after school because I would have to go to East Los Angeles to pick up my sister, come back, go and pick up my brother; by then it was already like 4:00 and then I get ready for work. So I

couldn't come for help. Like math last year, I really, really needed help, and I would come in the morning sometimes. I tried to skip PE [physical education]. I'd ask [the teacher] if I can go, and she would help me, but it was limited help. I wish there was Saturday help or something where we could come in the mornings or Sunday or something extra.

While Rose's recommendations for weekend tutoring at the school might be difficult for time-strapped teachers and budget cutbacks in schools, her comments confirm how after-school programs are often inaccessible to working students and students with family responsibilities.

Despite excelling academically and gaining admittance into a top California University, Rose knows that tutoring would have enhanced her academic opportunities. However, not only was she unable to attend after-school sessions, but the tutoring fees outside of school were also prohibitive for her family. In contrast, she observes how many of her IB classmates used their class privileges to hire tutors and acquire other resources:

Some of them, their parents buy them tutors so that they help them to do their regular homework. It's like, "Dang, I wish I had that at my house". . . . I couldn't afford it; so, I didn't take SAT school, which I wish I could have because I probably would have passed. There's some people in my class who spend thousands of dollars on SAT school, and it's like, "Dang, you're lucky!" . . . Or the ability to buy those books, they're expensive, and they come with a whole stack of books. I could only buy one 'cause that's all I could afford.

Rose is aghast that some students have tutors to help them daily with their homework, and she longed for the SAT class and workbooks her peers could afford. Such differences in resources punctuate the disparities in class backgrounds. They are also among the "hidden injuries of class" or the "feeling of vulnerability in contrasting oneself to others at a higher social level, the buried sense of inadequacy that one resents oneself for feeling" that poor and working-class students may experience (Sennett and Cobb 1972, 58). Similarly, since scores on the SAT have been found to influence self-confidence, access to competitive programs, and the ability to secure scholarships, not having the additional test preparation support to help bolster test results may have "unforeseen effects on both opportunity and motivation of Latino students who score poorly" (Gándara and López 1998, 34).

Such disparity has fueled some animosity by Rose against her Asian American classmates:

It kind of gets me mad like how some of these Asians, I'm sorry, some of these students, how their parents just get them a tutor and there you go; they're set 'cause the tutor helps them, and it's like, "Crap, I wish I had that!"

In school, where students are forced to compete for rewards, college admission, and scholarships, differential resources can fuel resentment by excluded students. In this case, it can possibly foster divisions between working-class and middle-class students as well as Latinas/os and Asian Americans. This can hinder social capital because students may not support each other and share their knowledge and resources. It also does not address the larger conditions in schools, where competition is encouraged over collaboration, there is a speed up in education to cover more material, and there is an intensification of the tutoring industry.

In spite of some resentment and the initial coldness and intimidation Rose encountered in the IB program, she was eventually able to establish friendships with her IB classmates. This was instrumental to her success in the program. Not only did she start to feel more like she belonged, but she credits her fellow IB students with helping her. They provided her with some of the tutoring she felt was lacking:

> People in IB who were going through it with me, those were the ones who helped me the most, 'cause whenever I needed help I could always ask one of the IB students. When it came to math, they'd teach me how to do it and show me over and over again until I finally got it, or if I had a question about homework or I needed help 'cause I could never really turn to my parents, I'd call one of them, "Oh, can you help me 'cause I don't understand?"

As Rose juggled her work and family responsibilities with her courses, occasionally she "just wanted to give up." Knowing that her peers were receiving additional help aggravated the situation, but at critical moments Rose was able to rely on these same students to assist her with homework.

Though Rose accomplished her goal of completing the IB program, more students leave the program than complete it. Perhaps feeling marginalized in the program and seeing the disparities in resources and the limited responses by the school to rectify them, they too feel intimated or that they do not belong and opt out of a program seeped with so much inequality.

"I Don't Know Where [to Get Help]": Albert Ortiz's Wishes

With students separated by academic track and race/ethnicity and class, many outside of IB and AP/honors courses or in different friendship circles are unaware of the world of tutoring. Possessing different social networks and forms of cultural capital, they may be uninformed of the extensive academic assistance that some of their schoolmates receive or, as sophomore Albert Ortiz describes, they may not even know how to access such tutoring.

As a struggling student enrolled in college preparatory courses, Albert believes that tutoring could help him. However, he feels that he has few options and limited knowledge about how he can improve academically. This was not always the case. Born and raised in a working-class Latina/o community, Albert and his mother selected SCHS over his neighborhood school because of their high aspirations: "My mom thought it was better for me to get a better education. So I said, 'Alright.'" Drawing on their networks, the Ortizes sought out SCHS because of its positive reputation:

> People around [middle] school talked to me, and then my next-door neighbor comes here too. [My mom] heard it from her, and [my mom] was like, "Is it good?"

Albert is the child of Mexican immigrants who instilled in him that "they don't want me to suffer." His mother earned a third-grade education, and his father completed eleventh grade. So they always emphasize to "study hard." Unfortunately, these messages, along with Albert's determination, have not been able to counterbalance the detrimental school practices constraining Albert's educational aspirations.

During his early years of schooling, Albert did well: "Classes were all right. Teachers were all right . . . I was pretty smart like from little kid to fourth grade and a little bit fifth grade." However, between fifth and eighth grade, there was a change:

> That's when I started getting in trouble, getting suspended and all that 'cause they make you wear uniforms. Tuck [your shirt] out, they get mad, and the principal's unfair. It's not fair at all. She'll like you if you're a little sucker, but after that if you get on her bad side, she'll try and blame you for everything.

At a young age, Albert was already being typecast and his clothing was heavily regulated through school suspensions. These suspensions for not following the school uniform policy increased. Having been forsaken by school officials, who seemed more concerned about appearances than how Albert was experiencing school, Albert began "mess[ing] around" and "not paying attention" in class. His suspensions started getting longer—"three days, then five days, and a whole week."

Those middle school years, when he felt blamed for everything, influenced his relationship to school. His scaled-back desire and the days he missed cost him:

I just started messing up and I didn't care anymore, and now that I'm starting to care, it's harder for me to do it 'cause I didn't learn the basics. I know stuff, basics and stuff, but I don't know them all . . . I regret doing what I did in the past because now it's harder for me to understand and learn and get my good grades like I want to.

Feeling that he lacks the academic foundation necessary to perform well in his courses, Albert is frustrated with school. At the time of his interview, his English class was causing him the most anger:

Writing is easy, but [my teacher] wants all this, and I'm like, "Damn. I don't know most of that, and I don't know how to do it," and I just say the F word in my head. Sentences, run-on sentences, commas—I don't know where they belong.

Remorsefully, he declares, "Damn, I should have paid attention. That's what I regret the most, not paying attention."

As she did when he was younger, Albert's mother continues checking on him academically:

[When she asks,] "Do you have homework?" I just tell my mom, "No." If we do, and I do it, I'm like, "Oh, yeah." I tell her, "This is all I had." She's like, "Nothing?" I'm like, "No, he just wanted us to read something, and I read it." She's like, "Okay."

While she is one of his biggest supporters, Albert finds that his mom cannot always assist him. When asked if there is someone who can aid him with the basics he missed during middle school, he is at a loss:

No, unless I go to tutoring somewhere where they can teach me, but I don't know where. So I don't know. My mom don't know; my mom does know, but doesn't know that much. My dad can't help me because all he does is speak Spanish, and my brothers are always busy, and my little sister, she has her own drama.

Like his schoolmate Rose Gonzalez, Albert has a supportive and encouraging family who has taught him much. However, he is not part of the network of students in the IB or AVID programs who share academic information or can afford tutoring. He is not even sure how to find the tutoring he desires. Embarrassed that he lacks the knowledge required for high school, Albert "just won't ask for help." Without the necessary support and the information needed for acquiring that support, Albert seems resigned when he is asked what is blocking him from improving academically:

> I guess the fear of failing, and even though I'm failing, but I try and do good at raising my grades, and then like something hard comes. I guess I try to avoid it, but I also try and do it, but I'm a slow learner, and it's really hard for me to get it right away.

Since peer groups are so separate, Albert is unaware of the extensive tutoring that some students receive. In a few cases, even Latina sophomores enrolled in honors English classes are unaware of its prevalence. For example, when asked what percentage of students at SCHS they think have tutors, Paula Calderon and Robin Lopez reply, "I don't know. I think it might be like 5 percent or less." This knowledge gap regarding the extent of tutoring can fuel racialized constructions of Asian Americans as smart compared to Latinas/os and it may account for the internalization that leads Albert to blame himself for being "a slow learner."

In spite of the many difficulties he encounters, Albert continues trying. Football helps to motivate him:

> 'Cause without grades I can't play, so that's why I'm trying to chill right now and trying to do everything. Mostly at nights, I'm up late trying to see if I can meet their expectations, but sometime I can't. That's what stresses me out—that I can't do as good as my family wants me to. I feel like I can't make them proud of me.

Since his classes don't provide him with the academic foundation he needs and he is ashamed of his skills, Albert could benefit from any of the private or free tutoring programs described by the IB and AVID students. This additional help could provide him and other students with the skills and confidence to achieve their dreams and the aspirations of their families. Instead, students who may need the most assistance often receive the least, and in Albert's case he is finding that he increasingly "hate[s] school" to the point that "I just don't want to be here."

With a son who also struggled at SCHS, the Cadenas can empathize with Albert and the lack of support he receives at school. They saw how their son was left to his own devises at the school. As a college graduate and an educator, Ana Cadena has the financial resources to help her son academically, but unlike Albert, who blames himself for the difficulties he encounters, she draws from her teaching experiences to provide a scathing critique of the practices at SCHS:

> It seemed like they didn't get any math help. [Our son] struggled through math, and we ended up having to seek outside tutoring for him to get ahead. It would be out-of-pocket and just to reach the minimum for him to pass his class. [The school] calls you, and they let you know, "I'm sorry. There's nothing we can do. He's failing the

class." It's on your lap. I felt so helpless as a parent, as an educator. I thought, "My goodness, at my school, we go above and beyond. We offer tutoring." We bend over backwards to get this child that's struggling, to get him to a certain level where he'll pass the class. But at SCHS, I feel that my son was just left high and dry.

Ana Cadena's feeling of being "helpless" mirrors Albert's reaction to the lack of support he is receiving at school. However, Albert's sense of helplessness is compounded by the fact that he is not able to access the tutoring he desires. As uncovered in the previous chapter, instead of receiving academic assistance, he confronts similar forms of policing and control that he encountered in middle school—the very dynamics that have fueled some of the conditions that hurt him today.

"Anyone Can Have a Tutor": Judgment and Simmering Resentment

Not all Latinas/os express such a strong desire for tutoring. During a two-hour discussion, sophomores Marisa Cadena, Jenn Vanderhol, Vicki Pardo, and Fran Padilla animatedly share some of their reservations. Their reflections also reveal the significance of class and a budding resentment against some of their peers.

Throughout our meeting, these four friends continually critiqued the academic profiling that pervades SCHS. Their experiences as Latinas in honors courses where Marisa and Jenn are also pre-IB students have made them very aware of people's misperceptions:

> JENN VANDERHOL: We don't fit the stereotype. We aren't Asian.
> VICKI PARDO: But we are smart. We are in honors.

This climate where they must always confront other's stereotypes shapes their sense of selves as well as their perspective on the tutoring programs used by some of their Asian American classmates:

> MARISA CADENA: Everybody knows the stereotype, but most Asians say that their parents are the ones that push them, that that's why they are smart.
> GILDA OCHOA: So what do you think about that?
> JENN: I mean, my parents push hard.
> VICKI: Yeah, mine do too.
> FRAN PADILLA: Yeah maybe a lot of Asian parents do push hard, but that doesn't mean that other parents don't push hard.
> JENN: I feel like they have extra help after school, like they have tutors.
> VICKI: Yeah, most of them have tutors.
> JENN: Which I don't want to do, so—

FRAN: Yeah, I don't want to do either.

VICKI: I mean anyone can have a tutor. It's not like we can't be like them—

Challenging the pervasive biological and cultural assumptions that construct Asian American parents and students as distinct from Latinas/os, these friends argue that their parents also "push hard." They realize that both groups of parents can push hard; to say that some parents have high expectations does not preclude the fact that other parents may as well.

Just as they emphasize that their parents are not different, they also argue that if they want, they can be like many of their Asian American classmates and have tutors too. However, as their conversation unfolds, it appears that they may be more than just opposed to outside academic programs:

FRAN: My neighbor, she is Japanese, and I remember two summers ago, I would go to the mall and her parents sent her to an IQ academy, the whole summer. My other friend, her parents sent her to a pre-SAT academy the whole summer, and my parents would never make me do that. They would be like, "You can do that if you want, but we are not going to force you 'cause you're getting good grades."

VICKI: Yeah, my parents don't even want me to. They don't want me to just [do] school, school, school.

JENN: Like twenty-four hours.

VICKI: I mean school is the main priority, but they just say, "You have to live your life." I always hear my mom say, "You are only a kid once. You better appreciate these years, 'cause I wish I was a kid again. I have to do all this stuff now and have so many responsibilities."

As these students critically discuss summer programs, they distinguish themselves from their Asian American peers, who they assume are spending numerous hours in tutoring and are too focused on school. Perhaps in response to the more positive academic image that Asian Americans have at the school, these comments become reactionary and judgmental when these friends favor their own families' approach to education over their perception of their Asian American classmates.

Similarly, in spite of their initial declarations about these outside academic programs, it is not clear that all four of the students really have no interest in participating in such programs. As they continue, it appears that just as racialized assumptions may shape their opinions, financial cost may also underlie their desires:

MARISA: But it's also a choice 'cause my cousin, she lives in Mexico, and this past summer she went to Harvard for two months. It was a summer program, and she is a sophomore or junior, and she said it was really hard, but it taught her a lot of stuff but it was her choice. Her parents didn't make her.

FRAN: I had the same thing. I wanted to go to a writing program at Stanford last summer 'cause I was selected, but it was like $4,000, so I really wanted to go and it was my choice but my parents were like, "No, you can't go. It's too expensive."

Unlike students such as Rose Gonzalez and Albert Ortiz, who explicitly regret not having access to tutoring, these sophomores present a slightly different perspective. Initially, they seem to outright ridicule tutoring and summer programs. However, as the conversation continues, a more nuanced narrative emerges—one that suggests that some of their animosity may actually be fueled by others' assumptions that only Asian Americans are smart and have parents that encourage education and that all students should follow a similar path to excelling academically. Thus the students' critiques may stem from multiple factors. They might be a challenge to racialized assumptions, but the criticisms could also emerge from students' resentment toward stereotypes that they then direct at Asian Americans. Finally, as Fran's final example of the writing program at Stanford indicates, their strong sentiment against such programs may also reveal an economic reality that not all parents can afford them.

Comparing the experiences by Rose Gonzalez and Albert Ortiz with these sophomores, there are important class differences that might also account for their distinct desires and perceived need for tutoring. Unlike Rose and Albert, these four students come from homes where all their parents have been able to graduate high school and most have also graduated from college. In particular, Marisa and Fran have teachers and a lawyer as parents. Thus while Rose and Albert feel that they have "no help" at home when it comes to schoolwork, this does not seem to be the case for these friends.

"Tutoring's Kinda a Waste": Nathan Yi's Boredom

Like a few of their Latina/o schoolmates, several Asian American students are also critical of tutoring. However, for Asian Americans, this criticism comes from students who have had private tutoring, and as sophomore and pre-IB student Nancy Chang expresses, it stems from a belief that "tutoring's a waste of money" and time. Having had the privilege of paid outside support, they purport that students who really want to achieve academic success can do so on their own without tutors. What the narrative of sophomore Nathan Yi also suggests is that when tutoring relies on approaches that emphasize memorization and fill-in-the-blank responses frequently used in standardized test preparation, it can become overly rigid and outright boring.

Born in Taiwan, Nathan immigrated to the United States when he was in fourth grade, and a couple years later, his mother enrolled him in a program that he attended from sixth through ninth grade:

> It's private tutoring at someone's house with a group of students. It helped me with math because that's what she's good at, but English-wise it didn't really. We started studying SAT at probably seventh grade, and I don't get any of it 'cause SAT, you're supposed to keep practicing and practicing; I get really bored doing those problems. I was like, "Whatever, I'm just going to guess and just sit there and do nothing."

Although Nathan found the assistance he received with math useful, the emphasis that his tutor placed on preparing for the SAT years before he would be taking the exam was dull to him:

> It's not like I do anything there. She asked me to do my homework, but what could she do? It's not like she could force me to, so I just sit there and stare into empty space.

While Nathan did nothing, his mother paid $300 a month for him to attend tutoring for three hours each day after school. Based on his experiences, Nathan concludes, "Tutoring is like babysitting. They just make sure you do what you're supposed to do and wait until your parents get off of work and pick you up."

Nathan's equating of tutoring with babysitting captures a reality for working mothers like his own. As a new immigrant, private tutoring may have provided Nathan's mother with the double benefit of day care and learning opportunities for Nathan. However, Nathan did not find the structure of the program compelling, and by the time he was a high school sophomore, he no longer participated in it.

At the time of our meeting and as recounted in the previous chapter, Nathan struggled with his chemistry class and was preparing to repeat it during his junior year. However, since his tutoring program emphasized SAT preparation, there is no indication that staying in the program would have provided Nathan with the support he actually needed to pass chemistry. Experiences such as Nathan's may explain why a couple of Asian American students who had private tutoring now criticize it. As was the case with Cristina Perez's daughters discussed earlier, the tutoring they were receiving may have been too test-centered, not providing the depth of understanding necessary for students to pass their higher-level classes.

"They Have Already Seen Everything That's in the Book":
Tutoring Altering Expectations, Assignments, and Pedagogy

According to parents and staffulty, the prevalence of private tutoring is impacting more than individual students. It is also affecting what happens in the classroom. As teacher Bryan Lee explains, "The tutoring programs have students reading and discussing novels that we use in class." Some students in accelerated tutoring are studying their high school course material even before their teachers introduce it. Hence prior to coming to class, these students have already completed teacher's assignments in their tutoring sessions. This causes a ripple effect as part of the tutoring cycle where select teachers are subtly or even overtly pressured to alter their expectations, curriculum, and pedagogy. Students without access to tutoring are then left to fend for themselves, and even students who have tutors critique some teachers who "expect us to know everything because we're IB or AP students, and they don't really teach us." Within the context of contemporary schooling, where standardized tests increasingly dictate education, some tutoring programs are reinforcing the emphasis on quantity over quality.

With decades of experience, teacher Val Sherman is critical of the changes in education. In particular, within the past ten years, she has seen a growth in the use of private tutoring among her students—a practice she believes is antithetical to public education:

> Most of my honors students have at least at one point in time been
> tutored concurrently or in acceleration. For me, as a public school
> math teacher, it's a frustrating thing because it's sometimes unneces-
> sary for students to get extra help.

Val Sherman is not opposed to all tutoring. However, she disagrees with the use of private entities doing the work of public schools, especially when such programs are used to bolster the image of individual students. They may also undermine the work of public school teachers:

> What parents are trying to do, in my opinion, is make their students
> look smarter by giving them Algebra 2 in the summer with a tutor
> and then starting Algebra 2 that fall, where they have already seen
> everything that's in the book. When I go, "What do you think the A
> means in this equation?" [Students respond,] "I know! I know!" And,
> of course, to me, if I didn't know that student was being tutored, I
> would say, "Wow, this bright student has already figured out what the
> A means in the equation, and nobody else knows."

As teacher Sherman describes, there is an element of unfairness in such accelerated tutoring. This inequality coincides with the competitive structure of schooling: select students are given additional resources to help ensure that they beat their classmates to the answer, enabling the chances that their teachers positively label them.

Val Sherman realizes that parents are aiming to aid their children as best they can, but she worries too about the enduring impacts of extensive tutoring on youth:

> I think that parents sometimes are doing their students a disservice because they won't be tutored the rest of their life, and they're going to have to be on their own at some point. I don't know if they're going to be able to really manage without the crutch, and some of these students have had that crutch every year since they were seven or eight years old. I have parents who tell me, "But he's being tutored in chemistry, math, and English," and it's the same tutor he's had since he was in seventh grade.

Coupled with her concern of tutoring becoming a "crutch" is Sherman's observation that students appear less able to apply their knowledge to math problems that require innovative approaches. She compares students in her Algebra 2 honors courses, a class she has taught for years:

> One thing that I do consistently is give them "Problems of the Week," and these are problems that are not necessarily tied to any of the curriculum that I'm teaching at the time. They're usually something that's a little more difficult, a little bit challenging; they have to think about it—sometimes pull back from their previous courses like geometry. And what I'm noticing as time passes is that I have many fewer students who are coming up with creative solutions who can even solve a problem that's quite difficult.

Observing the difficulties students are having with such math problems, she has altered her expectations by extending the amount of time students have to complete these assignments, and she is providing more assistance:

> I'm getting to the point where I give them two or three days to figure out the solution, and nobody's figured it out, and I have to actually give them a hand or get them started or they wouldn't be able to solve it at all. Some of them go to their tutors, but I've already told them that that was one of the things that they were not to do. So without going to their tutors, then they are stuck with how to solve things. Whereas five to ten years ago, I was easily able to have one or two people in every classroom come up with a solution.

While she has reluctantly revised her expectations of students, Val Sherman has encountered more extreme demands from tutoring that she refuses to accommodate. Rolling her eyes, she reveals the pressure she faced by a tutor and a parent to alter her teaching:

> There was a complaint from a parent about my class and a tutor accompanied the parent. It was about my [advanced math] class. It was a very unpleasant experience about five or six years ago. The tutor felt it was right to teach things his way and that my students should be able to do things his way. I was, "I'm sorry; I'm the teacher. When they leave my class, I don't care how they do it, but in my class, I expect them to do a certain kind of problem the way I've asked them to do it. If they don't do it that way, and I can't follow the way they did it, I can't give them credit, and I won't give them credit."

While no other teacher described similar demands expected of them, some parents, staff, and students believe that a couple of teachers are changing their methods because a majority of the students have already received instruction from outside tutors. For example, when students in one of her son's classes were speeding through course assignments and no longer listening to the teacher, Ah Kum Chan realized that the students had already learned the material from their tutors, leading the teacher to slowly stop teaching. She explains how, during a conversation with her youngest son, she came to this realization:

> I said, "How is your [science class]?" Do you know what he told me? "Mom, [our teacher] gave us the worksheet. The students finished in five minutes. I haven't finished the first question yet, and they finished already." The tutor already gave them the material. They studied it already.

When Ah Kum asked her son about the students' behavior in the class once they were done with the assignments, what she discovered was also revealing: "[My son] said, 'They are just making all kinds of problems. They talk a lot. I cannot concentrate on my work.'"

These revelations contradicted what she knew was the case several years earlier, when her older son had the same teacher:

> [The teacher] changed his teaching because everybody goes to tutors. Nobody is listening to him now. When my first son was in his class, [the teacher] taught. When my second son came, he didn't teach. He switched to another way of teaching. Why? Because he's thinking, "Not many students are listening. They know everything already."

As a result of these observations and conversations with other parents, Ah Kum deduces that the tutors acquired the course material that the teacher uses and now the instructor no longer teaches because a segment of students are not paying attention in class.

Junior Stephanie Yep concurs that she too has observed a lack of teaching. This is in her college preparatory math classes:

> She just tells us, "Go on the website, pick up your homework there, and just look at it there, and get your notes from that website." She's not really teaching us in class; so we can't really understand where she's coming from. She teaches in a weird way, and so I don't understand.

When asked if her teacher expects students to have tutors, Stephanie continues,

> I don't know, 'cause she expects us to do tests, and she's like, "I didn't teach this, but it's on the test." And I'm like, "Oh great!"

Perhaps because of experiences such as these, a few school counselors are known for warning students that they will not pass the advanced math and science courses without tutoring. Ah Kum Chan even remembers her son reporting how a teacher told students in an AP class, "Go find a tutor. Only one or two of you will survive without a tutor." No wonder first-year student Diana Muñoz has already deduced that there is a correlation among advanced classes, race/ethnicity, class, and the need for tutoring:

> The Asians are mostly in AP and honors classes 'cause their parents put them into tutoring; they have to do tutoring . . . For honors or AP, the people have money for tutors.

Overall, along with excluding students who do not have the resources for outside tutoring, these experiences reveal a catch-22: The extensive assistance select students receive may favor these students; stifle original thought; and instigate a change in teachers' homework assignments, expectations, and pedagogy. However, to the extent that a growth in tutoring causes teachers to alter their teaching, tutoring may become required, further influencing what happens in the classroom and reproducing the following cycle: tutoring, changes in the curriculum, and tutoring in ways that privilege students with extra support.

Tutoring and Standardized Tests: Cramming without Learning

In spite of the growing power of the tutoring industry, it is not alone in impacting teaching and learning. It is functioning synergistically with the simultaneous ratcheting up of standards-based curriculum and standardized tests that have intensified with No Child Left Behind and A Race to the Top. Thus, in addition to PSAT, SAT, and AP test preparation, within today's educational climate, where students, schools, and teachers are increasingly evaluated on students' performances on standardized tests, some tutoring programs also offer classes on these mandated tests. As described in chapter 1, the increasing emphasis on standardized tests narrows curriculum and emphasizes rote memorization over critical thinking and active engagement (Wood 2004; Ochoa 2007).

Math teacher Val Sherman has felt "the brunt of the testing assessment," forcing her to change her teaching methods. This is negatively impacting student learning and creativity:

> Compared to how it was fifteen to twenty-five years ago, we had a lot more freedom to not teach this topic, teach something else, or take some time off and do a project. Which we really feel compelled not to do anymore because of so much pressure to get the students to know all the standards and test well on them . . . There were projects we used to do that we just don't do anymore, and it frustrates me a little bit . . . [H]aving lived through the CSTs [California Standards Tests] for the last five years, I'm thinking, maybe I shouldn't worry about it so much. Maybe I should just concentrate on teaching what I want to teach, the way I want to teach it, and the way I think the students would learn the best, and not worry whether or not I'm teaching all twenty-five standards in Algebra 2. In the end, we shortchange the students because we're trying so hard to get everything in that we don't spend enough time to make sure that they understand everything.

The requirement to cover so many standards leaves some questioning whether students are actually learning. This fast-paced mode of schooling puts a premium on quantity over quality—in this case more material at the expense of student understanding.

The irony of this speedup in education is that it may in turn fuel the belief that students need tutoring to actually learn all the material that is being introduced in class. As researcher Mai Thai writes, parent Melanie Tan expressed this sentiment:

> When I asked her what issues she thought some of the parents faced at SCHS, she said that it was "kind of funny," because there were "a lot of students" she had "a chance to talk to" . . . [She believes that] they need the tutoring to catch up, like AP tests, SAT tests, and that "they have to apply to some kind of class to catch up."

Together, the interaction of outcomes-based schooling, standardized testing, and tutoring for test performance may be fueling the emphasis on quantitative measurements of performance such as SAT scores and grade point averages (GPAs) as opposed to process and inquiry-based education. Val Sherman laments how this climate influences student learning:

> We have a student body that is probably typical now of being concerned with grades and getting into college and not so much with whether they are learning anything of significance. If I look at my thirty-plus-year career, that's not too atypical in a high school, but over the last ten or fifteen years, the students that I teach have gotten more that way and are less willing to do a project or an assignment, which forces them to think about things and put things together. They're more concerned about "what will get me a high score on the SAT, a good score on the AP?" and all those external things that are going to get them into UCLA or Berkeley or wherever. When I start to say, "Don't you want to know what this is 'cause it's interesting?" [They say,] "Not really."

Conclusion: An Accumulation of Privileges and Losses

An analysis of tutoring and its many variations reveals the often unspoken accumulation of privileges, where students with the most types of school-sanctioned capital—economic, social, and cultural—are able to build additional forms. Their parents have the funds and networks to pay for and access accelerated and long-term tutoring programs that also facilitate connections to institutional agents and peer relations. For such students in the IB program, there is a tutoring cycle. As students progress through years of tutoring, they may move from tutee to tutor, where they are able to amass additional capital that assists them on their paths to higher education. This reinforces a cycle of privilege, and it compares with students who have no tutoring or short-term, as-needed tutoring where enduring ties with tutors and fellow tutees are less likely.

In spite of the benefits that accrue to some students from tutoring, there are important losses. To the extent that tutoring reproduces the current direction of schooling, regimented and narrowly focused programs may fuel an emphasis on competition and quantitative evaluations of performance over creativity, inquiry, and a love of learning. Furthermore, the tutoring enterprise and its financial supporters benefit economically by exploiting parents' fears and desires for their children. All this leaves unaddressed important questions about why so many students feel the need for tutoring, what is happening in classes and schools that propel this perceived need, and how public schooling benefits private interests. Finally, in its current form, tutoring is another practice that divides students and reproduces hierarchies. The divisions, resentment, and even outright hostility that too many students have for one another is intensified in the racialized climate detailed in the following chapter.

PART III

Everyday Relationships and Forms of Resistance

CHAPTER FIVE

"They Just Judge Us by Our Cover"

Students' Everyday Experiences with Race

Once the Star-Spangled Banner is done, the two large screens at the side of the stage show a mock news broadcast. A student of Asian background, Tanya Song, is the news reporter and tells the viewers of a reported crime. Unaga, the chief investigator, is a young man of Asian background that shows up on the screen speaking English in an exaggerated East Asian accent. Initially, he says some nonsense words like "Mitsibishi." His demeanor is frantic, and Tanya seems to want to laugh at his exaggerated accent.

—*Field notes, Mai Thai, May 23, 2008*

The opening of the school's final rally of the year encapsulates the racialized climate permeating SCHS and shaping everyday experiences. Organized by a student group and attended by students and staffuly, this rally used music, dance, and the quoted storyline to announce awards such as Most Improved Students, Salutatorian, Valedictorian, and Club of the Year. Like schools across the nation, it publically congratulated students who have been able to fulfill dominant expectations of schooling. In so doing, it reinforced the power-evasive discourses detailed in chapter 1 and the beliefs of individualism and meritocracy. The disparate resources influencing academic success were ignored. The assumption is that individual talent and work ethic are solely responsible for academic success. Similarly, by beginning with the Star-Spangled Banner and mocking accents and Asian immigrants in particular, this rally reproduced an assimilationist imperative that maintains the racial/ethnic hierarchies undergirding students' relationships and perceptions.

Shifting from a focus on the macro and meso factors fueling a socially constructed *academic* hierarchy at SCHS that position middle-class and upper-middle-class Asian Americans as a group at the top and working-class Latinas/os at the bottom, this chapter centers the narratives of students to understand how they experience and enact these dynamics in their relationships in ways that foster both academic *and* social hierarchies. Whereas Asian Americans are perceived as "smart" and expected to outperform their classmates academically, they are often positioned near the bottom of a *social* hierarchy. The results are differential experiences of invisibility on campus. Relative to one another, academically, Latinas/os may be underestimated and not seen, while socially, Asian Americans may be forgotten.

As with the many intersecting factors influencing an academic hierarchy, the dynamics shaping a social hierarchy are equally as complex. In particular, students' narratives highlight the significance of two dominant ideologies linked to the cultural deficiency perspectives and the silence surrounding whiteness detailed in chapter 1. They are at the crux of these hierarchies and maintain White supremacy: an assimilationist imperative and a "model minority" myth. An assimilationist imperative expects all to integrate into U.S. society by acquiring the English language and middle-class U.S. values and traditions. While this imperative has fluctuated during the past century—from justifying Americanization programs through the 1950s to the continual debates surrounding English-only practices, bilingual education, and immigration, it has been a mainstay in the United States. Oftentimes underlying it is the belief of Anglo superiority where the Spanish language, Asian languages, and those who speak these languages are perceived as inferior to the English language and U.S.-born residents.

The "model minority" myth has worked in tandem with this imperative by positioning Asian Americans as the example for successfully adapting to the United States. Within this construct, Asian Americans are depicted as hard working, passive, compliant, and malleable in opposition to Latinas/os and African Americans (see Espiritu 2000). Asian Americans are positioned as "good" students and "proper" members of immigrant groups who presumably follow school expectations relative to Latinas/os and African Americans who are deemed "bad" (Lee 2005, 5). Yet, on the other hand, Asian Americans are often cast as social outsiders who are "forever foreigners" (Tuan 1998). As Nazli Kibria describes, as part of this construction, "Asian American students are often stereotyped as overly studious and socially awkward nerds who raise the grading curve and so make life difficult for everyone else" (2002, 133). Thus there is a double bind. Asian Americans are often seen as exceptional and used as exemplars to discipline Latinas/os and Blacks, and yet they may not be seen as good enough *socially* to be fully accepted as "Americans."

Such assimilationist and "model minority" ideologies are, in the words of Yen Le Espiritu (2000), "ideological assaults." Along with perpetuating and justifying racialized academic and social hierarchies, they pit groups of color against each other, and they maintain whiteness as the unnamed norm and in a privileged position (Feagin 2001; Lee 2005). At SCHS, the racial privilege of Whites is ignored, and White students appear to encounter greater academic flexibility and options to select peer groups. As detailed in this chapter, the manifestations of these "ideological assaults" reverberate microscopically in the perceptions and messages of staffulty, families, and students. Such beliefs are part of a racialized climate that influences students' sense of selves, fuels their separation, and fosters the invisibility and privileging of whiteness.

Staffulty's Racialized Messages and an Academic Hierarchy at SCHS

As chapter 1 details, many of the staffulty adopt biological and cultural arguments to understand educational outcomes. These frameworks rooting academic achievement in assumptions surrounding innate intelligence and differing values by race/ethnicity are often enacted inside the classroom, where students encounter disparate expectations and treatment based on racialized assumptions.

Students, such as sophomore April Lee, are keenly aware of teachers' expectations that position Asian Americans at the top of the school's academic hierarchy:

> When a teacher looks at you and your face, [they think,] "Oh, you're Asian." She must be really smart, or she must be really good at math . . . They have that expectation that Asians have to be in honors. If they're not in honors, something's wrong.

Sophomore May Tran concurs:

> They expect a lot from me because they think I'm smart. When they look at me, people will say, "Oh, she's smart" because I'm Asian, but I'm not taking honors classes or anything, and then they'll just assume I'm smart. And then when I get a bad test score or something, they'll say, "Oh, why did you get this score?"

Both April Lee and May Tran are labeled as "smart," and if they do not abide by others' expectations and enroll in honors courses or perform well on tests, it is assumed that "something's wrong" with *them*. Such assumptions overlook the multiple structures and school practices shaping students' experiences.

Believing that all Asian Americans are the same is constraining for students, and it ignores students' diverse backgrounds. For April and May, among their differences are their generations, ethnicities, socioeconomic backgrounds, and interests. Born in Japan to Chinese parents, April spent her early years in China. She and her mother then moved to Southern California before April started elementary school. Her parents earned college degrees—her father in China and her mother at California State University, Los Angeles. Her mother is an accountant for a large firm, and her father manages a golf course in China. In addition to participating in mock trial and playing the piano, she enjoys taking pictures, dancing, swimming, and playing tennis. In comparison, May's family migrated from Vietnam two decades before the Lees. They live in a working-class community where May's mother maintains the home and her father is a mechanic. May spends her free time on the computer and "hanging out" with friends. Such differences are integral to how the two students perceive of themselves, and they illustrate their unequal resources. Nevertheless, the application of the "model minority" myth masks these differences and blames Asian Americans when they do not meet staffulty's high expectations.

Part of being positioned at the top of the school's academic hierarchy is the unequal treatment junior Becky Han characterizes as being racist toward or favoring Asian Americans in the classroom:

> I don't know if there's a trend, but I do know sometimes my honors teachers like Asians . . . They usually talk to them like friends, and then for other people they're like, "Why are you complaining?"

Becky knows that such preferred treatment comes with a cost. Not only does it typecast students, but it can also be rescinded if students do not comply with teachers' expectations. Socially, it is known to breed resentment from students who are treated inferiorly and can limit students' opportunities to build cross-racial/ethnic relationships (see Rosenbloom and Way 2004). With an awareness of these injustices, Becky advocates,

> I'm Chinese, and lots of people pressure you to do good, and they want you to succeed more. It's kind of not fair to other races. I think everyone should be pushed, but we get pushed more than Mexicans, Blacks, and Whites.

Recalling his physical education (PE) teacher, senior Mike Song agrees that staffulty differentially treat students even to the extent that their inaction fuels student divisions:

> Some of the teachers kind of take sides too. Like, in my freshman PE, some of the Mexican girls were like, "Oh, let's do a Mexican versus Asians game." So we were playing baseball, and we were Mexicans versus Asians and then the teacher doesn't do anything . . . I don't know if he was kidding or not, but [the teacher] actually said, "I honestly don't like Asians."

This condoning of race/ethnic-based teams, along with explicit displays of favoritism, aggravates already precarious relationships that are unequally structured at the school.

Just as members of the staffulty are critiqued for placing high expectations on and favoring Asian Americans, the opposite often exists for Latinas/os. Teacher Michele Mesa shares a concern articulated by several Latina/o teachers:

> I've had Hispanic students cry to me saying, "I'm so frustrated because I don't know what to do because no matter what I do it will never be good enough for teacher A because she or he favors the Asian students, gives them more attention, will ask the discussion questions only of them, and ignores us like we are not even there."

Sitting in during one of her colleague's after-school tutorials because of what she had learned from a Latina family member, teacher Mary Dupont observed this differential treatment:

> Some teachers on this campus focus primarily on one ethnic group . . . I went to all the tutoring and I watched. I even snuck in the back to see, and never once did [my family member] get attention. The Asian students that were on the left side of the room, immediately the teacher was over there, and there was my [family member] sitting with other kids. Two of her friends that were with her were Asian and the other three were Hispanic; and [they received] *nothing*, which boggled my mind.

Even teachers encounter these inequalities such that there is imbalanced support among their colleagues for working with Asian Americans and Latinas/os. Teacher Manuel Cadena explains,

> There is an underlying understanding that when you deal with Latino students, it's almost like [administrators and teachers] tell you, "Good luck." We wanted to start a MEChA [a Mexican American student organization], "Good luck with that," or we wanted to help out the Latino students or make a Latino parent group, "Good luck with that." Where anything that deals with Asian students, [we get,] "That's awesome." Everyone congratulates you. When you start a club with the Asian students, people automatically stamp "success"

> on it, and they support you 100 percent . . . It's an underlying, "I
> don't think you're going to make it" kind of thing [with Latinas/os].

Staffulty's comments send powerful messages about students' supposed abilities. For Korean-identified Patty Song, teachers' judgments "kinda hurt" because "we can't be different. We have to stick to a certain crowd." It is assumed not only that Asian American students are smart and good students but also that they will befriend other supposedly smart and dedicated Asian American students. Likewise, a similar form of racialized lumping occurs that reinforces racist beliefs that Latinas/os will not succeed. These messages and unequal treatments result in a self-perpetuating academic racial/ethnic hierarchy that also emerges from some of the messages conveyed by students' families.

Families Socializing Racial/Ethnic Inequality

Several Asian American students report how their parents have socialized them to keep their distance from Latina/o students because they believe that Latinas/os are dangerous and lazy, and at least one Mexican American student's father questioned why she remained in advanced placement courses with so many Asian Americans. These comments can influence students' perceptions of themselves and of their peers.

Junior Margaret Kang is one among several Asian American students who described being raised with a pejorative perception of Latinas/os and forbidden by her Taiwanese immigrant parents to befriend them. She explains by juxtaposing her beliefs with her parents:

> [Latinos] are very open. Like less conservative, compared to Asians,
> and I think they're carefree, and they could care less about school, but
> that's not a bad thing. But then my parents call Latinos stupid, and
> they told me not to hang out with them.

Margaret Kang echoes prevailing representations of Latinas/os and Asian Americans that permeate the interviews. However, she does not place a value judgment on this supposed difference, but neither does she deconstruct these assumptions. Instead, she critiques her parents for stereotyping.

Second-generation Chinese-identified Tommy Huie observes individual forms of racism by his father and other Asian American parents who have accepted these assumptions:

> From what I've seen, like a lot of Asian people are really racist and
> they say everything good about their own people and they just disre-
> gard everything else. Personally, my dad is freaking racist, to the max.

He went to China and he saw a Black guy in a line for a restaurant and in Chinese he yelled out loud, "What is this Black guy doing here?" and the Black guy turns around, and he speaks in perfect Chinese. He's like, "I'm here to buy food," and my dad just shuts up.

Tommy is critically conscious of these exclusionary beliefs and actions. Nonetheless, given their prevalence, they still seep into his thoughts, stilting his relationships. He recalls with interviewer Chris Fiorello his initial opinion when he was one of the few Asian Americans enrolled in a college preparatory geometry class:

> TOMMY: The first day when I walked in there, it was like my parents were saying, "Oh, Mexicans are dangerous." I sat in my own corner by myself. But after a while, I just relaxed and then got to know some of them.
>
> INTERVIEWER CHRIS FIORELLO: What do you think the kids were thinking of you when you were sitting in the corner?
>
> TOMMY: Who's that little nerdy kid over there? [Laughs.] And you know what I was thinking and I knew what they were thinking? We didn't really match up together, but after a while it was like, whatever.

Although some Asian Americans are instructed by parents to draw boundaries around themselves and away from Latinas/os, as Mexican American parent Ramon Vasquez reveals, his daughter stays away from Asian Americans. In this case, he attributes this distance to their low placement on the school's *social* hierarchy:

> They're a lot of the Asian nerds, and she didn't want to hang around them. She's very social, athletic, etcetera, and those kids just didn't hang around the same circle.

Even though most of his daughter's classmates in the school's advanced placement courses are Asian Americans, Ramon Vasquez believes "she wouldn't get close to them." By juxtaposing his daughter who he considers "very social" with "those kids," Ramon reinforces a binary construction that lumps Asian Americans together and favors one way of being over another. He emphasizes the importance of students being not so "driven and compulsive towards the academics":

> Back to my point about all these Asian kids being so unbalanced, and not participating in regular athletic events. Even if they're unorganized, just regular throwing the ball, kicking the ball and running around, that type of thing' [they don't do].

This middle-class and U.S.-centric conception of "balance" puts a premium on participating in sports and doing well academically—traits Ramon Vasquez associates less with Asian Americans than with Latinas/os such as his daughter.

Rather than completely disregarding all Asian Americans as, earlier, Margaret Kang's parents seem to do with Latinas/os, Ramon Vasquez attributes some positive characteristics to this panethnic group, even while he homogenizes them:

> I think the Asians are good. For whatever reason, they value education a
> lot, and they work very, very hard. It's no secret they know hard work.

Although he apparently praises Asian Americans, such generalizations do not allow for variations, and these characterizations may fuel divisions between groups since the implication is that other groups do not possess a similar work ethic.

Family's racialized messages not only influence children's friendships, but in the context of similar prevailing beliefs and exclusionary practices, these messages can hinder how students perceive themselves too. Junior Miriam Liang, who believes that Asian American parents exert more pressure on their children to excel than other parents do, shares how occasionally she regrets being Asian American because of these pressures:

> My mom compares me to other people, and when I don't get good
> grades, she goes, "How come so and so can get good grades, and I
> don't see you trying hard enough?" I try to explain to her and she's
> like, "You always use excuses." She doesn't want to hear it. It's
> sometimes really hard because it's kind of stressful. Sometimes I wish
> I wasn't Asian, but unfortunately I am.

At times, children may get angry and wish they had different parents, but in this example, Miriam gets mad at more than her mother. She is upset that she is Asian American. Miriam does not individualize her mother's expectations of her. Instead, she attributes her mother's messages to being Asian. Such generalizing to all Asian American families may stem from Miriam's knowledge of others' high expectations of her and the assumptions that frame Asian Americans as hard working and academically successful. Thus the same homogenizing processes that do not allow Asian Americans to be seen as individuals may be influencing Miriam's perception of her mother and of her own racial/ethnic identity.

To cope with these pressures to excel, Miriam has adopted two approaches. She imagines not being Asian, and as she explains, she has altered her approach toward schooling: "When I was little, I used to care a lot and try, but right now, I don't really care, well maybe. I can't be something that I'm not." Such comments reveal the power of other's expectations. They also suggest that maybe Miriam is trying to carve out her own sense of self. Perhaps this self-awareness will squelch the pressure she feels to distance herself from being Asian and even from her mother.

While Miriam is constrained by narrow constructions that equate Asian Americanness with being high achieving and having strict parents, Mexican-identified Summer Reyes is also limited by others' assumptions. For Summer, these constraints are a reflection of the socially constructed Asian American–Latina/o academic binary. Like Miriam, Summer feels these larger pressures intimately within her own family.

Introduced in chapter 3, Summer is the child of Mexican immigrants and among a small group of Latinas/os enrolled in the school's honors and advanced placement courses. At times, the isolation and awareness of the racial/ethnic skewing in her courses are difficult. It has taken awhile for her to feel that she belongs in these classes. However, this sense of belonging has been complicated by her family's judgments. One time when her father visited SCHS and observed the demographics of Summer's math class, Summer was again forced to rethink her place in these courses:

> My precalc class, I'm the only non-Asian. I sometimes feel like I
> shouldn't belong there because the class is really hard. I remember for
> back-to-school night, my dad came back home, and he's like, "Are
> you the only non-Asian?" I was like, "Yeah." And he's like, "I don't
> think you should go there anymore."

When Summer asked her father why he felt she should not return to the class, he offered no explanation. This left Summer unsure and speculating about her abilities. In the context of the school climate, one wonders if Summer's father was trying to shield her from others' negative perceptions or if he actually thought that maybe she did not have the capability to excel in precalculus. After all, as Summer shares, although she identifies as "completely Mexican," given her academic success where she has a 4.0 grade point average, her family teases her that she is not really Mexican:

> In my family, around my cousins, I'm the smartest one, supposedly.
> One of them looks up to me, and the rest just ignore me: "Oh, she's too
> good for us. She's an Asian." They constantly like making fun of me.

Such jokes about Summer's identity are hurtful. Not only does she encounter a racial/ethnic academic hierarchy at school that impacts her sense of belonging in top courses, but even with some members of her family, she feels shunned because she does not fit into their image of Mexicans. Having to endure such comments has also influenced Summer's sense of self, as the previous example was among the first she shared when she was asked how she identifies. As long as fixed constructions exist and school officials and family members reproduce them, students will have a difficult time contesting them.

Strained Peer Perceptions and Relationships

With limited cross-racial/ethnic and class interactions and scant knowledge about racial/ethnic histories provided to them in their courses, students often rely on stereotyped messages as their main source of information about one another. These stereotyped messages are part of the "ideological assaults" on people of color that are often replicated in everyday exchanges.

The Four Ss and Academic and Social Hierarchies

Early in their sophomore year, friends Vivian Chen, Terra Lee, and Lauren Chan sat down with then a student at the Claremont Colleges Kendall Parker for two separate hour-long discussions. They joked, built on one another's ideas, and discussed the perceptions of their peers and how these conceptions influence their relationships:

> VANESSA: People think of Asians as really smart and [says low and nervously] Mexicans are like stupid, and then African Americans are scary. That's how people separate them.
>
> INTERVIEWER KENDALL PARKER: So how do you feel that has affected you?
>
> LAUREN: We stay away from them.
>
> VANESSA: We stick together, I guess.
>
> INTERVIEWER KENDALL PARKER: Why do you stay away?
>
> LAUREN: Because they might make fun of us or something.

Vanessa and Lauren describe some of the "controlling images" that shape racial/ethnic hierarchies and peer relations at SCHS (see Collins 1990). In the words of sociologist Patricia Hill Collins, "These controlling images are designed to make racism, sexism, poverty, and other forms of social injustice appear to be natural, normal, and inevitable parts of everyday life" (2000, 69). By typecasting and then blaming groups of people, the larger factors shaping inequalities are ignored.

Along with the binary association of "smartness" and "stupidness" with Asian Americans and Mexicans, a prevailing construct of African Americans at the school is that they are "scary." Other students refer to African

Americans as "sports" or "sporty." These characterizations are what I refer to as the four Ss. They are among the dominant images of students of color at SCHS that fuel academic and social hierarchies; they exist in relationship to one another, and they often are linked to student separation.

Senior Jessica Su's comments capture the extent of her schoolmates' beliefs:

> I hear these jokes a lot. If you are Asian, you have to be smart. It is like the most common thing at this school . . . I am not the smartest kid out there, but if I discuss what I got on a test and I got a D, my Hispanic friend goes, "What? But you are Asian!"

Sophomore friends Nat Punyawong, Mark Ku, and Kathy Hsin concur that these images of Asian Americans are pervasive, fostering academic as well as social hierarchies:

> NAT: They probably typecast us as Asian people.
> MARK: Depends on what race they are.
> NAT: Yeah, that's one thing.
> MARK: Pretend these guys, Mexicans, don't know me, they would be like, "Oh, he's smart, yeah. He's a nerd."
> NAT: They'll probably say we have no friends.
> MARK: They just judge us by our cover.

Sophomore friends Gloria Camacho and Rebecca Ramos illustrate Nat and Mark's point, and they react to these dominant beliefs by reinforcing additional stereotypes:

> GLORIA: I kind of feel awkward with a lot of Asian people. I just feel different.
> GILDA OCHOA: How come?
> GLORIA: Usually, they're way smarter than us.
> REBECCA: That, too, they feel above us.
> GLORIA: They feel like they're better . . . Also, maybe inside we get jealous a little 'cause they're way smarter, and we're always talking about, "Oh, Asians don't know how to drive. They always crash." I think that's true; they always crash.
> REBECCA: It's 'cause they can't really see good 'cause of their eyes.

This dialogue between Gloria and Rebecca was direct and very serious, indicating that they seem to believe these biological arguments about intelligence and driving capabilities.

Even students who appear to offer more nuanced descriptions of their Asian American schoolmates still reinforce dominant images connected to academics and conceptions of popularity. For instance, senior Mallory Walker believes that with further assimilation into the United States, Asian Americans move from being "smart" and "nerdy" to "cool":

> The [Asians] that have an accent, they are really smart. The ones that don't have accents, those are the ones that are cool . . . When they come here, they are really nerdy. But when they already were here, a lot of times they are cool 'cause they're not that close to their parents. They aren't all strict, so they are more laid back like everybody else.

By naming the characteristics determining "coolness" at school—being U.S. born, speaking without an Asian accent, and being more "laid back"—Mallory illustrates the expectation of assimilation. However, given the previous comments by Mark and Nat, one wonders if such assimilation necessarily results in "coolness" for all Asian Americans. To the extent that they are prejudged, they may still be typecast and seen as not American and not cool.

Similarly, sophomore Jung Kim, who qualifies his characterizations with words such as "sometimes" and introduces the significance of class in influencing types of students, depicts Asian Americans in just two main ways:

> The smart people, which are mostly Asians, sometimes they play basketball. A lot of times, they wear their sports uniforms during lunchtime and class times, and I don't really like them because they think they're all that. They're like, "Oh, I play basketball. I'm so cool. I'm into all the latest fashions." I don't know what it's called, but there's something like Spitch or something, or Abercrombie, I don't know the brand.

As a Korean-identified student, Jung offers a more complex and multidimensional description of the Asian American students he labels as "smart." In his estimation, they also play basketball and are able to afford the latest name brand clothes such as Abercrombie and Fitch. This equation of brand name clothes with popularity reveals the role of class in influencing popularity. Furthermore, given several marketing strategies used by Abercrombie and Fitch—such as in 2002 when Asian Americans were caricatured on store t-shirts and in 2006 when CEO Mike Jeffries described how the company "go[es] after the attractive all-American kid"—the correlation of this brand with coolness may also be assimilationist since Abercrombie and Fitch presents an image of revering thinness, middle- and upper-classness, and whiteness (see Strasburg 2002; Denizet-Lewis 2006).

Continuing with a description of his peers, Jung Kim includes a second type of Asian American student:

> There's the Asians, not all Asians, but the Asians who are kind of
> nerdy, kind of outcasts, but they're all into the Japanese stuff, anime,
> or they're just too much into—I'm into games, but then I don't go
> around talking about them all the time.

Interestingly, Jung does not perceive of himself in either of these prevailing images of "smart" or "nerdy," revealing the limitations of these characterizations. As he describes "nerdy" students, he realizes that he too plays video games, but he clarifies that he does not fit into this description.

While Jung is unique among the Asian American participants, in that most presented more complex descriptions of other Asian Americans, the power of the "model minority" myth on one's sense of self is still undeniable. The myth negatively affects some students like sophomore Nancy Chang, who occasionally feels "ashamed of [being Chinese] 'cause everyone judges us so differently, like how they say, 'Oh, you must be smart,' and you know it's not like that." She explains, "'Cause whenever I'm doing something, it's kind of the racial theme, so like, 'Aren't you Asian?' 'Yeah, but I don't have to go with the stereotype.'"

On the flip side of associating Asian Americans and "smart" is the similar recurring pattern of equating Latinas/os and occasionally African Americans with the other extreme as "stupid." Junior Jennifer Cortez illustrates,

> A lot of the Asian kids at school, they try to make it seem as though
> all Hispanic kids are dumb, which really aggravates me . . . [I]n my
> [precalculus] class, this one kid's all, "Oh, wow, this is rare, a Mexi-
> can [student] is teaching an Asian person how to do math."

Jennifer is frustrated by the constant judgment she encounters. Thus, in an attempt to thwart the stereotypes used against her, like Gloria and Rebecca, Jennifer invokes an equally harmful stereotype about Asian Americans:

> I'm like, "Dude, you guys can't even drive a car and that's common
> sense. If you don't have common sense, that doesn't mean you're
> smart." I'm sorry, but how can you be smart without common sense?

Angered by others' assumptions, students often apply other stereotypes in order to defend themselves. As hurtful as this response is and even though it complicates prevailing conceptions of "smartness," it does not alleviate the insecurities and additional tensions that arise from the constant academic profiling. Jennifer continues,

> Yesterday in my precalculus class, some of the Asian kids, they didn't
> really understand it, but I did. So it actually made me feel better
> about myself. Usually, they try to make it as though Hispanic people
> are dumb. I'm like, "You're wrong dude. I actually understand it and
> you don't." So that gave me some more pride in myself.

The construction that Asian Americans are more intelligent and perform better at school is so powerful that some Latinas/os may act on it as truth, or even if they do not act on it, their behaviors may nonetheless be interpreted through dominant assumptions. For example, junior Ricky Liu and his friend are convinced that the following illustrates how some of their schoolmates have internalized prevailing beliefs:

> My Korean friend, he took summer school 'cause he failed the
> course . . . Blacks and Mexicans come up to him and say, "Oh, let us
> borrow your homework." They automatically assume that he knows
> how to do his work, and he doesn't; he's not like automatically bright,
> so I guess they expect that Asian people are going to be automatically
> smart and nerds, even if they're in a remedial class.

Regardless of whether Ricky and his friend's analysis is correct, by asking for their classmate's homework, the students in this summer class end up reinforcing the prevailing stereotypes about Asian Americans and themselves. While it is not unusual for students to ask each other for their homework, given the prevalence of racial lumping where Asian Americans, Latinas/os, and Blacks are often not seen as individuals, their actions are interpreted through the school's racialized climate.

Just as "smartness" is juxtaposed with "stupidness," so is the assumption that Asian Americans are good, dutiful, law-abiding students in comparison to Latinos and African Americans, who are typecast as engaging in illegal and threatening activities that make them "scary." Sophomore Nat Punyawong, who earlier critiqued being judged superficially, here perpetuates assumptions about Mexicans:

> MARK KU: I guess we do that too [judge people by their cover]—
> NAT PUNYAWONG: We do that too, but prove us wrong.
> KATHY HSIN: We're nice.
> NAT: Yeah, we're nice about it. Prove us wrong. Prove me wrong that
> like 80 percent of Mexican people at this school don't do drugs.
> Prove me wrong.

Part of the characterization of illegality and "scariness" is the belief that Latinos and African Americans are "gangsters." Junior Eric Han is convinced that this is not a stereotype but a fact:

> To be honest, I think, a lot of students, I'm not stereotyping at this point because it's true, especially Hispanics and Blacks, some are gangsters; some think they are all tough and everything.

Although Eric softens his language from "a lot" to "some," he still uses a broad stroke to portray his schoolmates. Similarly, sophomore Jung Kim, who earlier described Asian Americans as either "smart" or "nerdy," locates Latinos along the other end of the spectrum:

> The gangster people, they all think they're bad and they wear the bandannas sometimes, but they're not allowed to. They wear really long shirts or they talk in like Black talk. I don't know what they call it, but slang, and then those people usually don't work in class . . . mostly Mexicans who do that, 'cause there's not many African Americans here. They kind of intimidate people. They look intimidating, but then if you talk to them they're kind of cool, but then, they're pretty strong, and they look pretty scary.

The assumption underlying Jung's characterization is that at SCHS those who are "gangsters" and less concerned about school are mostly Mexican, but if there were more African Americans at the school, they too would fall into this category. After all, Jung claims that "Black talk" is the equivalent of the "slang" used by those he assumes are in gangs. In spite of these generalizations, Jung clarifies that while these typecasted students "intimidate people," there are exceptions. When he has had the opportunity to interact with some, he has realized that they are OK; they just look "scary."

Jung Kim is not alone in associating both "scariness" and "coolness," especially applying them to African American males. Senior Mike Song applies these representations and adds to them the belief that Blacks excel in sports as well:

> There's another group, I don't hate them but I fear them a little bit and those are Blacks or African Americans. I think they're really cool 'cause, I know I'm making a generalization again, but most of them that I meet are really good at sports. They're really big, and they can dunk.

These racialized and gendered assumptions of "scariness," "coolness," and "good at sports" are rooted in racialized hegemonic constructions of masculinity that place a premium on physical size and athletic ability. They are also part of a legacy of differential representations of men of color where dominant media constructions and public perceptions simultaneously criminalize and hypermasculinize Latinos and African Americans while Asian Americans are often emasculated (Davis 1981; Espiritu 2000; Feagin 2001). These racist images have a long history in the dominant imagination and have been constructed as a pretext for White hostility (Frankenberg 1993) and used to justify intensive policing and anti-immigrant policies. In contrast to these images, prevailing representations of White heterosexual men cast them as the model of masculinity by which all others are compared.

For a couple of students, their equation of Blacks with "sports" is rooted in long-standing racist beliefs they learned from their parents. Junior Matt Lee's reflections on the school's basketball team are illustrative:

> MATT: I heard that the basketball team is all Black students. The junior varsity team is like all the Asians and Hispanics and then, even though it is like 2 percent Blacks in the school, most of the varsity is Black.
>
> INTERVIEWER MARKUS KESSLER: And why do you think that is?
>
> MATT: I heard that Blacks are naturally buffer and have smaller lung capacity that sort of thing.
>
> INTERVIEWER MARKUS KESSLER: Where did you hear that?
>
> MATT: My parents. So Black people can't swim. They can lift heavy weights and stuff. That's what they say. I have no proof.

Ironically, at roughly 80 percent of the players, Asian Americans are the group overrepresented on SCHS's basketball team. Nevertheless, Matt, who reports that he has no support for his beliefs, still accepts his inaccurate biological claims.

According to junior Ricky Liu, these constructions of masculinity position Black males higher on the school's *social* hierarchy than Asian American males:

> Automatically, if you're Black, you get more respect. If you're Black, they won't mess with you. If you're Asian and you're small, you're not going to get any respect. If you're walking around, people are going to bump into you. They don't give a crap. Um, if you're White, I don't know [laughs].

Within the context of the derogatory perceptions of African Americans at SCHS, Ricky's application of the word "respect" is overstated. However, the testimonials of a couple of Asian Americans suggest that they may be subjected to different types of peer harassment than other young men of color on campus. Sophomore Jung Kim recalls attempts by students to steal his money during lunch, as campus security looked on:

> I'm standing in line, and these bunch of Mexicans behind me, they just open up my backpack and start taking out all my stuff, and the security guard is standing right next to me, and he didn't do anything. He saw the people taking stuff from my backpack, and thank god I had my money in my pocket.

Jung remembers this incident as a violation by his peers and by an adult who did nothing to stop it. Likewise, Mike Song recounts multiple experiences where Latinas/os have jostled him:

> Me and my friend were walking pretty close 'cause we were talking about something, and then all of a sudden this Mexican girl pushes me out of the way.
>
> There's lots of cases where some Mexican girls always used to touch my butt or something. It's so random. I know they're messing around, but I don't know.
>
> There's this one time where I was walking up the stairs right here, and then one of the Mexican kids, they just touched my ass. So I was like, "What's your problem, man?" Then he's like, "What, you homo[sexual]?" I was like, "Yeah, I'm homo. I'm homophobic."

Asian American men were the only students to describe such experiences. As Susan Rosenbloom (2010) has also recounted in her research in a multiracial high school, these experiences, where Asian Americans are being pushed and grabbed, may stem from Latinas'/os' resentment toward the relative academic privileging Asian Americans typically experience compared to Latinas/os. However, given the hegemonic construction of Asian American men as effeminate and asexual, such sexualized grabbing may also be an attempt to threaten a student's masculinity. Espiritu describes, "Disseminated and perpetuated through the media, these stereotypes of the emasculated Asian male construct a reality in which social and economic discrimination of Asian men appear defensible" (2000, 91). The SCHS school climate fuels animosity, negative perceptions, and hostile campus spaces, especially since such harassment is often left unaddressed. In fact, Jung Kim and Mark Song expressed some of the most disdain for their schoolmates. As is evident in Mark's third example earlier, he responded by proclaiming he is homophobic, and earlier in his interview, he stated, "I don't like Mexicans for some reason. I know I'm making a hasty generalization about this one incident, but then these incidents multiply."

Because they have had limited experiences with Latinas/os and Blacks, Jung and Mark have little context to understand these incidents. If they and the students they describe had other, more consistent, collaborative, and nonhierarchical interactions, it is possible that Jung and Mark would be better able to understand such incidents or that such hostile exchanges would be replaced with more productive and less hateful relationships (Ochoa, Enriquez, Hamada, and Rojas 2012).

Overall, the equation of different racial/ethnic groups on campus with the four Ss work in tandem with larger ideologies, school structures, institutional practices, and the staffulty's messages to perpetuate racialized academic *and* social hierarchies that fuel students' separation. Senior Maggie Cordova best illustrates these dual academic and social hierarchies, where as a self-identified Mexican, she is ignored by the school's predominately Asian American newspaper staff, but outside of the journalism class, Asian Americans are the ones who are disregarded:

> When it comes to journalism, I'm the minority . . . [I]n that environment, I'm treated like I'm not really anything; I'm just there. And it's funny how, outside of journalism, like at lunch, no one talks to the Asians. They're just randomly here, and like the rest of us—the Hispanics, Blacks, and Whites—are the majority.

As others have also found, invisibility often symbolizes a group's low status (Ellison 1947; Rollins 1985; Romero 2002). Thus these dual examples of invisibility may reflect the simultaneous marginalization of Latinas/os academically and Asian Americans socially.

Even students who wish to contest exclusionary thinking and divisive relationships find it difficult to cross racial/ethnic divides because of the power of school structures and others' beliefs. Focusing on the role of controlling images in hindering friendships, juniors Miriam Liang and Jenny Tuan explain to interviewer Laura Enriquez,

> MIRIAM: It's just Asians hang out with Asians and other races hang out with the same races. Yeah, it would be really nice if we could all get to know each other more, like different backgrounds.
>
> INTERVIEWER LAURA ENRIQUEZ: So why do you think Asians hang out with only Asians?
>
> JENNY: Well, I don't think this way, but some Asians think they're higher because of their grades and their background, so they don't want to hang out with anyone who's lower than them 'cause they think that's not going to help them in any way. And maybe Mexicans, they don't

want to hang out with Asians because they think we're snobbish or
something. So they don't really like us.

Junior Tommy Huie agrees that transgressing racialized boundaries is difficult. Not only must he contend with the racist beliefs transmitted since
he was young by his father that he shared earlier, but he must also navigate the exclusionary belief of many of his classmates:

> Going out of my bubble into the Mexican world, not world, but it's really
> different for us and they look down on us sometimes, saying we're not
> outgoing and stuff. So when we try to reach out to them, they shun us.

Without the support of the school in creating nonhierarchical opportunities for students to work together or in providing students with the
skills to deconstruct hegemonic images, those who try to cross socially
constructed lines may encounter yet again the four Ss. Likewise, in some
cases, these images are confounded by additional racialized representations described next.

Overestimating Asian Americans and Underestimating
Latinas/os: "The Yellow Peril" and Latina/o Invisibility

Although Asian American are 46 percent of the SCHS students compared
to Latinas/os, who are 43 percent and the group who is gradually increasing
in numbers at the school, there is a common perception by Latinas/os that
Asian Americans dominate the school demographically. Art Casas's comments are illustrative: "The school is mainly Asian, so [Asian school] is the
first thing that comes to mind [when I think of SCHS]."

Using words such as "Asian" and "non-Asian," even students' language
reveals this belief that most students at the school are Asian Americans.
Junior Sandra Mendez reflects,

> There are sooo many Asians, like they overpopulate our school. I
> have honors classes. So we feel like a minority . . . Whenever we do
> group projects, we always get together, and it is always the non-Asian
> and everybody else that are together. They look down on us. We
> know they do, 'cause they think we are stupid.

Sandra's comments mirror a prevailing trope within the United States that
portrays Asian Americans as assumed foreigners, invaders, and threats.
During different economic and political time periods, the U.S. media and
politicians have strategically portrayed various Asian countries and Asian
Americans as the "Yellow Peril." Historically, this image of being a threat

justified the Chinese Exclusion Act, the internment of Japanese Americans during World War II, and the war in Vietnam (Espiritu 2000). Today, it frames the image of North Korea, and in growing Asian American communities, it fuels anti-Asian hostility and English-only ordinances (for examples, see Saito 1998). These pervasive representations influence conceptions of Americanness and belonging. At SCHS, the image that Asian Americans are "overpopulat[ing] our school" could fuel the marginalization of Asian Americans as not belonging because the assumption is that they are not part of "our" school.

When highlighting the school's demographics, students occasionally draw on other racialized references that naturalize the idea that Asian Americans should be the majority in the school's top academic classes. The discussion of sophomore friends Araceli Castro and David Kim about the school's curriculum tracks is illustrative:

> ARACELI CASTRO: More Asians in the honors classes.
>
> DAVID KIM: Majority, yeah. It's more Asians. I mean the school is a majority of Asians, don't you think? Either way, [the honors classes] would be majority [Asian]. It's like saying, "How many Black people in the NBA and how many Whites would pass it?" It's the majority anyways, same exact thing.

Here again, the percentage of Asian Americans at the school is inflated. For David, this supposed higher percentage partially accounts for the larger number of Asian Americans in honors courses. However, he believes that even if Asian Americans were not a majority at the school, they would still predominate in these courses. To illustrate his point, he references the NBA (National Basketball Association) and assumes that the current higher participation of Black players over White players is natural, just as he implies that it is expected that Asian Americans excel academically. Thus, along with exaggerating the number of Asian Americans at the school, he draws on other stereotypes, naturalizing the assumption that Asian Americans are "smart" and Blacks excel in "sports."

As a dominant ideology, "Yellow Perilism" removes attention from structural and institutional practices that reproduce inequality, and it divides students. For example, as indicated earlier in her description of the school's demographics, Sandra Mendez is frustrated by the racial/ethnic skewing in the honors and advanced placement courses and the marginalization she experiences in these classes. However, by rooting all the blame in Asian Americans and excluding them from what she refers to as "our" school, a critique of the institutional factors and everyday exchanges that divide and rank students is lost. Blaming Asian Americans removes responsibility from the school and society for the unequal distribution of students in the top classes, and it also makes it more difficult for students to recognize their shared connections.

When analyzed in isolation, the overestimating of Asian Americans at SCHS may not always be a contemporary example of "Yellow Perilism." Overstating the percentages might be a reflection of students' friendship groups or classmates. However, it could also result from the simultaneous ignoring of Latinas/os academically based on some teachers' biases for Asian Americans or perhaps the school's public recognition in rallies and assemblies of select students who are often in the International Baccalaureate (IB) program and advanced placement (AP) courses and who tend to be middle-class and upper-middle-class Asian Americans. Since student invisibility often mirrors the marginalization of affected groups (see Lee 2005), in this case, it may indicate the lower *academic* positioning at SCHS of working-class Latinas/os. Thus, in the context of the historical construction of a supposed "Yellow Peril" and the other phenomena at the school—including anti-immigrant labeling detailed later, the overestimating of Asian Americans implies that they do not belong or are taking over. Similarly, the underestimating of Latinas/os may reflect the school structures and practices that marginalize many Latinas/os academically. In both cases, the over- and underestimating of students reproduce the larger dynamics occurring on campus.

Anti-Immigrant Sentiment, an Assimilationist Imperative, and Cross-Generational Tensions

Some of the same factors fueling cross-racial/ethnic divisions among students are replicated across generations. The child of Vietnamese immigrants, Billy Su succinctly illustrates the following:

> BILLY: We don't call them immigrants.
> GILDA OCHOA: Okay, then what do you call them?
> BILLY: FOBs [laughs].

Throughout their interviews, students frequently talked about immigrants. However, Asian Americans were most likely to label immigrants "FOBs" or fresh off the boat. Occasionally, like Billy, they applied the term to all immigrants distinguishing between students who are U.S. born and those who are not. Other times, they differentiated based on extent of assimilation. A few students laughed or stammered when using this label, revealing an understanding that it is a pejorative term, but in some cases, the term rolled off of their tongues as though it is part of their everyday conversations. The normalization of this label and the overall distancing from immigrants by many Asian Americans and a few Latinas/os reinforces an assimilationist imperative and a racial/ethnic hierarchy privileging the English language and other dominant values and norms.

Of all the students, Asian Americans were most likely to distinguish themselves from immigrants. As senior Jean Kim illustrates, this is often done through labeling and based on degrees of assimilation:

> I'm Korean, but then I am more Americanized than Koreanized. There are the FOBs; we call them fresh off the boat. They talk Korean amongst their friends, and then there are Asians. We, me and my friends we just talk in English, and we watch English movies and American televisions shows, but then when we talk with our FOB friends, everything is cool. It's just different what we like.

As the child of Korean immigrants, Jean was born in Chicago and raised in Los Angeles. She grew up bilingually, follows Korean traditions, celebrates Korean holidays, and watches movies and television in English. As a result of her bicultural upbringing, she feels more "Americanized" than her immigrant schoolmates, who she refers to as her "FOB friends" in comparison to those who she simply calls her friends. Jean indicates that there is no judgment behind the label "FOB," that it is used like "Asian" to acknowledge differences. Yet, just as Billy's laughter in the earlier interview implies, her qualifying language regarding her friends and her "FOB friends" suggests otherwise.

Often accompanying students' use of the acronym is a disparagement of immigrants and a blaming them for their position at the school. The following two Asian American sophomores, who earlier described the multiple Ss at SCHS, capture some students' rage toward immigrants:

> VANESSA CHEN: Then there's the FOBs.
> TERRA LEE: They don't speak English.
> VANESSA: Yeah, and they're really irritating because they are always speaking their own language.
> TERRA: Yeah, very loud.
> VANESSA: And it is like, "Just speak English!"

Although Vanessa and Terra are bilingual, and Terra came from Taiwan at the age of five, they are annoyed by schoolmates who do not abide by assimilationist expectations that include speaking English and in a relatively low tone when in public.

Along with language, divisions are drawn based on students' styles, suggesting the link between consumerism and Americanness (Lee 2005, 54; Olsen 1997). Second-generation Billy Su and May Lee offer the following description:

BILLY: The FOBs just choose to hang out together, and they have their own style.

GILDA OCHOA: So what's their style?

MAY: Like clothes.

BILLY: And their hairstyle is really long.

MAY: They decided to dye their hair bright. The guys have long hair like a lion [laughs].

As in this example and the earlier one about Abercrombie and Fitch, hairstyles and clothes may become important indicators used by students to mark group memberships and to physically differentiate themselves from other students (Bettie 2003, 62).

For some students, part of drawing boundaries around immigrants is to blame them for the generational separation on campus. Ivan Tam, an immigrant from Malaysia who moved to Southern California when he was seven years old, argues that immigrants are responsible for the divisions because, unlike him, they are not assimilating:

There's a lot of FOBs here. I'm a FOB, but people don't really see that in me because I don't really have an accent when I talk English and that's why they don't believe it when I say I wasn't born here. Other students, like the Asian students that come here from China or Taiwan, they choose to just keep on speaking Chinese. I know some FOBs that they don't really wish to learn English. Instead, they just hang with their close group of friends that are also FOBs, and they just talk in Chinese.

Agreeing with Ivan that recent immigrants opt to separate themselves, second-generation David Kim discusses with friend Araceli Castro why he thinks immigrants eat lunch away from students who are deemed more popular:

DAVID: The Asians, all the FOBs sit up there. I don't know why, but you never see an immigrant around here—

ARACELI: I don't really ask; it doesn't bother me where you were born, it's just—

DAVID: I think they put themselves in that position, too. They down themselves. When I'm talking to someone, [they have their] head down, kind of walking around. [I think,] "What are you doing? It's not like we hate you; it's just you hating yourself."

ARACELI: Some act like they're uncomfortable.

DAVID: That's why they sit up there. I think they just don't wanna be spotted or being by people who can speak perfect English and talking and having fun. I don't see why they don't just come down. It would kinda be weird, maybe, in the first week, but then, if they did, we'd get used to it. It's cool.

Where students eat lunch is a reflection of their position on the social hierarchy at school. Juniors and seniors, football players, cheerleaders, and members of the student leadership are typically among the students who eat downstairs at the school's lunch tables, under trees, and near where the food is sold. In contrast, younger students and Asian immigrants often gather upstairs in the less desirable part of campus where there are no tables. They eat their lunches outside in circles on the dusty cement floor or leaning against the brick walls of their classrooms. To understand why immigrants often sit upstairs, David initially blames them. When Araceli explains that some may feel uncomfortable, he then speculates that maybe they stay away from people "who can speak perfect English."

As someone born in the United States and who lived in Taiwan for seven years before beginning middle school in Southern California, Margaret Kang knows firsthand the value placed on speaking English and how English-language skills fuel divisions between her Chinese American and Chinese immigrant schoolmates:

> People look down more on immigrants here in high school . . . People
> would call each other FOBs, like fresh off the boat, or ABC—
> American-born Chinese, and then they'd respect those that speaks
> English as their primary language over those that do not.

According to Margaret, the high school campus has been a contentious space where intragenerational divisions emerge. She remembers a very different scenario when her family returned to Southern California from Taiwan as she was beginning fifth grade:

> I couldn't speak English, and so there was always this group of girls,
> they could speak Chinese with me, and then they would help me
> translate with the teacher.

This assistance and inclusion that Margaret felt early in her schooling shifted in high school at an age when students are developing a stronger sense of their identities and a greater consciousness of anti-immigrant and English-only sentiments. A campus climate that does little to affirm students' backgrounds fosters these social hierarchies that Margaret and her schoolmates describe at SCHS.

In a few cases, these tensions have escalated into serious threats and fights at the school. At the start of a recent academic school year, a student posted a death threat on the Internet site Wikipedia to various members of the school's predominately Asian American badminton team and "almost every single FOB." In response to the shooting threats, the school temporarily closed. Fortunately, physical violence in that case was averted, but longtime teacher Val Sherman recalls what she referred to as a "lynching" off campus six to ten years earlier, where second-generation Asian Americans attacked Asian immigrants:

> They took them up to the gated community, closed the gates, and
> they couldn't get out. And there was one car of students and then like
> thirty other students who just attacked them.

According to Val, this case surprised the staffulty:

> That was really a shock to us. We didn't realize that there was that
> kind of animosity until that happened . . . [W]e just went, "What?"
> And they were honors students and were in our classes.[1]

These examples underscore the potential severity of student divisions and suggest the staffulty's lack of awareness that such hierarchies exist.

Just as U.S.-born Asian Americans may draw boundaries around their Asian immigrant peers, some of the immigrant students who are targets of these slurs and potential violence reciprocate with their own derogatory labels. They assert their own identities in opposition to their U.S.-born classmates. During a discussion with Billy Su and Mike Song, senior May Lee explains what some Asian immigrants call Asian Americans:

> Oh, bananas [all three students laugh]. Umm yellow on the outside,
> white on the inside [friends keep laughing]. That's what they say. I
> don't know if you guys hear, but that's what they call you [all laugh
> again]. They'd call me that, but then it's just like in a joking manner
> for me 'cause I am actually friends with them.

As Billy and Mike laugh about the label, May continues,

> And then they talk about my friends: "Why do you hang around with
> them? They're so American. They don't have any pride in their cul-
> ture." And I am like, "No that's not true. It's just we've been here all
> our lives." They get really discriminatory because we listen to White
> music and like rock music.

Despite the hurtful impact that reciprocal name-calling and boundary drawing may have on students, these distinctions are not the same. As Margaret Kang described earlier, there is an unequal power relationship in that English is the privileged language. A focus on speaking English and an overall correlation of popularity with being more Americanized can be traced to such institutionalized preferences in the United States. Teacher Laura Cooper observes how these preferences materialize at SCHS:

> The popular kids are fairly diverse in their group. You will have some Hispanic kids, some Black kids, some White kids, and some Asian kids that are more Americanized.

This social hierarchy privileges U.S.-born students and the English language and maintains an assimilationist imperative that all should speak English and abide by dominant customs and values. Laura Cooper's qualifying statement that "Asian kids that are more Americanized" are among the popular students assumes that Asian Americans are less assimilated than other groups. Furthermore, as Stacey Lee (2005) also finds in her research with Hmong American youth, it may also imply that Asian Americans are never really perceived as "American"; either they are Americanizing or they are "more Americanized."

While not as often as their Asian American schoolmates, a few Latinas/os discuss the cross-generational divisions on campus. Capturing this separation, Mexican American–identified Alicia Vasquez describes campus divisions by focusing on Asian immigrants:

> They dress differently than everyone else. They have different hairstyles. They talk differently. We don't converse with them. We don't really acknowledge each other from either side. We know that they are there, and I'm sure that they know we are here.

Of the few Latinas/os who expressed anti-immigrant or an assimilationist perspective, several mentioned the label "FOB." However, they typically equated it with a slur used by Asian Americans against Asian immigrants, and they occasionally spotlighted its usage in a way that debased Asian Americans for perpetuating student divisions. Summer Reyes illustrates, "The smart Asians, they treat their FOBs really bad. They're like, 'Oh, they can't even speak English.' So you see discrimination even within their own group." Critical of the exclusion she has felt in her honors and advanced placement classes, Summer blames Asian Americans who think that "they really are better than everyone else." Perhaps as a result of her experiences, Summer emphasizes the negative treatment she has observed against Asian immigrants and uses this treatment as an example to prove her assumption that Asian Americans in general are hostile and competitive toward not only Mexicans but also Asian immigrants.

Friends Rebecca Ramos and Gloria Camacho concur:

> REBECCA: I was talking to this Asian girl, and I was joking with her and was like, "You should make friends with that girl over there." She's

like, "Oh, she's an Asian from Asia, and us Asian Americans don't talk to them. They're different; we do different stuff."

GLORIA: Yeah, there's a lot of people here that just came from over there, and they don't know a lot of people. The other Asians don't interact with them.

Assuming that all Asian Americans should get along, Rebecca admits to joking with a classmate that she should befriend another student. However, when Rebecca is told that the two students have different interests, she and Gloria are surprised and judgmental. They imply that this unwillingness to befriend another student because of generational differences is unique to Asian Americans. Nevertheless, they soften their criticism when I asked them about Latinas/os:

GILDA OCHOA: What about the Mexicans or Latinos here? Do they do that too?

GLORIA: A little bit.

REBECCA: Yeah, kind of. I've noticed this group; they speak Spanish all the time.

GLORIA: Oh yeah, it's rude to talk Spanish in front of people that speak English 'cause they don't know what you're saying. And all they do is speak Spanish. When you need to talk to the people, you talk to them in English, but then they go back and all they talk is Spanish.

REBECCA: Yeah, that's what we think of Asians that when they're talking Asian we don't know if they're talking bad about us or if they're just having a conversation.

Highlighting a recurring theme, Gloria and Rebecca shift momentarily from criticizing Asian Americans to argue that it is "rude" when people speak Spanish in public. They then apply this assessment to Asian immigrants.

One group of Latinas applied the epithet "FOB" to Latinas/os, but Asian immigrants and speaking English were still the focus of this label:

VICKI PARDO: The FOBs, the people who don't speak English and they dress very ugly . . . Other people make fun of that. They say "fresh off the border" or like "fresh off the boat."

FRAN PADILLA: "Fresh over the border."

GILDA OCHOA: I haven't heard that, "over the border." But when you were saying "FOB," what did you mean?

FRAN: I meant the Asians.

VICKI: Yeah, that's why I was laughing.

FRAN: FOB is for anybody who wasn't born here—was born in either Asia or Mexico or something, and they emigrated here after their childhood and a lot can't speak English, and what I hate is how you would be talking to them or be near them and they will all be talking another language that you cannot understand and then they will laugh.

VICKI: And they will look at you and laugh and you'll be like, "Are they talking about me?"

FRAN: That's one thing that bothers me 'cause I don't just like go up to a group of Asians and start talking in Spanish with my friends and laughing and pointing at them.

Even in this example, where Vicki and Fran use the phrase "fresh over the border" in reference to Mexican immigrants, they still focus on Asian immigrants and English-language skills. As with Gloria and Rebecca earlier, they echo a familiar argument given by proponents of English-only policies that they are fearful of being talked about by immigrants and not being able to understand.

In spite of the examples of the two previous friendship groups, U.S.-born Latinas/os tend not to distinguish between themselves and Latina/o immigrants. Instead, students explain either that there are few if any Latina/o immigrants at the school—suggesting their invisibility on campus—or as ninth-grader Jose de Leon believes, that it is a touchy topic, so Latina/o students avoid talking about immigration status:

> Sometimes we really don't want to ask them because sometime they cross the border without papers. So we don't want to make them feel bad because their parents crossed the border without papers. They're like the lower Mexicans so we really don't ask them.

This general silence by U.S.-born Latinas/os about Latina/o immigrants at the school contrasts significantly with other studies that detail how Latinas/os may display parallel forms of cross-generational tensions that exist among many Asian Americans at SCHS (see Ochoa 2004; Bejarano 2005). Rose Gonzalez, a second-generation and self-identified Mexican student, offers a compelling explanation for this difference between Asian Americans and Latinas/os at SCHS:

> The cool Asians are the Americanized Asians . . . They make fun of each other by calling each other FOBs. But what's weird is for Mexicans, they don't call us "wetbacks." I've never heard someone call me or call anybody a "wetback" or a "chuntie" or a "paisa" or something that we'd be called in a regular school. Like in a school with Asians and a whole bunch of Mexicans, they don't really make fun of that.

Prior to SCHS, Rose attended several different schools where most of the students were Latina/o, and anti-immigrant name-calling was common. Researching a predominately Mexican American high school in Texas, Angela Valenzuela (1999) found that curriculum tracking divided Mexican American and Mexican immigrant students, and course materials devalued Mexicanness. Thus such practices in Rose's former schools and in the Texas high school fueled student divisions and negative perceptions of immigrants. However, perhaps in a school such as SCHS where Asian Americans are academically favored, Latina/o students may form a sense of solidarity in *opposition* to their Asian American schoolmates that in turn reduces intra-Latina/o tensions. As such, this reveals how racial/ethnic tensions and their causes are situational and contextually specific.

Other possible explanations for why Asian American students at SCHS may make more distinctions by language and generation than their Latina/o schoolmates is that there are more Asian immigrants in the community, and non–Asian Americans may engage in a pattern of racial lumping where generational differences are overlooked. As a result, some Asian American students may attempt to disassociate with a group that is often stigmatized socially and perceived to be not American (see Lee 1996; Danico 2004). Since dominant conceptions of Americanness have long been equated with whiteness such as Anglo ancestry and speaking English, Asian Americans are often believed to be non-Americans or "forever foreigners," regardless of how many years and generations they have resided in the United States (see Tuan 1998), and students may do all that they can to avoid such immigrant lumping and stigmatizing by putting down other students to deflect attention away from themselves. Sometimes such distance drawing occurs between ethnic groups in the form of intraracial divisions.

Intraracial Divisions

At SCHS, students describe intraracial divides much less frequently than the aforementioned cross-racial/ethnic and generational strains. Nevertheless, these divisions are also significant for capturing the racialized climate and social hierarchies on campus. Among Asian Americans, a few detail negative exchanges between Korean Americans and Chinese Americans. Korean-identified senior May Lee shares with two of her classmates:

> When you think of Chinese people, Koreans have this certain word
> that means, umm, it's really bad. In Korean it means like Chinese
> bitch. So they look at Chinese and that's what they call them without
> them knowing. That's what they call them [friends all laugh]. The

guys would always say that 'cause most of my friends are Chinese. So they'd be like, "Oh, why are your friends all, umm, Chinese bitches?"

When asked why some may hold such degrading views, May and fellow Korean Mike Song confer,

> MAY: They're really discriminating though towards—
> MIKE: Everyone.

Chinese-identified student Charles Lin demonstrates how these divisions are contextually specific and stem from the peer dynamics fostered within the school:

> Outside of school, everyone's a pretty good person overall, but when they're with their friends, then I think that most people act differently. Like if a Korean person saw me outside of school, we would probably be really cool and talk about things, and he would be a nice person. But at school, it might come to the point where he ignores me if I say, "Hi."

Charles's analysis captures the role of the school environment and student cliques in inhibiting relationships among students on campus.

The competitive, hierarchical structuring in the form of tracking coupled with racial profiling and limited multicultural curriculum inflame divisions. They keep students separate and prevent greater awareness of the factors shaping students' relationships and conceptions of selves. As Mike Song recounted earlier how his physical education teacher did not intercede when students formed teams based on race/ethnicity, sophomore Nicole Alexander's example also illustrates how classes are places that can breed tensions:

> In Spanish class, I'm the only girl from Argentina, and it's a group of Mexicans in the class and they're always baggin' on Argentina. They're like, "Argentina this, Argentina that." I am like, "What's the point of that? What are you getting out of talking bad about the country my parents are from?" They're like, "Ohhh Argentina sucks, and na na na." I'm guessing it's a soccer thing 'cause there's a rivalry, but still it's kind of uncomfortable; I'm just sitting there, and I don't want to say anything bad, but . . .

According to Nicole, her Spanish teacher does not hear when students make these comments. However, the teacher seems aware that students express prejudices, and she tries to preempt them:

> She's told us that if you put down another race or if you say that another race isn't good then you're just making yourself look worse and cheap, but they still do it.

Without a systematic deconstructing of the multifaceted factors bearing on society, schools, and students, such general comments by teachers do little to thwart peer harassment or tackle the entrenchment of racial/ethnic and in this case national hierarchies. As Nicole concludes about her classmates, "They still do it."

For some students, intraracial tensions are directly connected to the narrow conceptualizations of what it means to be Asian American and Latina/o. Just as these conceptualizations result in academic profiling, students also reinforce them when they use static criteria to determine Asianness, Latina/oness, and whiteness, or when they reinforce class hierarchies. Senior Art Chen, who moved from an East Coast school with predominately White students to SCHS, explains his transition where he is scrutinized as not possessing the socially constructed expectations of what it means to be Asian at the school:

> I feel kind of awkward sometimes 'cause I'm so Whitewashed, and they joke about me being a White kid even though [laugh] I'm Asian but, umm, for the most part it's really cool.

He adds,

> I'm kind of with the Asians. They accept me 'cause for academics, but, umm, I'm in the White group sometimes 'cause culturally speaking I'm not all Asian sometimes. They are speaking Chinese, and they have this different mentality that I can't get accustomed to.

When asked how his friends would describe him, Art elaborates:

> We are pretty much really similar; we do academically well, and they'll probably say, "Oh he's a Whitewashed kid," and they don't listen to my music or anything like that. They listen to their Asian music or the opera and so they just think I'm good academically but just a White kid that's not White [laugh].

Comparable to the name-calling May Lee recounted earlier when she hears Asian immigrants label some Asian Americans "bananas," Art experiences equivalent jokes from friends who tease him for not being authentically Asian American. Culturally, he is assumed to be more White than Asian American, but his friends still seemingly accept him because he does well academically—a trait they associate with being Asian American. On the surface, these jokes may appear innocuous, but they are examples of the power of dominant images and static racial/ethnic categorizations. Just as Asian Americans are often thought to not be American, students such as Art encounter a double bind where because of his interests and upbringing, he is perceived as not really Asian. The belief that there are certain authentically Asian cultural practices camouflages the vast diversity that exists within this panethnic group as well as the multiple factors shaping people's experiences.

Junior friends Laura Cadena and Monique Martinez also employ the label "Whitewashed," but they do so to describe themselves in opposition to some Latinas/os:

> LAURA: We're the Hispanics that are kinda like Whitewashed.
>
> GILDA OCHOA: Tell me what Whitewashed means to you.
>
> LAURA: Whitewashed, I mean I'm proud to be a Hispanic, but I don't like how they're supposed to dress. It's like in the ghetto attire. I don't like that.
>
> GILDA OCHOA: So how are they supposed to dress?
>
> LAURA: Their Nike's and their tight, tight jeans, their tight, tight shirts that show their boobs.
>
> MONIQUE: The big hoops. That's what they dress like.
>
> LAURA: The big hoop earrings.
>
> ART CASAS: Whitewashed—they think they're well off, not rich but have money.

In contrast to Art Chen, who seems to not impose a value judgment when he describes Asian Americans who "have this different mentality that I can't get accustomed to," Monique and Laura draw class-based distinctions among Latinas symbolized in styles of dress. By belittling some Latinas' styles, they reinforce racialized class hierarchies that are present on campus but rarely discussed in the classroom curriculum.

The preceding examples also illustrate students' nuanced uses of the label "Whitewashed" to draw boundaries. The meanings of Whitewashed shift slightly depending on racial/ethnic identities and context. However, the implications are similar—one is assumed to be less Asian or Hispanic. While Art Chen's Asian American friends call him "Whitewashed" because of his musical preferences and language usage, self-described Hispanics Monique and Laura use it in reference to their fashion styles based on being financially "well off." By equating whiteness with being "well off" and Hispanics with being "ghetto," these friends boost assumptions that Whites "have money" and that Latinas/or are poor or working class. Overall, strict racial/ethnic categorizations are maintained with such labeling. As detailed later, these narrow and imposed labels for people of color contrast with the general invisibility and greater flexibility of Whites on campus.

White Student Invisibility, Flexibility, and Limited Antiracist Models

Just as chapter 1 revealed how some White staffulty are reluctant to discuss their own identities and whiteness is rarely named, White students are also largely invisible at SCHS. When asked about their White schoolmates, students frequently misjudged their numbers. About 7 percent or almost 150 students were classified as White during the time of the research, but comments such as these were common:

> VANESSA CHEN: I have only seen one [White student]. NO! I've seen two [laughter].
>
> MALLORY WALKER: Not that many [White students]. I only know my brother and my sister and then everybody else has some sort of Mexican traits. They look White, but they're not.

White students at SCHS are often undercounted and hidden. However, their invisibility is different from the *academic* invisibility or underestimation of Latinas/os and the *social* invisibility of Asian Americans. In general, White students have the privilege of being perceived as more heterogeneous by staffulty, and they appear to have greater flexibility of movement. Nevertheless, the lack of interrogation of whiteness, especially as it intersects with class inequality, limits understanding and the development of an antiracist and positive White identity.

In contrast to the homogenization that students of color typically encounter, White teachers tend to emphasize White student diversity. Teacher Mark Durand's comments are illustrative:

> White students are very diverse. There's ones that sort of fit in to that stereotypical Asian mold or just really focus on college all the way down to the other end of just getting through. I think they have the most variability within their group.

Although Whites compose a relatively small percentage of students at the school, Mark Durand believes that academically they are the *most* heterogeneous group on campus. He overlooks or is unaware of the range of backgrounds and experiences among Asian Americans and Latinas/os. Instead, he reinforces the static categorization of Asian Americans by simply referring to "that stereotypical Asian mold." Newer teacher Mike Williams agrees that there is a range of White students academically: "Usually, White students run the whole gamut from advanced down to the lowest of the low." It is unclear why these teachers perceive more academic diversity among Whites at the school, but their positions as self-identified Whites may be influencing how they distinguish and characterize students.

As Whites themselves, they may be more attuned to within-group heterogeneity among Whites.

Teacher Mary DuPont, who tended to highlight the diversity among
all students, expanded on this diversity most when she too reflected on
White students:

> Our White students fall right in the middle. In my experiences in the
> classes, some of 'em are lazy; some of them, they're right up there. I
> have them in my honors. I think I have maybe five total—no probably
> about ten total.

Although initially undercounting White students and explaining that
they are in the "middle," Mary's sentiment parallels Mark's and Mike's.
Being perceived as "diverse," running "the whole gamut," or even "in the
middle" allows Whites, relative to students of color, more freedom to transcend the narrow binaries used to label Asian Americans and Latinas/os.

The percentage of White students interviewed was slightly less than
their percentage in the school. However, of those interviewed, a couple
echoed the previous teachers' observations regarding their span across the
academic hierarchy. Junior Sandy O'Brien details,

> The Asians are more of the top academically. Then you have a thin
> line of minority kind of half in the higher academics and half in the
> lower. And then most Mexicans are in the lower, which is sad to say.

Sandy defines White and Black students as minorities at the school, given
their smaller numbers, but unlike the previous teachers, she astutely
attributes the racial/ethnic positioning on the academic hierarchy to socioeconomic class: "The lower classes are normally at the bottom. The higher
classes are normally at the top."

Ninth-grader Susan Drake characterizes the position of Whites slightly
different from Sandy, but the implications are similar—Asian Americans
and Latinas/os are seen as divergent, but Whites are undefined:

> I don't want to define them as a race "all Asians are smart," but I
> think a majority of them are because it's their culture . . . I think a
> lot of Mexican people are more family-oriented because they love
> their families . . . I don't know anything 'cause I'm White. I feel like
> I have no background. Like, you're just White. You have nothing
> specific about you.

Reflecting some of her White teachers' opinions presented in chapter 1,
Susan follows a similar pattern of believing that Whites have "nothing
specific." This sense of having "no background" is one that others have

described as "being cultureless," a belief that reinforces the invisibility of Whites and whiteness as the unstated norm (Frankenberg 1993). This feeling and treatment of not being defined or being unmarked may be one of the factors that allows some to perceive White academic diversity at the same time that they overlook the heterogeneity of other racial/ethnic groups on campus.

In addition to staffulty expressing a more acute awareness of White students' academic diversity, they describe White students as having greater flexibility *socially* in terms of identity and friendship groups. This too diverges from the racial lumping of students of color, who are often categorized in the four Ss and who have a difficult time transgressing racial boundaries and others' expectations. Whites, by comparison, are believed to blend in with students across race/ethnicity. Teacher Marie Silva observes,

> For the Caucasian students, they fit in anywhere. I see some Caucasians that fit more with the Asian groups, and some fit more with the Latino groups, and some are in between.

Newer teacher Laura Cooper expands,

> I've had a couple of White students, and I think that they just are. There's no expectation of them really. They're friends with whomever they want to be friends with. They have that opportunity; it's kind of like they blend, and whatever they want to do they can do. So if they want to hang out with the Asians, they can hang out with the Asians. They want to hang out with the Mexicans, they can hang out with the Mexican kids . . . It can go either way, and they do go either way.

Sophomores Rebecca Ramos and Gloria Camacho agree. Within the socially constructed binary that they characterize as Mexican and Asian, Whites "mix in":

REBECCA: There's a few [White students], not that many.
GLORIA: That's why they just mix in with the rest of the people. To me they act kind of Mexican.
REBECCA: Yeah.
GILDA OCHOA: In what ways do they act Mexican?
REBECCA: I don't know. They just act like us. They don't act Asian. To me, it's normal.
GILDA OCHOA: What does it mean to act Asian?
REBECCA: Like speak Asian, dress Asian.

Being defined as "normal" as opposed to "other," which in this case is "Asian," Whites are rarely singled out by their race/ethnicity in the ways that students of color are. As Arturo Madrid notes, the difference of being perceived as "normal" and "other" is substantial:

> Being *the other* means feeling dissimilar; is awareness of being distinct; is consciousness of being dissimilar. It means being outside the game, outside the circle, outside the set. It means being on the edges, on the margins, on the periphery. Otherness means feeling excluded, closed out, precluded, of disconnectedness, of alienation. (1995, 12)

Given the racialized boundaries and rigid friendships encountered by Asian Americans and Latinas/os, the ability to move across and between groups of students is a privilege. As teacher Laura Cooper elaborates, White students may be able to strategically form their peer groups in classes in ways that are beneficial to them:

> It is almost like an advantage because very rarely do you see a mix between Asian and Hispanic students when we group up [in class], and I let them choose their partners. But Whites, I have seen them group up with both. So whatever is most advantageous for them at that period of time.

Students with diverse friendships benefit from expanded networks. By introducing students to multiple perspectives and a wider range of people, these networks can increase students' access to more resources including additional cultural capital.

Not only do teachers observe how Whites have more liberty of movement between peer groups, but as teacher Laura Cooper highlights, "They just are. There's no expectation of them." Not being racially/ethnically pigeonholed by others' expectations may not be the case for all Whites, but it certainly contrasts with the experiences of Asian Americans, Latina/os, and African Americans who are often narrowly categorized and encounter limited expectations. Thus Whites can typically be perceived as individuals rather than as exceptions to their race/ethnicity or as Whitewashed when they fall outside of expectations.

Like their teachers, a few students believe that White and Black students have greater social flexibility. They are able to move across campus and between groups of students. Senior Art Chen describes, "There are White people and Black people, but they just kind of blend in and have their own crowd." Junior James Tuan concurs: "Whites and Blacks are everywhere. They can go anywhere. They're usually the popular, sporty [students]." Given the cultural hierarchy within the school, where immigrants are referred to derogatorily, length of time in the United States, English-language skills, and styles of dress are among the factors shaping student popularity.

This cultural hierarchy intersects with a racial hierarchy to privilege Whites and position them near the top of the school's social hierarchy. A few students are explicit in their adoption of White supremacist beliefs. For example, reflecting on her previous experiences in a predominately working-class school where Latinas/os were the majority, Mexican-identified Patricia Salas is convinced that Whites make SCHS stronger:

> Over here, there are more White people than Mexicans, and I think that the schools are better over here because of the White popula-tion . . . They like to have everything organized, clean and stuff. They don't like seeing the ghetto in their area.

While factors such as the age of schools and area resources influence facili-ties, Patricia is convinced that the physical quality of SCHS is due to Whites' believed penchant for cleanliness relative to Mexicans'. Likewise, even though Whites are a fraction of the students and community mem-bers, Patricia credits them for the school's appearance and perpetuates the invisibility of Asian Americans and Latinas/os.

Despite the general privileging of whiteness at the school and in society, when looked at through an intersectional lens that considers socioeco-nomic class, all Whites do not experience SCHS equally. Junior Sandy O'Brien alluded to these differences earlier when she emphasized the sig-nificance of class on track placement, but these disparities and how they influence everyday perceptions also emerge in other students' narratives. Given class-based hierarchies, these disparities are most apparent in the attitudes toward poor and working-class Whites. For example, Art Chen, who before transferring to SCHS attended an East Coast high school with middle-class and upper-middle-class Whites, was most explicit in his derogatory class-based labeling of Whites at SCHS:

> The White people here are not like the ones I'm used to, like the ones from a European descent. Here, I don't want to say it, but they are kind of like redneckish [laugh]. They are kind of backward and drive a pickup and listen to country music. I'm used to a Jewish community where I lived and a lot of people from different European descents. But people here I think they're just descendants from Oklahoma.

Art's comments expose class-based judgments and stereotyped images that prevail in the United States against poor and working-class Whites. Furthermore, along with rooting class inequality in "backward" views and tastes in cars and music, like a similar derogatory phrase "poor White trash," the epithet "redneck" "suggests that color and poverty and degenerate lifestyle so automatically go together that when white folk are acting that way, their whiteness needs to be marked" (Bettie 2003, 128). Finally, such labels assume that racist views stem from "backward" individuals and not ideologies and institutions.

Perhaps it is the negative associations some make with being White and working class that influence Sandy O'Brien's perception of herself:

> Being White, I am a minority. I like being a minority, personally, because it makes me different. But I think a lot of people look at it as, at this school, "If you're not Asian, you won't succeed." That's a big, big thing here. If you're not Asian, you're not smart. So me being in the honors classes and being one of the only White people in those honors classes, it kind of gives everybody else hope. So I think that's how my background and me being White affects everybody else and affects me in a way too because it does push me down sometimes because I am a minority I have everybody pushing on me and a lot of pressure. But it helps as well.

On first read, Sandy's reflections appear as though she positions herself as the supposed great White hope that can lift all other students if she excels. As such, she appears not to recognize her White privilege. However, her position as one of the few working-class students in honors courses may be among the factors influencing her perspective. After all, as previously indicated, Sandy is keenly aware that socioeconomic class is intimately connected to track placement at the school. Similarly, an interview with one of her good friends, Jennifer Cortez, demonstrates how Sandy identifies herself:

> My friend [Sandy], she's White, but I just say that she's like Mexican, like Hispanic-washed 'cause she's always with Hispanic people. She says herself she doesn't like White people that she prefers more the Latino community. I don't know why, but that's what she was telling me.

Raised in a predominately working-class Latina/o community and enrolled in AVID (Advancement via Individual Determination) with a majority of first-generation college-going Latinas/os, Sandy's socialization seems to influence how her friends see her and even how she views herself. However, one wonders how the school culture where students are provided with few structured opportunities to discuss systems of power and inequality and identity may also be preventing a positive White identity—one where Sandy does not have to disavow her background and all Whites.

The impact of disparaging constructions of working-class Whites and the limited development of a positive White racial identity is captured in junior John Jansen's identity:

> JOHN: Well, I'm White [laughs]. Everybody says that, but it's kind of funny, but it's true. I'm really White. There's not a lot of White people here; there's like, maybe ten of us, and we all hang out together, so people would make jokes.
>
> GILDA OCHOA: What jokes would they make?
>
> JOHN: [laughs] They'd call us the KKK and stuff, but it's joking around, and it's cool; it's like whatever. It's funny. We go along with it, and the people don't really bug me about it. I don't have any problems.

While initially John claims not to be bothered by such labeling, his responses to other questions expose how such teasing is not so innocuous:

> GILDA OCHOA: So what's it like being one of the few White students?
>
> JOHN JANSEN: I don't do a lot of things that I'm not supposed to 'cause I always think about my last name . . . I try not to mess up, because when I mess up, it's like a bad mark on my name, so I don't want that because I know it will affect my family. I guess I'm trying to put that as the fact that I'm White. So I try not to mess up, since I don't want that to reflect on other White people to make us look bad 'cause there's not a lot of us here.

Given asymmetrical power differentials, dominant images, and the racial/ethnic demographics of the United States, this experience of not being seen as an individual but instead as a representative of one's racial/ethnic group is more commonly encountered by people of color. However, on a campus where there are few White students, John is concerned about how his actions might reflect on his family and Whites in general.

Along with feeling the pressure to positively represent Whites, the racialized climate is also shaping his friendships in ways that complicate staffulty's earlier assumptions of White social flexibility and cross-racial/ethnic friendships:

> JOHN JANSEN: Most of the people I hang out with are Caucasian.
>
> GILDA OCHOA: Do you have any thoughts on why you hang out with other White students?
>
> JOHN: We got to stick together.
>
> GILDA: You feel that way?
>
> JOHN: Yeah, I do 'cause there's not a lot of us. So we might get singled out. I don't know, it feels better . . . I feel kind of stronger walking

with somebody. [I]t's not just White people. I just don't like to be alone. I'm just a people person. If I'm alone, I get really lonely, and I don't know what to do with myself.

John feels compelled to befriend Whites for fear of being singled out on campus. This sentiment limits John's networks and has the frightening potential of fostering more than racial/ethnic separation. As history has demonstrated, it can fuel separatist ideologies, a backlash against people of color, and exclusionary movements. As social psychologist Beverley Daniel Tatum argues, what is needed to facilitate White students' healthy conceptions of selves is adult support for the unlearning of individual racist beliefs and a consciousness of institutional racism (1997, 94–95). Continuing, Tatum advocates,

> We all must be able to embrace who we are in terms of our racial and cultural heritage, not in terms of assumed superiority or inferiority, but as an integral part of our daily experience in which we can take pride. (107)

Overall, in contrast to many of their White teachers described in chapter 1, who typically grew up in all White communities and articulate power-evasive frameworks in the form of "color-blindness," this was not the case for the White students interviewed at SCHS. White students such as ninth-grader Susan Drake seemed more reflective of their identities and of the history of White supremacy. Susan's exchange with interviewer Laura Enriquez is revealing:

INTERVIEWER LAURA ENRIQUEZ: Thinking about your racial/ethnic background, how do you identify yourself?

SUSAN: White [laughs], and I'm half Portuguese.

LAURA ENRIQUEZ: Okay, and is this background significant for you?

SUSAN: I don't know (slightly embarrassed laugh). It doesn't really matter. I don't really care about people's race that much. A lot of people care about their race, and they're all proud. I'm not putting down anyone, but just an example, Mexican people are all proud, "Yeah I'm Mexican." And I'm not like, "Yeah White." No, no, I'm just like, "Ok, I'm White, whatever."

LAURA ENRIQUEZ: Why do you think they're all like, "Yeah I'm Mexican"?

SUSAN: 'Cause they're proud of something that they are. They're proud of their background. I'm not because a lot of bad things happen with White people.

LAURA ENRIQUEZ: Like what?

SUSAN: Like the racist stuff they used to do. So I don't really like that so I'm not, "Oh White power!" I'm not like that at all.

As did most of the students who identified as White, Susan laughs when she says she is White.[2] The source of this laughter is unclear, but it may suggest a level of discomfort talking about her race. Susan's quote conveys her understanding of unequal power relations, where in the context of a racial/ethnic hierarchy that privileges whiteness, Mexican pride is qualitatively different than exerting White pride. As others have also found, this greater awareness compared to Whites socialized in all White communities could be attributable to White students' closer contact with people of color given the demographics of the SCHS and the surrounding neighborhoods (Perry 2002; Morris 2006). In spite of the potential that this awareness can mean for fostering antiracist students and an antiracist campus climate, little is provided to enhance students' understanding and analyses. Likewise, the school practices are kept intact in ways that continue to differentially advantage students by factors such as race/ethnicity and class.

Conclusion: A Parent's Vision

Beaming as she speaks, parent Mei Chee praises SCHS as a place where so many different racial/ethnic groups come together:

I think it's wonderful. I feel comfortable with the culture of diversity. So you get a chance to talk with Black, with Latino, with Korean, Japanese. It's a small scale of this society. Especially in California, Latino is like 30, 40 percent already. So, it's a great opportunity to expose our children in this small, great part of society.

Schools such as SCHS can be ideal sites to foster understanding and community among students. However, when dominant ideologies, structures, and practices divide and rank students and differences are overlooked and treated as liabilities, these opportunities are undermined. As students' narratives convey, hegemonic images, assimilationist imperatives, the privileging of Americanness, and the disparagement of immigrants prevail. Lacking opportunities for greater awareness and understanding from the school, these dynamics fuel a racialized climate of academic and social hierarchies, name-calling, and the formation of different peer groups. Thus important connections between students are stifled. Rather than share their cultural and social capital across generations and peer groups, students tend to stay away from one another, primarily interacting with students who are in their courses and who they perceive to be most like themselves (see Valenzuela 1999). As a result of such separation, opportunities for the development of healthier identities and deconstructing exclusionary beliefs and practices are reduced.

The dominant ideologies, structures, and practices that are inherited and reproduced in schools such as SCHS cannot miraculously be undone. However, when students are provided with structured opportunities to learn about power and inequality, dialogue about identities, and engage in cross-racial/ethnic interactions, they may develop a greater sense of understanding. Until then, as discussed in the following chapter, individual students and staffulty will do all that they can to resist the barriers and messages that contaminate the school climate. These individual and collective acts are empowering, but one thing is definite, in the absence of large-scale change, community-building strategies, and courses offering counterhegemonic frameworks, the dominant images, student divisions, and inequalities are sure to persist.

CHAPTER SIX

"Breaking the Mind-Set"

Forms of Resistance and Change

The stereotypes are so rigid here about what Hispanic students can accomplish versus what Asian students can accomplish, and you know the Asian students, even though they're the ones who perhaps have the more positive stereotypes, they feel just as confined by them as the Hispanic students feel confined by the stereotypes that plague them.

—*Michelle Mesa, teacher*

The dominant discourses, institutional structures, and everyday practices detailed in the preceding chapters converge to reproduce the stereotypes that teacher Michelle Mesa critiques. In spite of the power of these stereotypes and the exclusionary practices that accompany them, not all at SCHS are passively accepting others' dictates. Some students and teachers are engaged in everyday and organizational forms of resistance to the very discourses and practices that shape schooling, relationships, and opportunities.

Scholars have written about many forms of students' resistance. Most have focused on what has been considered "self-defeating resistance," where students may critique schooling, but they engage in activities such as classroom outbursts or leave school, which does not help students transform their positions in society or alter exclusionary school practices (for a critique of this scholarship, see Solorzano and Delgado Bernal 2001). Rather than focus on these types of activities, I center the everyday perspectives and organizational activities aimed at what high school junior Ashley Cordero refers to as "break[ing] that mind-set, that stereotype type of thing" that is so entrenched at SCHS and in the larger society. These types of resistance are intimately connected to the conditions at the school and students' varied experiences based on race/ethnicity, class, and

gender. They include (1) everyday perspectives and actions, such as affirming identities and playing with and defying stereotypes, and (2) creating
transformative spaces. While some students adopt perspective and actions
that reflect a critical awareness and affirmation of self and community,
others carve out politicized and conscious-raising spaces. These two forms
of resistance—everyday and organizational—are complementary, overlap-
ping, and convey the importance of considering the multiple and nuanced
forms of individual and collective agency. Together, they also reveal students' resilience and navigational skills as they make their way through
the educational pipeline (see Yosso 2006).

While the examples of resistance included in this chapter are aimed at
"break[ing] that mind-set," given how entrenched exclusionary images
and practices are, some of these acts occasionally reinforce binaries, divisions, and hierarchies. For example, even when students contest others'
mandates and play with stereotypes, their strategies and justifications are
so constrained by the dominant discourse that their articulations may perpetuate exclusionary thinking, oftentimes inadvertently. In other cases, as
in the student organization MEChA (Movimiento Estudiantil Chicano de
Aztlán), students and even their supporters encounter additional policing
and barriers as they contest dominant stereotypes. Nevertheless, even in
these contexts, students continue to persist. Thus the following examples
reveal the complexities involved with resisting the discourses, divisions,
and disparities at schools such as SCHS.

Everyday Forms of Resistance

While excluded from traditional conceptions of activism and resistance
that focus on visible and public activities such as elections, strikes, and
demonstrations, for many marginalized or excluded groups, claiming a
sense of self is a form of resistance. As social critic bell hooks (1989) writes,

> For many exploited and oppressed peoples the struggle to create
> an identity, to name one's reality is an act of resistance because the
> process of domination—whether it be imperialist colonization, rac-
> ism, or sexism oppression—has stripped us of our identity, devalued
> language, culture, appearance. (109)

At SCHS, where power-evasive discourses, racial/ethnic hierarchies,
and an assimilationist imperative prevail, some students are claiming
their identities, affirming their backgrounds, and striving to prove people
wrong. Within the context of externally imposed categorizations, these
techniques of saying who they are, playing with stereotypes, and defying

typification are all individual acts of resistance. They are grounded in strategies for survival and perseverance.

Claiming Identities: Self-Definition

Students provide nuanced descriptions of themselves. Their identities are based on multiple and at times intersecting factors, including ancestry, culture, and experiences of racism and discrimination. Comments by junior Ricky Liu, who began his interview with "I'm a sixteen-year-old Asian, totally ABC," are illustrative:

> ABC, American-born-Chinese, it's colloquial where it means that we're born in America, and we don't really know Chinese culture. And our parents are hard core Chinese traditional, but we don't really know that, don't really buy into it.

As the product of parents who migrated from the countryside of China to Southern California shortly before he was born, Ricky feels that ABC best captures his sense of self. With his family, he feels "kind of disconnected because I don't speak Chinese that well," and yet he realizes that he cannot disregard his race/ethnicity because not only is he influenced by his upbringing but others academically profile him:

> Even if I try to ignore what ethnicity a person is or try to forget that I'm Asian or I'm Chinese, this is not acceptable; it still affects you. As a Chinese, I don't know why people expect us to study hard, or be good at math, and the problem is I live up to that expectation . . . You don't really want to fulfill that stereotype, but at the same time, it's true. It's what you do. It's what your parents force you into.

Although he believes that he meets other's expectations, Ricky critiques them and adopts a nuanced sense of self. His identification as ABC blends together his experiences as a second-generation child of immigrants raised with the contradictory messages in the United States that he should forget his background and at the same time perform in accordance to others' racialized expectations.

Like Ricky, junior Melanie Park also carves out a strong sense of her identity in the context of her upbringing and the many messages she receives:

> I'm really, really proud of being a Korean American, and if someone says a racial slur or something, if they bring up Virginia Tech and I've heard this before, "Oh Melanie's gonna shoot up blah, blah, blah." I'm like, "Dude, shut up. You're stupid."

As a second-generation Korean American woman, Melanie encounters distinct stereotypes. In particular, after the 2007 Virginia Tech shootings, where a mentally troubled Korean American college student killed thirty-two people, her schoolmates ridiculed her, claiming that she too would commit such an act. Melanie verbally contests such accusations and racial lumping, where all Korean Americans are assumed to be the same. She is unwavering in her pride, but she is not unscathed by such comments. As she reflects, "I was brought up to be really proud of who I am, and although we all have insecurities, I think I've gone past that. I'm not sure yet though."

These statements of pride, especially in opposition to the racialized climate at the school, are apparent in many students' self-descriptions. First-year student Jose de Leon proclaims, "I'm proud to let people know that I'm Mexican . . . My parents, they've always taught me like even though Mexicans are not rich, they are still good." Similar to Melanie, Jose's pride has been instilled by his immigrant parents and is informed by external characterizations. In his example, he includes others' pejorative class assumptions associated with being Mexican. Such negative associations are precisely why first-year student Diana Muñoz exudes her Mexicanness:

> My parents were born in Mexico, so I'm proud to be Mexican. I'm
> not offended by it . . . A lot of people don't really like to say they're
> Mexican, or don't really like to speak Spanish. I am proud to do that.

Aware of a stigma at the school associated with being Mexican and an assimilationist thrust privileging English speakers, Diana proudly speaks Spanish, wears jerseys from Mexican soccer teams, and listens to Spanish music. As she boasts, she does all this in spite of others' perceptions of her, including her Mexican American friends who prefer to identify "as White not Mexican." For many, this emphasis on pride emerges from a critical awareness of marginalization.

Underlying the affirmation of some students' identities is a desire to be unique. A few Asian American students express this sentiment, such as second-generation Marvin Lee, who explains, "Being Chinese is different than anything else. Not that much different, but it just stands out a little." This emphasis on "stand[ing] out" was most common among Latinas/os—especially those identifying as Central American or with multiple Latina/o countries. At SCHS, where there are fewer students with these backgrounds, sophomore Mandy Esquivel shares,

> They always think I'm Mexican, but I'm not. I'm Salvadorian . . .
> Sometimes, I feel unique because there's so many Mexicans, and it
> feels kind of cool; you're the only one that's Salvadorian.

Given the history of the U.S. Southwest, U.S. labor recruitment in Mexico, and the proximity of Mexico, many Latinas/os at SCHS are of Mexican descent, and Salvadorians such as Mandy are often thought to be Mexican.

Like Mandy, junior Monique Martinez feels similarly when she proclaims that she is Mexican and Costa Rican:

> When I learned my mom wasn't Mexican she was Costa Rican, I thought that was cool. So now when I meet people, I'm, "I'm Mexican and Costa Rican." I'm just not Mexican 'cause there's a lot of just Mexicans out there. It's kind of cool to twist your name around and be, "I'm Costa Rican."

Initially, it appears that Monique is distinguishing herself from being Mexican because of the stigma that Diana Muñoz describes. However, Monique clarifies, "It makes me proud to be Mexican. It does; it does." Junior Art Casas concurs with the value of difference, and his emphasis here on being Puerto Rican when he identifies as Puerto Rican and Mexican reveals some of the contradictions involved in wanting to be unique: "I think it's important because of this school. It's nice to have different [groups], because there's not many Puerto Ricans in this school. So it's cool to say that you're Puerto Rican." For such students, this emphasis on being "different" challenges the assimilationist thrust that puts a premium on sameness. However, to the extent that it is an unspoken attempt to distance oneself from more stigmatized groups—in this case Mexicans—it may reinstate hierarchies.

For some students, stressing distinctiveness stems from a realization that peers and others are unaware of panethnic heterogeneity. Senior Angelica Vega explains,

> Just 'cause I'm dark-skinned, look like the regular Mexicans, they always assume that I'm gonna be Mexican. They never consider anything else. Just like they consider Asians all the same; they're not. They're Asians, Chinese; they're all different. Just like Central America and Mexico are two different things, and they consider me Mexican.

Angelica challenges such assumptions, which sometimes includes racist slurs:

> I just let them assume until they actually realize, or I tell them that I'm not. They assume something, like they say a racial comment, like Mexican beaner, and I'm like, "First, you don't know me. You don't know where I'm from. I don't like that."

Racist encounters such as these, when combined with a critical understanding of history and society, lead a few students to strategically claim their own politicized identities. For example, sophomore Robin Cadena identifies as Chicana, an overtly political term that gained popularity during the 1960s Chicana/o Movement for social justice, national pride, and self-determination. Despite the fact that many of Robin's schoolmates are unaware of this politicized identity, and members of Robin's family are critical of the term, Robin is asserting her own sense of self that is rooted in a larger history, struggle, and community. Both verbally and visually, Robin displays her Chicana/o identity:

> I am learning a lot about Chicanos and our history, and I just recently bought this shirt . . . my Grandma considered it like a bad word. She is like, "You are not a Chicano."

At the time of our interview, Robin was wearing her new t-shirt with "Chicana" on it. However, as she shares, she has received some flak from her grandmother, for whom Chicana/o connotes a negative association—historically, some used it as a pejorative term to refer to poor and working-class Mexican Americans. While Robin is unusual among the students in her explicit adoption of a Chicana identity, she attributes her growing knowledge of Chicanas/os to her Spanish honors course, where she has the rare opportunity in high school to learn about Chicana/o history.

Implied in their definitions and apparent throughout the school culture are the ways that unequal structures, dominant ideologies, school practices, and everyday messages impinge on students' sense of selves and their peer groups. The effects vary from politicized articulations to the unintentional reinforcement of hierarchical divisions. However, the implication underlying all these examples is how some students struggle to construct their own identities and claim connections to family, community, or history in the context of these larger factors.

Playing with/into Stereotypes

A small group of students demonstrate their critical awareness and strategic use of stereotypes by playing with and playing into them. This technique serves as a coping mechanism and may even help as they navigate through school and life. However, as with some of the other strategies, it may also take its toll by reinforcing hierarchies and the internalization of stereotypes. Junior Eric Han's comments are illuminating:

> I'm the type of person who typically doesn't like stereotyping. Sure, people every day make fun of each other, but I find that to be ironic.

In fact, Abraham Lincoln, first he didn't really realize how important African Americans were, but later he made them citizens. Eventually, we're going to come to the fact that everyone's going to be the same, no matter what. Sure today, they stereotype me, but I just laugh a way; I don't really care.

Eric draws strength from the struggle of African Americans to deal with the stereotypes he encounters as an Asian American male from Taiwan. Finding solace in history, he is confident that there will come a day when "everyone's going to be the same." In the meantime, he "just laugh[s] away" the stereotypes. Although this technique may be effective, that Eric replied with the earlier statement at the beginning of the interview when he was asked to share a little bit about himself reveals the influence of stereotypes on his sense of self. As Mia Tuan reveals in her work on the experiences of Chinese and Japanese Americans, such "self mocking strategies" might help in the short term, but for some their "psychological costs" may have "longterm consequences" of anger, shame, and humiliation (1998, 83–85).

Similar to Eric Han, senior Rose Gonzalez deals with the stereotypes about Mexicans with laughter and additional joke making. As introduced in previous chapters, Rose is one of the only Latina/o students in the school's International Baccalaureate program and the required theory of knowledge (TOK) class. In these spaces, she is often the focus of jokes, but she aims to deflect and redirect them:

[My teacher] with the class, he'll make a little Mexican joke to see if I'm paying attention. I'd be like, "What the heck!" He's just like, "Oh, it's 'cause she's Mexican" . . . I'm like, "Ha, ha, ha" [fake laughter], and sometimes in TOK, they'll say Mexican jokes. I'll be, "Ugh, you guys are dumb," and we'll make Asian jokes. But it's just to mess around; everybody's cool about it. I'm cool about it. I don't take it seriously.

Given his position of power in the classroom as a teacher and the only White man in the space, Rose's teacher's jokes are indefensible. They are an example of how jokesters who ridicule others tend to have more power and prestige (see Robinson and Smith-Lovin 2001). Similarly, one might question whether the jokes Rose and her Asian American peers make are actually "cool," especially given the prevalence of these beliefs and the fact that Rose is often the sole Latina/o in these classes. Instead, such jokes may contribute to what scholar Bernice Sandler has called a "chilly climate" that singles out a particular group and can lead to diminished participation, self-esteem, and ambition. Nonetheless, in comparison to her early experiences of intimidation in her IB classes, Rose feels that her classmates have "warm[ed] up" to her. Within this context, these exchanges could be a way for Asian Americans and Latinas/os to affirm their shared encounters with stereotypes by laughing at them together and, as Kimberle Crenshaw (1993) has described, "ridicul[ing] racism." It may even be a technique to name inequalities and perhaps even challenge stereotypes by reducing them to jokes. After all, not only does Rose talk back to these comments, but she is also excelling in the IB program—proving them wrong.

For at least one group of Asian American friends, playing with stereotypes and joking involves pushing boundaries by pretending to be White. Senior Patty Song explains,

> We have jokes between us. So we pretend sometimes that we're White because it's just like a better lifestyle. So when people are like, "What are you?" We go, "Oh, we're White." "But you're Asian." "No, we're White." [We] just kind of goof off about it.

While they may overlook the fact that because of various class positions not all Whites have "a better lifestyle," Patty and her friends are keenly aware of the disparities that plaque the United States and unequally privilege Whites as a race relative to Asian Americans. Patty experiences it firsthand when her Korean American family leaves her neighborhood:

> When we go to different place, people just look at us, "Oh Asian people." It is very different. It is just social status, like rights . . . It is hard sometimes because we haven't really done anything to deserve that kind of treatment.

Experiences of feeling "kind of low" because of such treatment influence her identity and behaviors:

> Sometimes I'm like, "Oh yeah, I'm Korean! I'm proud of it," but sometimes I'm just like, "Oh, I'm Korean yeah, but I'm an American too." In the different settings we're at, it's just different. Sometimes . . . when you are in more of an American setting, it is not always good to be totally all Asian about it.

This critical conscious of race, power, and place informs Patty's perspective and her friends' approach to playing with racial categories. By joking that they are White, they simultaneously demonstrate how race is a sociopolitical construct that is still meaningful in shaping lives. Furthermore, by calling attention to such disparities, Patty and her friends also disrupt the assumption that race does not matter. Nevertheless, the privileging of whiteness and the assimilationist imperative also leave their mark when Patty expresses some shame and occasionally feels the need to minimize her background.

Capturing the complexities of students' strategies and recognizing both external factors and students' individual agency, teacher Michelle Mesa argues, "I think sometimes students will play into those stereotypes if it helps them get to where they need to be." She offers two examples illustrating this strategic maneuvering, the first from an African American male:

> He was saying that his primary emphasis from high school were sports because he felt that he wasn't going to be able to do it academically and because of the stereotypes . . . I don't know if it's something that was perpetuated by his family, and I can't recall if he had older brothers who had fallen into sports and that's how they were able to get through, but socioeconomics played a big part for them because their family could not afford to send them to school. So he had to put an emphasis on sports to know that if he can just skirt by here and get somewhere where they might give him a scholarship through college then that was his goal.

While Michelle Mesa realizes the significance of socioeconomic class in influencing students' life goals and chances, she also believes this student may have participated in sports because of the construction that often associates Black males with sports. She reflects,

> Sometimes I have some of my students say, "Well, we all know that Blacks are really good at sports" . . . So I don't know if it's—he as Black himself giving into that as well, "This is the only shot I have. Because I can't do it academically so I have to do something with sports."

In the context of prevailing expectations, this student may have done all he could to advance academically by "playing into" stereotypes.

Michelle Mesa has observed some Asian American students employ this similar strategy based on the divergent ways that they are racialized:

> I have some of my Asian students who admit that even though it's very stressful and a lot of pressure associated with having to be on top all the time and to perform at this high level that the stereotypes [assume], they rather have that stereotype than the stereotype of being dumb or lazy. So they see the benefits . . . [E]ven though it's very stressful for them, they can justify it in their mind because there's

some payoff for them at the end. Whereas, there doesn't really seem to be a payoff for Hispanic students.

Just as Michelle describes, many students acknowledge the differential stereotypes they encounter, and compared to their Latina/o peers some Asian American students play with these stereotypes as a form of what Linda Võ has termed "image capital" in reference to Asian American professionals. As Võ explains, such capital is "manipulated into currency to leverage" some gain, even at the expense of various negative consequences (2004, 94). This playing with or leveraging of stereotypes was evident among Asian American students who are considered academically successful. IB student Marisa Yep reveals, "There's like the stereotype that Chinese are really smart. So then I can just pretend I'm smart even though I'm like, 'Eh?'" While Marisa jokes that she can play with the stereotype and act smart, later in her interview, she clarifies that she nonetheless believes "that the smart Asians are basically the us, the IB program, AP [advanced placement] students." Like the previous examples, Marisa's comments can destabilize dominant discourses by calling attention to them and labeling them as false. However, her approach may also reinforce dominant assumptions because students might feel pressure to embody them, and hierarchies based on race/ethnicity and curriculum track persist.

Being "Different" and "Proving Them Wrong": Defying Typification

Another way students contest dominant ideologies and controlling structures is by defying typification. Contestation takes several forms and is influenced by specific types of academic profiling. In particular, Asian American students are more likely to emphasize their distinctness from prevailing constructions with comments such as "I'm Asian, but . . ." or "My family is different." While as a whole Latinas/os tended not to say, "I'm Latina/o, but . . . ," they spoke more explicitly about wanting to dispel stereotypes by "proving them wrong." In such examples, students are aware of the academic profiling they experience, but given the low expectations they encounter, Latinas/os express an additional burden of wanting to correct misperceptions by favorably representing the group with which they are associated. Taken together, the following descriptions reveal students' desires to challenge preconceived ideas. Whether by race/ethnicity, class, or gender, students are working to broaden conceptions that limit their full development and holistic sense of selves.

Several Asian American students began their interviews by emphasizing their differentness from prevailing constructions. Senior Patty Song's introduction is an example of such a technique:

> I'm different than the Asian stereotype of my school because I do
> study, but I don't really focus on that as much as I should . . .
> [E]veryone at our school thinks that all Asians are smart and that
> they don't go out and they just listen to their parents and they're
> kinda like geeks. But I'm different than that.

In this distancing strategy, Patty clearly distinguishes herself from the
"model minority" stereotype. Initially, while listening to such introductions,
I considered how students might have begun their interviews by drawing
boundaries between themselves and hegemonic images because they saw me
as a teacher, a Latina, someone who is not Asian American and assumed
that I too would lump all Asian Americans together. However, I listened
more and noticed that this was a similar pattern other scholars have also
documented in their research (see Kibria 2002; Louie 2004).

Responding to dominant images of Asian Americans, words such as
"different" and "atypical" pepper the interviews of many of the Asian
American students. After saying, "It's not a big deal, but it's really cool
being Chinese . . . We're expected to do stuff," junior Garfield Tan clarifies, "Well, I'm not the stereotypical Chinese Asian. I suck at math and
science. I'm good at liberal stuff." Comments such as these are illustrative
of the ways that many of the Asian Americans are aware of others' high
expectations.

While Garfield seems to appreciate being Chinese and the high expectations that he encounters, in spite of the fact that they do not represent him,
a few Asian American students were more critical of these stereotypes—
especially if they saw themselves as diametrically opposed to them. This is
the case for sophomore Nathan Yi, who was bullied when he first moved
from Taiwan at the age of ten. This bullying gradually escalated into fights
and school suspensions in middle school. Now Nathan's grades are plum-
meting, and he contests the implications of the "model minority" myth:

> I hate that kind of stereotyping because I'm getting bad grades doesn't
> mean I'm any lesser than anybody else. Just because I'm Asian doesn't
> mean I have to get straight As and study all the time.

Responding to such pressures and negative evaluations, Nathan articulates his life philosophy:

> You spend one-fifth of your life studying and then you spend about
> two-fifths of your life like working and you only have two-fifths of
> your life to do whatever you want, and by that time you're sixty years
> old and you can't do anything fun . . . My philosophy is why study so
> hard all the time? Just get a passing grade and go on with your life.
> Get an easy-going job; you don't have to be a CEO of some company.

> You don't have to be a big shot at everything because when you die
> you aren't going to take it all with you.

As a sixteen-year-old, Nathan has developed an astute perspective that helps him defy other's assumptions. However, one wonders if he was allowed to explore his interests without being so narrowly pigeonholed, if he might have developed another perspective on schooling and life.

Just as some Asian American students contest assumptions about themselves, without prompting, several were quick to emphasize how their families are also distinct. Senior Tracy Fuji stresses about her parents, "They've never been strict on me. It's the opposite; they're not the typical Asian parents." Junior Robert Wong also characterizes his parents in this way:

> This is atypical of the Asian parents, but my mom has been telling
> me that it is important to enjoy life because she's been seeing that I
> have been studying a lot. And she always tells me that when she was
> younger, she didn't really take advantage of her childhood. Since I'm
> almost graduating high school, she thinks that I should spend more
> time enjoying the freedom I have as a child.

Senior Yi Lin, who in chapter 5 shared his tutoring experiences as an IB student, begins his reflection on his family's messages in a similar way:

> My family is not like the typical Asian family . . . We're pretty liberal
> about things like education . . . They barely even look at my grades,
> and they don't even ask about anything. It's not like my mom knows
> that much anyways, but I think they just look at the report card and
> as long as the grades aren't low grades, I'm good. So they didn't really
> force me to do anything, it's just "This is helpful. It's up to you. What
> do you want to do?" So even for the classes, they never told me what
> to do. Maybe because my mom's always busy so it's always been me
> choosing my own classes and taking what I'm interested in.

While Yi strongly begins by proclaiming that he believes his family is atypical when it comes to courses and grades, he then looks for answers as to why his mother might be different. Thus, rather than outright challenge the homogenous image of "the typical Asian family," he instead assumes that his mother is "always busy," and so that might explain why she and his family are exceptions.

By contesting the stereotypes for themselves or their families, such students indicate, even if unintentionally, support for the stereotype. By labeling themselves as different, the implication is that most Asian Americans fall within these dominant constructions. This subtle acceptance of a homogenous Asian American student and family could have the detrimental effect of fueling a sense of personal failure and a distancing from other Asian Americans who are believed to fit the expectations (see Kibria 2002). As SCHS counselor Carrie Paz has found, some of the students she works with even describe themselves as "fake Asians" or "not really Asian" because they do not perceive themselves as "smart, like all the other Asians." Overall, while many of these students presented examples and statements countering constraining representations, the fact that they defined themselves in relationship, even if in opposition, to this dominant image reveals its magnitude and its influence on their sense of selves.

Latina/o students adopt a slightly different approach to defying typification. That is, like sophomore Nathan Yi, they tend to outright verbally contest stereotypes and the controlling constructions of all Latinas/os. These differing approaches may be rooted in the disparate racialized constructions that Asian Americans encounter relative to Latinas/os. However, while both constructions are confining, they have differing implications.

Aware of the negative stereotypes about Latinas/os, some students turn these stereotypes into motivating factors to excel. When asked how, if at all, her background has influenced her experience at SCHS, AVID (Advancement via Individual Determination) student Iris Pedraza explains, "We Hispanics expect more of us because people say Hispanics just work on farms, and we want to prove them wrong, be teachers, be engineers, be business people." Thinking about his father who fled the political and military violence in El Salvador in the 1970s, AVID student Rafael Avila concurs:

> Sometimes people judge me by the way I look and not by the way I am . . . A lot of Hispanics don't go to four-year universities or colleges, and I want to try not to be like that. I want to make a difference for Hispanics and for me.

Many Latinas/os, especially AVID students, echoed this sense of resolve and will to "prove them wrong" and "make a difference." Just as students' knowledge of their family struggles motivate them, as detailed in chapter 2, the support and sense of community that AVID students describe as instrumental in fostering social and cultural capital may also shape this collective determination that both Iris and Rafael possess.

As one of the few Latinas/os to participate in the school's IB program, junior Ashley Cordero draws on what she calls her background as Puerto Rican, Dominican, Mexican, and Spanish along with her academic successes to also contest others' assumptions:

> There's a mind-set here . . . The Asians are the smart ones . . . The Lati-
> nas and Latinos are the ones that are not as smart and are too lazy . . .
> I'm glad that I was mixed. It breaks that mind-set, that stereotype. Also,
> it makes others become more motivated 'cause they're like, "Oh, wow."

Critical of the unequal expectations placed on students, Ashley emphasizes how being "mixed" enabled her to transcend others' limitations. On
first read, it might appear that Ashley is highlighting the significance of
being "mixed" because she accepts the biological assumptions that racial/
ethnic categories are innate, fixed, and unchanging. However, instead,
she articulates a more complex conception that defies labeling by shatter-
ing paradigms. She adopts a "mestiza consciousness—an identity that is
fluid, resilient, and oppositional" (Delgado Bernal 2006, 127). Like her
Latina/o schoolmates Iris and Rafael, Ashley adopts a consciousness ben-
efitting more than herself. By participating in the IB program, she believes
that her actions both inspired and corrected some of her classmates:

> I know I motivated many . . . and then I kind of changed the mind-set
> within IB. Students within IB, they'll be, "Oh my gosh, you're in IB?
> You're Hispanic." And I'm, "Your point is?" And they're like, "No,
> I'm just saying, it's just, there's never been."

For some Latinas/os, "proving them wrong" also involves participating in school activities where students see themselves as underrepresented.
This was one of the major motivators for senior Maggie Cordova and two
of her Black and Latina friends to join the school newspaper:

> We're the only three that aren't Asian on the staff . . . [W]e did it
> because that's actually what we want to do; it's the career path we
> want to take, and we're like, "Let's just do it in high school." We
> thought it's breaking the barrier because yearbook and journalism
> and everything except ASB [the associated student body] are done by
> the Asian community.

Maggie and her friends were also committed to working toward a heterogeneous staff more reflective of the student population:

> You can't have only one demographic of the school, one ethnicity of
> the school running something that is the paper that is supposed to tell
> the students about the day, the life, the week of the school. I thought it
> was weird to have one perspective from them. So that's why I joined it.

When discussing trying out for the newspaper, Maggie was confident and
self-assured. Her determination to be a journalist and to disrupt racial/
ethnic inequities impelled her to join, and it fuels her lifetime goals.

Similar to racial/ethnic disparities in school participation, there are also gender expectations that a few participants contest. For example, junior Andy Tellez is only one of several men in the over thirty students in the school's ASB, where the school's activities are planned and organized. Andy reflects on the factors driving this unequal gender distribution:

> There's more girls in ASB and in all my classes. I think a lot of guys
> are just afraid of being involved in something. I don't know. Maybe
> just their maleness is not as male.

During a discussion I had with all the group's members, other students echoed Andy's perception that men may feel threatened participating in ASB. With comments such as "guys do the heavy lifting," the athletics commissioner is a more "manly position" in ASB, "females run the show," and "girls are more interested in rallies and dances," such assumptions pervade thinking about who should be involved in ASB and the type of work they should perform. Within this context, Andy Tellez disrupts the gendered expectations that are limiting men's participation in certain campus activities:

> I think it is just based on the person. I don't care because this is
> something that is good, and I'm glad I'm doing it, and I wish there
> was more guys. I tried out for the cabinet, and I didn't make it. It's
> just because people view women as more responsible. That's not true
> to everyone.

Countering other's assumptions about what he should do and that women are "more responsible," Andy adopts an "I don't care" attitude that contests strict gender binaries that contain interests. As he argues, "It is based on the person." He applies this same fluid approach to gender and interests to his enrollment in Spanish honors:

> In my Spanish honors class, there are a lot of girls. I think it is just
> based on a lot of things. Just everything, a lot of girls do better at, but
> I think, the guys are trying to break that. I am.

While young Mexican American men are underrepresented in honors courses and face high push-out rates, Andy draws strength knowing that he is disrupting these patterns, and he does so with a more inclusive, unstable, and flexible understanding of gendered expectations.

A couple of Latina/o students are determined to "prove them wrong" not only at school but also at home. AVID student Art Casas is compelled to dispel the low expectations of his friends and parents. As explained in chapter 2, he recently switched from taking junior English to an AP English course. While the overcrowded, standing-room-only English class was part of the reason for his switch, the flack he received from his friends who are in the AP course also played a role:

> My basketball team is mainly Asian. So all of my friends are Asian. All
> of my friends are in [AP English], so another reason I joined that class
> is to prove them wrong. They always make fun of me because I'm Mex-
> ican. They're talking like, "You're gonna go to [community college]."

While earlier Art proudly identified as Puerto Rican because of its uniqueness at the school, here he explains that his friends emphasize his Mexicanness when belittling him academically. Perhaps given the hegemonic constructions of Mexicans at SCHS, it is this aspect of his identity that his friends ridicule suggesting that part of Art's earlier emphasis on being uniquely Puerto Rican may actually be an attempt to distance himself from the stigma he and other students experience. Furthermore, just as he contends with friends' ridicule, Art explains that he must prove his parents wrong too: "They don't really think I can get an A in that class. They think I should've stayed in English 3, got an A and not do English AP and get a C."

Senior Angelica Vega, who in chapter 3 described being referred to as "Mike Tyson" by school officials because of a fight she had early in her schooling, is equally as committed to proving her family wrong. For her, this involves leaving home after high school graduation:

> I want to be the one that gets out of the house—the youngest one
> being independent, proving them all wrong. My family, they're all still
> there. That's why I wanted to move. Just to be on my own, indepen-
> dent, leave young now, not [when I'm] thirty-eight years old like my
> brother.

As the youngest of seven, Angelica feels that she grew up "faster" and is more "settled" than her brothers and sisters who have relied on her mother. Thus she wants to move out and help her mother:

> Proving to them that I'm better than what they expected . . . I'd
> like to prove to them, "Hey, I'm not like you. I'm not still at home,
> twenty-five years old, married with a husband and still living there."
> I don't want to do that . . . I don't want to be the last one to take, to
> drain her . . . I want to help her.

By leaving the house and going to community college in another town, Angelica will simultaneously be contesting the limited expectations many at SCHS have for her, and she will follow the lifestyle she envisions and not had by her siblings.

For some students, defying typification involves playing down their backgrounds. After identifying himself as "Latino because my parents are from Mexico, and they're both Mexicans and I was born here," AVID sophomore Felipe Perez explains, "I don't think your background matters; everybody's the same." Similarly, senior Rose Gonzalez, who explains how "it's harder" because she is among the first generation in her family to go to a university, nevertheless believes that "when it comes to academic matters, I don't think [social class] matters at all because it's more what you have in your head than what you have in money." Initially, it seems that comments dismissing the salience of inequalities based on background are part of the prevailing belief that we live in a so-called postracial or postclass society where the assumption is that there is a level playing field. However, for students from stigmatized backgrounds or who transgress gender binaries, such minimization of one's background and discrimination may be a strategy that enables them to realize that, in contrast to people's negative expectations, "everybody's the same." As Linda Võ considers in her research on Asian Americans, such responses may be a "pragmatic survival strategy" because "naming racism means acknowledging that others might perceive one as 'less than'" (2004, 88–89). Comments by senior Andrew Moreno, who identifies as Mexican, are suggestive: "It doesn't really matter, 'cause everyone has their own little race." He explains why he rejects the importance of backgrounds when people talk about Asian Americans:

> Most people at this school see them as, "Oh, those are the smart kids.
> Their parents probably beat them to get straight As." But it's just
> everyone talking. People just say that 'cause they're Asian, but I just
> see them as another person.

Given the context where a cultural determinist discourse positions Asian Americans as superior to Latinas/os, denying the salience of racial/ethnic backgrounds is a challenge to hegemonic and hierarchical constructions. After all, affirmations of identity are not always liberating; they may be structures that discipline and regulate. Sociologist Steven Seidman explains,

> Identity constructions function, if you will, as templates defining
> selves and behaviors and therefore as excluding a range of possible
> ways to frame one's self, body, desires, actions, and social relations
> (1994, 173).

Overall, these examples of defying typification are not unusual. Disclaimers by Asian Americans of being different relative to what is perceived as "typical Asian achievement" are common (Kibria 2002, 135). Similarly, studies have also documented Latina/o students' determination to prove people wrong when confronted with a stigmatized identity (Flores-Gonzáles 2002; Yosso 2006). However, not all students respond to others' expectations and negative exchanges in the same way. For Asian Americans, the "model minority" myth creates "an imagined yardstick" that is impossible for many to achieve (Kibria 2002, 136). As a result, this has resulted in what Vivian Louie (2004) describes as "a set of psychological burdens" on students (87). Likewise, Latina/o students who have been made to feel academically inferior may internalize others' low expectations of them and underperform. Thus while defying typification is certainly a form of resistance, no student should have to face and then challenge the narrow, exclusionary, and sometimes downright hostile attacks on their identities. Patty Song succinctly captures many students' yearnings: "I don't want to fit into a stereotypical image; I want to be an individual."

As students struggle with confining messages, some are actively creating, maintaining, and affirming a sense of self that is influenced by their positions within larger racial/ethnic, class, and gender hierarchies. Whether affirming their identities, playing with stereotypes, or aiming to prove others wrongs, these forms of resistance enable students to navigate unequal and unjust terrain. Some students combine these individual acts of resistance with the following to transform spaces.

Creating Transformative Spaces

In schools like SCHS, where most students are of color, speak multiple languages, and have immigrant ties, there are rare spaces on campuses where students are provided with the tools to help them process their experiences and the multiple messages they receive about race/ethnicity, immigration, class, and gender. With the exception of so-called foreign language classes such as Spanish and Mandarin, students are often expected to leave their families' histories, languages, and experiences at school gates or classroom doors. Nonetheless, there are select teachers and students who aim to create what Emma Pérez (1993) refers to as *un sitio y una lengua*—a space and a language of critical reflection, deconstruction, and change (for examples, see Darder 2002; Ochoa 2007).

SCHS students emphasized two spaces that have been instrumental in enhancing empowerment and critical awareness—the student organization MEChA and advanced placement courses taught by teacher Michelle Mesa. Both of these spaces are important. However, perhaps because they generally involve different students—working-class Latinas/os and middle-class and upper-middle-class Asian Americans—are associated with different struggles, and entail varied practices beyond the classroom, they have not been equally supported. While MEChA is met with additional barriers that test students' and teachers' resolve to persist, Michelle Mesa's advanced placement course is frequently praised by the school administration. In both of these spaces, activist teachers, or what Daniel Solorzano and Dolores Delgado Bernal (2001) describe as "transformational role models," are instrumental in nurturing students' critical consciousness about inequality and a concurrent commitment to social justice.

"We Just Empower": Merging Critical Theory and Activism through MEChA

After a slow, singular clap that gradually gained strength, speed, and volume as more students joined in, students ended a May 2007 MEChA meeting with a call and response: "Who are we?" "MEChA" "Who are we?" "MEChA!"[1] This unity clap or Chicano solidarity clap used by the United Farm Workers when they were looking for each other in the fields connects students to one another and to the past. Plus, the call and response is a sign of affirmation and a sense of belonging. After all, as student Summer Reyes details, she often has to explain MEChA to her classmates and teachers:

> Everybody calls us the "Mexican club." And I tell them, "It's not." "Well then, explain to me what you guys do." And I'm like, "Well, we just empower Latino culture, but we're not just Mexicans. There're all different types of people in our club." We actually had an Asian person in our cabinet this year. And I hate when people call it Mecca-ha. It's not Mecca-ha; it's Me-ch-a!

Although sometimes the misperceptions and lack of awareness anger Summer, she speaks proudly of her participation and the group. Her poise and critical analysis reflect the very empowerment that she describes as a goal of MEChA. Similarly, senior Christopher Zuniga beams as he eagerly shares the group's purpose:

> It's a Latino enrichment cultural club. We try to promote higher-level learning like college . . . We take students to the [local MEChA] conferences, and they get to see that there is more than just high school.

Conversations with such members and their advisors, observations at a few of their meetings, and letters in the student paper reveal the empowering and oppositional space that they have built. This is a space "developed to battle a hegemonic consciousness utilized by ruling groups to repress potentially empowering beliefs and behaviors of an oppressed constituency" (Morris 1992, 363).

The roots of MEChA are oppositional and linked to a history of resistance; the emphasis on empowerment, Latinas/os, culture, and higher education at SCHS has its origins in the formation of MEChA during the 1960s Chicana/o Movement. During that period, Mexican American high school and college students were increasingly voicing their dissatisfaction with inferior education through the promotion of Chicana/o self-determination, student protests, school strikes, the adoption of a Chicana/o identity, and the formation of student organizations (Gómez-Quiñones 1990; Gutiérrez 1995). In 1969, Chicanas/os met at the University of Santa Barbara to create a plan for higher education—El Plan de Santa Barbara. The plan detailed the purposes of MEChA:

> MEChA must bring to the mind of every young Chicana and Chicano that the liberation of her/his people from prejudice and oppression is in her/his hands and this responsibility is greater than personal achievement and more meaningful than degrees, especially if they are earned at the expense of her/his identity and cultural integrity. MEChA, then, is more than a name; it is a spirit of unity, of sisterhood and brotherhood, and a resolve to undertake a struggle for liberation in society where justice is but a word. MEChA is a means to an end.

Given its history and the larger focus on challenging prejudice and oppression, maintaining one's identity, and struggling for liberation, MEChA is a site of struggle that combines theory and action.[2] It is described as the "largest and longest lasting Chicana/o student activist network and organization" (Licón 2009).

While the original emphasis was on Chicanas/os, given changing demographics and political climates, SCHS students reflect a pattern found in other contemporary MEChAs (see Valle 1996). It is open to students across backgrounds who share similar interests or experiences. About eighteen to twenty students attended the lunch meetings in May 2007 as the group was selecting the cabinet for the following academic year. While more than half the students were Latina and about a third were Latino, there were several Asian American women also in attendance. Informal conversations indicated that the Asian American members were likely to come from predominately Latina/o neighborhoods and were the first members in their families to attend college. While not all the members of MEChA are first-generation college students, such shared experiences may influence students' perspectives, commitments, and identities.

At SCHS, MEChA is an avenue for students to unite in the push for Latina/o academic advancement. Teacher Thomas Rojas explains,

> There's a problem because I think a lot of our Latino kids are left behind at this school, and they're not informed what their options are and how important those honors classes are when they're thinking about applying to a four-year college. The way we tried to fix that is through MEChA.

Senior Dolores Anaya was inspired to join MEChA precisely because of the campus climate, where she too believes that Latinas/os are not urged to excel academically:

> As one of the very few Latinas involved [in school], I wanted to stand out or be involved in MEChA . . . Latinos in general in this school are not encouraged enough . . . I don't think they're expected to do as much.

Rather than ignore the disparities at SCHS or adopt the prevailing cultural determinist argument that blames students and their families, MEChA provides a space for students to systematically understand the differences in course placement, disrupt the assumptions, and change the patterns.

MEChA is a unique site where students across racial/ethnic, class, gender, generation, and curriculum track unite through a range of activities that extend their learning and activism outside of the classroom. These include attending conferences, visiting colleges, and participating in immigrant rights struggles. For example, during the annual Cesar Chavez Day, the group educated the campus by organizing a day of silence and having a sit-in during lunch with placards. They also host a yearly talent show and tutor students at Maple Grove—the predominately working-class Latina/o middle school that feeds into SCHS. Together, MEChA's activities emphasize higher education, and they provide students with support, historical and cultural awareness, leadership experiences, and critical thinking skills.

MEChA also creates a space of affirmation where students exude bicultural identities and are not expected to forgo their racial/ethnic identities as they advance academically. In fact, all three of these student organizers—Summer, Christopher, and Dolores—are part of the small group of Latinas/os enrolled in honors and advanced placement courses at the school. It is unclear which came first or if it happened simultaneously: these students were involved in MEChA and were then inspired to enroll in honors courses or vice versa. However, other studies confirm that students of color who possess a strong racial/ethnic identity have a more favorable disposition toward schooling than students of color who adopt a raceless identity (Harris 2011). As Bettie found in her work with a group of California high schoolers, through MEChA, Mexican American students are able to "do well in school and yet maintain a political-cultural racial/ethnic identity" (2003, 89). Given these benefits, student involvement in such organizations may be seen as a strategy that does not require complete replacement of one's values, norms, and traditions with dominant expectations. Instead, such involvement fosters "accommodation without assimilation" where students can excel academically and acquire knowledge of their backgrounds (Gibson 1988).

In spite of the positive outcomes from their involvement, participants experience some of the barriers that impelled the formation of the organization in the first place. That is, MEChA and its members are forced to contend with constant misunderstanding as well as with outright opposition. As Summer Reyes explained in the beginning of this section, she often has to clarify the purposes of the organization by correcting people's assumptions. However, what is more troubling is how the group has to defend itself and its activities. As a two-year member of MEChA, Summer was the most critical of the opposition she and the organization have faced—much of it by the school administration:

> When I took [a leadership position in MEChA], I was really sad to see how the administration treated us, like how they discriminated against us. I didn't really think it was possible to see it at a school. I thought it was only out in the real world. I was like, "This is a preview of the real world."

Hoping that schools would be inclusive, Summer has to contend with the reality that schools are not places immune to discrimination.

One of the ways that MEChA and those connected with it have experienced such discriminatory treatment is through hypersurveillance. For example, the group's talent show is a large and popular event organized in the school's theatre. It is one of the few student-run events that brings together a cross-section of the campus and community. However, rather than being praised and supported for their work, students encounter the opposite. Devoting her spring break to the organization of the talent show, Summer explains how the show was received by the administration:

> I broke down twice that week because sometimes we don't have enough support from the administration at school. That entire week they were telling us that we had to pay $1,500 for security alone because the past two years, there has been fights at the talent show.

They were like, "Oh you guys need more security." And they charged us that much, and we didn't have the money because [our teacher], kept telling me not to fund raise anymore because we had enough money . . . They almost canceled the show twice, which were the two times that I broke down.

Summer faced multiple barriers from the administration, causing her tremendous stress. Expanding on this sentiment, teacher Emily Saldana adds,

[The administration's] like, "Oh, we need a lot of security there. We need a lot of administrators there." Well, why are you saying that? Why is it different when it's the Chinese New Year? We needed to have all these police there. We needed to have all this extra security, and I brought it up to the administration, "Why do we need all this extra security? Why are you perceiving that of us? It's just a talent show. What type of student do you think is going to be there that's going to create havoc or chaos?"

Both students and teachers are frustrated by the unequal treatment of MEChA and what appears to be the administration's belief that the people who attend their events are more inclined to criminality than the presumably middle-class and upper-middle-class Asian American students who attend Chinese New Year activities. As teacher Emily Saldana knows, "That affects the kids. They ask, 'Gosh, why are they doing this to us? Why don't they support us?'"

The hyperscrutiny of MEChA and Latina/o students in general was especially revealing in 2006 when over forty thousand students walked out of Los Angeles area schools in opposition to the anti-immigration bill House Resolution 4437: the Border Protection, Antiterrorism, and Illegal Immigration Control Act. Summer Reyes recalls what happened at SCHS after students walked out:

I saw real discrimination. A lot of people were absent because they wanted to walk out and [the administration] went through the lists [of absences], and they only gave people citations to those with Hispanic last names . . . Some of my friends that have Hispanic last names, they were absent because they were really sick, and they got citations. [One of my friends], her mom talked to [a school administrator], and she was like, "She was sick." And he was like, "I don't believe you. I need proof."

The systematic citing of all students with Spanish-language surnames who were absent from school confirmed Summer's belief that the school discriminates against Latinas/os.

As recounted in chapter 3, Summer finds that such discrimination and the continued surveillance are intimately connected to being a Mexican woman involved in MEChA. Summer describes the confounding impacts of marginality, where as an activist Mexican-identified woman involved with a stigmatized organization, she is treated unfairly. Overall, extracurricular school activities confer different levels of prestige on students. Typically, students who are involved in the production of school-sanctioned dances, assemblies, newspapers, and yearbook receive special status from school personnel in ways that consumers of school activities and nonparticipants do not (Eckert 1989). Students who are in charge of these activities are often provided with leadership positions and greater freedom of movement on campus. However, Summer Reyes's experiences illustrate how not all student leaders are granted privileges and not all forms of campus involvement are equally valued. In Summer's case, she believes she faces surveillance and reduced status and prestige because of her identity as a Mexican woman and her involvement with an overtly political and less-assimilationist organization.

Not only are MEChA and Latina/o students in general presumed guilty, but even teachers, as transformational role models associated with the organization, feel scrutinized and blamed for students' activities. Teacher Emily Saldana highlights,

> We did not in any way tell students, "Walk out. Do all this stuff." I remember we were getting ready for the talent show, and we were meeting after school and we were looking at the bands. Some administrators had come by, and they're like, "What's going on? What are you planning?" It was the week that was going to be the walkouts; they thought we were getting ready. It's like all of these little underlying things. We feel like we are being targeted. I also remember in a staff meeting, a teacher said, "Oh, what are you going to do if the kids walk out? What's going to happen?" One of the administrators in front of the entire staff said, "I don't know. Emily Saldana, what's going on? What's going to happen?" Then when the walkouts did happen, we didn't know they were going to happen, but we get blamed for a lot of things.

Such experiences of "being targeted" and "blamed" can take a toll on teachers as well as students. These experiences have the effect of regulating behaviors and disciplining those who even appear to be transgressing rules and regulations. In this case, teacher Emily Saldana was not involved in the student walkouts, but her work with Latina/o students and MEChA, and perhaps even her own identity as a Mexican American woman, made her suspect.

These experiences of academic profiling are similar to the police pro-filing that many Blacks and Latinas/os encounter when they are stopped, questioned, and assumed to be suspect by police officers. This policing of politicized groups of color has a long history in the United States. One only has to consider the 1950s and the 1960s, when under the directive of J. Edgar Hoover, the FBI's Counter Intelligence Program (COINTELPRO) engaged in a series of covert activities aimed at monitoring, discredit-ing, and eventually eradicating various political organizations within the United States, including the Black Panther Party and the Brown Berets (Pulido 2006). While the intent may have been different in 1999 when members of SCHS's then-active Black Student Union (BSU) participated in the first ever Black College Expo at the Los Angeles Convention Center, the implications were the same—Black youth were treated as suspect and even criminal. An advisor of SCHS's previous BSU recalls,

> We were out having a good time, and I think because they saw kids
> that were dressed with the low-cut pants or they were youth. I don't
> know what tipped them off, but they came in with riot gear. We
> were separated from our parties. I didn't know where half the kids
> were, and if you were on the inside, you couldn't get on the outside;
> if you were on the outside, you couldn't get on the inside. It was an
> experience to see that and for the kids to see that because they didn't
> understand why are the police here in riot gear. So many of them
> [were asking], "Why are we being held hostage? We're just trying to
> get some information for college, and we're just trying to do our thing
> as young Black people."

After raising funds to cover the buses for transportation and excited to learn more about college, students and advisors at the Black College Expo were greeted by police in riot gear. Soon after this terrifying field trip, the BSU at SCHS was no longer active.

In addition to the barriers and outright discrimination encountered by those working in politicized groups, whether in the BSU or MEChA, stu-dents in these groups have been cast as the so-called problem and charged with *causing* divisions at SCHS. In 2001 while the organizations were growing and becoming more active, the debate about their roles on cam-pus permeated the pages of the school's newspaper. Sections from two student letters, one from the paper's editorial staff and another from a student at large, capture much of the critiques:

> America: a melting pot of different cultures and ethnicity. Our diver-sity defines our country, just as the backgrounds of [SCHS] students
> define our campus . . . At school, most students of the same race

huddle together into separate groups and cliques . . . Take for example the ethnic clubs. For each race, there is a different club. Shouldn't we be participating in activities that bring students together instead of isolating them into different factions?

The author of the second letter argues,

The whole point of clubs created with a cultural theme was, and still is, the root of the student body division problem.

This first letter uses the same symbolism as teacher Harriet Andrews when, in chapter 1, she drew on the image of the United States as a "melting pot." This discourse, along with the ideas presented in both letters, promotes more than integration. It expects students to forgo their identities, blames students for divisions, and overlooks the role of institutions in fostering both separation and inequality. This "power-evasive" approach assumes that all have equal levels of power, and it removes the responsibility of institutional practices such as curriculum tracking that unequally sort and divide students.

Responding to the sentiment at SCHS critiquing organizations such as MEChA and the then-BSU, one of the MEChA advisors also submitted an article to the school's paper. Using a power-aware framework emphasizing the importance of multicultural history and not assimilating or melting away, the letter sarcastically began,

Let's begin by making anyone who has an ethnic name like Jose, Maria, or Ji-Ling change it to Joe, Mary, and Bob. Next, let's force everyone to speak only English . . . Similarly, let's get rid of all the books that deal with race and culture. I mean, why learn about the Jewish Holocaust, the Native American Removal Act, the Japanese Internment Camps, the Bracero Program, the Zoot Suit Riots and slavery? Students don't need to know about the brave heroes of the past who died trying to change the oppressive system they lived in . . .

Echoing MEChA organizers, this teacher confirms that MEChA not only creates a space of affirmation but also provides crucial historical knowledge in the movement to eliminate oppression. Continuing with her sarcasm, she also punctuates that MEChA and the then-BSU foster empowered, engaged, and critically thinking students:

I suppose that [student members] have learned too much about the history of Chicanos and African Americans through MEChA and BSU, and have now been empowered to take on the "system." Bad, bad, students. You see, good students are supposed to just sit behind

their desks, take notes like sponges, and never ever question or criticize the world around them.

Adopting a student-centered approach to education, which challenges
the traditional "banking method of education" where the teacher is the
conveyor of knowledge and students passively receive information (Freire
1970), this MEChA advisor knows the power of dialogical spaces that
enable critical analysis. She realizes that it is this consciousness and sense
of solidarity that some fear:

> Look at what happened when Martin Luther King Jr. questioned
> the government because of its unfair practices against minorities, or
> when Cesar Chavez questioned the unfair practices of the farming
> industry toward migrant workers, or when Rosa Parks questioned the
> segregation of blacks and whites in public spaces. Yes, indeed, it is
> a dangerous thing when people start to question the powers that be.
> The next thing you know, people will start to demand changes and
> try to make life fair for everyone. Now that would be a terrible thing,
> don't you think?

MEChA is a site of resistance precisely because it remains resolute in
tackling disparities. It provides what some refer to as the "forgotten"
students with an arena of racial/ethnic affirmation, a path to higher education, historical knowledge, and a sense of empowerment. It also builds
inclusive spaces and connects with the surrounding community through
activities such as tutoring and the talent show. Perhaps because they are
part of a longstanding power-aware organization that is fostering critically conscious and actively engaged students outside of the classroom,
those involved with MEChA are subject to further obstacles. What has
been most difficult is the presumption of criminality that Latina/o students and their allies encounter. However, from these experiences and the
support and skills developed through MEChA, students such as Summer
Reyes have acquired a power-aware analysis for understanding the school
and society. As Summer shares, she has developed key strategies that
will enhance her navigational skills as she continues with her education.
She offers the advice she has received about how to contend with discrimination: "Like my teacher said, I have to work my way around the
system." This is a technique teacher Michelle Mesa employs through her
pedagogy and curriculum.

"My Own Little Crusade": Michelle Mesa's Mission in the Classroom

Even before meeting Michelle Mesa, I had heard about her and her advanced placement courses from administrators and students. They raved about her teaching, and months later, when Michelle Mesa shared her philosophy with me, it was apparent that her mission reflected what I had already learned about her:

> The more time that I'm here, the more I see that there's this longing
> to want to understand each other, but there are so many divisions
> and so many things that are in place that prevent that from happen-
> ing and so I have sort of taken it as my own little mission where I
> bring multicultural aspects and issues in the classroom.

While Mesa's work is equally important as MEChA's in the struggle to disrupt the dominant narratives and culture on campus, rather than being received with ambivalence or outright suspicion, she is applauded as a model teacher. Perhaps like students in journalism and yearbook, her teachings are school sanctioned because they cater to students designated as academically successful, and unlike MEChA, they do not typically entail the combination of theory and action in the form of collective activism *outside* of the classroom space. Individual classrooms, students, and relationships may change as a result of her engaged pedagogy, but a connection to a larger organization and visible forms of group action are not apparent. Thus Mesa's fostering of a transformational space within the classroom may be more palatable to administrators than the resistance demonstrated by MEChA.

Students credit Mesa for facilitating vibrant discussions that help them understand their experiences and have the potential to enhance the campus climate. Students value her classes for deconstructing stereotypes and breaking taboos of cross-racial/ethnic discussions. Senior Patty Song explains the importance of such a space:

> If a student were to try to address [the stereotypes], they would get
> beat up or something. But in my class last year, my teacher was very
> open; she let us discuss anything we wanted. And it was really fun
> because there were Mexicans and Asians in our class, and we were
> allowed to talk about the stereotypical images in our class, and
> I think that's the way to vent what are our images of our school.
> So that was really cool because we can't do that outside of the
> classroom.

Summer Reyes agrees that Mesa's classes are instrumental in inciting discussion and reflection:

In our class, we had a couple of debates. Like, we had four corners—gender, race, age, social economic, and we had to write a paper on how we were being discriminated . . . [T]he Asians were talking about the Virginia shooting and all this other stuff, like how they were being targeted. So then I told them about the walkouts, and this other girl said that one day when she was in fifth grade someone called her house and they were like, "Oh, can I speak to your mom?" and she's like, "My mom doesn't speak English; she speaks Spanish." And they're like, "Oh well then tell her to go back to Mexico." That's the [issue] we spent the most time on because everyone had something to say. And the teacher talked about it, and she's like, "One thing the school is concerned with is that it's like two schools, and they want to make it one, not two." So she asked the class for ways to unite everyone.

Students appreciate these opportunities that allow them to think about and share their experiences. These dialogues help break down misperceptions and build understanding. Likewise, including contemporary issues such as the 2007 school shooting at Virginia Tech and students' relationships to such events makes education relevant and helps inform students. As in the example of MEChA, students are treated as contributing members of the space rather than as passive consumers of knowledge. Their ideas and experiences form part of the curriculum.

The dynamics at SCHS have fueled Mesa's transformational pedagogical approach:

I felt the need to have these conversations in my classroom because I wasn't getting the dialogue from colleagues, and I wasn't seeing the dialogue going in the direction that I wanted to from my administrators. So why not go to the source and start my own little crusade?

As detailed in chapter 1, the narrow presentation of test results and the constant reference to a so-called gap hinder the dialogue among school officials. As Mesa explains, "If there are no examples or no conversations to take place, then how can we change?" Agreeing with her colleagues who have advised MEChA, Mesa believes that such change needs to disrupt not only the separation on campus but also the inequality that accompanies such division:

Everything is always very separate, and everything that is considered more favorable is always placed on the Asian population. There hasn't been enough attention in terms of recruitment or mentoring of our Hispanic students to [enroll], for example, in AP or honors classes.

Mesa's power-aware view and strong relationship with students allow her to see the inequalities occurring daily, but there is so much silence surrounding these disparities that she refers to them as the "elephant in the classroom" and "in staff meetings." She reflects, "I don't think that anyone, including myself has been open enough to really go there primarily out of fear. Fear of how to speak openly about these issues because in doing so you would reveal maybe your own shortcomings as an individual." As Mesa ponders, unpacking the campus dynamics and deep-seated stereotypes may provoke many concerns. These might include the fear of realizing how individuals internalize and reproduce exclusionary beliefs and practices, the fear of learning new ways of thinking and teaching to reach all students, the fear of acknowledging the depth of inequality and how difficult it is for one person to tackle systemic injustices, and the fear of losing control by opening up discussion.

In spite of these reservations, Mesa is committed to creating transformative classrooms that enable discussion and help shift the discourse surrounding Asian Americans, Latinas/os, and schooling. Whether it's through discussions, journals, or readings, Mesa reports that students are encouraged to openly reflect and share their thoughts—facilitating the process of critical thinking, unlearning, and relearning:

> This one student did a double entry journal in which he had to pick a passage and document why that passage was of interest to him . . . One of the comments was that he was under the understanding that all Latin women were interested in was sex, and I wrote back to him, "Where does this come from? Why do you think this?"

Left unnamed, such dominant images of Latinas as hypersexual are allowed to fester. They permeate the media, and as demonstrated in chapter 1, educators have used these constructions to justify unequal educational policies. Given her own position, Mesa feels compelled to disrupt these conceptions: "There was no one around to challenge those assumptions [of Latinas as hypersexual] except for me, and I had to challenge them because I thought to myself, 'Here I am as a Hispanic teacher; how is [this student] seeing me?'"

With her reflective assignments, Mesa is able to question dominant assumptions, expose fallacies, and foster student learning. She also provides strategies for students to mediate the multiple forces influencing their perspectives and their lives:

> I had a student last year who said that his mother felt that most Hispanics were lazy and dumb and wouldn't amount much to anything.

So you have the family, you have the school, you have all of these things operating in tandem. How does the student make sense of all of these variables? Then there are some students who are not performing as well. But is it that they're not capable or is it that they're succumbing to the stereotype because that's how they're choosing to mediate amongst these social, political, and economic forces? So we talk about this and the different ways that people can mediate in general when they're up against forces like this.

Just as Mesa's classes provide an avenue for students to challenge the compounding exclusionary messages they receive, they also offer strategies on navigating the forces that students may encounter. As such, she is engaged in what Janie Ward (1996) refers to as "raising resisters." In these examples, she is raising antiracist students and students who develop the skills to navigate the educational pipeline.

As part of her pedagogy, Mesa strategically couples her writing assignments and discussions with relevant readings:

I taught a novel two years ago, and it was absolutely profound . . .
It was a book primarily about a Hispanic boy who's confronted
with choice A or choice B. It's very much a coming-of-age novel,
and the students responded to it regardless of if they were Asian or
Hispanic . . . They could identify with being a teenager, choices,
dilemmas, morality, and consequences, and all those different things
that I think broke down those barriers for a while.

While this book is not owned by SCHS, Michelle believed it would inspire dialogue and reflection, so she asked students if they would be interested in reading and purchasing it. When they agreed, she successfully incorporated it into the course curriculum.

As transformative approaches to schooling, self, and relationships, such spaces are not easy. Unlike traditional classrooms where there is a one-way transfer of knowledge from teachers to students, these dialogical and student-centered spaces may be unpredictable and emotion filled (see hooks 1994). Student Summer Reyes remembers an especially sensitive classroom discussion:

We were talking about what parents think, and this Asian guy said
that they were at the store and that someone was stealing something
and his mom was like, "Oh, don't worry. It's probably some Hispanic." And he said that through his mind he saw a fat Hispanic lady
in slippers, and all of us were like, "What?" All of the Asians were
mad at him, and [Becky,] this Asian girl, she speaks her mind. She

doesn't care who it is. She started yelling at him and saying, "That's wrong." He started crying, and then our teacher felt really bad, "No, you guys have to be nice to each other, blah, blah, blah."

Since students are sharing relevant topics about their families, perceptions, and racial/ethnic constructions, they are more invested in participating. Thus not only may they have emotional and physical reactions to the course—as in anger and sadness that appear in raised voices and tears—but also they are actively finding their voices and reformulating their ideas. In particular, they do so by using the Socratic fish or fish bowl, as student Marsha Smith describes, "We put certain people in a circle and then there's an audience. So the circle's debating the text, and the audience is observing," Mesa removes the focus of the class from her and the traditional teacher-student talk. This allows students to shape the direction of the discussion and to dialogue among themselves. In this example, this Socratic fish not only uncovered the exclusionary beliefs of parents and a student but also demonstrated the antiracism of a vocal Asian American student who had a strong response to her classmate's comments. When necessary, Mesa stepped in to facilitate the conversation and ease the pain.

Mesa knows that nurturing student trust, learning, and relationships takes time. So before delving into such topics, she spends several days building community in the classroom:

> For me, respect in the classroom is huge; I for them, them for me, and them for each other. So I spend a lot of time in the beginning of each year really fostering that whole idea. I know some teachers get into curriculum right away. I'll spend a good two or three days on just students getting to know each other and doing a lot of classroom building.

In contrast to authoritarian classrooms, where teachers demand that students respect them, the democratic classrooms that Mesa builds involve the mutual formation of respect. Part of building this respect is getting to know one another. This may be difficult in contemporary schooling, where classes are increasingly scripted to meet the expectations of standards-based curriculum and standardized tests. In these spaces, teachers often feel that they have less control over the time and curriculum. However, rather than rush into the curriculum to cover as much material as possible, Mesa slows down the chaotic pace and focuses instead on nurturing open and inclusive classrooms where she employs a variety of community building activities:

> It could be things like getting to know you Bingo; I have an interesting getting to know you activity using toilet paper, and students just

think that's hilarious. So there's a lot of buy-in just because of the
toilet paper. They're wondering, what are we going to do with this?
I just try different things that are engaging, interesting, and funny to
them and that has been really helpful.

While these activities may be effective, they can be difficult for some
students, especially because most have been schooled in traditional classrooms, where they are expected to be silent, obedient, and only participate
when called on; their experiences and what they know are typically devalued in classrooms (Ochoa and Pineda 2008). Thus coming from such
classroom spaces and a school climate that privileges certain students
over others may produce inhibited students who would prefer being quiet
in the traditional classroom than actively engaged in a more student-
centered and participatory spaces. Knowing this, Mesa aims to create as
safe a space as possible and gain students' confidence:

I will never ask them to do something that I'm not willing to do myself,
and I think because I am willing to go there with them, it creates a sense
of safety in like, "Okay, she has our back. She's not here to expose us or
to humiliate us or to make us feel bad. It really just is what she says; it's
about us getting to know each other." I explain the importance to them
and that I'll be asking them to do a lot of things throughout the year—
mainly discussion, but in order for that they need to feel comfortable with
each other. So I find what works best is when I explain things to them.

Sharing the philosophy behind her pedagogy is part of the process of conveying respect and facilitating students' realization that they have a stake
in the class. It raises their consciousness that there are multiple ways of
running and being in a class; classes are constructed by those who occupy
them. As we saw with MEChA, these lessons can foster students' critical
thinking skills, active engagement, voice, and a more informed understanding about schooling.

By designing cooperative classrooms that combine students' experiences with course materials on a range of topics dealing with power and
inequality, Mesa offers one of the few spaces at SCHS for students to
deconstruct, imagine, and work toward changing perceptions and the
campus climate. The transformations that she has observed leave her with
the following conclusion:

I'm convinced that if you were to invite staff members and if they
could eavesdrop in some of conversations that I've had with my
students in my classroom, where some have broken down and have
cried and they really shared very personal experiences with me, that

they will see the need for [change]. Our kids should not be graduating
from here feeling dejected before they've even begun their lives.

Mesa is confident that if her colleagues are willing to break the silences by
discussing "the elephant" in the room, they too will be more inspired to
make the changes that need to happen at school.

Both the students and teachers involved with MEChA and Michelle Mesa's
classes are subverting dominant discourses and educational practices. However, too few students have access to these transformational spaces. While
MEChA is open to all students, many do not know about it or they feel
uncomfortable participating. This is not a critique of MEChA but of the
pervasive misperceptions and stark divisions that exist. MEChA students
and their allies should not carry the burden for breaking down these divides.
They need the support of their administrators and a more inclusive campus environment that fosters understanding and the dismantling of unequal
divisions. Until then, organizations such as MEChA and those affiliated
with it are put in the position of constantly having to explain themselves
and to defend their work. Similarly, having to form such intentional communities as in MEChA is also a burden that adds to the pressure that many
students of color and from working-class families already face in schools
(see Pineda 2002). Over time, these experiences take an unequal toll, such
as increased stress and a diminished sense of belonging on campus and
maybe even in society. For example, while some claim that the once-active
BSU is now defunct at SCHS because of a decrease in Black students on
campus, seeing their experiences at what was to be an exciting conference
and considering the difficulties encountered by MEChA on its own campus, I wonder if similar dynamics plagued BSU until it finally disappeared.

Just as MEChA students and their advisors are doing vital work that is
lacking at SCHS, so too is Michelle Mesa. Nevertheless, there are similar
limitations to what can be achieved through her classes. Most importantly,
only students enrolled in her advanced placement courses are directly exposed
to her curriculum and pedagogy. While these students certainly benefit and
other teachers at the school may be doing exciting work as well, during the
time that I was at SCHS, students cited Michelle Mesa's classes in particular
as being instrumental in trying to address the campus climate. Thus students
in the top classes are given this venue to think through contemporary issues,
and they are provided with additional critical thinking, analytical, and
speaking skills. By denying non–advanced placement students the opportunity to participate in such courses, inequality and division by curriculum
track persist.

Finally, administrators need to realize that simply touting Michelle Mesa's pedagogical approach is not sufficient. Not institutionalizing the type of perspectives and activities that she is employing and instead continuing to police the actions of MEChA marginalize the work of both Michelle Mesa and MEChA. Mesa's work is tokenized, and MEChA's is stigmatized.[3]

Reflections on Resistance and Pathways to Change

The students and teachers included in this chapter are engaged in multiple forms of resistance that name, destabilize, and reconstruct dominant discourses and institutional practices. While students employ various approaches—some of them influenced by their differential experiences of racialization, numerous factors enable their resistance, including family messages of pride, participation in supportive groups like AVID, and politicized and consciousness raising spaces such as MEChA. Students' tenacity reveals their "navigational capital," which helps them make their way through schooling (see Yosso 2006). The examples of MEChA and teacher Michelle Mesa also illustrate "resistant capital," or as Tara Yosso describes, "those knowledges and skills cultivated through behavior that challenge inequality" (2006, 49). These forms of resistance and critical consciousness have the potential for transformation. However, these actions alone are not enough to dismantle the ideologies, institutional practices, and structures fostering divisions and disparities at SCHS.

Schools and society cannot rely only on the actions of such students and teachers to carry the burden of responding to exclusionary beliefs and practices. The emotional labor involved in constantly trying to defend oneself and contest the wrongs of institutional practices influences the individual health and collective well-being of students and communities. As is evident in many of the examples included in this chapter, even those who contest "the mind-set" are still caught in a web of exclusionary beliefs and face additional constraints. Thus a radical rethinking and restructuring of schools and societies are needed to ensure that those who are already the most taxed by inequalities are not expected to pick up the slack of the very institutions and everyday practices that continue to subjugate. Without such a change, racial/ethnic, class, and gender hierarchies will persist. Bearing in mind the need for systemic change, the final two chapters consider the processes of working for transformation at SCHS and raise larger questions about the state of education and the possibilities of creating more loving and just schools.

CHAPTER SEVEN

Processes of Change

Cycles of Reflection, Dialogue,
and Implementation

> We always have such great ideas. They get put on paper and nothing
> happens. This gets frustrating.
>
> —*Monica Lopez, staffulty*

> We cannot have the status quo. There has to be change. It will involve
> tough love.
>
> —*Jackie Towne, staffulty*

After spending over a year at Southern California High School, I eagerly
presented what I had learned to school administrators, counselors, teachers, and other staff in the fall of 2008. I appreciated the chance to share
the work with many of the people who had welcomed students from the
Claremont Colleges and me onto campus. This was a unique opportunity,
one not often provided to researchers. While the school principals who had
influenced the research topic in 2001 and agreed to the study during the
2007–2008 academic year were no longer on campus, I was optimistic that
some of the recommendations would be considered and implemented. The
school would soon be undergoing an outside review by the Western Association of Schools and Colleges (WASC), and administrators and staffulty
were looking for ways to address what they characterized as "the gap."
A couple even justified my work by saying that it could "help with the
WASC." Likewise, comments by individuals such as Monica Lopez and
Jackie Towne at the conclusion of my presentations also left me hopeful.

As I prepared for my talks, I kept in mind the prevailing "power-evasive"
frameworks I heard at SCHS and that are described in chapter 1. These

frameworks blame individuals and groups for their experience in schools or their positions in society rather than considering the impact of larger factors on inequality (Frankenberg 1993). Realizing the extent of these discourses and how they bolster contemporary school practices and not wanting to alienate anyone by insinuating that teachers are the source of the school's problems, I aimed to counter these frameworks by providing a macro and meso context to understanding students' experiences. This included a brief discussion of the sociopolitical historical construction of race and the origins of the "model minority" myth. To capture the extent of what we are up against in the movement for educational change, I extended social psychologist Beverly Daniel Tatum's (1997) metaphor of the smog of racism to include dominant ideologies, social structures, school practices, and racist representations. Combined, these factors and misrepresentations are "like smog in the air" (6). We do not always see them, but we exist within them and ingest them. So it takes much work to cleanse our minds and society of the unjust practices and the "controlling images" that influence how people of color and members of the working class are seen and treated (see Collins 1990).

As I detail in this chapter, despite my assumed preparation for the talks, I was caught off guard. The comments I received and the outcome of the research results reflected my yearlong research. Similar frameworks as those detailed in chapter 1 emerged, and the dynamics that unfolded were a microcosm of the disparities in society. Perhaps none of this should have surprised me, but what I was least prepared for was how some invalidated, misunderstood, and even co-opted my research, words, and analysis. It was as though we were "talking past each other" (see Blauner 1999). We were talking about the same topics and many of us were even advocating for change. However, we were doing so from differing lenses, positions, and frameworks that I label from transformative power aware to cultural determinist. In the midst of all of this, I continued nurturing the relationships I was establishing with a group of progressive teachers and administrators. However, I slowly began to recoil from one of several roles that were being assigned to me—that of bridge builder—because I felt I was caught in the middle with little power. Overall, this experience and positioning left me uneasy, and I conclude this chapter with several lessons that I learned about navigating multiple terrains in the struggle for educational change—including the role I played in the events at SCHS. By honing in on the specific dynamics that unfolded at the school, I hope that other engaged researchers, administrators, staffulty, and students committed to social justice can draw from these experiences. After all, similar phenomena are playing themselves out in schools and other organizations throughout the United States.

Reflections on the Research

In October 2008, I stood in front of roughly one hundred SCHS employ-ees, ready to deliver my first of two scheduled presentations to the staff and faculty. Before beginning, a school member introduced me and the study, explaining, "This is a qualitative study, so it is subjective." I am usually one of the first people to challenge research methodologies that position researchers as so-called experts and make claims of neutrality, objectivity, and validity. However, since quantitative research is perceived by many to be more valid and rigorous, especially in our current educational period where quantitative measurements such as test scores drive education, this introduction to my research seemed to set a tone of minimizing the work and the stories of hundreds of people that I was about to share. Neverthe-less, I agree that *all* research—not just qualitative research—is subjective. Who we are influences what we research, the types of questions we ask, our frameworks, our interpretations, and how others see and respond to us.

After spending several minutes of the first talk detailing my research methodology, positionality, and longtime relationship to the location, I shared some of the findings on how students' overall perceptions of SCHS and their campus experiences vary by race/ethnicity, class, and track place-ment. I also considered the sources and ramifications of the divisions and disparities at the school. In the subsequent week's presentation, I critiqued how the narrow framing of an "achievement gap" reinforces racial/ethnic binaries and hierarchies and excludes an analysis of social and opportu-nity gaps. I concluded with several recommendations on the importance of fostering a greater sense of community at the school, leaving no students behind, and enhancing cross-racial/ethnic and class awareness. Following each of the presentations, we had fifteen to twenty minutes for questions and discussion. These comments, and the ones that I received after the presentations via e-mail and through conversations, can be categorized into the following three frameworks that capture the overall findings of this study and are helpful for contextualizing the difficulties involved in working for change.

Critically Hopeful: Adopting a Transformative, Power-Aware Framework

Several people sent clear messages of appreciation for the research and presentations. This is perhaps best captured by language arts teacher Marie Silva, who exclaimed, "Thank you! You shared, affirmed what many of us have known for a while." Feeling that their observations and experiences had been confirmed, they gave thumbs ups and OK signs and made comments such as "awesome," "excellent," and "really good." In general, these individuals articulated what I call a transformative power-aware framework, where they critique persisting inequalities of power and resources and are looking for avenues for change individually, institutionally, and/or structurally that disrupt the status quo.[1] These critiques and recommendations for change focused primarily on school and teachers' practices. For example, teacher John Alvarez followed the first presentation with a criticism of curriculum tracking by proclaiming, "I'm wondering about the extent of being in different classes like IB [International Baccalaureate], AP [advanced placement], and CP [college preparatory] and how that makes students feel." Likewise, Marie Silva shared with the group the importance of changing course curriculum to enhance community formation. She specifically teaches Sandra Cisneros's *House on Mango Street* because she believes it creates a space where Asian American and Latina/o students are more apt to see and share their commonalities. Such comments represent a transformative power-aware analysis; they do not blame students or their families for educational outcomes but instead seek change in school and classroom practices.

Just as several teachers agreed with the research presentation and adopted a transformative power-aware analysis, so too did staff members. For example, two Latina paraprofessionals, who did not feel as comfortable speaking publically because of their unequal positions in the school, shared with me how they too have noticed racist expectations by counselors and teachers. Leaving the presentations, Mari Ramírez explained how earlier in the year her son had gone to meet with his counselor with a course schedule that both mother and son had agreed upon. However, he left that meeting with a different schedule, one that included a non–college preparatory course that would impede him from completing the requirements for attending a four-year university directly after high school. When Mari complained to the counselor about this course change, she was reprimanded for informing the school too late and was told, "Your son can always take the required class during the summer." Similarly, another Latina remembered almost in tears how her own high school teacher humiliated her. Hearing familiar stories from the students at SCHS inspired her to go back to the school to inform the teacher of the negative impact he add on her life.

Overall, Latinas/os, members of the working class, and teachers of English courses tended to express such a transformative power-aware framework following the presentations. Some might argue that it is coincidental that these individuals felt more comfortable talking to me about their larger critiques of the school; however, I believe that their own experiences of prejudice and discrimination, their perception of me as a Latina who also adopted such a framework, and/or their access to a broader under-standing of society from the literature they studied and teach are important factors in influencing their perspectives. Just as sociologist Robert Blauner (1999) found that Blacks, in comparison to Whites, tend to understand racism as historical, contemporary, and structural, not something in the past, these staffulty who come from marginalized racial/ethnic and class positions seem to also adopt a broader framework on inequality. Their "outsiders within" status in schools where Latinas/os and working-class people are underrepresented as teachers and administrators seems to have provided them with a unique angle of vision to understand educational inequities that they are determined to see transformed (see Collins 1990). As will soon become apparent, some of the same individuals who articu-lated this framework showed the most anger at the following analyses offered by their colleagues, and they were exasperated by the slipping away of what they too hoped was the possibility of transformation at SCHS.

Resigned Acceptance: Adopting a Power-Aware Framework

After my initial presentation of the research findings, science teacher Tom O'Brien was the first person to raise his hand. It shot up from the back of the room, and he proclaimed, "What you described is what we see in the community, in society. So what can *we* do?" When he spoke I sensed defiance in his voice, so I was unsure if his question was rhetorical or if he really was searching for answers.

After talking to others, I realized that his comment was illustrative of sentiment expressed by a group of individuals who also seemed to adopt a power-aware framework. However, in comparison to comments by those who stated a more transformative approach, these comments usually focused solely on factors *outside* of SCHS—often ignoring how schools play a role in reproducing inequality. The comments also suggested a level of resignation. Teacher Tara Mendez summed it up when she expressed frustration with her colleagues who appear reluctant or unwilling to change. According to her, they just say, "That's the way things are; it's too hard to change." Another teacher was also annoyed with similar comments she heard by some who simply replied, "Duh, we know this already," when talking about the research findings.

Older White men who had been working at SCHS for many years were most likely to articulate this framework publically. During their decades of teaching, they have witnessed multiple school administrators and the ebb and flow of new programs. In fact, during his interview, teacher Jim Scott even critiqued the lack of completion of most projects: "I'm involved in the school senate, academic senate and the school site council and I have these notebooks full of minutes, and I don't see any follow through. It's just not been there." Perhaps their years of seeing little to no completion of ideas and plans on the part of the administration or watching working-class students from Maple Grove Middle School "get the dirty end of the stick," as one teacher explained, has fueled a sense of resignation that change is impossible. However, by focusing mainly on the economic, political, and social factors impinging on schools, they also appeared less aware of or less concerned about the role(s) of the school and themselves in sustaining disparities. Similarly, while the Latina/o working-class staffulty who adopted the transformative power-aware analysis seemed more enraged and invested in changing the school because of the impact it was specifically having on Latina/o students, those who appeared more resigned spoke less about the implications of power and inequality for Latinas/os in particular. While they seemed cognizant of larger structural factors and sometimes even class disparities, they tended to overlook the significance of race—their own race, whiteness, and racism—in shaping school dynamics and inequalities.

As with the transformative framework, I was left wondering about my role in influencing these responses. Since I had framed the research during the presentations with a macro and meso analysis in the hopes of subverting prevailing individualistic discourses, I wondered if I had gone too much to the extreme. Had I provided a framework that was now being co-opted by some who wanted to avoid asking difficult questions about SCHS and how they are implicated in the school's inequalities? Was this framework an easy way to avoid addressing the transformations that need to happen? After all, if historical precursors, societal structures, and school policies are so entrenched, did I give the impression that change was impossible?

Lest I imply that individuals can be neatly categorized into these frameworks, it is important to emphasize that these differing frameworks represent varied sentiments, not types of people. In some cases, there were people who articulated multiple perspectives. For example, Jackie Towne's comments that begin this chapter capture a determination for transformation. She made those comments at the last meeting I had with her coworkers. However, at a previous meeting, the following exchange between us ensued. In it she illustrates a power-aware framework, but she dismisses how some at SCHS reproduce class-based hierarchies associated with different colleges and the students who attend them. As evidenced by the loud collective response Jackie Towne receives from her peers, this reproduction of class-based hierarchies is not just happening somewhere else; it is present at SCHS:

JACKIE TOWNE: What we see here is part of a larger pattern from the colleges and universities that are increasing their enrollment requirements, like UC [University of California] raising the GPA [grade point average] requirement.

GILDA OCHOA: Yes, I agree with you, but some of the students in college prep classes who are the first members of their families to graduate from high school or attend college may not know the paths to college. Also, there is a hierarchy among colleges and universities that leads some students to look down on community colleges and the students who attend them.

JACKIE TOWNE: We don't see that here.

STAFFULTY FROM THE AUDIENCE: Ohhhh.

Jackie Towne's comments are helpful for revealing her awareness of some of the larger factors impinging on schools; they also demonstrate the difficulty of always realizing multiple injustices and how they not only exist outside of schools but school cultures may even reproduce them. While Jackie might have clarified her point after a group of staffulty strongly expressed their disagreement with her, further discussion was stopped by a school official who intervened to present her own analysis of the disparities at SCHS—an all too common cultural determinist argument.

Cultural Determinist and Other Individual/Group-Level Arguments

Just as the staffulty were about to respond to Jackie Towne's earlier point about the perception of colleges at SCHS, Ana Young interjected with what I believe is a classic cultural determinist perspective. She began, "Let me tell you the Asian parent perspective." It is unclear if she thought I had been presenting the "Latina/o perspective," but this prelude and what followed seemed to undermine what I had shared the previous two meetings—including my emphasis on the heterogeneity within panethnic categories that dispels the belief that there is just one "Asian parent perspective."

Claiming to speak for all Asian parents, she continued, "Asian parents push education . . . Students lose face if they don't go to top schools; that was my experience too . . . I know that all groups value education, but Asians *really* push education." She recounted how if a student gets a B, he or she "will be beat" and that for Asian parents, there is a fine line when it comes to abuse. According to her testimony, Asian American parents expect their children to get As even in physical education. After making her points, she looked at her watch and closed the meeting with, "Okay, we have two minutes before the bell."

As described in chapter 1, arguments emphasizing the role of supposed cultural and other individual/group-level differences on students' educational outcomes are pervasive at SCHS. And after my first day presenting, language arts teacher Anthony Castro concurred with Ana Young's sentiment: "Some of what we see doesn't emanate from here; it begins before students come here. Some students come from strong cultural backgrounds." While reflecting on similar responses to the findings, teacher Mary DuPont indicated to me that she is aggravated by her colleagues' belief that Latinas/os are culturally deficient. In particular, she critiques their sentiment that Latina/o students are lazy and that as an educated Mexican American woman, she is somehow "an exception."

Compared to the power-aware frameworks, cultural determinist and other individual or group-level arguments tend to ignore systems of power and the role of prevailing ideologies and institutional practices in reproducing inequalities. Thus these arguments are often referred to as "blaming the victim" because they root blame in individuals and groups for their conditions (see Ryan 1976). Sociologist Eduardo Bonilla-Silva uses the term *abstract liberalism* to capture how some use the ideas associated with political and economic liberalism such as "equal opportunity," "choice," and "individualism" abstractly to deal with inequality (2006, 28). In general, such perspectives are based on the belief that the United States is a meritocracy with equal opportunities for individuals and groups to advance by working hard. Oftentimes underlining this framework is the acceptance of a cultural hierarchy where some values, traditions, languages, and aspirations are seen as superior to others. As exemplified by some of the previous comments after my talks, Asian Americans are praised, and Latinas/os and African Americans have typically been seen as culturally deficient.

During the presentations and discussions, the staffulty expressed three points reflecting this framework: (1) Asian Americans' and Latinas'/os' cultures (which are seen as homogenous and distinct from one another) are to blame for differences in educational outcomes; (2) not all groups should or want to attend college; and (3) change, if it is to occur, should involve altering groups or making small-scale additions to schools that generally keep institutional practices intact.

While a cross-section of the SCHS staffulty accepted such individual and group-level approaches, as a school official, Ana Young was uniquely situated to influence the staffulty, the direction of the discussion, and the possibilities for change. She had the potential of stifling discussion and hindering the opportunity for transformation. Since she ignored structural and institutional inequities and presented instead a cultural justification for the educational differences between Asian Americans and Latinas/os, as detailed in the following sections, the outcomes of the research and the next steps in the process of sharing the work were even more fragile. Overall, the three frameworks that were influencing the staffulty's response to the research shaped how the staffulty heard Ana Young's comments and their own recommendations for change.

The Dynamics of Dialoguing: Determining the Next Steps

The school bell rang soon after Ana Young finished her comments. As the bell chimed marking the end of the two planned staffulty meetings about the research, I walked over to the table where some of the most vocal teachers had been sitting, and I thanked them for their contributions to the discussion. John Alvarez shook my hand and fumed about how "the powers that be" had stopped the dialogue. I subtly agreed with him. However, several people who espoused a transformative power-aware framework refused to allow the conversation and hope for change to end, including Chris Tapia, who urged me to advise her on what she might do.

That week, I received several e-mails from SCHS—including a scathing one critiquing what had occurred at the final meeting and pleading for change. The author wrote,

> First of all I want to thank you for doing a great job of presenting your findings. You covered an extraordinary amount of data that I felt, and I believe many others felt, teachers needed and wanted to react to. In fact, we were led to believe that we would have the opportunity to dialogue with you, but [Ana Young] took over . . . [I]f these two Monday morning meetings were simply fillers of time, and if all this energy that was expended is a ruse, and if we fail to respond in real time fashion to "The Gap" that incessantly exists in our community, then I'm afraid these two meetings were a waste of time. What good is this data if we are not going to rise up to create the sort of change that is needed? It's just more static information that fills our minds. It's useless!
>
> Here are two questions I ask us to consider at [SCHS]: What was the goal for having these two lengthy meetings? And now that the data has been communicated, what are we going to do about it?
>
> True change requires true change. Change can be uncomfortable. People's toes might get stepped on. Actually we can guarantee that they will get stepped on. Is this staff willing to work diligently toward that direction? It's a monumental endeavor. And I'm not convinced that it's going to happen. Having said that . . . I don't think it's prudent or fair

to the faculty to begin something that we are not willing to finish. It happens all too often.

In short, I really appreciate your well-articulated research. It is very insightful information. And again, I don't know what the powers that be have in store for bridging "the gap." One thing I do know though is that I don't plan on being duped into believing that the Latino Community's interests at [SCHS] are of high importance. I've been around the educational "playing field" too long not to see that coming. Crumbs are not filling.

This letter clearly conveyed the transformative power-aware framework endorsed by a small group of staffulty. Like me, they wanted "true change" at the school, but some were not convinced "that the Latino Community's interests at [SCHS] are of high importance."

Shortly after I received this e-mail, Ana Young wrote to me apologizing for running out of time and inviting me back to the school for the following week to facilitate a forty- to fifty-minute discussion with the staffulty. She explained, "[I]t is so important to take action on this serious cultural and educational gap we have at [SCHS] . . . [We] have agreed to postpone our original professional development next week in order to give our teachers the opportunity to dialog and come up with steps to improve our school culture and climate. I really hope you are available." Later, when we had a chance to meet, she referred to having "hogged" the discussion at the last presentation, implying that she had heard some of the complaints. At least one person confided in me that she believed Ana had silenced dialogue at the meeting, and she stopped future discourse too because "now we all know how she feels." Nevertheless, even if cultural deficiency frameworks, the language of the "gap," and all that these discourses obfuscate were omnipresent in how my invitations to meet with the staffulty were framed, I remained hopeful that there was the will for discussion and transformation. The ensuing dialogue was promising, but our differing recommendations and paths for change were trying.

Discussion on Enhancing SCHS

Given the desire for dialogue, I was committed to making the final meeting discussion based. So school official Chris Tapia and I worked together constructing the following questions that formed the base of this discussion:

- How can [SCHS] better meet the needs of *all* students (including by course placement, socioeconomic background, and post–high school interests)?

- How can [SCHS] enhance a sense of connectedness within its community? Consider relationships among students, staffulty, and its surrounding communities as well as creating a more inclusive campus environment for *all* parents.
- How can [SCHS] work toward reducing divisions and disparities among students by race/ethnicity and socioeconomic class? Consider changes in curriculum, instruction, counseling, student activities, adult–student interactions, and student–student interactions.

The goals of this discussion were to (1) address any questions and concerns about the research; (2) encourage dialogue; (3) work toward community, reflection, planning, and implementation; and (4) leave the meeting with a plan for the next steps. Chris Tapia predetermined the discussion groups of eight to ten staffulty, and she selected who she referred to as campus "change agents" to be the group facilitators. She envisioned that these "change agents" would come together afterward to help move SCHS forward.

The small groups participated in lively conversations about ethnic studies, disparities in rates of school detention, and inequalities in parent power at the school. They considered tough issues on the salience of race/ethnicity and the overall disadvantaging of Latina/o and Black students at the school. People seemed engaged, but teachers were doing most of the talking. Indicating their more privileged position at the school relative to most staff members, they also tended to sit at the center of the tables. In contrast, the instructional aides, clerical staff, and security guards sat more quietly and on the margins of their discussion groups. These disparities within the staffulty revealed how entrenched power and inequality are. Nevertheless, I left that meeting eager to review and disseminate the groups' notes. The next day, I compiled all the notes from the discussion groups, organized them thematically, and e-mailed my summary to the school administrators. I suggested meeting to discuss the findings and expressed my interest in presenting to interested SCHS parents and students and also to teachers at the middle schools that feed into SCHS. I only heard back from one of the administrators with a short e-mail thanking me for the notes. However, as I understood, the notes would be distributed to the staffulty, who would continue their discussions during their departmental meetings.[2] This was just the beginning of a long and difficult process. Perhaps realizing this, at our last staffulty meeting, Ana Young explained that she did not know when she would be able to have me back for another one of the school's Monday meetings.

Recommendations and Frameworks for Change

As I reviewed the notes from each of the small group discussions, it was clear that the majority of the staffulty and I concurred that a sense of unity at SCHS needs improving. We also agreed on two ways to foster a stronger community—working with middle schools and using cooperative learning in the classroom. By emphasizing collaboration, both of these strategies have the potential to mitigate some of the divisive, individualistic, and competitive aspects that characterize U.S. schools and society. Despite these areas of agreement and some variation among the staffulty, in general, we differed on three other substantial points: the role of academic programs in perpetuating divisions and disparities, strategies for addressing class inequalities, and the value of ethnic studies. These differences confirmed what I had learned during the months of interviewing: many of us were working under divergent frameworks for change—from transformative power-aware to cultural determinist perspectives.

Points of Agreement

The discussion groups echoed the importance of collaborating with the middle schools that feed into SCHS. They considered organizing assemblies with the schools and having academic departments meet to discuss curriculum and expectations. Like many throughout the country, the high school and middle schools basically work in isolation of one another. With little to no interaction, they are unable to share ideas and collaborate to enhance student learning. Cultivating relationships between these schools can facilitate students' academic and social transition. Likewise, a partnership can also help combat the racist and classist assumptions that exist about the different middle schools. As detailed in chapter 2, such assumptions foster unequal course placement and negatively influence peer groups.

With suggestions such as "Have students teach each other," "Students are a resource," and "Group together multiracial students," many members of the staffulty also emphasized the value of using cooperative learning in the classroom. Potentially, cooperative learning groups provide opportunities for students to work across racial/ethnic and class boundaries. These groups allow students to draw on their differing strengths and knowledge bases and develop critical thinking skills. In these spaces, students can also be more engaged contributors in the classroom rather than positioned as passive consumers of information. Also, cooperative learning groups can develop students' social skills and help students expand their peer groups and the social capital that comes from a wider network of friends. For example, in a community youth program that employed techniques aimed at "bridging difference," Natasha Watkins and her associates found that students formed cross group relationships, enhanced their understanding of diverse groups, and acted with greater awareness by decreasing discriminatory behavior and demonstrating a commitment to social justice and action (2007, 395). Similarly, studies indicate that students perceive friendlier cross-racial/ethnic relations when teachers assign more collaborative projects and students work in cooperative learning groups (Slaven 1995; Goldsmith 2004, 606). Despite the potential positive outcomes of collaborative learning, the odds of such cross-racial/ethnic partnerships in most classrooms are slim because of the often racial/ethnic and class segregation in course enrollment from college prep to International Baccalaureate.

Points of Disagreement

Initially, it appeared that the majority of the staffuly and I agreed on the limitations of the school's rigidly defined academic tracks and programs. We seemed to support the idea that public and comprehensive schools such as SCHS must serve all students and should offer more electives. Thus when I advocated for broadening course offerings and increasing access to social and academic support, I did not sense any opposition. However, what became more apparent after the small group discussions is that while we might have agreed on this overall sentiment, in general, different frameworks seemed to be informing specific components of our opinions.

As detailed in chapter 2, students are keenly aware of which students and programs are recognized, privileged, and preferred and which are not. Those outside of the school's IB and AVID (Advancement via Individual Determination) programs report far less access to counselors and other systems of support. Such differential treatment and its intersections by race/ethnicity, class, and gender reproduce inequalities and hegemonic constructions. Clear illustrations of this are students' extensive references to the four Ss—that Asian Americans are "smart," Latinas/os are "stupid," and Blacks are "sports" or "scary." Likewise, many of the IB students who are predominately middle- and upper-middle-class Chinese Americans have adopted the school's labeling and treatment of themselves as the "elite."

Given the way that these academic programs at SCHS divide students and reinforce inequalities, SCHS and schools like it need to ensure that no students are left behind. The perpetuation of curriculum tracking where the students in the highest tracks receive the most and other students are ignored or dismissed is a civil rights issue. All students should have access to challenging curriculum that prepares them for fulfilling lives with multiple opportunities.

One of the changes that must be made is a rethinking and restructuring of which students receive most of the schools' resources, energy, and attention. Not only should all students have access to school resources, but schools should also devote more of their attention and resources to struggling students. In many schools, including SCHS, the same students often receive the most: the challenging classes, school officials' encouragement and affirmation, and academic awards.

Working from a transformative power-aware perspective, I aimed to critique the academic tracks and especially the IB program because of their reproduction of inequality. While there were teachers such as John Alvarez who also found fault with the unequal tracking system, other than a couple of people mentioning that more Latinas/os should be included in the IB program, most people said nothing about the IB program during the presentations and discussion. Outside of the staffulty discussions, a school official had informed me that the school receives thousands of dollars for the IB program. So there was hope by at least a few that this program would not be publically critiqued.

In fact, rather than dismantle any of the academic programs or paths, many of the staffulty instead argued for *additional* academic differentiation. They advocated that "SCHS needs more courses available to non–college bound students." "We need remedial courses for kids not ready for college preparatory"; they argued for the need to "re-introduce our Industrial Arts Program" and to have more "blue-collar/hands-on" electives. I understand these recommendations for more electives, which some of the SCHS students also suggested. The electives could offer a broader and more inclusive curriculum; they could also help shift the privileging of certain types of knowledge and skills over others. However, unaccompanied by a radical rethinking of the racialized and classed hierarchies within SCHS and society, the return of remedial courses such as the transitional English class that initiated this study would fuel even greater disparities and divisions between and among students. As has typically been the case, remedial or transitional classes may become even more unequal "Mexican classes"—as SCHS student Alberto Perez described his class back in 2001 when I met him and his peers. Like segregated classrooms and schools of the past, they may fuel the existing social and economic order by preparing Latina/o and working-class students to fill the role of low-wage workers (see Gonzalez 1990).

The language of "choice" such as "we don't provide choices" for students was common in staffulty's arguments. While I also endorse the concept of student choice, given the patterns at SCHS and schools across the United States, I worry that these paths will not be a choice but instead, as is already the case nationally, that working-class, Latina/o, and Black students will be steered into these non–college preparatory courses with limited opportunity to change academic tracks. Similarly, the language of choice implies that we all have equal options and face the same consequences for our "choices."

Cultural determinist and other individual/group-level analyses underlie some of these arguments for remedial classes and "choice." In several cases, the implication was that not all students want to go to college and even that "not all students are college bound." So as one person wrote in the discussion group notes, the school should "not enroll students into courses for which they are not qualified." As has been the case historically, this characterization may be used to justify teaching students in disparate classes. Furthermore, it appears to place all the blame on students for their desires, abilities, and levels of preparation without considering larger factors that influence students' opinions and backgrounds as well as staffulty's perceptions of students. In addition, while some of the staffulty may have been thinking about generic students not being "college bound" or not "qualified," one person specifically wrote, "There are more Asians in Honors classes; if we let Hispanics in, they fail"—reinforcing what has emerged throughout this book that some of the staffulty assume that Latinas/os are the unqualified students.

Absent in such cultural determinist and other individual/group-level frameworks is an analysis of class. As discussed in chapter 1, at SCHS, there tends to be an ignoring or even an acceptance of the ways that schools maintain and are a reflection of capitalism. Likewise, few discuss the salience of socioeconomic status on schooling and how schools privilege middle- and upper-class students. Since talking about class is characterized as taboo by some at SCHS and in most spaces within the United States, during the staffulty research meetings, I emphasized the following often hidden ways that school practices, class positions, and students' experiences interact at the high school: (1) With the exception of the less than 10 percent of students in the school's AVID program, most first-generation college students are less informed at school about paths to college, and they are also more concerned about how to fund college than their second-generation college-going and middle- and upper-class peers; (2) some poor and working-class students are excluded from high-status extracurricular activities at the school such as band and cheerleading because of the extensive financial costs attached to them; and (3) academically, Asian American students from middle- and upper-class backgrounds were more likely to have access to the academic resources such as outside tutoring, computers, and the Internet that were helping them in their advanced courses.

To counteract such reproduction of class inequality, I critiqued the rigid academic tracks, but I also recommended that the school increase student support and access. Students in the IB and AVID programs should not be the only ones who have frequent and easy access to counselors, and public schools should ensure that poor and working-class students are not denied access to school activities or prohibited from completing course assignments because they lack expected resources.

During their small group discussions, a couple of the staffulty encouraged teachers "to keep an open mind" about students and to consider "students with limited resources." However, along with an emphasis on providing students "choices" in courses and non–college alternatives, much of the focus was on working within the established practices at the school. The staffulty advocated for more funding to support AVID and other school programs. In fact, several people mentioned how "AVID has gradually lost funding," and there was concern that "programs just come and go." In addition, some of the staffulty suggested "peer tutoring" and organizing activities such as "Career Week/College Week" and "more open times for the Career Center." While helpful, these recommendations, especially expanding AVID, would likely not change the overall structure or culture of the campus. While a few more select students may benefit from participating in AVID, there is no guarantee that students outside of the program would be given additional information about college or contact with their counselors. Likewise, elaborate costs may still exclude poor and working-class students from participating in key campus activities. Thus power and inequality is left intact by such cultural determinist and individual/group-level approaches.

While I offered several recommendations throughout the presentations, I advocated most strongly for the teaching of ethnic studies. As is the case with many schools, the wealth of experiences and knowledge of the community are dismissed at SCHS. An assimilationist thrust permeating U.S. schooling persists. Consequently, in spite of the demographic composition of SCHS, the school practices and curriculum could make it almost any school in the United States. The varied histories of migration and diverse racial/ethnic and class backgrounds are underappreciated and undeveloped assets at the school. Building on them could help emphasize the school's uniqueness, enhance school pride, foster student unity, and improve students' academics.

As I presented the idea of ethnic studies to the staffulty, I envisioned students from across curriculum tracks and with varied racial/ethnic and class backgrounds learning together about the multiple histories, perspectives, and experiences of groups who are typically marginalized in mainstream curriculum—such as Latinas/os, Asian Americans, African Americans, and poor Whites. Unlike traditional curriculum, ethnic studies courses do not center the histories and approaches of middle- and upper-class European American heterosexual men. Likewise, ethnic studies courses are not based simply on a diversity model that touts cultural differences by celebrating holidays, food, and styles of dress. Emerging in the 1960s as a result of demonstrations and opposition to traditional curriculum and forms of schooling, ethnic studies classes combine analyses of systems of power, privilege, and inequality with multiple histories, literatures, and contemporary issues; they encourage critical thinking and tackle the historical origins and contemporary patterns of racism, often using intersectional approaches that combine analyses of race/ethnicity, class, nation, and gender. Pedagogically, they are known for challenging the traditional "banking method of education" in which the teacher deposits knowledge into students (Freire 1970). Instead, students are often treated as knowledge producers and change agents, and classrooms may be extended beyond the school gates to encourage students to learn from and work with various communities (Solorzano 1997; Ochoa and Ochoa 2004).

As I have experienced in my own teaching and research, such courses help students see themselves and their families in what they learn; affirm their families' histories and knowledge; understand how all lives are interrelated and influenced in distinct ways by historical, political, and economic factors; and envision possibilities of change (Anderson and Collins 1995). While contested and now banned in places like Tucson, Arizona, these courses benefit students socially, politically, and academically. Students learn best when their backgrounds are affirmed by such curriculum and analyses (Ladson-Billings 1994), and Tucson's Mexican American Studies Department even found that students completing such coursework performed better on standardized tests than did similar students not enrolled in such courses. Likewise, such courses encourage students to be active, critical, and engaged participants in schools and society (de los Ríos and Ochoa 2012).

To demonstrate the feasibility and provide models of how California public school teachers design and lead such classes, I brought to the presentations copies of high school course syllabi, books with relevant curriculum, and lists of suggested readings. Among the materials I shared was a collection of teaching activities and assignments gathered by Edith Chen and Glenn Omatsu (2006) titled *Teaching about Asian Pacific Americans* and articles from *Rethinking Schools*, an independent activist magazine advocating for equitable public schools that practice social justice.

Some staffuty endorsed the idea of offering ethnic studies. During their small groups, they discussed its importance and considered ways that the social studies teachers could teach such classes. At least one group thought ethnic studies should "start early" in ninth grade because of the role these classes could have in providing a "healthier campus environment." Some advocated "extending the cannon of literature" in general and using history "to highlight the origins of racial/ethnic divides and how these were/ are resolved." One person even mentioned creating opportunities in the curriculum for "student-based solutions to racial/ethnic/economic issues on campus."

Despite this support by some, in general, the staffuty were much more likely to endorse "cultural nights," "multicultural days sponsored by clubs," "multicultural food," and "mix it up days," where students are encouraged to interact with students they do not know from different racial/ethnic backgrounds. One person proposed what several people echoed: "What if we do a culture a day or a week where we spend ten to fifteen minutes via video bulletin talking about this? I can't really do this in [my science classes]."

If accompanied by a larger historical and political framework and with curriculum transformation, there is nothing inherently negative about such celebrations of cultures. However, typically, these celebrations are removed from the historical understandings and interrogations of power and inequality that are foundational to ethnic studies. Cultural celebrations are often conducted in tokenistic ways that do not disrupt the status quo. A focus simply on eating different foods and participating in certain festivities may also give a false assumption that one is suddenly familiar with or knows a culture, its histories, and its people. Meanwhile, racial/ ethnic stereotypes and inequalities are often uncontested. Instead, such cultural celebrations may actually end up reinforcing inaccurate conceptions about groups' cultures by depicting them as homogenous and unchanging. Finally, to the extent that cultures and groups other than Whites are celebrated or on display, these groups are positioned as "exotic" or "different" while whiteness is centered as the norm. Warning against such tokenized diversity, social critic bell hooks writes that we must avoid the current fashion in which "ethnicity becomes spice, seasoning that can liven up the dull dish that is mainstream white culture" (1992, 21).

Overall, what these responses and recommendations reveal is that there was interest for change at SCHS. However, since our standpoints and perspectives differed, so too did the types of changes we proposed. Although there was variation of opinions among the staffulty, some of the overall recommendations appear easier and more palatable to implement without altering the structure of the school or classrooms. They do not represent the "true change" that those adopting a transformative power-aware perspective envisioned. Instead, as illustrated by their push for *more* academic differentiation and cultural celebrations, many of the staffulty advocated for changes that can be *added into* the traditional running of the school and classroom without disrupting the status quo. These recommendations are also less threatening because they do not implicate anyone or the school in perpetuating hierarchies.

When placed in the context of the larger research findings, the staffulty's overall ideas suggest a general acceptance of a cultural determinist-individual/group-level perspective. However, some of the staffulty's belief that there is little opportunity for more holistic change might also be influencing their frameworks and strategies for change. In fact, as indicated by some who argue a power-aware framework, several feel resigned because of the current top-down state and district policies that are hindering teacher and school autonomy to shape curriculum and the direction of the school. A few critiqued how the state pressures to perform on standardized tests and follow strict pacing guides limit the time teachers can devote to the racial/ethnic and class divisions and disparities at the school.

The reactions, reflections, and differing recommendations regarding the research reveal the extent of the work needed at SCHS and in the educational system in general. Following the presentations and discussions, I tried to facilitate some of this work. I met with individual staffulty, applied for external grants, and volunteered to organize critical reading and discussion groups. However, as explained in the following section, this work was difficult, and it highlighted the limitations of my role and the lessons that I have learned as part of this larger process.

Critical Reflections on My Role(s) and Lessons Learned

While I was aware of my positionality throughout my time at SCHS, I became especially attuned to how the staffulty viewed me during and after the two presentations and discussion. For most, this was the first time they saw me present my ideas in a public forum, and for several reasons, this was a more complicated experience than I was used to. I shared what I learned from some of the same people I had interviewed. This is not customary in traditional positivistic approaches, where researchers typically collect data, leave the research site to write, and then present their findings in academic journals and conferences to people who are often geographically and experientially far removed from those in the study. However, as a Latina feminist following an ethos of reciprocity and a commitment to social justice, my work is informed by critical methodological approaches in Chicana/o–Latina/o studies, sociology, education, and women's studies. This includes centering personal experiences as forms of knowledge, sharing research findings, and linking research with community and social change.[3] While I had shared my work with participants involved in other research that resulted in *Becoming Neighbors* (2004) and *Learning from Latino Teachers* (2007), I was less accustomed to sharing the work when the stakes were higher. In this case, I was led to believe that there was a possibility for impacting larger school change, but I knew that I needed to earn the respect and support of enough staffulty to better facilitate this process. I had nurtured relationships with several key individuals at SCHS, but if a significant number of staffulty did not agree with what I said or how I said it, it would be harder to continue working toward progressive change. Likewise, I did not want to misrepresent what the participating staffulty had shared in their interviews, and I wanted to do justice to students' narratives. That was more difficult to negotiate because, as detailed in the earlier chapters, some students were very critical of SCHS and the interactions they had with the school officials who were in the meetings.

These experiences of presenting my research and working for change forced me to think hard about my role—perhaps more than at any other time during the research. Since meeting the twenty students in the transitional English class, described in the preface, I was committed to exposing the injustices at SCHS and hopeful that the school would take them seriously. While I think that happened, the two overarching lessons that I learned as part of this process are the importance of collaborating for sustainability and maintaining a strong sense of purpose.

Collaboration for Sustainability

Before and after the process of collecting and sharing the research, I cultivated relationships with several individual staffulty and various students from the Claremont Colleges who worked on this research. These relationships were key for enhancing understanding of the campus dynamics, and in the case of the staffulty, they were also significant for trying to reciprocate the time, experiences, and energy that people shared. While I was at SCHS, I spoke in several teachers' classes about college and careers; I arranged for students from the Claremont Colleges to facilitate class discussions, and I met with individual members of the staffulty to brainstorm how they might apply the research findings to their work. These last exchanges were important because after the presentations, several teachers asked to meet individually to discuss the research and the possibilities of change. So we met during teachers' lunches, their preparation periods, after school, and over dinner. I also extended an invitation for several of us to attend a daylong workshop at another high school on breaking down barriers between students. Three of those named by Chris Tapia as "change agents" at the school met me at this workshop.

Months after presenting the research, I collaborated with two of the school administrators to apply for outside grants. Working with Pomona College colleagues, we applied for a grant from the Kellogg Foundation. Through our project, SCHS and Pomona College proposed partnering to offer human development workshops, community-building activities, and ethnic studies curriculum to address racial/ethnic divisions and disparities. Seventeen high school teachers and their classes were to work with seventeen trained Pomona College students to facilitate these workshops and discussions in cross-racial/ethnic classes. I also applied for a smaller grant through the American Sociological Association to expand work I had been completing for the past several years with my brother, Enrique Ochoa, and a group of students from SCHS through an after-school ethnic studies program that we had started when the students were in middle school. Regrettably, neither of the two grants was funded.

In addition to these collaborative attempts, I was also fortunate to partner with various students from the Claremont Colleges throughout the research. As indicated in the acknowledgments, there were two main research teams of three students each that met often as collectives to plan, conduct, and reflect on the research.[4] It was important for me to foster a series of research teams to provide college students with the experience of completing original research and to follow an ethic of collaboration. All six of these students presented the research at the California Sociological Association Conference in 2008. In 2012, I coauthored "[De]Constructing Multiple Gaps" in *Transnational Crossroads* with members of the first team: Laura Enriquez, Sandra Hamada, and Jenniffer Rojas.

In spite of these relationships, I realized while sharing, reflecting, and strategizing for change that more cohesive ties were necessary. The need for such ties was made clear when individual staffulty who seemed to have the same interests were not working together. People would confide in me their concerns about SCHS, but they were not necessarily speaking with other staffulty who I believed felt similarly. Without a united group of staffulty to work with for change, there were times I felt that I carried too much of the onus. This feeling was enhanced by comments such as the ones made by Chris Tapia: "Tell me what I can do. I'm sure you don't want all of the research to go to waste . . . [W]ithout you this may fail."

Greater cohesion would have enhanced the infrastructure needed to sustain the work, energy, and commitment required for "true change." Thus rather than recommending the establishment of reading groups for staffulty *after* the research presentations, it would have helped to have formed discussion groups earlier in the process. Even focus group discussions during and after the research would have helped. These groups would have allowed more time for reflection and community building, and these groups could have more powerfully articulated and pushed for change than individual staffulty. Finally, when I needed to scale back my work at the high school because of my other responsibilities, there would have been a group of staffulty already meeting about the research findings and working together to more effectively sustain the movement.

As with the staffulty, I should have tried to incorporate the SCHS students more during the research and reflection processes. It would have been helpful to collaborate with a group of high school students in the same way I did with the Pomona College research teams. In this capacity, interested high school students would have developed their critical thinking and research skills. Most significantly, they may have felt invested in the research findings and the recommendation for changes if they had played a role in collecting the research. As such, they could have been key change agents in the school. I regret not collaborating or sharing the research results more systematically with the students. The SCHS students my brother and I were already working with could have been a group of students to partner with for this research. However, at the time, I remember not wanting to blur the original purposes of that program and the research. Unfortunately, I realized too late that the intents were complimentary, and the two could have worked well synergistically. Since students' perspectives were the impetus for this research, I wonder how I had inadvertently silenced the very voices that the staffulty needed to hear.

Similarly, my previous work in the struggle for bilingual education had taught me the powerful role that parents play in critiquing dominant structures and advocating for their children and the community (see Ochoa 2004). However, since so much of my focus and time on this work involved listening to students during school hours, I was unable to establish enduring ties with parents at the school. This hindered my ability to work in solidarity with parents and other community members.

Maintaining a Strong Sense of Purpose

During the process of sharing and discussing the research, administrators and staffulty were assigning different roles to me and evaluating my approach. I was considered a teacher, consultant, mentor, bridge builder, and instigator. Sometimes, I was positioned in one of these roles, and at other times, I felt as though I was assigned all of them. For example, when my recommendation for an ethnic studies class was supported by some of the staffulty, Ana Young told me, "You should teach the course." She preferred that an "outsider" teach the class rather than her because of what she called "her biases." She also thought a Pomona College professor would bring "greater prestige."[5] Along with appointing me to a teacher role, Ana Young mentioned that I might help departments consider changes to the curriculum; Chris Tapia used the word "consultant" to define the role she envisioned me playing. When I was contacted by select staffulty to discuss ways of enhancing their programs and interactions with parents, I felt like a consultant. However, when the staffulty confided in me about the school, I felt like I was tasked with uniting people who had similar commitments but were reluctant to work together.

I was comfortable with most of these roles. However, the role that SCHS perhaps needed the most was the one I was least able to perform—bridge builder. Without support or authority to impact change, the emotional labor involved in being a bridge builder is daunting (Rushin 1983). It involves mediating between different people with varying views and disparate levels of power. If I undertook this role, I feared some would be less invested in working toward change because there would be an impression that the work was already being done. In this way, the work I did risked being tokenized, co-opted, or even for naught. Thus I avoided being placed in this role. As I describe in the following e-mail response to the critique about the "powers that be" inhibiting dialogue, I preferred being a conduit to share the research and to support the transformation at SCHS.

> Thanks for your e-mail. I hope that you and other committed faculty and staff are able to draw upon the research to ask the tough questions that you posed in your e-mail and to advocate for (and implement) change. I have been told that there is an interest in having these ideas and the movement for change come from the faculty and staff. I will continue to offer whatever support I can to address the inequalities at the school and am willing to meet with interested faculty, staff, parents, students . . .

As of now, I have been asked to come back on Monday to participate in the dialogue to come up with steps to improve the campus culture. I agree with you that this process will not be easy, but my sense is that there are teachers and staff who will not stand for the status quo that is shortchanging too many students. Hopefully, we will hear from many of these people at Monday's meeting and their ideas for addressing the racial/ethnic-class disparities. I remain optimistic, but I understand that there are many deep-seated misconceptions and embedded practices that must be confronted.

Please feel free to e-mail me your suggestions, ideas, etc. for Monday's discussion. I think time for both large group and smaller group discussion will be important. What are your thoughts for what might work best for Monday and that won't stop the process? I hope to be able to facilitate or (at least) help structure Monday's discussion. So, please I welcome your feedback.

Perhaps because the staffulty had varied expectations of me and of the possible outcomes of the research, some interpreted my presentation in ways I had not anticipated. In particular, I found it odd and a bit disconcerting that two members of the staffulty individually described my approach and the presentations as "politically correct." While they may have meant that I chose my words carefully—especially when referring to racial/ethnic groups—or that I was being politically strategic in what and how I presented, in one-on-one conversations they each said that I could have been even more critical of the school. For example, Chris Tapia explained how "some expected you to present even worse things or to be even harder," and teacher Cati Sato said that I was "safe; teachers need to hear it." On two previous occasions presenting to teachers, I actually received very different critiques. For example, after speaking to a group of school officials about Latinas/os and education, one Latina teacher angrily told me that she felt like I was blaming teachers when in fact they are so dedicated (see Ochoa 2007). Similarly, after leading a daylong workshop with a group of teachers in another school district, several of them voiced their outrage for what they described as my continual presentation of "cases of discrimination" and "sob stories" from students (see Ochoa 2009). Thus the comments by Chris Tapia and Cati Sato left me wondering if these earlier experiences and the varied dynamics I was negotiating at SCHS had inadvertently led me to soften my analysis, thereby inhibiting some from seeing my social justice perspective. I also speculated about how I appeared "safe" and what more they may have wanted to hear. Perhaps their interpretations were informed by their own hopes for transformation and the larger role they thought I could perform in that process.

Experiences such as these affirmed for me the importance of being clear with oneself and participants of the role(s) one is willing and able to occupy. While these role(s) might fluctuate over time, as they did with my work at SCHS, constant reflection and dialogue about what is feasible and what is expected is necessary to facilitate greater understanding among all involved.

As someone committed to reciprocity, social justice, and critical methodological approaches centering personal experiences, sharing research findings, and linking research with community and social change, there were other ways I could have approached my role and this work. Juana Mora and David Diaz's push for "a new vision and practice in Latino communities" is most applicable here. They argue that researchers "will need to view themselves as facilitators of a community process of inquiry rather than assuming the principal investigator roles that traditionally give the researchers much power over the entire research enterprise" (2004, 6).

A Lost Opportunity?

Just as the students' voices in the transitional English class are still with me, so too are Chris Tapia's comments: "Tell me what I can do. I'm sure you don't want all of the research to go to waste . . . [W]ithout you this may fail." Her comment left me feeling that I had failed the work. I thought, "Had I worked more in community, perhaps she and others would have asked instead, 'What can *we* do. *We* don't want all the research to go to waste . . . [W]ithout *us* this may fail.'" Even now as I reflect on what she said and my own complicity in what transpired at SCHS, the comments from students in the transitional English class remind me how quickly some of us are to adopt individualistic discourses that blame ourselves and other individuals. Individuals certainly have a role, but as the previous chapters have detailed, there are multiple forces impinging on schools and the movement for educational transformation.

What was confirmed during my presentations is how the narrow focus in today's schools hinders institutional transformation and enlarged visions of change. Policies from the No Child Left Behind Act (NCLB) and A Race to the Top circumscribe actions, discourses, and beliefs. Just as staffulty are compelled to abide by the teaching and testing mandates, many echo the discourse of an achievement gap and seem tied to working within this framework.

Overall, just as the systems of power and inequality are so entrenched, so are the larger frameworks that influence our beliefs, actions, and the types of change we are willing to work for. Whether within the K–12 system or in institutions of higher education, we continue to be constrained by top-down polices and influenced by hegemonic ideologies that are steeped in years of exclusion. We must do all we can to eliminate this "smog" structurally, institutionally, ideologically, and individually (see Tatum 1997). Despite the difficulties, Chris Tapia's pleas and the ones that began this chapter capture the determination that many of us have for eliminating the divisions and disparities in schools such as SCHS. Thus what we learn from this extended example is that the processes of change are never easy. There are no quick fixes, and altering such enduring institutions and engrained perspectives is an unending process. However, as long as there are individuals committed to transformation, we must find ways to collaborate to sustain the work, energy, and commitment required for "true change." This will take patience and much unlearning on all of our parts.

Possibilities and Pitfalls in Any School, U.S.A.

As a new school year was beginning and I was preparing for my classes, I was surprised by an e-mail from one of the SCHS administrators. Months had passed since we had last spoken, so I eagerly clicked on the message. Along with thanking me for "the impact" I made at the school, the e-mail invited me to campus to learn about the newly implemented AFFIRMS (Achieving Fantastically through Individual Responsibility and Motivating Success) program that was designed to "close some of the achievement gap between the two main subgroups" at the school.[1]

A week later, I was back at SCHS. Walking up to the school gates, I was greeted by two security guards who were a familiar presence at the school. We spoke briefly, but our conversation was cut short when the administrator called out for me. By the time I turned to the sound of my name, I was being warmly embraced. The administrator's enthusiasm to share the school's new program was palpable, and I was quickly swept into the administration building to hear all about AFFIRMS.

There were several changes made since my eighteen months of research at SCHS. The administrator was now having regular coffee meetings with parents and teaching a class to both "better understand students" and to follow the expectations required of teachers: The belief was that if teachers are compelled to abide by standards, then this too should be mandatory for the administrator. However, the biggest change was organizational. The previous spring semester, nearly two-thirds of the teachers had approved a daily twenty-three-minute AFFIRMS class comprising twenty-five grade-level students across curriculum track, race/ethnicity, and socioeconomic class.[2] As part of AFFIRMS, the twenty-five students were to remain together in this class with the same teacher during their high school years. The classes were designed to be smaller than many courses on campus to better facilitate a sense of community. The teachers were described as "responsible" for the students and would even read their names together at graduation. The class was to focus on tutoring, mentoring, and social awareness with the goal of "improving academic performance, attendance, and behavior."

As the administrator gushed about AFFIRMS and thanked me for "planting the seed," I began thinking about how such a program could potentially move the school toward the "true change" that some of the staffulty were advocating for at our last meetings together. Bringing students together in a shared classroom space with the same teacher for four years could enhance a sense of belonging and stronger ties among students and with their teachers. It could also help chip away at some of the racial/ethnic stereotypes because students would not be kept so separate. To the extent that barriers are reduced, students' social and cultural capital also expands (Valenzuela 1999). This could nurture a more community-centered campus climate where all students are valued and feel like they belong—factors known for enhancing academic engagement (Stanton-Salazar 2004). If teachers use the time for team building, goal designing, and discussing social issues and current events, as the first six week schedule of AFFIRMS indicated, there is the possibility that such a class could also foster students' understanding of contemporary issues and improve their critical consciousness. The possibilities are promising.

However, the twenty-three-minute class time is short, and there is no guarantee that the classes will not become study halls; as the administrator explained, it was agreed that the classes would at "minimum" be places to complete homework. After all, these classes were added on to teachers' already time-strapped schedules, and it was not clear that teachers were being prepared to lead multicultural, power-aware courses that emphasized team building and breaking down barriers. Moreover, much of the rationale used to justify the program is couched within the language of the so-called achievement gap, and one of the goal sheets to be completed by students early in the academic year even requires them to list their individual rankings (far below basic, below basic, basic, proficient, or advanced) based on their performance on California's state tests. Also, as I later learned, with the classes scheduled just before lunch, students were being rewarded for accomplishing certain school requirements by being let out *early* from their AFFIRMS class to have longer lunch periods. By privileging certain students and actions, this practice seemed to undermine the value and potential of the program. It also casts the program as a form of punishment that is best avoided.

The idea and possibilities for AFFIRMS were exciting, but I was left wondering if such a program alone really could help move schools in a different, more holistic and humanizing direction. Reflecting on this larger question and the overall findings of this study, I was reminded of one of the last interviews I had at SCHS. It was with Chris Tapia; her characterization of the campus and the feelings that she expressed about the school were becoming increasingly apropos:

> It's diverse according to national demographics, but not. Divided amongst students and staff. There's a clear division. I'm really disillusioned. So it's hard for me to praise the school because right now it doesn't feel good.

When analyzed through the macro-meso-micro framework used throughout this book, these three Ds—diverse, divided, and disillusioned—capture the complexities that we are up against in changing the direction of our schools. After all, within the national context of assessment, individual accountability, and racial/ethnic and class inequality, the dynamics occurring at SCHS make it any school, U.S.A., both in terms of the applicability of the school's culture and because the unique aspects of the students and their communities are overlooked and undermined. In spite of the school's demographics and the surrounding communities, the running of the school appeared very generic. The school could have been located in many different areas of the United States.

The Masking and Misrepresenting of Diversity

As a school with a majority of Latina/o and Asian American students and smaller percentages of Whites and Blacks, SCHS may appear racially/ethnically diverse. However, that diversity is masked and misrepresented, and the opportunity to build on the students' and communities' strengths is missed.

Diversity at SCHS is undermined by federal policies, school practices, and individual beliefs that have been shaped by neoconservative and neoliberal frameworks emphasizing assimilation and being "color blind." For example, the age of assessment in schools, which is based on rigid testing and standardization by definition, omits individuality and creativity; it ignores the larger factors influencing test performance, and students, teachers, and schools are reduced to numbers and categories based on test results (McNeil 2005, 103; Valenzuela 2005). In particular, with NCLB assessing schools based on racial/ethnic performances on tests and little emphasis placed on learning about the heterogeneity within the panethnic categories of Latina/o, Asian American, White, and African American, students' differing histories, backgrounds, and experiences are largely ignored. Similarly, discussions of these histories, backgrounds, and experiences are absent in most staffulty meetings, in the course curriculum, and even in campus events where instead whiteness may be normalized and affirmed. Furthermore, as some staffulty share, little is said about gender and class because they are not discussed in relationship to test results; talking about class in particular is said to be "taboo" because of individualizing discourses that blame the poor and working class for their positions in society.

This masking and overall lack of discussion prevents an awareness of how racism, sexism, and class disparities are crucial in shaping students' experiences. At SCHS, this is key when one considers how Asian Americans and Latinas/os have been racialized differently. It is also significant given class differences at the school that are linked to migration patterns and U.S. policies. Many (but not all) Asian American students come from families whose parents were able to receive college educations. As a result, Asian American students at the school often have access to middle-class and upper-middle-class resources, including private tutoring and knowledge about college. This is generally not the case for their largely working and lower-middle-class Mexican American schoolmates who may be the first members of their families to be able to attend college. As a result of such silences, students too tend to know little about each other's backgrounds and experiences; in some cases, they even reinforce the racial/ethnic and class hierarchies and the assimilationist thrust that prevails in the United States by ridiculing immigrants and emphasizing English.

When diversity is not being masked by silence or the homogenization of panethnic categories or erased by assimilationist practices, it is misrepresented as a liability. This takes three predominant and intersecting forms. First of all, because of the power of high-stakes testing in shaping school cultures, one of the few times that racial/ethnic categories are considered is when these categories are accompanied by test scores at the beginning of the school year and quantitative data are used to illustrate a so-called achievement gap. The results of this continual pairing of racial/ethnic categories with test scores is the fueling of academic profiling, where Asian American students become especially valued because they are believed to raise test scores. Latinas/os, in contrast, are assumed by some to be hurting the school's ranking; they are seen as liabilities. Both groups are compartmentalized in these static ways, and their complexities are minimized. Second, instead of discussing the structural and institutional factors shaping educational outcomes and the heterogeneity within racial/ethnic categories, when race/ethnicity is named, it is usually through deficiency frameworks, where groups are stereotyped and academic profiling prevails. This takes the form of many staffulty and students adopting biological and cultural deficiency ideologies that see Asian Americans as "smart" and hard working in opposition to Latinas/os who are cast as "stupid" and not valuing education. Finally, diversity is perceived as a liability when it does not fit the normative and expected ways of being. This was most apparent in the fueling of social hierarchies among students at school based on generation, language usage, and styles of dress.

Occasionally, diversity is highlighted as an asset of the school and the surrounding communities. However, this celebration is often superficial or tokenized, especially when considering its general absence in the school organizationally and culturally. Racial/ethnic and class diversity is not equitably distributed across positions of power and curriculum tracks. Furthermore, SCHS is not diverse in terms of the campus culture, where racial/ethnic, class, and gender academic and social hierarchies are reinforced and created. The wealth of student, family, and community histories, experiences, and cultural assets are ignored by stereotypic and panethnic homogenization. In spite of the important exceptions of MEChA (Movimiento Estudiantil Chicana/o de Aztlán) and teacher Michelle Mesa's courses detailed in chapter 6, school activities and the school curriculum often exclude multicultural histories and power-aware perspectives. Thus rather than finding affirming spaces, students are inundated with exclusionary messages that infiltrate the staffulty's perceptions, students' peer groups, and even self-conceptions.

Thus while some may tout the school's diversity if they are only looking at the student demographics quantitatively, this framing leaves the multiple levels of assessing diversity underanalyzed. By simply naming Asian Americans and Latinas/os when they talk about the school, as so many of the staffulty seem to do, the prevalence of whiteness is ignored, and the assimilationist culture and unequal schooling that are hallmarks of the U.S. educational system persist. Without an interrogation of the multifaceted dynamics that are colluding to mask and misrepresent diversity, schools will not be able to foster a type of schooling grounded in self-love; students' positive sense of their classmates; an understanding of multiracial/ethnic, class, and gender histories; and global awareness.

Divided: Separated and Unequal

As Chris Tapia highlights, like schools across the nation, SCHS is divided. Students are divided by separate middle schools, curriculum tracks, unequal policing, differential access to tutoring, and stereotyped conceptualizations. School cultures of individualism and competition are also divisive. As *Academic Profiling* illustrates, these divisions are not inconsequential. There are clear separations by race/ethnicity, class, and gender that replicate hierarchies of power and inequality. For Latina/o and Asian American students, these divides are reinforced and informed by larger belief systems such as the "model minority" myth. They are propagated by school structures, academic programs, school policies, and individual practices. Students are provided with vastly different levels of support and other resources, and the opportunities to create inclusive and community-centered spaces are lost.

Staffulty too are divided, even those who have shared interests and perspectives. Whether it's curriculum tracking or standardized tests, some of the same factors that divide students also separate staffulty. For example, the ranking of students into different courses spills over onto teachers who find that what and who they teach may determine how much value and how many resources they too are afforded. As described in chapter 2, the fact that teacher John Alvarez was initially denied the opportunity to use a particular book in his classroom because it was for honors-designated students and not for college prep classes is one significant indication of such divisions. Similarly, with more testing, reporting, and paper work, teachers are kept busy by the increasing bureaucratization in schools. With less time and autonomy, teachers also feel the stress that students encounter from testing, especially because test scores are used to ascertain their worth too. Just as these conditions and the fueling of divisions are not healthy for students, they are also detrimental for teachers' morale, and they may deter a larger sense of belonging and an ethos of working collaboratively.

Whether it is because their phone calls are not returned, their wishes for their children's classes are ignored, or they do not find the support that they desire, some parents also experience a sense of separation from the high school. As is the case elsewhere, this separation is often connected to race/ethnicity and class, so that working-class, immigrant, and Latina/o parents may encounter unwelcoming school environments and schools that schedule unaccommodating meeting times (Shannon 1996; Ochoa 2004). Most glaringly is the fact that while SCHS had a paid Chinese parent liaison who was instrumental in holding helpful meetings and supporting the school's Chinese American Parent Association, during the time of this research, there was no comparable paid liaisons working with other parents in the same manner, including Latina/o parents.

In spite of such separate and unequal schooling, the repercussions of these social and opportunity gaps are absent in most contemporary discussions and educational policies. In an era where primacy is given to standardized tests, "achievement gaps," and individual accountability, public attention is diverted away from the *qualitative* inequalities that are manifested within and plague our schools. Thus public discourse and public policy is not aimed at improving schools for the greater good.

Disillusioned and Finding Hope

It is within such a climate that Chris Tapia expresses her disillusionment with SCHS. Others are equally frustrated, leading them to question more generally the purpose of schooling. Perhaps one of the more haunting expressions is by Mary Dupont, a nine-year veteran science teacher, who critiques how assessment-driven education is draining students, teachers, and schools:

> These kids are dying to get out of here. They don't want to be
> here . . . Testing is just killing them . . . And it's killing me because
> I got into this career for the kids . . . I'm here because I enjoyed the
> kids, I loved this school, I loved where we were at, and I loved what
> we were doing. And I just don't think we're there anymore.

It is easy to become disillusioned when multiple factors are taking a toll on students and staffulty and are literally killing their love of youth, learning, and communities.

In spite of the damaging conditions shared throughout this book, many continue to question, imagine, resist, and plan. It is this individual and collective resilience that reveal the desire and inspiration. Like Chris Tapia and Mary Dupont, many hope to improve schooling, knowing that what we are up against is not easy to overcome. The foundations of schools are built on inequality. Nevertheless, perhaps it is precisely the love of youth, the commitment to learning, and seeing the value of creating socially responsible people that motivate some. I believe that it is on this basis and intent that the administrator proposed and the majority of the teachers approved AFFIRMS. Working within the multiple constraints and pressures shaping schools—especially in the era of high-stakes testing, they created AFFIRMS, and even with the potential pitfalls, programs such as AFFIRMS can be important interventions. However, what the testimonials and perspectives uncovered in *Academic Profiling* reveal is that such programs and good intentions alone are not enough. They do not tackle the systemic separation and inequality that persists. Without a deconstructing of the political, economic, and social factors perpetuating inequality and a radical rethinking of education, the possibilities are lessened, and programs such as AFFIRMS may unintentionally become a reflection of all that still needs to be changed in schools and society.

Student Participants, Staffulty, and Parents

Latina/o Student Participants						
Name	Year in school	Academic program	Racial/ethnic identity	Generation	Parents' education (mother, father)	Parents' work (mother, father)
Melvin Acuña	12th	College prep	Hispanic	2nd	BA, BA	Teacher, police officer
Nicole Alexander	10th	Honors	Argentinean	2nd	BA, HS	Teacher, owns contracting company
Karina Alvarado	10th	College prep	Mexican American	2nd	HS, HS	Substitute worker, NA
Dolores Anaya	12th	AP	Mexican	2nd	HS, HS	Assistant, contractor supervisor
Rafael Avila	9th	College prep, AVID	Hispanic	2nd	Some college, HS	
Megan Ayala	11th	AP	Mexican American	2nd	HS, some college	Own a meat market
Laura Cadena	12th	College prep, AVID	Mexican American	4th	MA, JD	Teacher, lawyer
Marisa Cadena	10th	Honors	Hispanic	2nd	JD, BA	Lawyer, teacher
Paula Calderon	10th	AP	Mexican American	NA	NA, HS	NA, NA

(*continued*)

Latina/o Student Participants (continued)

Name	Year in school	Academic program	Racial/ethnic identity	Generation	Parents' education (mother, father)	Parents' work (mother, father)
Gloria Camacho	10th	College prep	Chicana	2nd	7th, 6th	Home, landlord
Art Casas	11th	AP, AVID	Puerto Rican and Mexican	2nd	Some college, HS	Home, owns trucking business
María Castillo	10th	College prep	NA	2nd	Some college, HS	Human resources, printer
Araceli Castro	10th	College prep	Latina	3rd	HS, HS	Sales, mechanic
Ashley Cordero	11th	AP	Puerto Rican, Dominican, Mexican, and Spanish	4th	MA, HS	Teacher, restaurant manager
Maggie Cordova	12th	Honors	Mexican	2nd	Some college, GED	Restaurant manager, trucker
Francisco Cortez	12th	Non–college prep	Salvi	2nd	HS, some college	Home, construction worker
Jennifer Cortez	11t	AP, AVID	Latina	2nd	HS, some college	Home, owns copy service
Miguel Cortez	9th	College prep, AVID	Mexican	2nd	BA, BA	School worker, VP card company
Becky Cruz	10th	AP	NA	2nd	HS, HS	IT manager, NA
Hector de la Torre	10th	College prep	Mexican American	3rd	NA, NA	Sells plane parts, construction worker
Jose de Leon	9th	College prep, AVID	Mexican	2nd	NA, some college	Home, car painter
Mandy Esquivel	10th	College prep, AVID	Hispanic	2nd	8th, 8th	Crossing guard, welder

(continued)

Latina/o Student Participants *(continued)*

Name	Year in school	Academic program	Racial/ethnic identity	Generation	Parents' education (mother, father)	Parents' work (mother, father)
Joe Figueroa	10th	College prep	Mexican American	3rd	Some college, some college	Home, construction worker
Isabel Fuentes	10th	College prep	Mexican	NA	NA, NA	NA, NA
Rose Gonzalez	12th	IB	Mexican	2nd	10th, some college	Bank teller, asst. store manager
Daniela Gutierrez	10th	College prep	Mexican	2nd	BA, 10th	Phlebotomist, construction worker
Samuel Heredia	12th	College prep	Mexican American	2nd	HS, AA	Health care, truck driver
Eva Hernandez	10th	College prep	Mexican	2nd	HS, MA	Own a restaurant
David Kim	10th	College prep	Korean and Argentinean	2nd	HS, NA	Manager hair salon, NAs
Robin Lopez	10th	AP	Mexican American	3rd	AA, HS	Nurse, software company
Laura Luna	11th	College prep, AVID	Mexican	2nd	NA, NA	NA, NA
Claudia Macias	10th	College prep	Mexican	2nd	None, 8th	Own a restaurant
Cindy Marquez	12th	Non–college prep	Mexican American	4th	AA, AA	Accountant, disability
Monique Martinez	11th	College prep, AVID	Costa Rican and Mexican	2nd	HS, HS	Waitress, restaurant owner
Sandra Mendez	11th	AP	Mexican	2nd	BA, BA	Teacher, owns fire tech company
Shelly Mendoza	10th	College prep	Latino/ Hispanic	2nd	HS, some HS	Secretary, trucker

(continued)

Latina/o Student Participants (continued)						
Name	*Year in school*	*Academic program*	*Racial/ethnic identity*	*Generation*	*Parents' education (mother, father)*	*Parents' work (mother, father)*
Manuel Mesa	12th	Non–college prep	Latino	2nd	8th, HS	None, none
Lisette Michaels	11th	College prep	Mexican and Italian	2nd	AA, NA	Nurse, NA
Marcy Michaels	12th	College prep	Mexican	2nd	AA, NA	Nurse, NA
Andrew Moreno	12th	College prep	Mexican	3rd	NA, HS	NA, construction deliverer
Diana Munoz	9th	College prep, AVID	Hispanic	2nd	8th, 10th	Domestic worker, gardener
Albert Ortiz	10th	College prep	Mexican	2nd	HS, 3rd	Elder care, retired
Karla Ortiz	12th	College prep	Mexican and Indian	2nd	Some college, MA	School aide, store manager
Cathy Padilla	12th	College prep	Scottish-Mexican American	3rd	Some college, BA	Insurance manager, court house manager
Fran Padilla	10th	Honors	Mexican	2nd	MA, some college	Teacher, MTA manager
Vicki Pardo	10th	Honors	Hispanic and European	2nd	BA, HS	Business, car technician
George Paz	10th	College prep	Mexican American	3rd	10th, GED	Home, truck driver
Iris Pedraza	11th	College prep, AVID	Hispanic Mexican	2nd	none, 4th	Home, retired window installer
Felipe Perez	10th	College prep	Latino	2nd	HS, HS	Office work, factory work
Rebecca Ramos	10th	College prep	Mexican	2nd	HS, HS	Fast food, country club worker

(*continued*)

Latina/o Student Participants *(continued)*

Name	Year in school	Academic program	Racial/ethnic identity	Generation	Parents' education (mother, father)	Parents' work (mother, father)
Summer Reyes	11th	AP	Mexican	2nd	Some college, some college	Day care, mail carrier
Monica Ruiz	10th	College prep, AVID	Mexican	2nd	8th, 7th	Teaches catechism, service writer for car dealer
Patricia Salas	9th	College prep, AVID	Mexican	2nd	3rd, 5th	Motel worker, disabled
Rosalyn Saldana	9th	College prep, AVID	Mexican	3rd	11th, 11th	Sales manager, construction
Christian Sandoval	12th	College prep	Mexican American	2nd	11th, 4th	Home, factory manager
Edmund Sosa	10th	College prep, AVID	Mexican	2nd	HS, HS	Secretary, valet
Eduardo Telles	9th	College prep, AVID	Mexican	2nd	11th, NA	Factory worker, NA
Andy Tellez	11th	College prep	Mexican American	5th	HS, HS	Sales clerk, truck driver
Edwin Tobias	12th	Non–college prep	Latino	2nd	HS, NA	Childcare, NA
Tanya Valdez	12th	College prep	Mexican	2nd	5th, 10th	Office worker, sales
Brenda Valle	12th	College prep	Latina	2nd	AA, HS	Church translator, technician
Jenn Vanderhol	10th	Honors	Caucasian and Mexican	4th	Some college, BA	Air quality, store owner
Alicia Vasquez	12th	AP	Mexican American	4th	MA, JD	Home, judge

(continued)

Latina/o Student Participants *(continued)*

Name	Year in school	Academic program	Racial/ethnic identity	Generation	Parents' education (mother, father)	Parents' work (mother, father)
Elisa Vasquez	11th	College prep, AVID	Mexican	3rd	NA, NA	NA, NA
Angelica Vega	12th	College prep	Hispanic	2nd	HS, NA	NA, NA
Elizabeth Villa	10th	College prep, AVID	Mexican American	2nd	BA, some college	Robbery investigations for bank, disabled factory worker
Christopher Zuñiga	12th	AP	Mexican	3rd	MA, HS	Teacher, postal service

Asian American Student Participants

Name	Year in school	Academic program	Racial/ethnic identity	Generation	Parents' education (mother, father)	Parents' work (mother, father)
Elisa Brown	10th	College prep	Mexican and Asian	3rd	Some college, HS	District store manager, Time Warner
Lauren Chan	10th	Honors	Chinese	2nd	Some college, NA	Accountant, sales
Rebecca Chan	11th	AP	Chinese	2nd	BA, MA	Teacher, accountant
Frank Chang	11th	AP	Chinese American	2nd	BA, BA	NA, NA
Pablo Chang	10th	Honors	Chinese	1.5	Some college, some college	Sells shoes, carpet installer
Nancy Chang	10th	Pre-IB	Chinese	2nd	BA, NA	NA, retired chef

(continued)

Asian American Student Participants (continued)

Name	Year in school	Academic program	Racial/ethnic identity	Generation	Parents' education (mother, father)	Parents' work (mother, father)
Carmen Chee	11th	AP	Taiwanese American	2nd	BA, BA	Nurse, writes for Chinese magazine
Art Chen	12th	IB	Chinese	2nd	Some HS, BA	Home, finance manager
Sarah Chen	11th	AP	Chinese American	1.5	BA, BA	Custom house workers
Vanessa Chen	10th	Pre-IB	Asian	2nd	BA, BA	Own seafood business
David Chu	12th	College prep	Korean American	1.5	HS, 3rd	Own a liquor store
Marilyn Cruz	10th	College prep, AVID	Filipina	2nd	BA, BA	Nurse, nurse
Matt de la Cruz	12th	AB	Filipino	1.5	BA, HS	Nurse, NA
Tracy Fuji	11th	AP	Japanese	2nd	BA, BA	Real estate agent, real estate agent
Samuel Fujimoto	12th	College prep	Japanese	4th	Some college, BA	Kaiser, retired from Boeing
Terra Lee	10th	Honors	Asian	1.5	BA, BA	Home, company manager
Becky Han	11th	AP	Chinese	2nd	BA, BA	Writer, computer programmer
Eric Han	11th	AP	Chinese	1.5	NA, NA	Private teachers
Kathy Hsin	10th	CP	Chinese	2nd	BA, BA	Accounting, owns computer company

(*continued*)

Name	Year in school	Academic program	Racial/ethnic identity	Generation	Parents' education (mother, father)	Parents' work (mother, father)
Asian American Student Participants (continued)						
Tommy Huie	11th	AP	Chinese	2nd	NA, NA	Works for social security office, owns car repair shop
Mary Hwang	10th	Honors	Chinese	1.5	HS, BA	Owns business, materials supervisor
Margaret Kang	11th	AP	Chinese	1.5	BA, some college	Accountant, home
Jung Kim	10th	College prep	Korean	1.5	BA, BA	Waitress, owns trading company
Mark Ku	10th	College prep	Chinese	2nd	MA, NA	Own construction company
Jennifer Lai	12th	IB	Chinese	1.5	BA, BA	NA, business
April Lee	10th	Pre-IB	Chinese	1.5	BA, BA	Accountant, golf course manager
Marie Lee	11th	AP	Korean	1.5	HS, HS	Home, car company
Marvin Lee	11th	AP	Chinese American	2nd	Some college, HS	Secretary, construction
Matt Lee	11th	AP	American Asian	2nd	Matt Lee	11th
May Lee	12th	IB	Korean	2nd	BA, BA	Own restaurant
Terra Lee	10th	Honors	Asian	1.5	BA, BA	Home, company manager
Miriam Liang	11th	AP	Taiwanese American	1.5	NA, BA	Hairstylist, bakery
Todd Lim	12th	AP	Taiwanese American	2nd	BA, MA	CPA, accountant

(continued)

Name	Year in school	Academic program	Racial/ethnic identity	Generation	Parents' education (mother, father)	Parents' work (mother, father)
Charles Lin	12th	IB	Chinese	1.5	Some college, some college	Home, travel agent
Yi Lin	12th	IB	Chinese	1.5	MD, MD	Poker host, NA
Zixin Lin	11th	AP	Chinese	1.5	BA, BA	Real estate, construction
Ricky Liu	11th	IB	American-born Chinese	2nd	HS, HS	Home, contractor and construction manager
Mark Milton	10th	College prep	Half Chinese and half different groups[1]	3rd	MA, BA	Information services, substitute teacher
Melanie Park	11th	AP	Korean American	2nd	BA, BA	Airline reservationist, owns supplier company
Stephanie Park	11th	AP	Korean	1.5	BA, BA	Own restaurant
Nat Punya-wong	10th	College prep	Thai	2nd	HS, MA	Accounting, government job
Mike Song	12th	IB	Korean	2nd	BA, BA	Employment officer, engineer
Patty Song	12th	AP	Korean	2nd	BA, BA	Bank manager, store manager
Sonya Song	11th	AP	Korean American	2nd	BA, BA	Dentist, photographer
Billy Su	12th	IB	Asian	2nd	Some college, HS	Post office, machine operator

(continued)

Asian American Student Participants (continued)						
Name	Year in school	Academic program	Racial/ethnic identity	Generation	Parents' education (mother, father)	Parents' work (mother, father)
Jessica Su	12th	AP	Korean American	2nd	AA, some college	NA, NA
Ivan Tam	11th	AP	Malaysian	1.5	HS, BA	Own a coffee business
Garfield Tan	11th	AP	Chinese	1.5	MA, BA	Import/export business
James Tan	11th	AP	Filipino and Chinese	2nd	BA, BA	School counselor, medical technician
May Tran	10th	College prep	Asian	2nd	NA, NA	Home, mechanic
James Tuan	11th	AP	Chinese	1.5	Some HS, some HS	Clerk, shipping
Jenny Tuan	11th	AP	Chinese American	2nd	NA, BA	Home, business
Rudy Wang	11th	AP	Asian American	2nd	BA, BA	Home, runs a factory
Bryan Wong	11th	AP	Chinese	2nd	MA, MA	NA, NA
Robert Wong	11th	AP	Californian and Asian	2nd	BA, PhD	Computer information, engineer
Sandra Wu	12th	IB	Chinese	2nd	BA, BA	Loan dealer, engineer
Timothy Yan	11th	AP	Chinese	2nd	BA, BA	Employment officer, engineer
Nathan Yi	10th	College prep	Taiwanese	1.5	NA, NA	NA, NA
Marisa Yep	12th	IB	Chinese	2nd	Some college, HS	Bank supervisor, contractor
Stephanie Yep	11th	College prep, AVID	Chinese	2nd	NA, AA	Owns a flower shop, UPS

(continued)

Asian American Student Participants *(continued)*

Name	Year in school	Academic program	Racial/ethnic identity	Generation	Parents' education (mother, father)	Parents' work (mother, father)
Kathy Yu	10th	College prep	Chinese	2nd	HS, HS	Own restaurant
Daniel Zhao	11th	AP	Asian American and Polynesian	2nd	BA, BA	NA, NA

1. Several different European groups were named.

White and Black Student Participants

Name	Year in school	Academic program	Racial/ethnic identity	Generation	Parents' education (mother, father)	Parents' work (mother, father)
Yvette Belan	12th	College prep	French, Chinese, Greek, and Italian	1.5	Some college, PhD	Business, business
Susan Drake	9th	College prep, AVID	White	2nd	Some HS, HS	Concrete inspector, NA
Melvin Jackson	12th	Non–college prep	Black	NA	BA, HS	Nurse, trucker
John Jansen	11th	College prep	White	6th	AA, BA	Bartender, NA
Tomas Medina	10th	College prep	White	2nd	MD, MD	Dentist, dentist
Sandy O'Brien	11th	AP, AVID	Half Irish and half Dutch	4th	HS, NA	Factory worker, NA
Julia Rios	10th	Pre-IB	White	3rd	MA, PhD	Teacher, professor
Marsha Smith	12th	AP	Black	NA	MA, MA	Property management, retired from air force
Mallory Walker	12th	College prep	White	NA	BA, NA	Teacher, laser technician

Staffulty

Name	Position	Years in occupation	Racial/ethnic background/identity
Alison Adams	Teacher	2	Caucasian
Margaret Albert	Teacher	40	European
John Alvarez	Teacher	9	Hispanic/Latino
Harriet Andrews	Teacher	30	American
Joe Berk	Administrator	10	White
Todd Brown	Teacher	35	Black
Manuel Cadena	Teacher	4	Latino
Ana Camacho	Teacher	4	Chicana
Anthony Castro	Teacher	5	Mexican
Ah Kum Chan	Staff	11	Taiwanese
Elaine Cobb	Teacher	24	American
Laura Cooper	Teacher	2	White
Tom Delgado	Staff	10	Mexican American
Mary Dupont	Teacher	9	Mexican American
Mark Durand	Teacher	12	White
Marilyn Garcia	Teacher	5	Vietnamese
Nancy Gardiner	Counselor	1	White
Beth Hill	Teacher	7	White
Jane King	Teacher	5	Caucasian
George Lakin	Teacher	25	Jewish / Eastern European
Bryan Lee	Teacher	NA	Chinese American
Scott London	Teacher	4	Caucasian
Michele Mesa	Teacher	4	Hispanic
Tracy Mori	Counselor	13	Japanese American
Carrie Paz	Counselor	4	White
Sandra Perez	Staff	14	Hispanic
Mari Ramirez	Staff	NA	Hispanic
Thomas Rojas	Teacher	6	Latino
Jonathan Ryan	Teacher	38	NA
Emily Saldana	Teacher	5	Mexican
Jim Scott	Teacher	39	White
Val Sherman	Teacher	39	Asian American
Marie Silva	Teacher	5	Caucasian

(*continued*)

Staffulty

Name	Position	Years in occupation	Racial/ethnic background/identity
Chris Tapia	Administrator	7	NA
Mallory Tate	Teacher	38	White
Jackie Towne	Counselor	12	NA
Rudy Valdez	Counselor	< 10	Mexican
Mike Williams	Teacher	4	White
Joan Young	Teacher	30	Bolivian

Parents

Name	Racial/ethnic background/identity	Generation	Education	Occupation	Parents' education (mother, father)
Maribel Anaya	Mexican	1st	NA	NA	NA, NA
Ana Cadena	Mexican American	2nd	MA	Teacher	AA, NA
Miguel Cadena	Mexican American	3rd	JD	Lawyer	NA, NA
Mei Chee	Chinese	1st	BA	RN	HS, BA
Bob Chen	Chinese	1st	MA	Finance manager	NA, HS
Pat Jackson	African American	NA	Some college	LVN	Some college, HS
Tammy Liu	Chinese	1st	HS	Home	5th, 3rd
Wendy Milton	Chinese	3rd	MA	Information services	BA, BA
Cristina Perez	Mexican American	3rd	Some college	Accounting	HS, HS
Melanie Tan	Chinese	1st	Some college	Owns cabinet business	PhD, NA
Ramon Vasquez	Mexican American	3rd	JD	Judge	Some HS, HS
Iris Zuñiga	Mexican American	2nd	MA	Teacher	HS, 8th

NOTES

Preface

1. To ensure the privacy of the participants and their families, I have changed all names (including the names of schools). The name changes were selected to approximate participants' names by gender and race/ethnicity.
2. Unless otherwise noted, I use quotation marks here and throughout this work to indicate that these are sentences, phrases, and words used by the participants in this work.
3. Throughout this book, I use "race/ethnicity" and "racial/ethnic" not to conflate them or to assume that they are biological, cultural, or static categories but instead to acknowledge that they are two interrelated systems and social-political-economic-cultural constructs that influence life chances and perspectives. I use the panethnic categories "Asian American," "Asian Pacific Islander," "Latina/o," "White," "Black," or "African American" to be inclusive. However, most of the students in this book identify as Asian, Mexican, or Mexican America, and many of the Asian students are children of Chinese and Korean immigrants.
4. The *Mendez v. Westminster* case resulted in the elimination of de jure segregation for Mexican students and was crucial in the passage of the 1954 U.S. Supreme Court decision that overturned the national practice of racial segregation in schools, *Brown v. Board of Education* (Gonzalez 1990).
5. All the research assistants are listed in the book's acknowledgments. At any one time, I worked closely with one to six college students.
6. The differences involved with being 1.5 or second generation can be significant (see Danico 2004). Some of these experiences are considered in chapters 5 and 6.
7. At various stages of the project, Dianna Moreno, Laura Enriquez, Sandra Hamada, Mai Thai, Jenniffer Rojas, Francisco Covarrubias, and Markus Kessler all submitted thoughtful and detailed field notes.

8. As part of Chicana/os–Latinas/os and Education, a course that I teach, students Celia Camacho, Zoë Folger, Sarah Garrett, Alex Geonetta, Camille Sheffield, Charity Soto, and Jessica Villaseñor facilitated classes at SCHS on topics such as college, the fast food industry, and the prison industrial complex.

9. With the helpful assistance of Martina Ebert at Pomona College, I collaborated with two SCHS administrators and Pomona College colleagues María Tucker, Sergio Marin, and Sefa Aina to apply for a $400,000 grant from the W. K. Kellogg Foundation. I also worked with one SCHS administrator to apply for a much smaller grant through the American Sociological Association Spivack Community Action Research Initiative. More about these experiences are discussed in chapter 7.

Introduction

1. As I have described in *Learning from Latino Teachers* (2007), my upbringing in an immigrant and biethnic family, schooling and work experiences, and critical feminist and ethnic studies approaches have shaped my vision of education.

2. Data accessed from http://www.ed-data.k12.ca.us.

3. At the same time that Mexicans have been recruited for their labor, they have faced rampant anti-Mexican policies including waves of deportations. During the Great Depression in the 1930s, nearly one million people of Mexican descent, including thousands of U.S.-born children, were deported and repatriated to Mexico (Balderrama and Rodríguez 1995). Under what was called Operation Wetback, similar deportation campaigns occurred during the post–Korean War recession where the Immigration and Naturalization Service (INS) deported two million Mexican immigrants and their Mexican American children (Acuña 1988).

4. The freeway bifurcated the area's school district, and most students residing in the older working-class community to the north continued attending the high school on the other side of the freeway.

5. This act brought a gradual increase of Korean Americans to the area. Many Koreans migrated because of limited economic and social opportunities in South Korea, and they saw the United States as a means of mobility for themselves and their children (Lee 2002, 33). U.S. military, economic, political, and cultural connections in Korea are significant in shaping this migration (Min 2011).

6. The percentage of Mexican immigrants who are high school graduates is increasing. Likewise, years of education increase for second-generation Mexican Americans such that 89 percent have a high school diploma and 17 percent are college graduates (Brick, Challinor, and Rosenblum 2011).

7. The Los Angeles area has been the major point of destination for highly educated Taiwanese immigrants, and New York has been the preferred location for many from mainland China who are more likely to be working class (Saito 1998).

8. As Min Zhou (2009) describes, nationally, since 1960, the "Chinese American community has increased 13-fold: from 237,000 in 1960 to 1.6 million in 1990 and to 3.6 million in 2006" (43).

9. Koreans have faced similar forms of hostility and resentment as Chinese Americans and Latinas/os where their Americanness is questioned and they have been blamed for downturns in the economy. This was especially apparent during the 1992 Los Angeles Uprisings where government and police officials delayed responding when two-thousand Korean-owned businesses were being damaged or demolished by fires, totaling about $400 million in losses (Takaki 1993, 5).

10. The California Department of Education designates a student socioeconomically disadvantaged if the student is eligible for free or reduced lunch or if both of the student's parents do not have a high school diploma.

11. About one in four Mexicans in the United States is living below the poverty line (Ramirez 2004), but there is also a growing Mexican American middle class.

12. Data accessed from http://www.ed-data.k12.ca.us.

13. The pressures, uncertainties, and scapegoating of immigrants that often accompanies economic downturns follow students from their neighborhoods into their schools in the form of divisions, tensions, and animosity.

14. In particular, I draw from the work of Frankenberg (1993) and her use of Omi and Winant's (1986) stages in the scholarship and discourse on race/ethnicity. Because of the problematic equation of the term *color-blindness* with a physical disability, I prefer to use Frankenberg's concept of *power-evasiveness*, which more accurately captures this dominant ideology.

1. Framing the "Gap"

1. I use Frankenberg's (1993) three-part definition of whiteness, which includes (1) "a location of structural advantage, of race privilege"; (2) "a standpoint, a place from which white people look" at themselves, others, and society; and (3) "a set of cultural practices that are usually unmarked and unnamed" (1).

2. In comparison to Asian Americans and the students in the honors and advanced placement courses, college preparatory and Latina/o students were more likely to discuss the California High School Exit Examination that is required for high school graduation.

3. While talking to the IB students at this meeting, who were mostly Asian American, this school official made no direct racial/ethnic distinction, but the racially coded language of "bright" and "light" were used in reference to smartness—revealing how language reflects and may even reinforce racial hierarchies even if at a subconscious level. In this case, that "light" or White is better intellectually.

4. The interview with Anthony Castro was not tape-recorded. So the excerpts from his interview are not verbatim. They are from the notes taken during and after the interview.

5. Thanks to Isaac Medina for emphasizing this.

6. This is not the case for all the White teachers interviewed. For example, one shared how she did not start developing a critical consciousness of race/ethnicity until her graduate school program that focused on social justice.

7. In his research on the nearby community of Monterey Park, Saito (1998) describes similar reconstructions of history and the "whitening" of Southern California's Mexican past.

2. Welcome to High School

1. When asked to define "ghetto," students tend to focus on the appearance and quality of the school grounds, school resources, and surrounding community. However, in a few cases, as with Monique Martinez, this term is used to refer to students' styles of clothes and music: "The girls who draw in the eyebrows and the girls who crunch their hair with hairspray so it looks wet all days and the boys who wear white shirts. You know, the ghetto people. You could just tell. They listen to rap music."

   Underlying such negative characterizations of "ghetto people" is a devaluing of (1) working-class and poor communities; (2) styles often associated with working-class, Mexican American, urban youth; and (3) musical preferences typically linked to working-class, Latina/o and African American urban youth. Concurrently, there is an implicit valuation of middle- and upper-class students and communities.

2. Thanks to Laura Enriquez for noticing this.

3. In schools without racial/ethnic tracking, more positive cross-racial/ethnic relations are reported (Goldsmith 2004).

4. Thanks to Isaac Medina for making this point.

5. Teacher Thomas Rojas expands, "We have a person that gets hours from the district that gets paid in the office to be the contact person between the Chinese community and SCHS. And we don't have something like that for Latinos."

6. These less regimented classes may also allow more space for what Marie Silva describes as "freethinking" students to share their perspectives.

7. As described earlier in this chapter, this includes criticism of the additional resources provided to the IB program.

3. "I'm Watching Your Group"

1. In pairs, students shake hands and try to pin their opponent's thumb down to their finger.

2. Thanks to Laureen Adams for pointing this out.

4. "Parents Spend Half a Million on Tutoring"

1. In 1965, the Elementary and Secondary Education Act Title 1 was established to provide federal funding to educational agencies serving low-income families in concentrated areas.
2. Lew (2006) finds important class differences between Korean American high schoolers and their participation in tutoring programs. While the parents of working-class Korean American students could not afford to send their children to tutoring programs or after-school academies, many of the middle-class Korean Americans in her study participated in such programs. These middle-class students highlighted how in the United States their immigrant parents continued a pattern from Korea of sending students to private programs as early as kindergarten (40).

5. "They Just Judge Us by Our Cover"

1. Although Val Sherman did not describe this attack as one by gang members, newspaper reports around the time of the attack claimed that some of the instigators of the beatings may have been members of an Asian gang.
2. Thanks to Dani Bernstein for noticing this.

6. "Breaking the Mind-Set"

1. I thank Laura Enriquez, Sandra Hamada, and Jenniffer Rojas for first hearing about the MEChA meetings at SCHS.
2. In some MEChAs, part of this struggle has also been one of privilege and exclusion marred by nationalism, sexism, and heterosexism (Tijerina-Revilla 2009).
3. In April 2013, I was informed that MEChA is no longer active at SCHS.

7. Processes of Change

1. Building on Frankenberg's (1993) concept of "power-evasive," I use the idea of "power-aware" to capture how some people were attuned to how power and inequality historically, structurally, institutionally, and/or individually shape lives and opportunities.
2. I do not know if these notes were ever sent to the staffuly. Informal discussions with a couple of teachers suggest that they never received them.
3. For more discussion, see Muñoz (1989), Collins (1991), and Delgado Bernal (1998).
4. Laura Enriquez, Sandra Hamada, and Jenniffer Rojas were part of the first research team. Afterward, Mai Thai, Francisco Covarrubias, and Markus Keesler worked together for a shorter period of time.

5. While I understood "her biases" as a reference to the detailed comments she made at the end of the second staffulty meeting, I do not know why she initially thought a SCHS faculty member could not the teach the course. I indicated my interest in teaching the course but explained that my own work responsibilities would prevent me from attending all the classes. At last check, such a course has yet to be offered at the school.

Conclusion

1. The name of the program has been changed to ensure the anonymity of the school.
2. According to the administrator, some teachers were reluctant about the program. Concerns included a shortening of lunch to accommodate the class and the time required to prepare for an additional course. There were also questions about whether students would take AFFIRMS seriously because no grades are attached to it. Given these concerns, it was agreed that at the end of the academic year, teachers would vote again on the program.

REFERENCES

Abelmann, Nancy, and John Lie. 1995. *Blue Dreams: Korean Americans and the Los Angeles Riots.* Cambridge, Mass.: Harvard University Press.

Acuña, Rodolfo F. 1988. *Occupied America: A History of Chicanos.* New York: Harper and Row.

Advancement via Individual Determination. 2012. "Overview." http://www.avid.org/sec_overview.html.

Almaguer, Tomas. 1994. *Racial Fault Lines: The Historical Origins of White Supremacy in California.* Berkeley: University of California Press.

Anderson, Margaret L., and Patricia Hill Collins. 1995. *Race, Class, and Gender: An Anthology.* Belmont, Calif.: Wadsworth.

Andriesse, Ann B. 1987. "An Oral History Interview with Anne Faure." The Workman and Temple Family Homestead Museum Oral History Project. City of Industry, Calif.

Apple, Michael W. 2001. *Educating the "Right" Way: Markets, Standards, God, and Inequality.* 2nd ed. New York: RoutledgeFalmer.

———. 2004. *Ideology and Curriculum.* 3rd ed. New York: RoutledgeFalmer.

Aurini, Janice, and Scott Davies. 2004. "The Transformation of Private Tutoring: Education in a Franchise Form." *Canadian Journal of Sociology* 29, no. 3: 419–38.

Balderrama, Francisco E., and Raymond Rodríguez. 1995. *Decade of Betrayal: Mexican Repatriation in the 1930s.* Albuquerque: University of New Mexico Press.

Barrera, Mario. 1979. *Race and Class in the Southwest.* Notre Dame, Ind.: Notre Dame University Press.

Bejarano, Cynthia L. 2005. *Qué Onda? Urban Youth Culture and Border Identity.* Tucson: University of Arizona Press.

Beres, Linda S., and Thomas D. Griffith. 2001. "Demonizing Youth." *Loyola of Los Angeles Law Review* 34: 747–66.

Berliner, David C., and Bruce J. Biddle. 1995. *The Manufactured Crisis: Myths, Fraud, and the Attack on America's Public Schools*. Cambridge, Mass.: Perseus Books.

Bettie, Julie. 2003. *Women without Class: Girls, Race, and Identity*. Berkeley: University of California Press.

Blauner, Robert. 1972. *Racial Oppression in America*. New York: Harper.

———. 1999. "Talking Past Each Other: Black and White Languages of Race." In *Race and Ethnic Conflict: Contending Views on Prejudice, Discrimination, and Ethnoviolence*, edited by Fred L. Pincus and Howard J. Ehrlich, 30–40. Boulder, Colo.: Westview Press.

Bobo, Lawrence, and Devon Johnson. 2000. "Racial Attitudes in a Prismatic Metropolis: Mapping Identity, Stereotypes, Competition and Views on Affirmative Action." In *Prismatic Metropolis: Inequality in Los Angeles*, edited by Lawrence Bobo, Melvin L. Oliver, James H. Johnson Jr., and Abel Valenzuela Jr., 81–166. New York: Russell Sage Foundation.

Bonilla-Silva, Eduardo. 2006. *Racism without Racists: Color-Blind Racism and the Persistence of Racial Inequality in the United States*. Lanham, Md.: Rowman & Littlefield.

Bourdieu, Pierre, and Jean-Claude Passeron. 1977. *Reproduction in Education, Society and Culture*. London: Sage Publications.

Bowles, Samuel, and Herbert Gintis. 1976. *Schooling in Capitalist America: Educational Reform and the Contradictions of Economic Life*. New York: Basic Books.

Bray, Mark. 1999. *The Shadow Education System: Private Tutoring and the Implications for Planners*. Paris: UNESCO.

Brick, Katie, A. E. Challinor, and Marc R. Rosenblum. 2011. "Mexican and Central American Immigrants in the United States." Migration Policy Institute. June.

Buchmann, Claudia, Dennis J. Condron, and Vincent Roscigno. 2010. "Shadow Education, American Style: Test Preparation, the SAT and College Enrollment." *Social Forces* 89, no. 2: 435–61.

Buchmann, Claudia, Thomas A. DiPrete, and Anne McDaniel. 2008. "Gender Inequalities in Education." *Annual Review of Sociology* 34: 319–37.

Butler, Brandon. 2010. "Princeton Review Bets on Online Learning." *Worcester Business Journal Online*, August 30. http://www.wbjournal.com/article/20100830/PRINTEDITION/308309977.

Byun, Soo-yong, and Hyunjoon Park. 2012. "The Academic Success of East Asian American Youth: The Role of Shadow Education." *Sociology of Education* 85, no. 1: 40–60.

Calavita, Kitty. 1992. *Inside the State: The Bracero Program, Immigration, and the I.N.S.* New York: Routledge.

California Department of Education. 2007. "Special Education Enrollment by Ethnicity and Disability." Education Demographics Unit, Sacramento. http://dq.cde.ca.gov/dataquest/SpecEd/SEEnrEthDis1.asp?cChoice=SEEthDis1&cLevel=State&cYear=2006-07&ReptCycle=December.

———. 2008. "Special Programs: Free/Reduced Price Meals, 2006–2007." Education Data Partnership, Sacramento. http://www.ed-data.k12.ca.us.

———. 2008. "Students by Ethnicity, 2006–2007" and "Teachers by Ethnicity, 2006–2007." Education Data Partnership, Sacramento. http://www.ed-data.k12.ca.us.

Chan, Sucheng. 1991. *Asian Americans: An Interpretive History.* New York: Twayne Publishers.

Chavez, Leo R. 2001. *Covering Immigration: Popular Images and the Politics of the Nation.* Berkeley: University of California Press.

Chavez, Linda. 1991. *Out of the Barrio: Toward a New Politics of Hispanic Assimilation.* New York: Basic Books.

Chen, Edith Wen-Chu. 2006. "Deconstructing the Model Minority Image: Asian Pacific Americans, Race, Class, Gender, and Work." In *Teaching about Asian Pacific Americans: Effective Activities, Strategies, and Assignments for Classrooms and Communities,* edited by Edith Wen-Chu Chen and Glenn Omatsu, 41–56. Lanham, Md.: Rowman & Littlefield.

Chen, Edith Wen-Chu, and Glenn Omatsu. 2006. *Teaching about Asian Pacific Americans: Effective Activities, Strategies, and Assignments for Classrooms and Communities.* Lanham, Md.: Rowman & Littlefield.

Chou, Rosalind S., and Joe R. Feagin. 2008. *The Myth of the Model Minority: Asian Americans Facing Racism.* Boulder, Colo.: Paradigm Publishers.

Clotfelter, Charles T. 2002. "Interracial Contact in High School Activities." *Urban Review* 34:25–46.

———. 2004. *After Brown: The Rise and Retreat of School Desegregation.* Princeton, N.J.: Princeton University Press.

Collins, Patricia Hill. 2001. *Black Feminist Thought: Knowledge, Consciousness, and the Politics of Empowerment.* New York: Routledge.

Collins, Thomas W. 1979. "From Courtrooms to Classrooms: Managing School Desegregation in a Deep South School." In *Desegregated Schools: Appraisals of an American Experiment,* edited by Ruy C. Rist, 89–113. New York: Academic Press.

Conchas, Gilbert Q. 2006. *The Color of Success: Race and High-Achieving Urban Youth.* New York: Teachers College.

Crenshaw, Kimberle. 1993. "Mapping the Margins: Intersectionality, Identity Politics, and Violence against Women of Color." *Stanford Law Review* 43: 1241–99.

Dang, Hai-Anh, and F. Halsey Rogers. 2008. "The Growing Phenomenon of Private Tutoring: Does it Deepen Human Capital, Widen Inequalities, or Waste Resources?" *World Bank Research Observer* 23, no. 2: 161–200.

Danico, Mary Yu. 2004. *The 1.5 Generation: Becoming Korean American in Hawai'i.* Honolulu: University of Hawai'i Press.

Daniels, Roger. 1988. *Asian America: Chinese and Japanese in the United States since 1850.* Seattle: University of Washington Press.

Darder, Antonia. 2002. *Reinventing Paulo Freire: A Pedagogy of Love*. Boulder, Colo.: Westview Press.

Davidson, Alex. 2008. "Sticking to Basics." *Forbes Magazine*, November 10. http://www.forbes.com/global/2008/1110/076.html.

Davis, Angela Y. 1981. *Women, Race, and Class*. New York: Random House.

de León, Jozi, and Linda J. Holman. 2002. "Standardized Testing of Latino Students." In *Educating Latino Students*, edited by María Luisa González, Ana Huerta-Macías, and Josefina Villamil Tinajero, 177–94. Lancaster, Pa.: Scarecrow Press.

Delgado Bernal, Dolores. 1998. "Using a Chicana Feminist Epistemology in Educational Research." *Harvard Educational Review* 68, no. 4: 555–82.

———. 2006. "Learning and Living Pedagogies of the Home." In *Chicana/Latina Education in Everyday Life: Feminista Perspectives on Pedagogy and Epistemology*, edited by Dolores Delgado Bernal, C. Alejandra Elenes, Francisca E. Godinez, and Sofia Villenas, 113–32. Albany: State University of New York Press.

Delgado-Gaitan, Cocha. 1992. "School Matters in the Mexican-American Home: Socializing Children to Education." *American Educational Research Journal* 29, no. 3: 495–513.

de los Ríos, Cati V., and Gilda L. Ochoa. 2012. "The People United Shall Never Be Divided: Reflections on Community, Collaboration, and Change." *Journal of Latinos and Education* 11, no. 4: 271–79.

Delpit, Lisa. 1995. *Other People's Children: Cultural Conflict in the Classroom*. New York: New York Press.

Denizet-Lewis, Benoit. 2006. "The Man behind Abercrombie & Fitch." Salon.com, January 24. Accessed May 13, 2013. http://www.salon.com/2006/01/24/jeffries/.

Denner, Jill, and Bianca L. Guzmán. 2006. *Latina Girls: Voices of Adolescent Strength in the United States*. New York: New York University Press.

Díaz-Cotto, Juanita. 2006. *Chicana Lives and Criminal Justice: Voices from El Barrio*. Austin: University of Texas Press.

Eckert, Penelope. 1989. *Jocks and Burnouts: Social Categories and Identity in High School*. New York: Teachers College.

Ellison, Ralph. 1947. *The Invisible Man*. New York: Vintage.

Epstein, Cynthia Fuchs. 1988. *Deceptive Distinctions: Sex, Gender, and the Social Order*. New Haven, Conn.: Yale University Press.

Espinoza, Roberta. 2011. *Pivotal Moments: How Educators Can Put All Students on the Path to College*. Cambridge, Mass.: Harvard Educational Press.

Espiritu, Yen Le. 1992. *Asian American Panethnicity: Bridging Institutions and Identities*. Philadelphia, Pa.: Temple University Press.

———. 1997. "Race, Gender, Class in the Lives of Asian Americans." *Race, Gender, and Class* 4, no. 3: 12–19.

———. 2000. *Asian American Women and Men*. Walnut Creek, Calif.: Altamira Press.

Fabienke, David. 2007. "Beyond the Racial Divide: Perceptions of Minority Residents on Coalition Building in South Los Angeles." Tomás Rivera Policy Institute, Policy Brief. June: 1–18.

Feagin, Joe R. 2001. *Racist America: Roots, Current Realities, and Future Reparations.* New York: Routledge.

Feliciano, Cynthia. 2005. *Unequal Origins: Immigrant Selection and the Education of the Second Generation.* El Paso, Tex.: LFB Scholarly Publishing LLC.

Fields, Jessica. 2008. *Risky Lessons: Sex Education and Social Inequality.* New Brunswick, N.J.: Rutgers University Press.

Fleury-Steiner, Benjamin. 2008. *Dying Inside: The HIV/AIDS Ward at Limestone Prison.* Ann Arbor: University of Michigan Press.

Flores-González, Nilda. 2002. *School Kids/Street Kids: Identity Development in Latino Students.* New York: Teachers College.

Frankenberg, Ruth. 1993. *White Women, Race Matters: The Social Construction of Whiteness.* Minneapolis: University of Minnesota Press.

Freire, Paulo. 1970. *Pedagogy of the Oppressed.* Translated by M. Bergman Ramos. New York: Seabury Press.

Gándara, Patricia. 1995. *Over the Ivy Walls: The Educational Mobility of Low Income Chicanos.* Albany: State University of New York Press.

Gándara, Patricia, and Elías López. 1998. "Latino Students and College Entrance Exams." *Hispanic Journal of Behavioral Science* 20, no. 1: 17–38.

Gándara, Patricia and Frances Contreras. 2009. *The Latino Education Crisis: The Consequences of Failed Social Policies.* Cambridge, Mass.: Harvard University Press.

Gans, Herbert. 1979. "Symbolic Ethnicity: The Future of Ethnic Groups and Cultures in America." *Ethnic and Racial Studies* 2, no. 1: 1–19.

Garcia, Arnoldo, and Elizabeth Martínez. 2006. "What Is Neoliberalism?" In *The Line between Us: Teaching about the Border and Mexican Immigration,* edited by Bill Bigelow, 20. Milwaukee, Wis.: A Rethinking Schools Publication.

Garcia, Lorena. 2012. *Respect Yourself: Protect Yourself: Latina Girls and Sexual Identity.* New York: New York University Press.

Gibson, Margaret A. 1988. *Accommodation without Assimilation: Sikh Immigrants in an American High School.* Ithaca, N.Y.: Cornell University Press.

Ginorio, Angela, and Michelle Huston. 2001. *Sí, Se Puede! Yes, We Can: Latinas in School.* Washington, D.C.: American Association of University Women Educational Foundation.

Giroux, Henry. 1983. "Theories of Reproduction and Resistance in the New Sociology of Education." *Harvard Educational Review* 53: 257–93.

Glazer, Nathan, and Patrick Moynihan. 1975. *Ethnicity: Theory and Experience.* Cambridge, Mass.: Harvard University Press.

Goldenberg, Suzanne. 2005. "Why Women Are Poor at Science, by Harvard President." *The Guardian,* January 18. http://www.guardian.co.uk/science/2005/jan/18/educationsgendergap.genderissues.

Goldsmith, Pat A. 2004. "Schools' Role in Shaping Race Relations: Evidence on Friendliness and Conflict." *Social Problems* 51, no. 4: 587–612.

Gómez-Quiñones, Juan. 1990. *Chicano Politics: Reality and Promise, 1940–1990.* Albuquerque: University of New Mexico Press.

Gonzalez, Gilbert G. 1990. *Chicano Education in the Era of Segregation*. Philadelphia, Pa.: Balch Institute Press.

Gonzalez, Juan. 2000. *Harvest of Empire: A History of Latinos in America*. New York: Viking Press.

Goode, Judith, Jo Anne Schneider, and Suzanne Blanc. 1992. "Transcending Boundaries and Closing Ranks: How Schools Shape Interrelations." In *Structuring Diversity: Ethnographic Perspectives in the New Immigration*, edited by Louise Lamphere, 173–213. Chicago: University of Chicago Press.

Gregory, Anne, Russel Skiba, and Pedro Noguera. 2010. "The Achievement Gap and the Discipline Gap: Two Sides of the Same Coin?" *Educational Researcher* 39, no. 1: 59–68.

Gutiérrez, David G. 1995. *Walls and Mirrors: Mexican Americans, Mexican Immigrants, and the Politics of Ethnicity*. Berkeley: University of California Press.

Hallinan, Maureen T., and Ray A. Teixeira. 1987. "Students' Interracial Friendships: Individual Characteristics, Structural Effects, and Racial Differences." *American Journal of Education* 95: 563–83.

Hallinan, Maureen T., Ray A. Teixeira, and Richard A. Williams. 1989. "Interracial Friendship Choices in Secondary Schools." *American Sociological Review* 54: 67–78.

Hamilton, Nora, and Norma Stoltz Chinchilla. 2001. *Seeking Community in a Global City: Guatemalans and Salvadorans in Los Angeles*. Philadelphia, Pa.: Temple University Press.

Harris, Angel L. 2011. *Kids Don't Want to Fail: Oppositional Culture and the Black-White Achievement Gap*. Cambridge, Mass.: Harvard University Press.

Harrison, Lawrence E. 1999. "How Cultural Values Shape Economic Success." In *Race and Ethnic Conflict*, edited by Fred L. Pincus and Howard J. Ehrlich, 97–109. Boulder, Colo.: Westview Press.

Henze, Rosemary, C. Anne Katz, and Edmundo Norte. 2000. "Rethinking the Concept of Racial or Ethnic Conflict in Schools: A Leadership Perspective." *Race, Ethnicity, and Education* 3: 195–206.

hooks, bell. 1989. *Talking Back: Thinking Feminist, Thinking Black*. Boston: South End Press.

———. 1992. *Black Looks: Race and Representation*. Boston: South End Press.

———. 1994. *Teaching to Transgress*. New York: Routledge Press.

Hursh, David. 2005. "The Growth of High-Stakes Testing in the USA: Accountability, Markets, and the Decline in Educational Equality." *British Educational Research Journal* 31, no. 4: 605–22.

International Baccalaureate Organization. 2007. "Country Information for United States" [Electronic version]. http://www.ibo.org/country/US/index.

———. 2012. "Mission and Strategy." http://www.ibo.org/mission.

Johnson, David W., and Roger T. Johnson. 2000. "The Three Cs of Reducing Prejudice and Discrimination." In *Reducing Prejudice and Discrimination*, edited by Stuart Oskamp, 239–68. Mahwah, N.J.: Lawrence Erlbaum.

Kao, Grace. 2000. "Group Images and Possible Selves among Adolescents: Linking Stereotypes to Expectations by Race and Ethnicity." *Sociological Forum* 15, no. 3: 407–30.

Karla, Scoon Reid. 2004. "Federal Law Spurs Private Companies to Market Tutoring." *Education Week* 24 (15): 1–19.

Kerstiens, Gene. 1998. "Studying in College, Then & Now: An Interview with Walter Pauk." *Journal of Developmental Education* 21, no. 3: 20–22.

Kiang, Peter N., and Jenny Kaplan. 1994. "Where Do We Stand: Views of Racial Conflict by Vietnamese American High School Students in a Black-and-White Context." *Urban Review* 26: 95–119.

Kibria, Nazli. 2002. *Becoming Asian American: Second-Generation Chinese and Korean American Identities*. Baltimore, Md.: Johns Hopkins University Press.

King, Mike. 2011. "Private Tutoring Market to Witness Huge Growth to Reach $100 Billion." *Business Wire*, July 22. http://www.businesswire.com/news/home/20110722005211/en/Private-Tutoring-Market-Witness-Huge-Growth-Reach.

Kochhar, Rakesh, Richard Fry, and Paul Taylor. 2011. *Wealth Gaps Rise to Record Highs between Whites, Blacks, Hispanics*. Washington, D.C.: Pew Research Center.

Koyama, Jill P. 2010. *Making Failure Pay: For Profit Tutoring, High-Stakes Testing, and Public Schools*. Chicago: University of Chicago Press.

Kupchik, Aaron. 2010. *Homeroom Security: School Discipline in an Age of Fear*. New York: New York University Press.

Kyburg, Robin M., Holly Hertberg-Davis, and Carolyn M. Callahan. 2007. "Advanced Placement and International Baccalaureate Programs: Optimal Learning Environments for Talented Minorities." *Journal of Advanced Academics* 18: 172–215.

Ladson-Billings, Gloria. 1994. *The Dreamkeepers: Successful Teachers of African American Children*. San Francisco, Calif.: Jossey-Bass.

Lamphere, Louise. 1992. "Introduction: The Shaping of Diversity." In *Structuring Diversity: Ethnographic Perspectives on the New Immigration*, edited by Louise Lamphere, 1–34. Chicago: University of Chicago Press.

Lareau, Annette. 1987. "Social Class Differences in Family-School Relationships: The Importance of Cultural Capital." *Sociology of Education* 60, no. 2: 73–85.

———. 1989. *Home Advantage: Social Class and Parental Intervention in Elementary Education*. Bristol, Pa.: Falmer Press.

———. 2003. *Unequal Childhood: Class, Race, and Family Life*. Berkeley: University of California Press.

Lee, Jaekyung. 2007. "Two Worlds of Private Tutoring: The Prevalence and Causes of After-School Mathematics Tutoring in Korea and the United States." *Teachers College Record* 109, no. 5: 1207–34.

Lee, Jennifer. 2002. *Civility in the City: Blacks, Jews, and Koreans in Urban America*. Cambridge, Mass.: Harvard University Press.

Lee, Stacey J. 1996. *Unraveling the "Model Minority" Stereotype: Listening to Asian American Youth*. New York: Teachers College.

———. 2005. *Up against Whiteness: Race, School, and Immigrant Youth*. New York: Teachers College.

Lew, Jamie. 2006. *Asian Americans in Class: Charting the Achievement Gap among Korean American Youth*. New York: Teachers College.

Lewis, Oscar. 1966. *La Vida: A Puerto Rican Family in the Culture of Poverty— San Juan and New York*. New York: Random House.

Licón, Gustavo. 2009. "'¡La Unión Hace La Fuerza!' [Unity creates strength!] M.E.Ch.A. and Chicana/o Student Activism in California, 1967–1999." PhD diss., Department of History, University of Southern California.

Lindholm, Kathryn. 1995. "Theoretical Assumption and Empirical Evidence for Academic Achievement in Two Languages." In *Hispanic Psychology*, edited by Amado Padilla, 273–87. Thousand Oaks, Calif.: Sage.

Ling Nakano, Susie. n.d. "Pre-War Japanese Americans in the San Gabriel Valley."

Lipsitz, George. 2002. "The Possessive Investment in Whiteness." In *White Privilege: Essential Readings on the Other Side of Racism*, edited by Paula S. Rothenberg, 61–84. New York: Worth Publishers.

Lopez, Nancy. 2003. *Hopeful Girls, Troubled Boys: Race and Gender Disparity in Urban Education*. New York: Routledge.

Louie, Vivian S. 2004. *Compelled to Excel: Immigration, Education, and Opportunity among Chinese Americans*. Stanford, Calif.: Stanford University Press.

Lozano, Aliber, Karen M. Watt, and Jeffery Huerta. 2009. "A Comparison Study of 12th Grade Hispanic Students' College Anticipations, Aspirations, and College Preparatory Measures." *American Secondary Education* 38: 92–110.

Luttrell, Wendy. 1993. "The Teachers, They All Had Their Pets: Concepts of Gender, Knowledge, and Power." *Signs* 18, no. 3: 505–46.

Madrid, Arturo. 1995. "Missing People and Others." In *Race, Class, and Gender: An Anthology*, edited by Margaret L. Anderson and Patricia Hill Collins, 10–15. Belmont, Calif.: Wadsworth.

Martínez, Elizabeth. 1999. *De Colores Means All of Us: Latina Views for a Multi-Colored Century*. Cambridge, Mass.: South End Press.

Matute-Bianchi, Maria Eugenia. 1986. "Ethnic Identities and Patterns of School Success and Failure among Mexican-Descent and Japanese-American Students in a California High School: An Ethnographic Analysis." *American Journal of Education* 95: 233–55.

McGhee, Paul E. 1976. "Sex Differences in Children's Humor." *Journal of Communication* 26: 176–89.

McIntosh, Peggy. 1995. "White Privilege and Male Privilege." In *Race, Class, and Gender: An Anthology*, edited by Margaret L. Anderson and Patricia Hill Collins, 94–105. Belmont, Calif.: Wadsworth.

McNeil, Linda McSpadden. 2005. "Faking Equality." In *Leaving Children Behind: How "Texas Style" Accountability Fails Latino Youth*, edited by Angela Valenzuela, 57–111. Albany: State University of New York Press.

Min, Pyong Gap. 2011. "Koreans' Immigration to the U.S.: History and Contemporary Trends." The Research Center for Korean Community Queens College of CUNY, Research Report No 3. January 27.

Moody, James. 2001. "Race, School Integration, and Friendship Segregation in America." *American Journal of Sociology* 107, no. 3: 679–716.

Mora, Juana, and David R. Diaz. 2004. "Participatory Action Research: A New Vision and Practice in Latino Communities." In *Latino Social Policy: A Participatory Research Model*, edited by Juana Mora and David R. Diaz, 1–21. New York: Haworth Press.

Morris, Aldon. 1992. "Political Consciousness and Collective Action." In *Frontiers in Social Movement Theory*, edited by Aldon D. Morris and Carol McClurg Mueller, 351–73. New Haven, Conn.: Yale University Press.

Morris, Edward. 2006. *An Unexpected Minority: White Kids in an Urban School*. New Brunswick, N.J.: Rutgers University Press.

Muñoz, Carlos, Jr. 1997. "The Quest for Paradigm." In *Latinos and Education: A Critical Reader*, edited by Antonia Darder, Rodolfo D. Torres, and Henry Gutiérrez, 439–53. New York: Routledge.

National Commission on Asian American and Pacific Islander Research in Education. 2008. "Asian Americans and Pacific Islanders: Facts, Not Fiction: Setting the Record Straight." The College Board. http://professionals.collegeboard.com/profdownload/08-0608-AAPI.pdf.

National Commission on Excellence in Education. 1983. *A Nation at Risk: The Imperative for Educational Reform*. Washington, D.C.: U.S. Government Printing Office.

New York Civil Liberties Union. 2012. "Stop-and-Frisk 2011." http://www.nyclu.org/files/publications/NYCLU_2011_Stop-and-Frisk_Report.pdf.

Noddings, Nel. 1984. *Caring: A Feminine Approach to Ethics and Moral Education*. Berkeley: University of California Press.

Noguera, Pedro A. 2008. *The Trouble with Black Boys: And Other Reflections on Race, Equity, and the Future of Public Education*. San Francisco, Calif.: Jossey-Bass.

Nolan, Kathleen. 2011. *Police in the Hallways: Discipline in an Urban High School*. Minneapolis: University of Minnesota Press.

Oakes, Jeannie. 1985. *Keeping Track: How Schools Structure Inequality*. New Haven, Conn.: Yale University Press.

Oakes, Jeannie, and Gretchen Guiton. 1995. "Matchmaking: The Dynamics of High School Tracking Decisions." *American Educational Research Journal* 32: 3–33.

O'Brien, Eileen. 2008. *The Racial Middle: Latinos and Asian Americans Living beyond the Racial Divide*. New York: New York University Press.

Ochoa, Gilda L. 2004. *Becoming Neighbors in a Mexican American Community: Power, Conflict, and Solidarity.* Austin: University of Texas Press.

———. 2007. *Learning from Latino Teachers.* San Francisco, Calif.: Jossey-Bass.

———. 2009. "'A Nation of Cowards': Education and the Reproduction of Racism." *In Motion Magazine,* March 1. http://www.inmotionmagazine.com/opin/ochoa_gilda.html.

Ochoa, Gilda L., Laura E. Enriquez, Sandra Hamada, and Jenniffer Rojas. 2012. "(De)Constructing Multiple Gaps: Divisions and Disparities between Asian Americans and Latinas/os in a Los Angeles County High School." In *Transnational Crossroads: Remapping the Americas and the Pacific,* edited by Camilla Fojas and Rudy P. Guevarra Jr., 143–70. Lincoln: University of Nebraska Press.

Ochoa, Gilda L., and Enrique C. Ochoa. 2004. "Education for Social Transformation: The Intersections of Chicana/o and Latin American Studies and Community Struggles." *Latin American Perspectives* 31, no. 1: 59–80.

———. 2007. "Framing Latina/o Immigration, Education, and Activism." *Sociology Compass* 1, no. 2: 701–19.

Ochoa, Gilda L., and Daniela Pineda. 2008. "Deconstructing Power, Privilege, and Silence in the Classroom." *Radical History Review* 102: 54–62.

Ogbu, John U. 1991. "Immigrant and Involuntary Minorities in Comparative Perspective." In *Minority Status and Schooling: A Comparative Study of Immigrant and Involuntary Minorities,* edited by Margaret A. Gibson and John U. Ogbu, 3–33. New York: Garland.

Oliver, Melvin L., and Thomas M. Shaprio. 1995. *Black Wealth, White Wealth: A New Perspective on Racial Inequality.* New York: Routledge.

Olsen, Laurie. 1997. *Made in America: Immigrant Students in Our Public Schools.* New York: New Press.

Omi, Michael, and Howard Winant. 1994. *Racial Formation in the United States.* 2nd ed. New York: Routledge.

Ong, Paul, Edna Bonacich, and Lucie Cheng. 1994. "Capitalist Restructuring and the New Asian Immigration." In *The New Asian Immigration in Los Angeles and Global Restructuring,* edited by Paul Ong, Edna Bonacich, and Lucie Cheng, 3–35. Philadelphia, Pa.: Temple University Press.

Parsons, Talcott. 1951. *The Social System.* Glencoe, Ill.: Free Press.

Pearl, Arthur. 2002. "The Big Picture: Systemic and Institutional Factors in Chicano School Failure and Success." In *Chicano School Failure and Success: Past, Present and Future,* 2nd ed., edited by Richard R. Valencia, 335–64. New York: Routledge.

Pérez, Emma. 1993. "Sexuality and Discourse: Notes from a Chicana Survivor." In *Chicana Critical Issues,* edited by N. Alarcón, R. Castro, E. Pérez, A. Sosa Riddell, and P. Zavella, 159–84. Berkeley, Calif.: Third Women Press.

Perry, Pamela. 2002. *Shades of White: White Kids and Racial Identities in High School.* Durham, N.C.: Duke University Press.

Pew Hispanic Foundation/Kaiser Family Foundation. 2004. "National Survey of Latinos: Education." Washington, D.C.

Pineda, Daniela. 2002. "Analyzing the Formation of Social Support Networks and Intentional Communities among Latina Undergraduates at Liberal Arts Colleges." Unpublished senior thesis, Department of Sociology, Pomona College.

Pinheiro, Eugene Arthur. 1960. "A Historical Study of the City of La Puente." Master's thesis, Whittier College.

Pitch, Lisa, Gwen Marchand, Bobby H. Hoffman, and Arlene Lewis. 2006. *AVID Effectiveness Study*. Las Vegas, Nev.: Clark County School District.

Pizarro, Marcos. 2005. *Chicanas and Chicanos in School: Racial Profiling, Identity Battles, and Empowerment*. Austin: University of Texas Press.

Pulido, Laura. 2006. *Black, Brown, Yellow and Left: Radical Activism in Los Angeles*. Berkeley: University of California Press.

Quijada, Patricia D., and Leticia Alvarez. 2006. "Cultivando Semillas Educacionales (Cultivating Educational Seeds): Understanding the Experiences of K-8 Latina/o Students." In *Abriendo Caminos: The Latina/o Pathway to the Ph.D.*, edited by Jeanett Castellanos, Alberta M. Gloria, and Mark Kamimura, 3–17. Sterling, Va.: Stylus.

Ramirez, Roberto R. 2004. "We the People: Hispanics in the United States." U.S. Census Bureau, Census 200 Special Reports. December. http://www.census.gov/prod/2004pubs/censr-18.pdf.

Ramírez-Berg, Charles. 1997. "Stereotyping in Films in General and of the Hispanic in Particular." In *Latin Looks: Images of Latinas and Latinos in the U.S. Media*, edited by Clara E. Rodríguez, 104–20. Boulder, Colo.: Westview Press.

Risman, Barbara. 1998. *Gender Vertigo: American Families in Transition*. New Haven, Conn.: Yale University Press.

Robinson, Dawn T., and Lynn Smith-Lovin. 2001. "Getting a Laugh: Gender, Status, and Humor in Task Discussions." *Social Forces* 80, no. 1: 123–58.

Rollins, Judith. 1985. *Between Women: Domestics and Their Employers*. Philadelphia, Pa.: Temple University Press.

Romero, Mary. 2002. *Maid in the USA*. New York: Routledge.

Romo, Harriet D., and Toni Falbo. 1996. *Latino High School Graduation: Defying the Odds*. Austin: University of Texas Press.

Rosenbloom, Susan Rakosi, and Niobe Way. 2004. "Experiences of Discrimination among African American, Asian American, and Latino Adolescents in an Urban High School." *Youth & Society* 35, no. 4: 420–51.

———. 2010. *The Multiracial Urban High School: Fearing and Trusting Friends*. New York: Palgrave Macmillan.

Ruiz, Vicki L. 1998. *From Out of the Shadows: Mexican Women, Unionization, and the California Food Processing Industry, 1930–1950*. Albuquerque: University of Mexico Press.

Rushin, Donna Kate. 1983. "The Bridge Poem." In *This Bridge Called My Back: Writing by Radical Women of Color*, edited by Cherríe Moraga and Gloria Anzaldúa, xxi. New York: Kitchen Table Women of Color Press.

Russom, Gillian. 2012. "Obama's Neoliberal Agenda for Public Education." In *Education and Capitalism: Struggles for Learning and Liberation*, edited by Jeff Bale and Sarah Knopp, 109–34. Chicago: Haymarket Press.

Ryan, William. 1976. *Blaming the Victim*. 2nd ed. New York: Vintage.

Saito, Leland T. 1998. *Race and Politics: Asian Americans, Latinos, and Whites in a Los Angeles Suburb*. Urbana: University of Illinois Press.

Schlesinger, Arthur M. 1991. *The Disuniting of America: Reflections on a Multicultural Society*. New York: Norton.

Schofield, Janet Ward. 1991. "School Desegregation and Intergroup Relations: A Review of the Literature." *Review of Research in Education* 17: 335–409.

Schofield, Janet Ward, and H. Andrew Sagar. 1979. "The Social Context of Learning in an Interracial School." In *Desegregated Schools: Appraisals of an American Experiment*, edited by Ruy C. Rist, 155–99. New York: Academic Press.

Seidman, Steven. 1994. "Symposium: Queer Theory/Sociology: A Dialogue." *Sociological Theory* 12: 166–77.

Sennett, Richard, and Jonathan Cobb. 1972. *The Hidden Injuries of Class*. New York: Vintage Books.

Shannon, Sheila M. 1996. "Minority Parental Involvement: A Mexican Mother's Experience and a Teacher's Interpretation." *Education and Urban Society* 29, no. 1: 71–84.

Shor, Ira. 1992. *Empowering Education*. Chicago: University of Chicago Press.

Skiba, Russel J., Robert S. Michael, Abra Carroll Nardo, and Reece Peterson. 2000. "The Color of Discipline: Sources of Racial and Gender Disproportionality in School Punishment." Indiana Education Policy Center, Research Report SRSI. June.

Sleeter, Christine E. 1993. "How White Teachers Construct Race." In *Race, Identity, and Representation in Education*, edited by C. McCarthy and W. Crichlow, 157–71. New York: Routledge.

Solorzano, Daniel G. 1997. "Teaching and Social Change: Reflections on a Freirean Approach in a College Classroom." In *Latinos and Education: A Critical Reader*, edited by Antonia Darder, Rodolfo D. Torres, and Henry Gutiérrez, 351–31. New York: Routledge.

Solorzano, Daniel G., and Dolores Delgado Bernal. 2001. "Examining Transformational Resistance through a Critical Race and LatCrit Theory Framework." *Urban Education* 36, no. 3: 308–42.

Soto, Lourdes Diaz. 1997. *Language, Culture, and Power: Bilingual Families and the Struggle for Quality Education*. Albany: State University of New York Press.

Stanton-Salazar, Ricardo D. 2004. "Social Capital among Working-Class Minority Students." In *School Connections: U.S. Mexican Youth, Peers, and School*

Achievement, edited by Margaret A. Gibson, Patricia Gándara, and Jill Peterson Koyama, 18–38. New York: Teachers College.

Steele, Claude. 1997. "A Threat in the Air: How Stereotypes Shape Intellectual Identity and Performance." *American Psychologist* 52: 613–29.

Stolberg, Sheryl. 1992. "150,000 Are in Gangs, Report by D.A. Claims." *Los Angeles Times*, May 22, A1.

Strasburg, Jenny. 2002. "Abercrombie & Glitch: Asian Americans Rip Retailer for Stereotypes on T-Shirts." *San Francisco Chronicle*, April 18, A1.

Suárez-Orozco, Marcelo M., and Mariela M. Páez. 2002. "The Research Agenda." In *Latinos: Remaking America*, edited by Marcelo M. Suárez-Orozco and Mariela M. Páez, 1–37. Berkeley: University of California Press and David Rockefeller Center for Latin American Studies.

Swanson, Mary C., Hugo Mehan, and Lea Hubbard. 1995. "The AVID Classroom: Academic and Social Supports for Low-Achieving Students." In *Creating New Educational Communities*, edited by Jeannie Oakes and Karen H. Quartz, 53–69. Chicago: University of Chicago Press.

Takaki, Ronald. 1993. *A Different Mirror: A History of Multicultural America*. Boston: Back Bay Books.

Tatum, Beverley Daniel. 1997. *"Why Are All the Black Kids Sitting Together in the Cafeteria?" and Other Conversations about Race*. New York: Basic Books.

Teranishi, Robert T. 2010. *Asians in the Ivory Tower: Dilemmas of Racial Inequality in American Higher Education*. New York: Teachers College.

Tijerina-Revilla, Anita. 2009. "Are All Raza Womyn Queer? An Exploration of Sexual Identity in a Chicana/Latina Student Organization." *NWSA Journal: A Publication of the National Women's Studies Association* 21, no. 3: 46–62.

Trejos-Castillo, Elizabeth, and Helyne Frederick. 2011. "Latina Teenage Mothering: Meanings, Challenges, and Successes." In *Latina/Chicana Mothering*, edited by Dorsía Smith Silva, 125–40. Toronto, Canada: Demeter.

Tuan, Mia. 1998. *Forever Foreigners or Honorary Whites? The Asian Ethnic Experience Today*. New Brunswick, N.J.: Rutgers University Press.

U.S. Bureau of the Census. 2010. "U.S. Census American Fact Finder." http://factfinder.census.gov/servlet.

Valadez Torres, Martin. 2005. "Indispensable Migrants: Mexican Workers and the Making of Twentieth-Century Los Angeles." In *Latino Los Angeles*, edited by Enrique C. Ochoa and Gilda L. Ochoa, 23–37. Tucson: Arizona University Press.

Valenzuela, Angela. 1999. *Subtractive Schooling: U.S.-Mexican Youth and the Politics of Caring*. Albany: State University of New York Press.

———. 2005. "The Accountability Debate in Texas: Continuing the Conversation." In *Leaving Children Behind: How "Texas Style" Accountability Fails Latino Youth*, edited by Angela Valenzuela, 1–32. Albany: State University of New York Press.

Valle, María Eva. 1996. "MEChA and the Transformation of Chicano Student Activism: Generational Change, Conflict, and Continuity." PhD diss., Department of Sociology, University of California at San Diego.

Van Ausdale, Debra, and Joe. R. Feagin. 2001. *The First R: How Children Learn Race and Racism*. Lanham, Md.: Rowman & Littlefield.

Vigil, James Diego. 1980. *From Indians to Chicanos: The Dynamics of Mexican American Culture*. Prospect Heights, Ill.: Waveland Press.

Võ, Linda Trinh. 2004. *Mobilizing an Asian American Community*. Philadelphia, Pa.: Temple University Press.

Ward, Janie V. 1996. "Raising Resisters: The Role of Truth Telling in the Psychological Development of African-American Girls." In *Urban Girls: Resisting Stereotypes, Creating Identities*, edited by Bonnie J. R. Leadbeater and Niobe Way, 85–99. New York: New York University Press.

Waters, Mary. 1990. *Ethnic Options: Choosing Identities in America*. Berkeley: University of California Press.

Watkins, Natasha D., Reed W. Larson, and Patrick J. Sullivan. 2007. "Bridging Intergroup Difference in a Community Youth Program." *American Behavioral Scientist* 51, no. 3: 380–402.

Wessler, Seth Freed. 2013. "Harvard Students Demand Investigation into Heritage Researcher's Immigrant IQ." Colorlines.com, May 20. http://colorlines. com/archives/2013/05/harvard_students_demand_investigation_into_heritage _researchers_immigrant_iq_dissertation.html.

Williams, Christine L. 1995. *Still a Man's World: Men Who Do Women's Work*. Berkeley: University of California Press.

Williams, David L., and John T. Stallworth. 1983. *Parent Involvement in Education Project, Executive Summary of the Final Report*. Austin, Tex.: Southwest Educational Development Laboratory.

Woo, Deborah. 2000. *Glass Ceilings and Asian Americans: The New Face of Workplace Barriers*. Walnut Creek, Calif.: Altamira Press.

Wood, George. 2004. "Introduction." In *Many Child Left Behind*, edited by Deborah Meier, Alfie Kohn, Linda Darling-Hammond, Theodore R. Sizer, and George Wood, vii–xv. Boston: Beacon Press.

Yosso, Tara. 2006. *Critical Race Counterstories along the Chicana/Chicano Educational Pipeline*. New York: Routledge.

Zhou, Min. 2007. "Divergent Origins and Destinies: Children of Asian Immigrants." In *Narrowing the Achievement Gap: Strategies for Educating Latino, Black, and Asian Students*, edited by Susan J. Paik and Herbert Walberg, 109–28. New York: Springer Press.

———. 2009. *Contemporary Chinese America: Immigration, Ethnicity, and Community Transformation*. Philadelphia, Pa.: Temple University Press.

Gilda L. Ochoa is professor of Chicana/o–Latina/o studies and sociology at Pomona College. She is the author of *Becoming Neighbors in a Mexican American Community* and *Learning from Latino Teachers* and coeditor of *Latino Los Angeles.*